KU-692-028

ELECTRONIC AND EXPERIMENTAL MUSIC

Pioneers in Technology and Composition

Second Edition

Thom Holmes

ROUTLEDGE
NEW YORK AND LONDON

Published in 2002 by
Routledge
29 West 35th Street
New York, NY 10001

Published in Great Britain by
Routledge
11 New Fetter Lane
London EC4P 4EE

Routledge is an imprint of the Taylor & Francis Group.

Copyright © 1985, 2002 by Thom Holmes

Printed in the United States of America on acid-free paper.

All rights reserved. No part of this book may be reprinted or reproduced or utilized in
any form or by any electronic, mechanical, or other means, now known or hereafter
invented, including any photocopying and recording, or in any information storage or
retrieval system, without permission in writing from the publisher.

10 9 8 7 6 5 4 3 2 1

Cataloging-in-Publishing Data is available from the Library of Congress

ISBN 0–415–93643–8 (hb)
ISBN 0–415–93644–6 (pb)

This book is dedicated to every composer, musician, and engineer who dreams of music that has never been heard. May the voices of those who speak in these pages serve as inspiration and encouragement to you all.

About the Author

Thom Holmes studied composition with Paul Epstein at Temple University and was a member of Epstein's improvisation group in the early '70s. His work *3 Open Windows, 1 Small Antenna* (1973) for shortwave, synthesizer, and live vocalizations was premiered on a radio concert at WBAI in New York in 1974. He was the publisher and editor of the magazine *Recordings of Experimental Music* from 1979 to 1985. The first edition of *Electronic and Experimental Music* was published by Scribner's in 1985. With John Cage's help, he created and maintained the only authorized discography of Cage's music, which was originally published by the John Cage Trust. Holmes has been composing electronic music since the age of sixteen, when his favorite recording artists were the Yardbirds, the Beach Boys, John Cage and the Electric Prunes. His other passion in life is paleontology. He writes dinosaur books for young people. His website is thomholmes.com

CONTENTS

ACKNOWLEDGMENTS

I must first thank someone who is no longer with us; John Cage, without whose encouragement as a young composer I would not have developed such a passion for new music. I was pleased to include something in this volume that John wrote for me in 1985 but which had never been published (his thoughts on composing found in chapter 11). I also wish to thank Laura Kuhn, Executive Director of the John Cage Trust, who keeps the Cage legacy burning bright and whose unfailing organization and wit were extraordinarily helpful.

The first person I studied music with was composer Paul Epstein, who taught me how to compose beyond the moment and think about the *process*. The things I learned from Paul continue to influence the words that I write and the music that I secretly compose.

Many composers and electronic music pioneers gave generously of their time to share their thoughts with me for this book. I will single out Gregor Asch (DJ Olive), Robert Ashley, Bebe Barron, David Behrman, John Bischoff, Harold Budd, Wendy Carlos, Joel Chadabe, Charles Cohen, Nicolas Collins, Tetsu Inoue, Mimi Johnson, Annea Lockwood, Alvin Lucier, David Lee Miller, Ken Montgomery, Robert Moog, Thurston Moore, Ikue Mori, Gordon Mumma, Pete Namlook, Pauline Oliveros, Zeena Parkins, Maggi Payne, Matt Rogalsky, Marina Rosenfeld, Laurie Spiegel, and Karlheinz Stockhausen.

Thanks to Kim Gordon for stepping on my toe with her spiked heels at Tonic.

A special thanks goes to fellow music author Richard Kostelanetz, who urged me for many years to revise my older book and put me in touch with my editor, Richard Carlin, at Routledge. Richard Carlin, of course, has had more than a minor role in shaping this project and I thank him for his dedication to the work and his many excellent ideas for improving it.

Many people assisted me with the acquisition of photographs, a good number of which have never appeared in a print before. These sources are all documented in the photographic credits.

I must make special mention of Gordon Mumma. He accepted the burden of my questions with grace, good humor, and the utmost of help, providing me with many extraordinary photographs and documents from his personal collection. He and Ashley have very fat file drawers!

Thanks to Wendy Carlos for giving me the opportunity to document her deserving accomplishments and to writer Carol Wright for her valued opinion and for opening doors.

Thanks to Mercedes Santos-Miller, Museum Manager at Caramoor, the estate of Walter and Lucie Rosen, for granting access to the Theremin constructed for Lucie Rosen by the master himself.

My little history of the Theremin benefited greatly from the help of David Miller, who has documented the story behind the Paul Tanner electro-Theremin.

Many thanks to friend and consummate researcher Saul Fischer, who was surprised to find that I had a corner on some old movie trivia that he was unaware of. He helped research Samuel Hoffman's Theremin music for the movies and had many other helpful suggestions and edits along the way.

Jeff Winner keeps the flame alive for the Raymond Scott archives and was instrumental in making my version of the Scott story as accurate as possible.

Thanks to Michael Evans for reigniting my interest in the work of Oskar Sala. My story about Sala and the trautonium is much richer because of his help.

A thousand thanks to the many people who provided access to or photographs of homemade electronic music instruments for the photo gallery, especially Matt Rogalsky for his photos of David Tudor's gizmos, Robert Moog, Jeff Winner for the Raymond Scott material, Roger Luther of Moogarchives.com, Wendy Carlos, Zeena Parkins, and David Behrman, who keeps photocell mixers stashed in a box under his piano. It was Matt's photographic layout of David Tudor's electronics at the Tudor website which inspired my own photo gallery of homemade gizmos found within these pages. Not all of these photos made it into the final pages of the book, but they can all be seen at my website image gallery that accompanies the book (thomholmes.com).

Thanks to John Bischoff and Maggi Payne of the Center for Contemporary Music at Mills College for reading parts of the manuscript and improving its California story. The dialogue we started is fit for another book.

Finally, I need to thank Caroline and others at the Quantum Leap restaurant in Greenwich Village in New York for hosting many of my evenings of writing and editing this book. Their dinner menu and a lot of café mochas from local coffee shops kept me going for several months.

Introduction

NEW TECHNOLOGY, NEW MUSIC, NEW LISTENING

1951: Music is dead. Long live electronic music.
2001: Electronic music is dead. Long live music.

The novelty of making music with electronic instruments has long worn off. The use of electronics to compose, organize, record, mix, color, stretch, randomize, project, perform, and distribute music is now intimately woven into the fabric of modern experience. Just as digital visual effects have become so commonplace in movies that we often don't notice them, so too have we accepted the electronic seasoning that tenderizes every form of music imaginable.

Music as we know it today–in all of its many-faceted, genre-bending splendor—would not exist without technology. The explosive development of new musical ideas and materials during the last hundred years is a direct result of explorations with electronic instruments and recording technologies.

Composers now *think* differently about the music they make. Their aural vocabulary has no bounds, and the structures they impose, or choose to avoid, are all made possible by technology.

The audience now *listens* differently to music because recording has changed the way music is experienced. It can be presented live or through various communication media or a combination of the two, any variation of which alters the social context within which music delivers its influence on the human spirit.

All music today is electronic music.

Electronically produced music is part of the mainstream of popular culture. Musical concepts that were once considered radical—the use of environmental sounds, ambient music, turntable music, digital sampling, computer music, the electronic modification of acoustic sounds, and music made from fragments of speech—have now been subsumed by many kinds of popular music. Record-store genres including new age, rap, hip-hop, electronica, techno, jazz, and popular song all rely heavily on production values and techniques that originated with classic electronic music.

There was a time not so many years ago when the term "electronic music" had different connotations. It suggested a music of new and different ideas, never-before-imagined sounds, and creative impulses that were the aural brethren of abstract painting and dance. Electronic music was *new* music. It evolved during the twentieth century in parallel with the growth of industry and technology. It came into being *because* of new technology, and, ironically, much technology now exists because of electronic music.

This book is about new musical ideas and the parallel growth of electronic music instruments. It is about music that exists *because of the use of electronics* rather than music that simply *uses* electronics. Rock music, pop music, jazz, rap, movie music, house, techno, drum and bass, rhythm and blues, and other genres of music use electricity, but they are not the kinds of electronic music discussed between these covers. Here you will find the work of engineers and composers, tinkerers and performers, pocket-protector geeks and new music pioneers. These are people who have always had something different in mind when it comes to music. They share a desire to disrupt the musical norm and to fiddle with the expectations of human experience. Their musical space is one in which aural reality is recontextualized by new sounds, new rules for playing sounds, and new demands for listening.

If this book were only about the technology, then that would have been the end of it. I am not interested in writing about music technology for the sake of the gizmos themselves. As fascinated as I am with soldering and circuits, the real story of electronic music has always been the symbiosis that develops between the artist and the inventor, and the imaginative music that flows from these creative collaborations. This is a book with history, but it is mostly the history of the artistic desire to create music that has never been imagined before.

I visited Robert Ashley early in this project. His studio is a vast open floor in an old industrial building in the TriBeCa section of New York City. When I arrived the light was dim except for the lamp on a worktable at the other end of the space where he had been busy. All around him were boxes of files from his past, projects arranged in folders, like reams of time through which he had been sifting.

John Cage performing *Improvisation I—Child of Tree or Branches* (1975). It consisted of playing on cacti and plant materials that had been connected with contact microphones. "My reason for improvising on them," explained Cage, "is because the instruments are so unknown that as you explore, say the spines of a cactus, you're not really dealing with your memory or your taste. You're exploring." Used with permission of the John Cage Trust.

That was the first time I heard him say that not enough had been written about contemporary music from the '60s. The '60s "were an incredibly fertile period in American music," but the music of the times was not documented because publishers wouldn't produce books about it and record companies wouldn't release recordings. The true music history of that era, Bob claimed, only "exists in composer's file cabinets like mine, all over the United States." This is exactly what I have found in speaking with him and countless other generous composers who shared their thoughts with me for this book.

What you will find in this book is not intended as an exhaustive history of every composer and musician who has contributed to the rich history of electronic music composition; encyclopedias are better suited for that kind of reading. My intent is to offer insight into the work of key pioneers in the field whose ideas and methods set the course for many others to follow.

I have tried to write a book combining a rich history of technical invention with parallel ideas formulated in experimental music. In a world where technology now infiltrates every nuance of our existence, one must remember that the arts succeed where computers fail in elevating the human being in us all. The development of electronic music—itself a by-product of technology—exemplifies everything about being human that the arts can offer.

Chapter 1

WHAT IS ELECTRONIC MUSIC?

The field of music is full of uninformative labels and categories. Electronic music has not escaped this phenomenon. During the heyday of institutionalized electronic music in the '50s, even the founders of the music had difficulty agreeing on what to call it. Schaeffer and Henry called their combination of synthetic and natural sounds "musique concrète." Eimert and Stockhausen called their music of purely synthetic origins "elektronische Musik." Varèse called his combination of synthetic and processed natural sounds "organized sound." Luening and Ussachevsky called it "tape-music."

The situation is no less confusing today. Try and explain the differences between ambient, illbient, minimalism, new age, space music, electronica, techno, environmental, avant-garde, downtown (in New York), proto-techno, electro, Krautrock, world, dub, trance, house, acid house, rave, and just plain old electronic music. Most of these so-called genres exist as points on a single continuous spectrum of music that wouldn't be possible without electronics. Trying to define them any further than that is unhelpful.

I decided not to pigeonhole works of electronic music into those kinds of uninformative genres. Instead, it makes more sense to me to discuss the music from the standpoint of composition: the aesthetic and technological approaches used by a composer to work with the sound material. This requires an understanding of the technology that aids the composer, for in the field of electronic music the creative act is securely tethered to the equipment. A discussion of musique concrète must also be a part of a discussion of tape recorders, tape loops, and the kinds of sound manipulation that can take place because of tape editing. Other technology and approaches that drive the nature of a composer's work include process music, turntablism, and tools that can be used for real-time electronic music production in live performance. By discussing the music in this way I hope to acknowledge the unavoidable influence of technology on the composer while at the same time providing a framework within which different approaches to composition can be illuminated. It also allows for the easy grouping of works of similar conceptual and technical origins so that they can be compared and contrasted.

The stuff of electronic music is *electrically produced or modified sounds*. A synthesizer, sine wave generator, and a doorbell all use electrically produced sounds. An amplified violin connected to a wah-wah pedal, or a voice being embellished by electronic reverberation, are examples of ways to modify sounds.

This is perhaps as broad a definition as one can have of electronic music short of admitting that everything we listen to can be defined in this way. The lines are often blurred between sounds that originate from purely electronic sources and sounds from the real world that are synthetically modified. But I will use two basic definitions that will help put some of the historical discussion in its place: purely electronic music versus electroacoustic music.

Purely Electronic Music

Purely electronic music is created through the generation of sound waves by electrical means. This is done without the use of traditional musical instruments or of sounds found in nature, and is the domain of computers, synthesizers, and other technologies. It is the realm of programs, computer displays, and "virtual" instruments found in software.

Ensembles for Synthesizer (1961–63) by Milton Babbitt (b. 1916) is an example of purely electronic music. It is a twelve-tone piece exploring different "ensembles" of rapidly changing pitches, rhythms, and timbres. It was composed using the RCA Music Synthesizer at the Columbia-Princeton Electronic Music Center. *Switched-On Bach* (1968) by Wendy Carlos (b. 1939) is an example of purely electronic music in which Carlos performs keyboard music of Bach using only the Moog synthesizer.

Purely electronic music can be made through either *analog* or *digital* synthesis. The difference between the two merely lies in the way electricity is controlled. There are no aesthetic differences between the outcomes, and the listener will probably not be able to tell the difference.

In analog synthesis, composers work with continuous electrical current that is *analogous* to its corresponding sound waves. The sound begins as an electric current (alternating current, or AC). The vibrating pattern of the current can be controlled by the composer to create regular or irregular patterns. This current is then fed to an amplifier and loudspeakers, which convert the electrical oscillations into air pressure waves that can be detected by the ear. The resulting sound waves vibrate at the same rate as the electrical waves produced by the electrical sound source. The vibrations of the electric current are controlled by triggering devices such as rotating dials and piano-style keyboards. Analog sounds can be generated by something as simple as a buzzer or sound-wave oscillator, or by an instrument designed more specifically for musical applications such as an electric guitar or analog synthesizer.

Making sound digitally requires computer circuitry that can generate sound waves. Home computers, toys, digital synthesizers, and video games do this through the use of sound chips. Instead of working directly with the control of continuous electric current, a sound chip represents sound waves as binary information, coded into a series of "on" and "off" electrical pulses. This bitstream represents sounds using the same principles that a computer uses to represent numbers or letters of the alphabet. Different pitches are represented by different codes. Because human hearing is an analog process, digital signals must be converted to analog signals before they can be heard. To make the sound patterns audible, the computer converts the codes into an analog form of electrical current that can be amplified and used to operate a loudspeaker. This is done through what is called a digital-to-analog converter. Once the digital codes are converted into continuous electric current and fed to a speaker system, they sound the same as sounds produced through conventional analog means. The reverse process can be used to get analog sounds into a computer for digitization; they are converted using an analog-to-digital converter and then controlled by the computer.

The benefits of digitally generated sound synthesis are many. Like anything else that can be done on a computer, sounds can be controlled and organized with unprecedented ease, in comparison to the rigors of manipulating analog sounds on tape. Digital sounds can be cut and pasted, modified using special effects, made louder or softer, and structured to precise time measurements. Digital sound has the added benefit of being devoid of hiss and other audio artifacts of analog tape recording. The music that results can be copied directly to an audio CD for listening, storage, and distribution.

The term "synthesis" refers to the process of constructing sounds using electronic, or synthetic, means. The music synthesizer is a device designed to generate purely electronic sounds by analog or digital means. Prior to 1980, most commercially available synthesizers were analog.

Electroacoustic Music

Electroacoustic music uses electronics to modify sounds from the natural world. The entire spectrum of worldly sounds provides the source material for this music. This is the domain of microphones, tape recorders, and digital samplers.

The term "electroacoustic music" can be associated with live or recorded music. During live performance, natural sounds are modified in real time using electronics. The source of the sound can be anything from ambient noise to live musicians playing conventional instruments.

Cartridge Music (1960) by John Cage (1912–1992) is a work of electroacoustic music in which phono cartridges were used to amplify sounds that were otherwise nearly inaudible. *Rainforest IV* (1973) by David Tudor (1926–1996) used the amplified and processed sounds of vibrating objects freely suspended in the performing space. The sounds were amplified, filtered, mixed, and also recycled to make other objects vibrate.

The manipulation of recorded, naturally occurring sounds is the foundation of much electronic music. The classic art of composing electronic music using magnetic tape was not conceptually very different from what is called "digital sampling" today. The objective in each case is to capture sounds from the real world that can then be used, and possibly modified, by the composer.

The amplification of traditional musical instruments is a form of electroacoustic music, but for the purposes of this book such work only crosses the line into the realm of electronic music if the musician uses technology to modify the sound.

The interaction of live musicians playing electronically modified or processed acoustic instruments has been a popular approach with composers. In *Mikrophonie I* (1964) by Karlheinz Stockhausen (b. 1928), the sounds of a tam-tam are picked up by two microphones, amplified, and processed through electronic filters. *Wave Train* (1966) by David Behrman (b. 1937) which threw away all established techniques for playing the piano, consisted of controlled feedback caused by guitar pickups placed on the strings of a piano. *Superior Seven* (1992) by Robert Ashley (b. 1930) used real-time digital processing to extend and embellish the notes played by a flutist.

Electronic music exists *because* it is conceived and created with electronic instruments. Does this make it different from other kinds of music? Don't we listen to it with the same set of ears?

Aaron Copland observed that "we all listen to music, professionals and non-professional alike, in the same sort of way—in a dumb sort of way, really, because simple or sophisticated music attracts all of us, in the first instance, on the primordial level of sheer rhythmic and sonic appeal."[1]

As attractive as this observation is, I will argue that we listen to electronic music with different ears, and a different state of mind. One day this will not be the case. Our taste and perceptual constructs will evolve to the point where music of non-acoustic origins will be treated with the same objectivity as all other music, in Copland's "dumb sort of way." But today, hardly fifty years into the recorded medium of electronic music, we have barely been able to get past the technology and think only about the music. Composer-technicians are still most at home in this field. Anyone who composes with synthesizers, software, and computers knows very well that the technology of electronic music has not yet reached the "appliance" stage. When it does, the necessities of *composing* will preoccupy composers instead of the necessities of *mechanics*, the knowledge needed to push the correct buttons and plug in the correct components.

Electronic music is not entirely alien to us. It shares many characteristics with other music. It is emotionally charged and designed to absorb one's attention. Even the most colorless music, stripped of all ornamentation, is fraught with emotional implications. Charles Ives took the twelve-tone composers to task when he wrote, "Is not all music program music? Is not pure music, so called, representative in its essence? Is it not program music raised to the *n*th power, or, rather, reduced to the minus *n*th power? Where is the line to be drawn between the expression of subjective and objective emotion?"[2] The listening experience is psychological and fluid, moving forward incessantly, demanding that we take notice or miss out.

Seven Reasons Why Electronic Music Is Different

The sound resources available to electronic music are unlimited and can be constructed from scratch. One of the key differences between electronic music and music composed for traditional instruments is that *its sonic vistas are limitless and undefined.* The composer not only creates the music, but *composes* the very sounds themselves. Herbert Eimert (1897–1972), one of the founders of the Studio für Elektronische Musik in Cologne, expressed the innate potential of electronic music this way:

> The composer, in view of the fact that he is no longer operating
> within a strictly ordained tonal system, finds himself confronting a
> completely new situation. He sees himself commanding a realm of
> sound in which the musical material appears for the first time as a

malleable continuum of every known and unknown, every conceivable and possible sound. This demands a way of thinking in new dimensions, a kind of mental adjustment to the thinking proper to the materials of electronic sound.[3]

Any imaginable sound is fair game. The composer can invent sounds that do not exist in nature or radically transform natural sounds into new instruments. For *Thema–Omaggio a Joyce* (1958), Luciano Berio (b. 1925) used tape manipulation to transform the spoken voice into a myriad of sound patterns eerily laced with the tonalities of human communication. In the piece *Luna* (from *Digital Moonscapes*, 1984), Wendy Carlos modeled a digital instrument whose voice could be modified in real time as it played a theme, metamorphosing from the sound of a violin to a clarinet to a trumpet and ending with a cello sound. This sound wasn't possible in the world outside of the computer, but became possible with her library of "real-world orchestral replicas" that the GDS and Synergy synthesizers allowed.[4] For *Beauty in the Beast* (1986), she took this experimentation a step further by "designing instrumental timbres that can't exist at all, extrapolated from the ones that do exist."*

Electronic music expands our perception of tonality. The accepted palette of musical sounds was extended in two directions. On one hand, the invention of new pitch systems became easier with electronic musical instruments. Microtonal music is more easily engineered by a composer who can subdivide an octave using software and a digital music keyboard than by a piano builder. On the other hand, electronic music stretched the concept of pitch in the opposite direction, toward less and less tonality and into the realm of noise. All sounds became equal, just another increment on the electromagnetic spectrum. Varèse sensed this early on and introduced controlled instances of noise in his instrumental and electronic music. Cage accepted the value of all sounds without question and let them be themselves:

> Noises are as useful to new music as so-called musical tones, for the simple reason that they are sounds. This decision alters the view of

---

* Wendy Carlos, interview with Carol Wright, *New Age Voice*, <www.newagevoice.com>, November, 1999, copyright 1999 by Carol Wright (June 18, 2001).

history, so that one is no longer concerned with tonality or atonality, Schoenberg or Stravinsky (the twelve tones or the twelve expressed as seven plus five), nor with consonance and dissonance, but rather with Edgard Varèse (1885–1965) who fathered forth noise into twentieth-century music. But it is clear that ways must be discovered that allow noises and tones to be just noises and tones, not exponents subservient to Varèse's imagination.[5]

Electronic music only exists in a state of actualization. Igor Stravinsky (1882–1971) wrote that "it is necessary to distinguish two moments, or rather two states of music: potential music and actual music. . . . It exists as a *score*, unrealized, and as a *performance*."[6] You will rarely find an electronic work that can be accurately transcribed and reproduced from sheet music. It does not exist as "potential music" except in the form of notes, instructions, and ideas made by the composer. Conventional musical notation is not practical for electronic music. You cannot study it as you would a piece of scored music. Experiencing electronic music is, by its nature, a part of its actualization. The term "realization" was aptly adopted by electronic music pioneers to describe the act of assembling a finished work. Even those works that are transcriptions of conventionally composed chromatic music cannot be fully described on paper, because the elements of electronic instrumentation, sound processing, and performance defy standardization. A work of electronic music is not *real*, does not exist, until a performance is *realized*, or played in real time.

Electronic music has a special relationship with the temporal nature of music. "Music presupposes before all else a certain organization in time, a chronomony."[7] The plastic nature of electronic music allows the composer to record all of the values associated with a sound (e.g., pitch, timbre, envelope) in a form that can be shifted and reorganized in time. The ability to modify the time or duration of a sound is one of its most fundamental characteristics. Traditional instrumental music, once recorded, benefits from a similar control over the manipulation of a real-time performance. The equivalency between space and time that Cage attributed to the coming of magnetic tape recording—and which can be extended to any form of analog or digital sound recording or even MIDI control signals—has the liberating effect of allowing the composer to place a sound at any point in time at any tempo.

In electronic music, sound itself becomes a theme of composition. The ability to get inside the physics of a sound and directly manipulate its characteristics provides an entirely new resource for composing music. The unifying physics behind all sounds—pitched and unpitched alike—allow a composer to treat all sounds as being materially equal.

Electronic music does not breathe: it is not affected by the limitations of human performance. As Robert Ashley learned about electronic music early on, "It can go on as long as the electricity comes out of the wall."[8] The arc and structure of the music is tolerant of extremes in the duration and flow of sounds. The ability to sustain or repeat sounds for long periods of time—much longer than would be practical for live instrumentalists—is a natural resource of electronic music. In addition to its sustainability, electronic music can play rhythms too complex and rapid for any person to perform. It can play with more than two hands at the same time. The composer is freed of the physical limitations of human performance and can construct new sounds and performances of an intricacy that can only exist as a product of the machine.

Electronic music springs from the imagination. The essence of electronic music is its disassociation with the natural world. Hearing is a "distance" sense, as opposed to the "proximal" senses of touch and taste. Listening engages the intellect and imagination to interpret what is heard, providing "only indirect knowledge of what matters—requiring interpretations from knowledge and assumptions, so you can read meaning into the object world."[9] Having little basis in the object world, electronic music becomes the pulse of an intimate and personal reality for the listener. Its source is mysterious. "It is thought, imagined and engraved in memory. It's a music of memory."[10] In these ways, the human being becomes the living modulator of the machine product, the circuitry dissolves into the spirit of humanness that envelops it.

Chapter 2

ELECTRONIC MUSIC RESOURCES

Electronic music is an art that marries technology and human imagination. While becoming an electrical engineer is not a prerequisite for making or listening to electronic music, some background on how the music is produced can improve one's appreciation for it. Anyone with the added inclination to become a soldering composer should certainly take notice of the material attributes of sound.

The Components of Sound

Sound is produced by air pressure waves that cause the eardrum to vibrate. These vibrations are converted by auditory nerves into impulses that the brain recognizes as sounds. If the wave vibrates in a regular pattern, it is perceived as a pitched sound, such as those used in music. If the wave does not vibrate in a regular pattern, it is perceived as unpitched sound or noise.

The science of musical acoustics developed during the latter half of the nineteenth century in tandem with general discoveries in the field of electricity. The scientist Hermann von Helmholtz (1821–1894) was largely responsible for this work, with his landmark 1862 paper "Sensations of Tone." In it, he demonstrated that musical sound could be analyzed according to a few basic physical principles. Using combinations of tuning forks to illustrate his point, he showed that the quality (or timbre) of a tone was reliant on the intensity, order, and number of harmonics (overtones and partials) present in the note. A single musical note was not so simple after all. Helmholtz showed that it actually consists of a base, or fundamental, tone accompanied by related vibrations (harmonics) above the pitch of the fundamental, which create timbre, or tone color. Timbre is what distinguishes the sound of a violin from the sound of a piano, even though both instruments might be playing the same note. Every instrument exhibits its own unique mixture of harmonics. This theory suggested that sound could be analyzed by its component parts.

Helmholtz's analysis of the components of sound had a profound effect on many inventors and composers. The instrument builder Thaddeus Cahill cited Helmholtz in devising his technology for synthesizing sound. An understanding of the wave structure of sound led to a robust reassessment of tonal systems used by composers. Our entire understanding of consonance and dissonance stems from this scientific work. Helmholtz's theories also inspired a new, rational approach to analyzing sounds of all types, including noises. The Futurists transformed this science into a rational categorization of sounds into different types for the purpose of composing with them. Varèse's mentor, the musical visionary Ferruccio Busoni (1866–1924), saw in the scientific understanding of musical sound the possibility of a scientific or technical instrument for making new sounds. He wrote in 1907:

> Suddenly, one day, it seemed clear to me that the full flowering of music is frustrated by our instruments. . . . In their range, their tone, what they can render, our instruments are chained fast, and their hundred chains must also bind the creative composer.[1]

All of these people had set the scene many years before the arrival of composer John Cage. What Cage brought to the affair that the others did not was an artistic clarity about the nature of creating music. He did this partly by removing his emotions from the process and objectively examining the materials of music. He sought ways to let sounds be themselves, allowing the listener to provide whatever emotional or intellectual context he or she needed to assess the result. His approach was not unlike that of a scientist studying a natural phenomenon. He observed, measured, and experimented to carry out musical hypotheses in the form of compositions.

Like Helmholtz, Cage was fascinated by the constituent parts that make up sound. In 1937, he gave a talk to an arts society in Seattle in which he suggested that music should be defined by its four basic components: the timbre ("overtone structure"), frequency, amplitude, and duration of sounds.[2] By 1957 he had added a fifth component to the list: the "morphology," or envelope, of the sound, otherwise known as its attack and decay characteristics, or "how the sound begins, goes on, and dies away."[3]

When Cage first proposed these ideas he also related them directly to the potential of using electronic musical devices to broaden our sound spectrum and create a new kind of music. The special nature of "electrical instruments" was that they provided total control over the principal components of sound. In perhaps his most prophetic statement, Cage said in 1937, "I believe that the use of noise to make music will continue and increase until we reach a music produced through the aid of electrical instruments which will make available for musical purposes any and all sounds that can be heard." (*Silence*, pp. 3–4) Cage was by no means working in aesthetic isolation. He had the benefit of knowing and learning from several key figures in contemporary music, including Edgard Varèse, Henry Cowell (1897–1965), and Arnold Schoenberg (1874–1951). But in analyzing sound according to the five basic parameters—timbre, frequency, duration, amplitude, and envelope—Cage defined the common denominators by which all sound can be described. What set Cage apart was that he used these essentially scientific principles to rewrite the definition of music. Because all sounds are composed of the same primary components and because music *is* sound, then it must follow that all sounds can be defined as being musical.

Understanding the five components of sound is helpful for the appreciation of any music. They are especially pertinent to electronic music because the composer and musician are often working with direct control over these aspects of what you hear.

- **Frequency**: the pitch of a sound. Specifically, it is the number of vibrations per second, which, when in the audible range, are detected as a certain pitch. In electronic music, this pitch becomes audible as an expression of the alternating electrical current that is used to vibrate the cone of a loudspeaker at a certain rate per second.
- **Amplitude**: the loudness or volume of a sound. Amplitude is conveyed by a loudspeaker by the distance that the speaker cone moves back and forth from its neutral position. This varies from frequency, which determines how fast the speaker cone vibrates, but not how powerfully it does so. With acoustic instruments, amplitude is controlled by the performer playing softer or harder—pressing the key, blowing the horn, bowing the strings, etc. In electronic music, amplitude is driven by the electrical power of an amplifier that makes electronically produced sounds audible.
- **Timbre**: the nature or quality of a sound, sometimes known as tone color. Timbre is what distinguishes the sounds of different musical instruments playing the same note. All sound waves are complex and contain more than just one simple frequency or fundamental tone. These additional wave structures are called such

things as partials, overtones, harmonics, and transients. If one pitch, or fundamental, predominates, then the sound can be related to a note on the musical scale. When there is more competition for dominance or there are very complex sets of overtones present, a sound may take on highly dense and unusual characteristics.

- **Duration:** the length of time that a sound is audible. Acoustic instruments have a limited ability to sustain sounds. The piano was even designed with a special pedal just for the purpose of letting notes linger longer. Electronic instruments have the innate ability to sustain a sound indefinitely, making duration a key element in composition. Duration is closely allied with the principles of the sound envelope.

- **Envelope:** the attack and decay characteristics of a sound—the way it begins, sustains, and ends. This is essentially the shape of the amplitude characteristics of a sound as it occurs over time. *Attack* refers to the beginning of a sound and how long it takes to reach its maximum loudness. *Sustain* is the length of time that a sound lasts at its peak loudness. *Decay* is the time it takes for a sound to drop off and end. Visually, the shape of a sound can be depicted as a ramp that goes up, levels off, and then goes down again. In electronic music, the envelope of a sound wave can be controlled with great precision.

Waveforms

Sound waves can be represented graphically by their two basic characteristics, *pitch* and *loudness*. In electronic music, pitch is referred to as *frequency* and is defined by the number of vibrations that occur each second (also known as hertz, or Hz). The loudness of a sound is its *amplitude*. In a diagram of a wave, amplitude is represented by the height of the wave.

A complex tone is composed of several sound waves. It will have a *fundamental frequency* and additional sidebands or overtones. The fundamental is the wave with the lowest frequency or the highest amplitude and thus dominates the combination of tones. Overtones add color to the sound, giving it character or timbre.

While most of the sounds we hear in electronic music are combinations of multiple waves or are specially treated for added tone color, it is possible to catalog a few basic waveforms, or waveshapes, that serve as the building blocks of the electronic music composer. Computer sound cards and music synthesizers provide electronic audio oscillators capable of generating any one of these waves in an approximately pure form.

- **Sine wave:** This is the simplest type of wave. Theoretically, it should contain no harmonics or overtones. Although some liken the sound of a sine wave to that of a flute, even the flute has more body and depth than a pure sine tone. The sine is a thin, precise tone, similar to a whistle.
- **Triangle wave:** A triangle wave is similar to a sine wave but has a number of harmonics, or sidebands, added. Its sound has more body and depth than a sine wave and a more hollow effect, like that of a flute, trumpet, or musical saw.
- **Sawtooth wave:** This waveform has a sharp, angular shape like the teeth of a saw. It has twice as many harmonics as a sine wave. It has a full, buzzing sound, like a reed instrument such as the saxophone.
- **Pulse wave:** This waveform has the same number of overtones as a triangle wave but the grittiness and reedy sound of a sawtooth. The waveform jumps instantly from the lowest point of its waveshape to the highest. When diagrammed, it consists only of right angles and is often called a square or rectangular wave. A pulse wave has a sound that is somewhat like the combined sounds of a flute and an oboe. It can also be used to create sharp rhythmic sounds more easily than the other basic waveforms.

Each of these basic waveforms has a reliable structure that exhibits strict amplitude relationships between the harmonics and their fundamental. They can also be combined to create richer, more textured sounds or used to modulate the amplitude or frequency of another sound, techniques that will be explored below.

One more basic waveform needs to be mentioned. It is called *white noise,* and it does not exhibit the structural symmetry of sine, triangle, sawtooth, or pulse waves. In the simplest sense, white noise is to those four basic waveforms what the color gray is to the primary colors: it is a combination of all of them, with no particular element dominating the mix. White noise is made when all the frequency and amplitude characteristics of a sound occur at random within the audio spectrum. It is a continuous dense hiss. It can be filtered and refined to sound like such things as the wind or the ocean, and is a rich source of background sound and texture for the composer of electronic music. Composer Allen Strange (b. 1943) defined white noise more precisely as containing all audible frequencies between 18 Hz and 22,000 Hz. A distilled form of white noise is called *pink noise,* which Strange defined as containing all frequencies between 18 Hz and 10,000 Hz. At the other end of the audio spectrum, noise restricted to the frequency ranges between 10,000 Hz and 22,000 Hz would be *blue noise.*[4]

Making Electronic Music: A Lexicon of Materials and Techniques

The science behind sound waves and the electrical generation of music brings with it a battery of tried-and-true techniques that have been explored since the earliest days of electronic music. As in the worlds of medicine, metallurgy, paleontology, or any other science you wish to name, those who tinker in electronic music have a language all their own. Sit for an afternoon with an electronic music mechanic—a composer who builds his or her own instruments—and you will be immersed in the jargon of filters, subharmonics, triggers, gates, and a bevy of other terms that seem to have no relationship to music whatsoever. Pioneers in the field were obsessed by their own creative forces to develop and master techniques for synthesizing sounds that had never existed before. The equipment they used was borrowed from the world of vacuum tubes and audio testing equipment. Acetate discs and tape recorders were their only means of recording the results. Loudspeakers were the stage from which the music emanated. Through their work and collaborations with audio engineers, a library of techniques for electronically creating and modifying sounds became a known and practiced craft.

The most common functions and components associated with music synthesis are described below. Though rooted in analog devices that predate the transistor radio, most of these principles of sound manipulation are still used today because they are, in the parlance of the computer industry, "platform-independent" techniques. Digital synthesizers, computers, and synthesizing software may have replaced the actual knobs and hardwired components of analog hardware with chips and virtual controls, but the processing techniques of current electronic music systems are modeled after the analog methods first developed thirty to fifty years ago.

Oscillators

An oscillator generates an audio frequency tone in the range that is audible to the human ear, from approximately 20 Hz to 20,000 Hz. Some oscillators may actually reach frequencies above and below hearing range, say, from 1 Hz to 22,000 Hz. These subsonic and supersonic ranges, although inaudible themselves, can still be used to modulate other waveforms.

Oscillators are included on sound chips in keyboard instruments. The sound card provided with personal computers also includes some basic sound-making capability, and more robust chip sets can be purchased as add-ons to expand the computer's ability in this regard.

Synthesizer oscillators usually provide a selectable range of waveforms for use by the composer, generally including the four basic types that we've already discussed: sine, triangle, sawtooth, and pulse. Synthesizers with preset instrumental voices use predetermined combinations of the available oscillators to produce different instrumental timbres.

Controllers

An electronic music instrument needs a way to physically sense the movements and gestures of the musician. A class of devices called controllers do just that. Many kinds of controllers have been created over the years to make an electronic music instrument playable by a composer or performer.

Direct manipulation of controls. The composer uses patch cords, dials, and switches to trigger sounds. The original synthesizers made by RCA, Moog, and Buchla worked in this way. They did not have piano-style keyboards. This is because the early synthesizers were not viewed as performance instruments. They were used with tape recorders in the context of the electronic music studio, and the music was put together piece by piece through tape editing. Synthesizers are still widely available today as rack-mounted components without keyboards. These "slave" sound modules can be triggered by a musician using MIDI signals from either a single controlling keyboard or through software "patches" on a personal computer.

Piano-style keyboard. Keyboards are the most common form of controller used on synthesizers. Today's keyboards are polyphonic–capable of playing more than one note at the same time–but this wasn't always the case. Commercially available voltage-controlled analog synthesizers available during the late '60s and early '70s could only play one note at a time: the highest one being played on the keyboard at any given moment. Each key represented a different amount of voltage. The early synthesizers were not performer-friendly. Even the simplest chord had to be created through multitrack recording.

In addition to the familiar black and white keys, electronic keyboards often have expression controls for embellishing the sound. Keyboards are usually touch-sensitive, so that the harder a person strikes the keys the louder the sound becomes. Another common feature of electronic keyboards is control wheels for bending a note or adding the wavering effect of tremolo.

Ribbons, plates, wands, and other controllers. Not all electronic music is meant to be played on a keyboard. Many innovative alternatives to controlling the sounds of a synthesizer have been developed over the years. Even the earliest solo instruments—the Theremin and Ondes

Martenot—were a dramatic departure from the norm. The Theremin is played by moving the hands in space within the proximity of two antennae, giving a performance a unique theatricality. The Ondes Martenot used the same sound-generating principles as the Theremin, but provided a sliding ring that was moved with one hand over a diagram of a keyboard, thus enabling the performer to hit the proper notes more easily than on the Theremin. Other unique methods have been developed over the years for the control of electronic musical instruments. One of Moog's original options was a ribbon controller. It was a monophonic device for the linear control of voltage and essentially served the same function as the keyboard but without the keys. It was used by sliding a finger up and down a slender metallic ribbon to cause changes in pitch. Like the Theremin and Ondes Martenot, the ribbon controller was especially suited to creating glissandi and wavering effects with unbroken chains of rising or falling notes.

Donald Buchla (b. 1937), the *other* inventor of the voltage-controlled synthesizer, has been devising unique controllers throughout his career. Like the Moog, the original Buchla synthesizer developed around 1965 did not have a keyboard. Instead, the player controlled the triggering of pitches and voltage-controlled actions by using a set of touch-sensitive pads. Buchla continued to noodle with touch-pad controllers and in 1990 manufactured the Thunder, a MIDI-compatible touch-pad controller for performers. In 1991, he introduced the Lightning, an optical MIDI controller that uses infrared beams to transmit control data from handheld wands to any MIDI-compatible synthesizer equipped with a receiver. The speed and position of the wands can be used to trigger a variety of MIDI parameters, including pitch but also the panning of sound and volume level. In 2000, a Lightning II model was introduced, with the added bonus of a thirty-two-voice synthesizer, making it a complete, ready-to-play instrument. Yet another Buchla invention, the Marimba Lumina, translates the keys, program switches, and editing controls of a normal synthesizer into a marimba-like surface with controller strips instead of keys. The strips are played by four different programmable mallets. One can use the Marimba Lumina in place of a keyboard to control MIDI-compatible synthesizers.

Sequencers. The term "sequencer" was associated with voltage-controlled analog synthesizers. It referred to a module that could be programmed to store a pattern of DC voltages used to control a voltage-controlled oscillator. A sequencer could receive its control-voltage pattern from a keyboard, ribbon controller, or other voltage-control source. It allowed a series of notes to be programmed and played back at different speeds or with different synthesizer voicings. The Buchla synthesizer was the first to incorporate a sequencer, which soon became a common accessory for any voltage-controlled synthesizer. Before the introduction of MIDI in 1983, sequencers were the most popular method of storing strings and patterns of notes. They were typically used to provide steady rhythms and harmonic lines that could be repeated while other sounds were played freely at the same time. Sequencer music became synonymous with the steady, trancelike rhythms that characterized the music of such artists as Tangerine Dream, Kraftwerk, Isao Tomita (b. 1932), and Klaus Schulze (b. 1947). Although the term "sequencing" is often used today in reference to software that can record MIDI sequences of notes, the analog sequencer hardware that was once widely used has long since passed from the scene.

MIDI. By 1984, a significant step toward a standardized industry approach to digital synthesizer interface was reached with the introduction of MIDI—the Musical Instrument Digital Interface. MIDI permits instruments made by different companies to be linked electronically for control purposes during performance. It allows a single performer using a single keyboard or other controller (e.g., software) to play more than one instrument at a time, regardless of the make and manufacturer of the gear. The control signals from the single keyboard are transmitted through MIDI interface communications to the other synthesizers that are linked to it, thus permitting the orchestration of music using a variety of MIDI-compatible instruments.

MIDI was a natural outgrowth of the microcomputer and affordably married the electronic musical instrument to the computer. It remains the standard interface employed by all commercial makers of music technology.

The original specification for MIDI was the result of a collaboration between competitors in the then-explosive market for commercial synthesizers. Roland, Yamaha, Korg, Kawai, and Sequential Circuits all contributed to version 1.0 of the spec, which was completed in August 1983.[5] It was not a perfect standard and was mostly championed by those who were interested in the commercial application of electronic musical instruments for the making of popular music. This oriented MIDI toward keyboard music, not the cup of tea preferred by many composers in the field. Still, it succeeded in providing genuine compatibility among different instruments and the computer and led to explosive growth in the making of software and hardware for the music industry. It was the evolutionary leap that led to widespread growth in the music technology industry.

What does MIDI do? It communicates the values of notes played on the keyboard, including the pitch, amplitude, and duration. This should not be confused with *recording* the sounds played by the keyboard; MIDI "records" only a sequence of note values. The timbre, or quality of the sound, is the provenance of the synthesizer that receives the MIDI sequence. A sequence of MIDI note values is independent of the sound or voice of the instrument playing the notes. The same sequence of note values can be played on different instruments using different voices.

MIDI: Musical Conformity or Just Another Creative Tool?

By 1984, the makers of commercial synthesizers and PCs were feeling pressure from consumers to provide universal connectivity of their gear. No industry-wide standard existed at the time for allowing a PC to control or communicate with a synthesizer. When a manufacturer chose to connect a computer with a synthesizer, it did so using expensive and quickly outdated proprietary methods that were unique to its own products. The time had come for the industry to eliminate this problem.

The answer was a protocol called the Musical Instrument Digital Interface, otherwise known as MIDI. Introduced in 1984, it was the result of many months of behind-the-scenes cooperation and squabbling by several leading electronic instrument manufacturers, including Roland, Oberheim, Sequential Circuits, Yamaha, Korg, and Kawai.

The MIDI control signal can communicate several parameters about musical notes that are independent of the instrument on which they are played. These parameters include the pitch value, its amplitude (how hard a note is played), the effects of using a pitch-bend wheel, modulation wheel, and volume pedal, and how hard a key is pressed while a note is being sustained.

The MIDI interface was designed with two basic performance applications in mind:

- MIDI can connect standalone electronic music instruments and permit one instrument to control the sounds being made on several others. This can be done without a separate computer. The instruments may or may not have keyboards, although in a typical multi-instrumental setup there is at least one keyboard that triggers all of the activity.
- MIDI can connect standalone electronic music instruments with a PC. In this configuration, the computer is used to trigger sounds and patterns on the connected instruments. Many multiple MIDI channels may be operated simultaneously in this way.

As with any industry standard, the creation of the MIDI protocol was not completed without some compromises. The primary limitation of MIDI is that it was conceived with the production of keyboard music in mind. This was rightfully viewed as providing the most widespread commercial application of the standard, but it potentially left in the lurch many composers who had ideas unrelated to keyboard music. Over the years, however, MIDI has proved to be eminently adaptable by engineers and composers alike, so that today its limitations are often overcome in many creative ways. Not long after the introduction of MIDI, the same protocols used to generate control signals between keyboard synthesizers were being adopted for a wide variety of other musical applications. Wind instruments, drum machines, and effects boxes all became MIDI-compatible. David Rockeby in Toronto created a way to translate images from a video camera into MIDI signals. His Very Nervous System was used in 1991 to interpret and translate the images of a dancer into musical accompaniment. Donald Buchla has devoted his most recent years to the development of new controllers that can take advantage of MIDI. Results of his work include the Lightning, a wand controller that translates the physical movement of a handheld wand in space to MIDI input signals.

Since 1978, Michel Waisvisz, the director of STEIM (Studio for Electro-Instrumental Music) in Amsterdam has dedicated himself to the creation of gestural controllers for live electronic music performance. He was on the crest of the MIDI wave in 1984. He does not record his own music anymore, instead favoring "the reality of the concert hall: direct, in contact with the audience, tangible, sensitive, sweaty and excitingly real."[6] One of his earliest electromechancial controllers was called Hands, first used in 1984. It consists of a pair of metal plates shaped so that one can be worn comfortably on each hand. The Hands contain touch-sensitive keys that can be played by the fingertips as well as sensors that respond to tilt and the changing distance between the two Hands. They send control signals to sound modules to generate sound in real time.[7]

One might think that an iconoclast like Robert Ashley would have resisted the rigor imposed by MIDI, yet he embraced it almost immediately, because it freed him from having to enlist an orchestra of acoustic instruments for certain kinds of compositions that he was contemplating. One of these was *Superior Seven* (1986). He explains it this way:

> When *Superior Seven* was composed, the MIDI system was a barely workable technology, and I must say that because I did not own a computer then and because I was not much interested in "computer music," the idea of a composition that is so appropriate to MIDI could not have occurred to me. But *Superior Seven* is very appropriate to realization in MIDI, and MIDI—not an orchestra of acoustical instruments—is the technology of this recording.[8]
>
> The piano part of the work played cues for other instruments. The other instruments were intended to play the same notes in the same register in precise synchronization with the piano cues: "Thus, the cue lines serve the same function as a sequence of note-instructions from the computer, and the cue lines 'conduct' the entrances of all the other instruments in the orchestra."[9] If he had used a live orchestra to perform the work, Ashley likened the role of the conductor to that of "the mixer at a recording console." The use of MIDI provided an ideal solution for him.

Additive and Subtractive Synthesis

Synthesis is the ability to use the fundamental building blocks of sound to construct new sounds. The earliest electronic music composers had no synthesizers at their disposal. Armed only with waveform oscillators, filters, and tape recorders, they learned how to combine and modify existing sounds to make new ones from the simplest component parts.

The simplest form of sound synthesis is the combination of two or more sine waves into a more complex waveform. This process is called *additive synthesis* and can be used to create diverse sounds by building up layers of many individual sounds. Each wave source can be treated and varied independently. In the old days, this was done by combining the sounds of several audio oscillators to produce a new result. For example, a triangle wave could be constructed by using many individual sine waves. The base or fundamental sine wave would be the loudest, and additional sine waves would be added to build the overtone structure characteristic of a triangle wave. It was a tedious way to work and required much trial and error. The result was difficult to reproduce without precise details of the settings for each of the oscillators.

Just as waveforms can be constructed by the addition of one sound to another, they can also be altered through the systematic elimination of certain parts of the sound, such as overtones or the fundamental frequency. This practice is commonly achieved through sound filtering and is called *subtractive synthesis*.

A familiar example of a filter is the sound "equalizer" available on home stereo systems. This device permits the listener to filter out various bands of frequency, usually for the purpose of eliminating noise in the high ranges and adjusting bass and treble to more closely match the acoustic requirements of a given space. In a more novel way, equalizers are sometimes used to filter out the voice of a performer on a record in order to leave only the instruments playing.

As a synthesized sound passes through a filter, it allows some frequencies to pass and cuts off others. Filters designed for electronic music come with several specific purposes in mind.

Band-pass filter. Allows only those sounds *between* specified high- and low-frequency cutoff points to be heard. It removes the high and low frequencies from a tone at the same time.

Band-reject filter. Allows only those sounds *above* or *below* specified high- and low-frequency cutoff points to be heard. It removes the midrange frequencies from a tone.

Low-pass filter. Allows only frequencies *below* a specified cutoff point to be passed. It removes the high frequencies from a tone.

High-pass filter. Allows only frequencies *above* a specified cutoff point to be passed. It removes the low frequencies from a tone.

Filters may be part of a synthesizer console, a software component for processing sounds, or a standalone device used like an effects box between the instrument and the amplifier.

Envelope Shaping

The envelope of a sound is the way the sound begins, continues, and then ends. It is the result of amplitude modulation. A note played on the piano, for example, begins with a sharp attack but may be made to end quickly or slowly, depending on whether the sustain pedal of the instrument is depressed. Notes played on wind instruments, such as the saxophone or flute, typically begin and end sharply. Electronic musical instruments offer the unique ability to vary and control the envelope characteristics of a sound. This technique can be used to change the attack characteristics of all sounds activated by the keyboard. Rather than having abrupt, instantaneous attacks, like the notes played on a piano, the sounds can be made to have slowly rising attacks of increasing volume.

Amplitude Modulation (AM)

Amplitude modulation (AM) is the use of a control voltage to alter (modulate) the loudness of another signal. The sound that is being modulated is called the carrier signal. When a subaudio signal is used to modulate a given sound wave, the result is a slow, undulating effect called *tremolo* in which the volume of the sound becomes alternately louder and softer but without changing the pitch. The loudness rises and falls around a central amplitude.

All types of waveforms can be used as control signals. Using a sine wave to modulate the carrier will cause the loudness to rise and fall very gradually. A triangle wave will effect a gradual rise in loudness that sharply turns down and gradually falls, only to switch directions again very sharply. The use of a pulse wave as an amplitude-modulating signal eliminates the various gradients between loud and soft, and causes the carrier to switch instantly between the two extremes.

When the control signal is a waveform in the audio range, the changes in loudness become much more difficult to perceive because of their rapidity, and the resultant effect is the creation of audible *sidebands* of the carrier signal. Sidebands are the partials or harmonics that make up part of a total sound but do not dominate it. They add tone color or body to the sound. Sidebands are mathematically related to the carrier: the upper sidebands are equal to the sum of the carrier and control frequencies, while the lower sidebands are equal to the difference between them. When sidebands become audible, the carrier signal still remains the dominant signal.

Frequency Modulation (FM)

Frequency modulation (FM) is the use of a control voltage to alter the frequency (pitch) of the sound. A subaudio control voltage will produce a *vibrato* effect, which is an undulation of pitch around the central carrier tone. As in amplitude modulation, when the control voltage is in the audible frequency range, the resultant signal contains sidebands of the carrier wave. The complexity and harmonics of FM sidebands are much more intricate and rich than those produced by AM. Unlike AM, FM sidebands may actually dominate the carrier tone.

Ring Modulation

Ring modulation is a form of amplitude modulation in which special circuitry suppresses the carrier signal and reproduces only the sidebands. Two additional frequencies are created in place of the original carrier signal. One is equal to the sum of the two input frequencies, and the other is equal to the difference between them. If the input signal has many harmonics, such as a guitar or the human voice, the resulting output signal is complex and rich, a kind of ghost of the original sound. The analog ring modulator still being made by Robert Moog (b. 1934) has a second input signal in the form of an oscillator. This can be adjusted to narrow or widen the distance between the two frequencies generated by the effect.

Other Electronic Music Techniques and Effects

Amplification of sounds. A microphone and amplifier can be used to pick up any sound and feed it into a synthesizer or computer for modification. This puts the entire universe of sounds at the disposal of the composer. A microphone converts sound into analog electrical signals. The analog signal can be modified for input to a computer using an analog-to-digital converter.

Two kinds of microphones or pickups have been commonly used in the production of electronic music:

> **Conventional "air" microphones.** These are the most familiar type of microphone and are designed to react to pressure waves in the air. Condenser or electrostatic microphones are the preferred kinds for making accurate recordings of sounds such as instruments, voices, and ambient noise. These kinds of microphones can generally detect sounds in the full frequency response range of human hearing, say, from less than 100 Hz to about 20,000 Hz.

> **Contact microphones:** These microphones are designed to pickup vibrations while in direct contact with a vibrating or resonating surface. They are quite limited in their frequency response, only sensing a narrow band of frequencies of no more than a few thousand hertz, usually at the lower end of the scale. Even so, contact microphones are a familiar staple of electroacoustic music because of their ability to amplify quiet, undetectable sounds. They can be inexpensively constructed using a few dollars' worth of parts from Radio Shack.

Other kinds of pickups that can be used to detect sound waves include magnetic pickups found on guitars, and the humble phonograph cartridge. Around 1960, John Cage and David Tudor discovered that they could get some startling results by using a phono cartridge as a kind of contact microphone. The cartridge is designed to pickup the vibrations present in the groove of a vinyl audio recording. It does this by way of a needle or stylus that runs in the groove of the record. The vibrations are then converted into electrical signals that are amplified. Cage and Tudor made their new sounds by detaching the cartridge from its tonearm, replacing the phonograph needle with objects such as toothpicks, Slinkys, and straight-pins, and then amplifying the results of physical contact between the surrogate "needle" and other objects.

Feedback. Composer Robert Ashley calls feedback "the only sound that is intrinsic to electronic music."[10] Not only is it a natural effect that is available whenever a microphone or audio pickup is used, but it also introduces the use of sustained sounds, which is one of electronic music's inherent attributes. While it is certainly one of the most familiar and easily obtainable effects when using a microphone or amplified instrument, it is one of the most delicate and difficult to control.

Feedback is a wonderfully rich and expressive voice when incorporated into music. Ashley himself is famous for his piece *The Wolfman* (1964), a very early manipulation of feedback as an intentional part of the music. In this piece, the level of amplification is set very high, at the point of feedback for the given audio space. The performer delivers a set of vocal patterns while keeping his mouth in very close proximity to the microphone. Ashley described the effect:

> In *The Wolfman* the feedback is tuned for whatever place you're performing in. Then into that feedback are put different kinds of modulating materials on tape. That modulated feedback product is passing through the sole microphone in the space, the singer's microphone. That means that by just putting your mouth up against the microphone, and by doing very simple vocalisms, you can affect that whole feedback system in a very slow, modulation filtering sense. That's the principle of the piece. The feedback is a loop and the tape sound is being broadcast into that loop. The bottleneck in that loop is the microphone so that by treating the resonant cavity right in front of the microphone you actually create a model of the room in the size of the vocal cavity. It's a very simple principle. The room just keeps moving around and changing shape because of the way you shape your mouth. The act of doing it in the presence of that sound–the feedback–is so overpowering to the listener that no one ever understands how the sound is made.[11]

Steve Reich (b. 1936) arrived at his work called *Pendulum Music* (1968) by devising a way to manipulate the raw power of acoustic feedback using the mechanics of a swinging object. In this work, one or more loudspeakers were placed on their backs, aimed at the ceiling. Microphones were the source of the input signal. The amplitude was turned up to the point where feedback would occur if the microphones were brought within proximity of the front of a loudspeaker. The microphones, suspended from the ceiling on long cables like pendulums, were then swung so that they would pass just over the loudspeakers. As a microphone crossed the space above a loudspeaker it would create a whooping feedback sound. As the swing of the microphones eventually decayed, they came to rest directly over the loudspeakers, causing uninterrupted feedback until the amplifier was shut off.

Reich, whose highly determinist compositions stand in stark contrast to Cage's work, was amused by the combination of process and chaos that *Pendulum Music* represented:

> Over a period of ten minutes, which was a little too long for my taste, and as the pendulums come to rest, you entered a pulsing drone. Once it hit the drone, I would pull the plug on the machine and the whole thing ended. It's the ultimate process piece. It's me making my peace with Cage. It's audible sculpture. If it's done right, it's kind of funny.[22]

What began as a straightforward compositional process ended with the cacophony of an opposing process: uncontrolled electronic feedback.

New Yorker David Lee Myers (b. 1949) has been creating electronic music using *only* feedback for over twenty years. His is not feedback of the acoustic variety, however, for the sound does not result from the interference of a highly amplified signal in the proximity of a loud-speaker. He feeds electronic circuits back onto themselves to create interference noise that he can then mix, filter, and shape using audio processors:

> The idea is that an effects device is fed some of its own output—much like a squealing speaker which accidentally feeds the microphone supplying its input—and electrons begin to flow as they wish. The trick is to shape this flow, select the feedback paths which create an aesthetically pleasing, or whatever direction and shape. What is required is several devices whose business it is to bend sound into various shapes, and a routing scheme which allows them to speak to each other and to themselves.[13]

Using a variety of specialized "feedback workstations" that he has constructed over the years, Myers creates a music with no human origins—no keyboards signaling pitches, no dials setting frequencies, no musical interfaces whatsoever. The result is a music of the ether that he shapes as the elements allow. His sonic washes sometimes result in soothing drones. Other times they pulse with the beat of interfering electrical signals.

Japanese composer Toshimaru Nakamura (b. 1962) has recently borrowed a page from Myers' book. He wires a mixing panel so that its output line is plugged into its input line to create minimal sonic pictures resulting from his "no-input mixing." Whereas Myers explores the vast peaks and valleys that can be generated by internalized electronic feedback, Nakamura is intent on reducing the experience to a wire-frame representation of sound.

Reverberation. Unlike echo, reverberation does not involve the periodic repetition of a given sound. "Reverb" adds resonance and depth to a sound, much as singing in the bathroom or shouting in a large auditorium does. In a sense, reverb is really a sound with many echoes that are spaced so closely that they do not become distinct or separate from the original sound.

Reverb was first achieved electronically by running a sound through a metal spring before amplifying it. This created additional vibrations of the sound and the sound shadows associated with reverb. The amount of spring reverb could be controlled by adjusting the tension of the spring and the amount of amplification of the signal passing through it. Like echo effects, reverb is now created using digital circuits that model analog spring reverb but also provide greater control and precision in setting the level of reverberation desired.

Recording and sampling. The tape recorder was the original "sampler," allowing its user to manipulate recorded sounds and make them a part of an abstract musical composition. The entire body of tape music collectively known as musique concrète was based on the concept of sampling. It depended on removing sounds from their familiar surroundings and recontextualizing them as a form of musical expression. Sampling is done today using digital recorders, software editors, and specialized sampling keyboard instruments.

Chapter 3

MUSICAL PRECEDENTS TO ELECTRONIC MUSIC: ORIGINS OF THE AVANT-GARDE

Electronic music is an outgrowth of larger trends in twentieth-century music and culture. A new avant-garde was developing that rejected old rules of melody, harmony, rhythm, and composition. Electronic musical instruments were a liberating force behind new musical style. To understand the development of electronic music, we have to briefly review the early history of twentieth-century music.

The expression "avant-garde" was originally a French military term meaning "vanguard," as in the first wave of soldiers mounting an attack. These were the soldiers most likely to be killed while leading an assault on a well-fortified enemy compound. The term was borrowed by Parisian artists of the late nineteenth-century, no doubt because they too felt the somewhat daunting futility of putting their careers on the line while battling the more conservative tastes of the typical patron of the arts.

Historically, the avant-garde emerged during a time of great change in society. The industrial revolution spread new technology at an unprecedented rate. Electricity illuminated once-darkened nights. Telephony dramatically modified our concepts of time and space by allowing two people to communicate at the same time without being in the same place. The automobile allowed people to more fully explore the world beyond their neighborhood. It was a time of great hope but also of great struggle. The industrial revolution increased the stratification of society by expanding the ranks of the rich and the poor alike. It also fed the world's military powers with new and improved weapons of war, leading to conflict after conflict and eventually to World Wars I and II.

As has always been the case, artists are apt to reflect changes in society by making changes in their art. Beginning in the 1880s, composers responded with a revolution of their own.

Alternate Pitch Systems, New Scales, and Atonality

As the nineteenth-century drew to a close, some composers were beginning to question the limitations of the equal-temperament scale, the tuning system that had evolved in the seventeenth-century as the de facto standard for use in orchestral music. The adherence of this scale to twelve tones of equal intervals allowed for smooth transitions from key to key and was easily adapted to the tonal ranges of the orchestral instruments that had evolved by that time. The piano itself was a reply from the industrial age to the twelve-tone, equal-temperament scale: a musical machine with a fixed set of musical intervals that would stay in tune for a long time.

The equal-temperament scale, of course, is not universally found in all world music. Some systems use whole-tone instead of half-tone scales; others use scales with more or fewer tones and equal or unequal steps between them. By the turn of the century, Western composers became increasingly aware of alternative scales and the possibility that an octave might be divided into more than twelve equal steps. Any scale with more than twelve steps is known as a *microtonal* scale.

One of the first modern composers to experiment with different scales was Erik Satie (1866–1925). In 1887, after having dreamed away several years at the Paris Conservatoire, the young Parisian wrote his *Gymnopédies* (1988) and *Sarabandes* (1887) for piano. He had become bored with the contrivance of major-minor tonality as found in Germanic symphonies and operas, and was no more enamored of the self-conscious approach of "impressionist" music—then still a young movement. He was later to comment on his experience at the Paris Conservatoire, "My harmony professor thought I had a gift for the piano, while my piano professor considered that I might be talented as a composer." Satie set forth to create a new music of lucid clarity, stripped of ornamentation and "sauce," as he called it. The result was a blow for simplicity straight from the heart of this most original of composers.

Satie first applied medieval scales and the modes of Gregorian chant to his music in the *Gymnopédies* and *Sarabandes*. These haunting and unforgettable pieces employed delicate melodies in conjunction with floating harmonic blocks and unresolved chords to suspend the sound, with a kind of mystical aura. Some of the scores for Satie's early piano works omitted bar lines as well as time and key signatures.

Satie was eccentric in almost every respect. He notated his scores with humorous and banal instructions to test the performer's wit and engage him or her psychologically in the performance of his works. Written above the staff instead of instructions such as "Slowly" or "Moderately," one was more likely to find a performance indicator such as "A bit rococo but slow," "Dance inwardly," "Do not cough," "Cloisterly," "With tears in your fingers," "Like a nightingale with a toothache," or dozens of other instructions.

Satie's acerbic wit, indifference to public acknowledgment, and penchant for unusual titles (such as *Veritable Flabby Preludes, Chapters Turned Every Which Way,* and *Old Sequins and Old Carcasses*) gave his reputation an aura of self-imposed ridiculousness. Yet the experiments he undertook to free French music from the European traditions were the force underlying much of the impressionist movement. Debussy, for instance, went on to employ the pentatonic and other medieval scales and to a large extent receives credit for developing these techniques, which were in fact first attempted by Satie.

Debussy became *the* pivotal figure of modern music in France. In 1889 he attended the Paris Exposition, which marked the one-hundredth anniversary of the French Revolution. There he heard Balinese gamelan music for the first time. His exposure to this led him to experiment with the whole-tone scale, which is suggestive of Far Eastern modes. Debussy was brimming over with creative enthusiasm and seized every experience, every influence, as a means for mobilizing his own ideas. He was a marvelous assimilator of concepts, an archetype of the modern composer in a world that has fewer and fewer ethnic, and sonic, borders.

Debussy first met Satie in 1890, when Satie was performing as pianist at Le Chat Noir, a well-known cabaret in Montmartre. Satie, twenty-four, and Debussy, twenty-eight, became fast friends. Both were disillusioned with the current condition of music, and as they watched their peers wallowing in the mire of Wagner, each laid down plans to change the state of the art. By this time, both men had experimented with unusual tonal scales, suffered through an academic environment in which their ideas were met with indignation, and become charter members of the avant-garde social life of Paris. It was probably during one of their discussions at a French club that Satie uttered his famous line "We ought to have our own music—if possible, without sauerkraut!"

Satie shared some thoughts with Debussy on a lyric opera he was considering. As the story goes, Debussy was so influenced by this conversation that he went on to compose his only completed opera, *Pelléas et Mélisande,* which took him ten years to write. In the meantime, Satie continued to sculpt his whimsical, crystalline piano works with such titles as *Pièces froides* (Cold Pieces, 1897) and *Trois morceaux en forme de poire* (Three Pieces in the Form of a Pear, 1903).

Satie and Debussy perfected several distinct experimental approaches to music, including: the use of organum, in which two or more melodies are written in parallel so that they rise and fall in equal steps simultaneously; the application of the whole-tone scale and other scales consisting only of primary intervals and lacking major and minor steps like the half steps of the chromatic scale, as found on the piano; and the use of repetitive chords in a steady rhythmic pattern to achieve a suspension of motion and tension. Perhaps the foremost preoccupation of both composers was their effort to free melody from its traditional underpinning of keys and chords, allowing it to move and develop independently of any presupposed and melodramatic superstructures. This gave much of their music its detached, disembodied serenity.

Vexations (1893) was Satie's most enigmatic and abstract work. Comprising a score of only one page, it consists of 180 notes to be played on the piano with the following instruction written at the top: "To play this motif 840 times in succession, it would be advisable to prepare oneself beforehand, in the deepest silence, by serious immobilities." This previously unknown work was brought to the attention of John Cage in 1949, and in 1963 Cage produced its first performance using a relay team of ten pianists. The performance took more than eighteen hours. Had the term "minimalism" been in vogue at the time, *Vexations* would no doubt have been branded as its granddaddy. Cage summed up the performance in this way:

> The experience over the 18 hours and 40 minutes of those repetitions was very different from the thought of them or the realization that they were going to happen. For them to actually happen, to actually live through it, was a different thing. What happened was that we were very tired, naturally, after that length of time and I drove back to the country. . . . I slept an unusually long period of time, and when I woke up, I felt different than I had ever felt before. And furthermore the environment that I looked out upon looked unfamiliar even though I had been living there. In other words, I had changed and the world had changed. . . . It wasn't an experience I alone had, but other people who had been in it wrote to me or called me up and said that they had had the same experience.[1]

The score of *Vexations* is perplexing and defies a performer's normal musical instincts. It is not easy to play even once, let alone 840 times. It becomes an exercise in deep concentration, a transfixing experience that reprograms the consciousness of those who perform and listen to it. It is perhaps the first calculated example of a western composition made to create a new state of listening. In this way, it has an overtly spiritual function as music. Its performance has a reality-altering effect that is more like that of an Indian raga or Balinese mon-key-chant than a recital of European music.

During the same period that Satie and Debussy began using whole-tone scales, a number of other composers and theoreticians began to suggest even more elaborate approaches. Microtonal scales employ intervals that are smaller than the traditional half tones of the chromatic scale. A composer may devise any division of the octave that is desired. Early proponents including Shohe Tanaka and Carl Fitz created micro-tonal scales having from 20 to 104 notes per octave. Unfortunately, no instruments existed at the time for playing such music. These ideas clearly anticipated the need for new kinds of instruments, which was never satisfactorily addressed until the development of electronic music synthesizers that could be tuned in variable scales.

In 1888 a fourteen-year-old American named Charles Edward Ives (1874–1954) wrote his first song, *Majority*. In the piano accompani-ment, he used a tone cluster, which required the simultaneous playing of adjacent keys on the piano—a rebellious act for a beginning composer. This is probably the first documented use of a tone cluster in a score. Ives went on to employ the device in many later pieces. True to form, he remained a musical rebel throughout his career, developing into one of America's most original and prolific modern composers. He added sev-eral new techniques to the lexicon of composition, including polytonal-ity (the use of different keys simultaneously), polyrhythms (the simultaneous use of different rhythms), and polymeters (layers of differ-ing rhythms and rapidly changing meters). He also explored microtonal music, mostly through his piano work for quarter tones. The resource-ful Ives once tuned two pianos a quarter tone apart so that he could compose and play his *Three Quartertone Piano Pieces* (1923–24).

Following the early work of Satie, Debussy, and Ives, the explo-ration of alternatives to the standard chromatic tonal scale was champi-oned by many composers. They included Ferruccio Busoni (1866–1924), Béla Bartók (1881–1945), Arnold Schoenberg, and Anton Webern (1883–1945). In 1907, Busoni, a well-known Italian-German pianist, composer, theoretician, and teacher, read about the Telharmonium of Thaddeus Cahill (1867–1934) in *McClure's* magazine. He was inspired by the possibilities of using such an instrument to develop new tonal scales and was compelled to write about it in his famous manifesto *Entwurf einer neuen Ästhetik der Tonkunst* (Sketch of a New Aesthetic of Music):

> Dr. Thaddeus Cahill . . . has constructed a comprehensive apparatus
> which makes it possible to transform an electric current into a fixed and
> mathematically exact number of vibrations. As pitch depends on the num-

ber of vibrations, and the apparatus may be "set" on any number desired, the infinite gradation of the octave may be accomplished by merely moving a lever corresponding to the pointer of a quadrant.

Busoni came the closest to recognizing the value of the Telharmonium as a precursor of an experimental age of music. It took nearly sixty years for this vision of electronically generated microtonal scales to become truly practical with the development of the analog synthesizer.

In 1906 the Hungarian composer Béla Bartók began to incorporate elements of his country's native folk music into his compositions. This folk music impressed him with its use of old musical modes, lack of major and minor keys, and employment of pentatonic scales. His *Twenty Hungarian Folksongs* (1906) was an early work to exhibit this influence. Bartók became noted for using polymodality (combining different modes), polytonality (combining major and minor keys), percussive dissonance (anticipating Stravinsky), droning bass lines, repeated notes, repetitive rhythmic structures, and tonal dissonance.

Arnold Schoenberg composed his last piece of music to use a major or minor key signature, the *String Quartet No. 2 in F-sharp Minor*, in 1907, and turned his attention to creating what he called *twelve-tone music*. By the '20s, he had refined his technique so that it focused on a basic characteristic of the equal-temperament scale that had previously been avoided. In his system, the smallest atomic unit of the scale was not the chord, as had been previously practiced, but an individual note. Thus he discarded the time-honored rules governing tonal harmony and key relationships. He and his followers Alban Berg (1885–1935) and Anton Webern began to compose music based on the relationships of the notes to one another, regardless of key. Notes were free to be themselves without respect to traditional harmony. Schoenberg did not want to encourage total chaos, so he made up some rules. They could be applied to any adjacent set of twelve notes (black and white keys) you can play on the piano:

- The twelve notes must be arranged in a definite order (the tone "row").
- Each composition is created around its own tone row.
- The twelve tones can be used in a melody in any order, provided that no tones are repeated before any others are used.
- Each tone is given equal importance and is not reliant on a tonic (the keynote of a melody; in the key of C, the C note is the tonic).
- The tone row may be inverted or reversed.[2]

Music composed using this twelve-tone system is called *atonal* music because it lacks a tonal center or key.

With its emphasis on the tone row, this music avoided the use of familiar chord and melody structures, and employed a highly organized, often mathematical approach to building a piece of music from sequences of notes.

Webern elevated twelve-tone technique to extremely high altitudes, where the air is thin and time seems to slow. He extended Schoenberg's principles by applying them to tone color—the combination of instruments that he would allow to play at the same time. In his *Symphony* (1928) for chamber orchestra, the theme is brief and consists of seemingly isolated tones that bear little relationship to one another. Schoenberg's non-repeat rule is applied to tone color: each instrument is allowed to play only one note at a time and does not play another note until all the other instruments have been heard from in turn.

Webern's music is austere and threadbare, a clothesline without the clothes. He exploited the most radical portions of Schoenberg's doctrine, and suppressed all repetition in his work, feeling that this led to a continually renewable source of creativity. There is a nascent tendency in twelve-tone music toward time compression that Webern took to extremes. His works are shorter than short. The *longest* of his *Five Pieces for Orchestra* (1911–13) is only a minute. His life's output consists of only thirty-one works, and it only requires about three hours to play them back-to-back. "This is not much to show for a creative activity that extended over thirty-five years," remarks music historian Joseph Machlis, "but the music is so carefully calculated that it impresses one as having been written at the rate of a few notes a day."[3]

Webern moved toward the complete control of all tonal elements of a work, applying strict rules to the designation of pitch, timbre, and rhythm. Those that followed him—most notably Pierre Boulez (b. 1925) and Karlheinz Stockhausen—extended his ideas even further by seeking the total "serialization" of a piece of music, applying his technique not only to pitches, timbres, and rhythms, but to dynamics, densities, and amplitude as well.

Webern's life was cut short by a tragic case of mistaken identity. After surviving the Nazi regime in Germany, he was accidentally shot dead by an Allied soldier in 1945, five months after the end of the war, while violating a curfew to smoke a cigarette.

The "Art of Noise" In Music

By 1910, music patrons were politely humoring the eccentric approaches to tonality that could be heard in the works of Debussy, Ives, Schoenberg, Satie, and others. This set the stage for the next onslaught, for which they were hardly ready: the use of noise as an element in music. This movement began, appropriately, with the piano. In his *Allegro barbaro* (1911), Bartók suddenly began to pound loud, dissonant "chords" on the keyboard. Even more alarming, though, were the antics of a young composition student at the University of California named Henry Cowell. In 1912, Cowell took Ives's tone cluster to the next level, making it the centerpiece of many compositions. Whereas Ives had mostly restricted his clusters to two or three simultaneous notes, Cowell banged on the keyboard with his forearm, the flat of his hand, or a length of wood in order to depress an entire range of adjacent keys at the same time. Going even further, he plucked and struck the strings on the inside of the piano. His techniques were so well developed that he published a book called *New Musical Resources* in 1930 (written in 1918 when he was only twenty-one) to document his efforts. Cowell was one of the most durable members of the American avant-garde and gained notoriety for his performances during the 1920s and 1930s.

Even more startling was the Futurist movement, which sprang up in Italy in 1909. It was conceived and organized by poet Emilio Filippo Tommaso Marinetti (1876–1944), and while its primary focus was in the visual arts, some of its members became interested in new musical ideas. In 1911, the composer Francesco Balilla Pratella (1880–1955) published a manifesto, *Futurist Music*. In this work, he expressed sentiments not unlike those being put forth in Germany, France, and the United States. He was interested in expanding the range of harmonic music through the use of semitones and agreed with the use of a "chromatic atonal mode," as previously introduced by Schoenberg. He called this the "enharmonic mode," and although he claimed this development as "a magnificent conquest by Futurism," his formula does not seem to be vastly different from theories being considered elsewhere at that time. In addition, Pratella hoped to "crush the domination of dance rhythm" in order to create a freer approach to tempo, and to take charge of polyphony as a way of "fusing harmony and counterpoint."

In 1913, Pratella introduced his music at a concert at the Teatro Costanzi in Rome. He conducted his piece called *Musica Futurista* for orchestra, much to the delight of his Futurist compatriots. One painter, Luigi Russolo (1885–1947), was so inspired that he quickly wrote his own manifesto, *The Art of Noise* (1913). Russolo's ideas were more extreme than Pratella's. Pratella's objective was to develop new pitch and rhythm systems to expand the potential of existing instruments. Russolo envisioned entirely new ways of making music through the use of noise. He not only put his ideas on paper but immediately abandoned painting and devoted himself full-time to the design and invention of new mechanical noisemakers to produce his music.

Luigi Russolo and his assistant Ugo Piatti with Intonarumori, 1914. Used with permission of the Philadelphia Museum of Art, the Harry Lewis Winston Collection.

Russolo's manifesto is an impressive document and certainly an influential precursor of modern experimental music. Had the tape recorder been in existence during his time, Russolo probably would have invented his own form of musique concrète. Here are some representative statements translated from *The Art of Noise*:

> Ancient life was all silence. In the nineteenth-century, with the invention of the machine, Noise was born. Today, Noise triumphs and reigns supreme over the sensibility of men.
>
> At first the art of music sought purity, limpidity and sweetness of sound. Then different sounds were amalgamated, care being taken, however, to caress the ear with gentle harmonies. Today, music, as it becomes continually more complicated, strives to amalgamate the most dissonant, strange, and harsh sounds. In this way we come ever closer to *noise-sound*.
>
> The musical evolution is paralleled by the multiplication of machines, which collaborate with man on every front. Not only in the roaring atmosphere of major cities, but in the country, too, which until yesterday was totally silent, the machine today has created such a variety and rivalry of noises that pure sound, in its exiguity and monotony, no longer arouses any feeling.

On the other hand, musical sound is too limited in its qualitative variety of tones. . . . this limited circle of pure sounds must be broken, and the infinite variety of *noise-sound* conquered.

We Futurists have deeply loved and enjoyed the harmonies of the great masters. For many years Beethoven and Wagner shook our nerves and hearts. Now we are satiated and we find far more enjoyment in the combination of the noises of trams, backfiring motors, carriages and bawling crowds than in listening again, for example, to the *Eroica* or the *Pastorale*.

Away! Let us break out since we cannot much longer restrain our desire to create finally a new musical reality, with a generous distribution of resonant slaps in the face, discarding violins, pianos, double-basses and plaintive organs. Let us break out!

We want to attune and regulate this tremendous variety of noises harmonically and rhythmically.[4]

Russolo wanted to extend the accepted spectrum of music by introducing nonmusical sounds in a controlled fashion. With the help of the painter Ugo Piatti, he designed and built various mechanical noise-producing instruments. He called them *intonarumori* ("noise-intoners") and built them to produce "families" of sounds, ranging from "roars" (thunders, explosions, etc.) to whistles (hisses, puffs), whispers (murmurs, grumbles), screeches (creaks, rustles), percussive noises (metal, wood), and voices of animals and humans.

Russolo designed and constructed noise-intoners for each of his six categories of sounds. Outwardly, each instrument consisted of an oblong wooden box with a large metal megaphone attached to amplify the sound. Inside, there were various mechanical devices used to generate the desired sounds by turning cranks, tapping stretched membranes, and other means. Some had levers and wires to rattle pots or cardboard canisters filled with objects. One used an air bellows to create wind or breath sounds. Another used a skin stretched like a drum head that, when scraped or tapped across its diameter, produced a sequence of pitched tones. This last type of noise-intoner was used to imitate the starting of an automobile engine. Russolo also found that he could adjust the timbre of these stretched membranes by preparing them beforehand using various chemical baths. The noise-intoners were mostly played by holding a lever with the left hand to control the pitch range and turning a crank with the right hand to evoke the noise.

In addition to constructing his instruments, Russolo immersed himself in writing music for ensembles of noise-intoners. He was not a trained musician, so his scores consisted of verbal and graphic instructions, foreshadowing the use of graphical scores by electronic music composers decades in the future.

By April 1914, an entire orchestra of roarers, whistlers, whisperers, screechers, and howlers had been constructed, and Russolo's first concert was performed in Rome. The instruments were played in unison to create a variety of sound environments reminiscent of the city and nature. The works had titles such as *Awakening of Capital*, *Meeting of Cars and Airplanes*, *Dining on the Terrace of the Casino*, and *Skirmish in the Oasis*. This performance is legendary because of the public disturbance that ensued. Scores of rotten fruits and vegetables were hurled at the performers for the duration of the concert.[5] The event was topped by the arrest of Marinetti and Russolo for having incited a riot.

Bruised but triumphant, Russolo and Marinetti next presented a series of twelve performances in London in June 1914. The ensemble was arranged on stage with the megaphones of the noise-intoners aimed squarely at the audience. Behind the sizable boxes stood the musicians, each positioned with a music stand and Russolo's large sheet music perched on top. This must have been a comical and puzzling sight for most listeners, considering the music of noises that emanated from the stage. Marinetti remarked that playing the noise-intoners for the unsuspecting public was like "showing the first steam engine to a herd of cows."[6]

A critique of the event in the *Times* of London summarized the public's reaction to this music by likening the sounds to those "in the rigging of a channel-steamer during a bad crossing." This critic suggested that it had been "unwise" of the musicians to proceed after their first piece was greeted by "the pathetic cries of 'no more' from all parts of the auditorium." Marinetti himself claimed that the performances were a huge success and attracted as many as 30,000 people.

Russolo received a serious head injury during World War I, but after a long recovery period returned to Paris to continue his exploration of noise-making machines. One was the Rumorarmonio—the "noise harmonium"—which put several of his noise-making devices under the control of a piano-style keyboard. One firsthand account of the Rumorarmonio described it as an elaborately modified piano whose mechanical action struck metal plates, rattled porcelain, and drew croaking noises and "choked calls, cries" from its insides.[7]

Sadly, all of Russolo's scores and noise-intoners were lost during World War II, and only one extremely poor recording exists of one of his performances (Paris, 1921). Pierre Henry (b. 1927) composed an homage to the Futurists in 1975 that employed several newly constructed versions of Russolo's noise-intoners. In addition, the Foundation Russolo-Pratella has, since 1979, undertaken a revival of Futurist music using notes and firsthand accounts from Russolo's time to recreate his instruments and music.

Back in France, Erik Satie had joined forces with the playwright Jean Cocteau to present a "ballet" called *Parade* in 1917. With sets by Pablo Picasso and choreography by Leonid Massine, this work was a pivotal piece of avant-garde craftsmanship. Cocteau characterized the ballet as a manifesto of cubism. The stage was filled with a variety of nonsense activities, including the antics of a Chinese magician, a dancer who mimed the riding of a horse and swimming in a river, and a troupe of acrobats flying across the stage. It was Satie's music that caused the biggest uproar. Not only did it nonchalantly move from ragtime to classical motifs but it included such nonmusical sounds as the pounding of a typewriter, a steamship whistle, a siren, and an airplane motor. The audience revolted and the newspapers denounced the spectacle. In one reply to a critic, Satie simply wrote:

Sir and Dear Friend,
You are not only an arse, but an arse without music.

Erik Satie

Chapter 4

ELECTRONIC PIONEERS: CAHILL, THEREMIN, MARTENOT, TRAUTWEIN, AND HAMMOND

The technology of electronic music has a longer history than many might imagine. Rudimentary experiments in the electrical production of sound were taking place before the invention of the light bulb. The principles of electricity were hardly understood until the late 1800s. At that time, any discussions of oscillating electrical waves—or oscillating anything, for that matter—were strictly within the purview of science. The German physicist Hermann von Helmholtz, a prominent scientist of the late 1800s, illustrated many of his theories about electromagnetic wave action by using tuning forks and musical demonstrations. It wasn't long until inventors began to find a way to apply these ideas to the electrical creation of musical sound.

Some of the earliest devices that produced sounds electrically were the results of experimental accidents that remained largely misunderstood by their inventors. In 1837, one Dr. C. G. Page of Salem, Massachusetts, reported in the *American Journal of Science* that he had discovered a way of generating a "distinct ringing sound" by toying with the action of horseshoe magnets and a spiral of copper wire with its ends connected to a zinc-lead battery. He called the result "galvanic music," and although he was at a loss to explain the phenomenon, he had stumbled on a way of producing fairly pure electronic sounds. Similar experiments were conducted by others, but no one seemed successful in applying this discovery to the design of a musical instrument.

The first actual electronic musical instrument was invented in 1874 by American Elisha Gray (1835–1901). Professionally, he was involved in the field of telegraph communications. He obtained his first telegraph patent in 1867 and was employed by the Western Electric Company as a supervisor. Gray is best known for his contentious patent dispute with Alexander Graham Bell over the design of the original telephone in 1876.

In early 1874, Gray discovered that his young nephew had connected some curious electrical circuits involving batteries and a vibrating metal strip to a bathtub, and this produced an audible hum when the circuits were opened and closed. In essence, Gray's nephew had inadvertently devised a primitive method for transmitting vibratory currents created by the spring-loaded metal strip. Gray reproduced the experiment in his lab and began exploring a number of practical applications of the effect. One of these was the invention of a small keyboard device equipped with enough single-tone "transmitters" to play an octave. He called this the "musical telegraph," and took the instrument on tour with him to England in August and September of 1874. He also produced a two-octave version late in the same year. The unit was polyphonic and predated the introduction of the first practical electric organ by sixty years.

Any significance that this invention might have had to the world of music was lost when Gray dropped further research into its musical applications. Instead, he saw in the musical telegraph a primitive design for sending several telegraph signals at once, what we would today call a multiplexer. In 1885 a German, Ernst Lorenz, developed an elaboration of the sound-generating circuits demonstrated by Gray, and investigated ways of controlling the envelope of the sound. Although this device was patented, it apparently never enjoyed any practical use outside of the laboratory.

The "Singing Arc" of the English physicist William Duddell became a familiar novelty around the turn of the century. Duddell was trying to devise a way of eliminating the annoying whining sound that emanated from the era's carbon-arc streetlights. In 1899 he learned that he could actually control the irregular piercing tones that were produced through the use of a secondary circuit system connected to the direct current of the arc. This secondary circuit was used to modulate and control the oscillations of the arc. Duddell later attached a simple keyboard to his primitive voltage-controlling device and took his show on the road. The device was a very crude demonstration of frequency modulation using a controlling circuit.

Thaddeus Cahill and the Telharmonium

The haphazard experiments of Page, Gray, and Duddell were dramatically eclipsed by the work of Thaddeus Cahill (1867–1934). Cahill was a spirited American inventor who had the technical know-how, creative genius, and marketing foresight to complete what can only be described as the most ambitious electronic music project ever conceived. Not only was he working against great technological odds (his hard-wired instrument preceded the availability of vacuum tubes by fifteen years), but his unique idea to market live electronic music over a telephone network foreshadowed the concepts of Muzak, radio broadcasting, and cable television by decades. Cahill was the first man to have a sense for the commercial potential of electronic music as well as the means and persistence to fulfill his dream. Among his achievements, he was the first to build an electronic music synthesizer, one capable of several effects and sound shaping; he used a polyphonic keyboard with touch-sensitive (dynamic) keys; he was the first to perfect the sound-generating technique of the rotating tone wheel, later used by Laurens Hammond (1895–1973) for his famous electronic organ; and he transmitted his electronic music "live" over telephone wires.

On February 4, 1896, Cahill filed a patent for a machine to produce what he described as "electrical music." He was twenty-nine at the time, but his original theories and plans for this device dated back to 1884, when he was a seventeen-year-old enrolled in the Conservatory of Music of the Oberlin Academy in Ohio. The science of musical acoustics was becoming better known at the time because of the pioneering work of Helmholtz. It appears that Cahill was sufficiently inspired by this work to dream up his electrical method for purifying musical sound and putting the power of a synthetic orchestra in the hands of a single performer. He first filed for a patent for the device on August 10, 1895, but, finding the original design overly complicated and impractical, he assimilated its pertinent features into a better-conceived forty-five-page patent opus in 1896. In Cahill's own words, the "grand objects" of his invention were to "generate music electrically with tones of good quality and great power and with perfect musical expression, and to distribute music electrically generated by what we may term 'original electrical generation' from a central station to translating instruments located at different points." Cahill's plan was to build an electronic music device and pipe live music to remote locations. This device could imitate the sounds of familiar orchestral instruments or use the unusual electronic sonorities that were unique to it.

The patent that he obtained in 1896 described his system in great detail. The instrument itself became known by two different names: the Dynamophone and the Telharmonium. Cahill preferred the second. The original patent described a device with electrical tone-generating devices, dynamics-controlling devices for building and shaping individual tones, a keyboard for activating the tone-generating circuitry, and a speaker system for reproducing the sound. The opening paragraph of the patent even uses the word "synthesizing" to describe the way the Telharmonium would combine individual tones to create composite sounds, and we can credit Cahill with coining the term in this field.

The complexity of Cahill's early musical machine is surprising. The tone-generating mechanism of the first patent consisted of twelve "pitch shafts," or axles, on which were mounted a series of "rheotomes," or cogged metal tone wheels. These were, in essence, a series of elementary alternators that, when rotated rapidly by the turning of the pitch shafts, brought each tone wheel into contact with a metal brush, which was part of an electrical circuit. The rapid on-and-off contact of grooves in a tone wheel with a brush created an electrical oscillation of a given frequency or tone.

Each of the twelve pitch shafts corresponded to one note of the chromatic scale. All of the shafts were rotated in unison by a single motor using an elaborate wheel-and-belt system, therefore maintaining a steady rate of rotation and keeping all of the shafts spinning at a constant pace. This design assured that all of the pitch shafts would remain in tune with one another—unless, of course, there was some slippage in the belts. Cahill eliminated the latter possibility by later designing a direct-drive system using mechanical linkage.

To derive each of the twelve notes of the scale, Cahill had to cut the correct size and number of grooves in the surface of each tone wheel. Each individual tone wheel could produce a single pure sine tone, but Cahill's knowledge of the physics of tonal sound told him that he would need to add harmonics to each tone in order to create a full-bodied sound. He did this by employing multiple tone wheels for each note, with each wheel representing one partial of the designated base frequency. The first partial was identified as the "ground tone," and to this he added as many as five more tone wheels to provide overtones for any given note of the scale.

Cahill set aside one rotating pitch shaft for each note of the twelve-tone scale. To create octaves of a single note, he simply added corresponding groups of tone wheels to the appropriate shafts. Each shaft, therefore, was designed to hold a series of tone wheel groups, each corresponding to a different octave of the same note. The device described in the patent had seven octaves per note. The first five octaves each used six partials, while the sixth used four, and the seventh only two. Cahill based this design on the fact that at higher frequencies, musical sounds have fewer overtones and so become purer. The original Telharmonium design, then, included 84 notes or rheotome groups, corresponding to the 84 notes of a seven-octave piano. These notes employed 408 individual rheotomes to create all of the partials needed to create the tones.

The Telharmonium used a specially designed keyboard that was pressure-sensitive. Every group of tone wheels—each representing one note of the scale—was connected to an individual key through an electrical circuit. When depressed, each key served to close the circuit, thus producing a tone. The keys were made touch-sensitive through the use of a coil in the circuit-closing action. The harder a key was depressed, the closer the proximity of the coil and the louder the resultant sound. Unlike the pipe organ, but very much like a piano, the Telharmonium keyboard was sensitive to the amount of pressure applied by the fingers.

The tones being played were first combined in a "tone mixer" (transformer), where the individual components of the total sound could be controlled and balanced. Through creative mixing and filtering of the sound, Cahill was able to use the Telharmonium to imitate common orchestral instruments like the oboe, cello, and French horn. The sound was then directed through ordinary telephone wires to "vibration-translating devices." These were no more than common telephone receivers equipped with large paper horns to project the sound. His patent included a preferred design for an electromagnetic speaker outfitted with a wooden soundboard, but there is no evidence to show that he was ever successful in using this unique forerunner of the modern loudspeaker.

Cahill's design was for a complete electronic music synthesizer. In creating this instrument, he encountered all of the same basic technical problems faced by the designers of modern synthesizers: the method of tone generation, keeping the system in tune, purifying or modulating the tones, mixing and amplification, and the control of dynamic features for the shaping of sounds. Cahill was never able to build a Telharmonium that precisely followed his original specifications, although we will see that he came very close despite financial and technical difficulties. In all, he built three of these devices, each somewhat more complicated than its predecessor.

The first Telharmonium was a small prototype version. It was built in Washington, D.C., in 1900. Cahill constructed it purely for demonstration purposes, with the hope of gaining the financial backing that he needed to support full-scale production. This model contained only thirty-five tone wheels distributed over a single octave of twelve notes, thus allowing for only two or three tone partials per note, but it was impressive enough to interest investors in his idea. His first transmissions of electronic music over the telephone wire occurred during 1900 and 1901. These attempts were limited to sending the sound from his laboratory in one part of Washington to his home and office in other parts of town. In 1902, he sent some of his live telharmonic music to the home of George Westinghouse also in Washington, as well as to the

A musician, probably Karl W. Schulz, playing the Telharmonium in Holyoke in 1906.
The music that was triggered from this room was actually generated by the massive
Telharmonium installed in another part of the building. The music could be heard
through telephone receivers and horn speakers wired directly to the instrument.
(Smithsonian Institution Photo no. 77469. Used with permission).

office of a friend in Baltimore via leased telephone lines. Westinghouse
was a wealthy tycoon in the railroad air-brake industry, and through his
recommendation, Cahill was put in touch with his first financial back-
ers. It was during this same time that the eminent British mathematician
and physicist Lord Kelvin was taken on a tour of the Cahill lab and
reportedly gave his blessing to the young inventor.

Having secured financial support, Cahill moved his lab in 1902 to
larger facilities in Holyoke, Massachusetts. He finally had adequate
space in which to work, and he set to the task of building a much larger
machine for commercial applications. By 1904, Thaddeus and his brothers, George and Arthur, had submitted articles of incorporation for the
Cahill Telharmonium Company. Two plans emerged for the marketing
of telharmonic music.

The first telephone-based distribution network was to be launched
in Boston under the auspices of the New England Electric Music
Company, the head of which was one of Cahill's financial sponsors. This
network would have included 2,000 subscribers. The Telharmonium
was to be built in Holyoke and installed in Boston. A second machine
was planned for use in New York City by the New York Electric Music

Company. Construction went slowly, though, and by 1906, when the first large Telharmonium was completed, the plans for Boston were abandoned and all efforts were focused on getting a unit ready for the New York site.

Working under pressure from his sponsors, Cahill completed his second Telharmonium, which still did not live up to his original patent specifications. Even so, it was much larger and more functional than the prototype. He worked feverishly to complete an instrument in time to stage a demonstration for the local Holyokers. At the same time, he was building the additional components needed to upgrade the Holyoke model for use by the New York Electric Music Company, all of this to be shipped to New York by mid-1906.

Cahill's second model used 145 tone wheels instead of the intended 408. Because of this, five octaves were employed instead of seven, depriving the machine of some upper tonal ranges. In spite of these limitations, the device was versatile and sophisticated. It included two of Cahill's touch-sensitive keyboards mounted one atop the other in pipe-organ fashion. It included all of the "stops" and "expression devices" needed to vary tone color, introduce vibrato effects, and control the crescendo or diminuendo of sounds. Other enhancements included the use of a direct-drive mechanism for the rotating pitch shafts instead of the original belt-and-pulley system. Detail-minded as usual, Cahill even took the time to update his patent to reflect these improvements and preserve the rights to his invention.

The Holyoke instrument was unimaginably huge for a musical instrument. It occupied the better part of the factory building in which it was located. The 145 tone wheels were each attached to an eleven-inch section of a steel pitch shaft and divided into eight groups. This meant that each note (including six partials, for example) used almost six feet of shaft and that a shaft with five octaves measured almost thirty feet in length! The bed plate supporting all of this was comprised of eighteen-inch-thick steel girders mounted on brick supports and extending sixty feet. Nearly 2,000 switches were required to connect the keyboard with the tone wheels and various electrical devices needed to synthesize and amplify the sounds. The entire instrument weighed about two-hundred tons. To the casual viewer, this device probably resembled a power plant more than anything, and it must have created quite a racket when it was operating. The musician was stationed in a small room in the same building and had a telephone receiver so that he or she could hear the music that was playing.

Playing the Telharmonium was no small feat. In 1903, Cahill hired one Edwin Hall Pierce (1868–1954) to master the instrument and to teach junior members of the staff. Pierce, a professional pianist and organist, persevered gallantly to overcome the many technical problems he faced. Not only was he surrounded by a jungle of wires in a small room, but he had to control two keyboards and become adept at using two levels of expression devices. The first level of "stops" opened or closed the many individual partials of a single note. The second level, controlled by the hands and feet, permitted the shaping of the attack and decay of the sounds.

The first public demonstrations of the Telharmonium began on the weekend of March 16, 1906. The music was transmitted by telephone wire to the ballroom of the Hotel Hamilton, nearly a mile away. The sound was reproduced by a single telephone receiver equipped with a large paper horn and placed on a chair in the middle of the room. This image is remarkably reminiscent of the "loudspeaker concerts" of electronic music that were prevalent during the 1950s and 1960s.

What did this marvelous machine sound like? While no recordings of the Telharmonium exist, we are lucky to have some published accounts of the events that took place. The most widely read of these was by Ray Stannard Baker and appeared in the popular *McClure's* magazine in July 1906. He described the music as consisting of "singularly clear, sweet, perfect tones" and was amazed that the "whir of machinery" from the Cabot Street plant could not be heard at all. The music must have consisted of penetrating sine and triangle waves, and perhaps had the depth and presence that is associated with the Theremin. It was of sufficient amplitude to pervade all parts of the ballroom without revealing the precise location of the sound source. Baker was very moved by the experience and further described the sound as being "pure music, conveying musical emotion without interference or diversion." An account appearing in *Electrical World* also mentioned that the tones were "remarkably pure and beautiful" and that the result sounded nothing like the more familiar mechanical means for reproducing sound, the phonograph and the telephone.

On the occasion of this first public performance, the musicians succeeded in taming the Telharmonium quite well. One of the novel features of the instrument was its ability to imitate familiar orchestral instruments. The concert demonstrated this capability through the replication of oboes, flutes, French horns, bugles, and cellos. The settings for making these sounds were not stored or programmed, but were set manually like one would set the stops on a pipe organ. The musical selections played that night made generous use of vibrato effects, tone color, and various degrees of attack and decay. Among the pieces first played were Schumann's *Traumerei*, Beethoven's Trio in C Major for Two

Oboes and Cor Anglais, selections by Bach and Schubert, Stein's *Arkansas Traveler,* and a rousing imitation of a fife-and-drum corps playing *Dixie.*

After a number of well-received demonstrations, Cahill readied his equipment for the move to New York City during the summer of 1906. The equipment required more than thirty flatcars to be shipped to New York. The New York Electric Music Company occupied a new building in midtown Manhattan at 39th Street and Broadway, across the street from the original Metropolitan Opera House. The building was later dubbed Telharmonic Hall, and consisted of a main floor with a listening room. The Telharmonium keyboard console was located on a small stage in the listening space, tucked into an alcove and framed by giant ferns. Its jungle of wires were discreetly channeled through the floor to the bulky sound-generating dynamo located in the basement. The listening room itself was a posh as any lobby in a New York hotel. There were seats for more than 275 people. Romanesque columns and easy chairs surrounded a plush circular divan in the center of the space. Potted plants and ferns, many hiding loudspeakers, were strategically placed around the room.

Because this model still used only a third of the tone wheels originally specified in the patent, Cahill pondered ways to add more body to the sound without having to fabricate additional pitch shafts. Always up to the challenge, he devised a means to use each single tone wheel for more than one note of the scale through additional wiring and switches. This meant that a ground tone for one note might also be used as a partial for another. He also added a third keyboard to the instrument so that three different instrumental voices could be played at the same time.

Concerts in New York began on September 26, 1906. Subscribers were actively recruited up and down Broadway for the electronic music service. Technical problems began to arise in the practical matter of transmitting the music over telephone wires. Because of the massive amount of power needed to shoot the music through the telephone network, other telephone wires running alongside those used for the Telharmonium began to experience noise and crosstalk. The music of the Telharmonium was creeping into the conversations of unsuspecting telephone users.

Despite these early warning signs, Cahill and his partners were able to mount a successful concert season that first winter. A dozen leading hotels and restaurants became subscribers, including the Waldorf-Astoria, Victoria, and Café Martin.[1] Several wealthy clients began to have the music piped directly into their homes.[2] There was an active public concert series that increased from two to four performances a day. The public was even enticed by the promise of live telharmonic music being played on trolley cars through the overhead power wires.[3]

Technical, regulatory, and business problems soon took their toll, however. The instrument itself—being a miniature power plant of sorts—had its own peculiar problems. Cahill's own work for diverting the instrument's power to create additional harmonics stretched the electrical supply too far. The addition of notes or voices (keyboards) being played at the same time had the effect of sapping the power source so that the music gradually became quieter as more notes were played. Chords played more quietly than a single note.

Problems with the phone lines led the phone company to terminate its agreement with Cahill for disseminating telharmonic music. He and his company began going through the legal motions to obtain a permit to lay their own telephone lines, but by the time this came about the business was already in trouble. Dwindling subscribers, complaints from phone customers, and a lack of infrastructure to successfully transmit the music brought the final curtain down on Telharmonic Hall in February 1908.[4]

Cahill continued to pursue his dream. The Telharmonium was shipped back to Holyoke. He built a third, improved model, and succeeded in returning to New York City in April 1911, now into a building on West 56th Street. But even after a demonstration at Carnegie Hall, it seemed that the public, and the press, were no longer fascinated by the Telharmonium. The company declared bankruptcy in December 1914.[5]

Had Thaddeus Cahill attempted to build his Telharmonium twenty years later, with the availability of space-saving vacuum tubes and a more stable power supply in New York City, he probably would have met with some success. Unfortunately, none of that was to be, and the most ambitious achievement in the history of electronic music was soon forgotten. In spite of the fact that the mighty Telharmonium was apparently sold as scrap, its legacy lived on in the tone wheel principles used to develop the popular Hammond organ in the late 1920s.

The Theremin: Electronic Music for Everybody

With the widespread availability of the vacuum tube and radio electronics during the 1920s, many industrious individuals set to work on creating the first commercially available electronic musical instruments. Cahill's Telharmonium may have been a gigantic, temperamental monstrosity, but the vacuum tube allowed inventors to produce compact devices that didn't dim the streetlights when they were played. Perhaps even more importantly, each member of the new generation of instruments possessed a

Leon Theremin shows the circuitry inside of the Theremin's cabinet (circa 1928).
Photo courtesy of Robert Moog/Big Briar Inc.

unique electronic voice of its own and was not designed to mimic traditional instruments. Composers began to take notice.

One of the earliest instruments to capture the fancy of audiences and composers alike was the invention of Russian electrical engineer and cellist Lev Sergeyevich Termen, who was more commonly known by the anglicized version of his name, Leon Theremin (1896–1993). Originally called the Etherophone or Thereminovox but later simply the Theremin, this device was first built in Russia around 1920. Although Theremin applied for patents in Germany and America during 1924 and 1925, it wasn't until 1927 that Americans first heard public performances of the instrument. The Theremin was distinguished by the sound of sweeping, monophonic sine waves and a performance technique that lent itself to solo instrumental playing. Perhaps the strangest characteristic of the Theremin was that you played it merely by waving your hands in the vicinity of two antennae. This mystifying display not only baffled most onlookers but also added a high degree of theatricality to a performance. The Theremin was the first "space-controlled" electronic music instrument.

The Theremin operated on a modulation principle called *beat frequency oscillation*, as did numerous other early electronic music instruments that followed. Two electrical signals that were nearly equal in frequency were mixed. The combination of the two resulted in a third signal that was equal to the difference between the first two frequencies. The remaining, audible tone was the "beat frequency." The radio-frequency signal generators used in the Theremin were actually above the range of human hearing, but the difference between them was audible. The frequency of one of the oscillators was fixed, while the other could be altered by moving an object, such as the performer's, hand in the vicinity of a vertical antenna about eighteen inches tall.

As the hand entered the electromagnetic field of this antenna, the frequency of the oscillator would rise, resulting in a corresponding change to the audible beat frequency or pitch. The pitch was controlled by moving the hand back and forth in relation to the pitch antenna.

In addition to the pitch antenna, there was a secondary loop antenna, usually positioned horizontally, or a foot pedal, to control the loudness of the sound. Bringing the hand close to or touching the volume antenna would silence the sound.

The sound of the Theremin was very close to that of a pure sine wave but with enough sidebands to add depth and body to the tone. The original Theremin is said to have had a range of five octaves. The sound was continuous unless the hand was moved in and out of the vicinity of the antenna. Special effects such as vibrato were easy to produce with simple movements of the hand.

Being monophonic, the instrument was melodic in nature and enjoyed some notoriety in the public eye during the 1920s and '30s. Leon Theremin signed a licensing agreement with American radio maker RCA to manufacture and market a commercial version of his instrument to the public. The RCA Theremin was introduced in 1929. It had a range of about three and a half octaves, the highest note being about 1400 Hz. The RCA service manual for its Theremin described the instrument as:

> a musical instrument operating entirely on electrical principles and played by the movement of the hands in space. Having no limitations such as keyboards, stops, etc., exceptional individuality of expression may be obtained.[6]

Though easy to describe, the Theremin proved quite difficult to master. Only five-hundred were sold by RCA. The instrument remained a quaint novelty at music recitals throughout the 1930s. Most composers did not have a clue when it came to composing for the instrument. Its repertoire was filled with trivial and programmatic solo parts, any of which could have been played as easily on a violin or cello. Theremin himself first demonstrated the instrument by playing familiar pieces for

Clara Rockmore was the foremost interpreter of classical Theremin music (circa 1932). Photo courtesy of Robert Moog/Big Briar Inc.

cello. The most devoted thereminist of the day, Clara Rockmore (1910–1998), knew the inventor and made the rounds of classical music recitals playing conventional music on this unconventional instrument. Her selections frequently included adaptations of string parts in works by Rachmaninoff, Saint-Saëns, Stravinsky, Ravel, and Tchaikovsky. She once likened it to playing an entire string concerto on only one string. One had to literally learn how to pluck a series of notes out of thin air with great accuracy. There was little room for error. Rockmore is lovingly remembered as the greatest master of the instrument, and fortunately some audio recordings survive of her stunning performances.

Not surprisingly, many felt that the promise of the Theremin was trivialized by using it to perform conventional instrumental music. John Cage echoed the sentiments of many serious composers when in 1937 he said:

> When Theremin provided an instrument with genuinely new possibilities, Thereminists did their utmost to make the instrument sound like some old instrument, giving it a sickeningly sweet vibrato, and performing upon it,

with difficulty, masterpieces from the past. Although the instrument is capable of a wide variety of sound qualities, obtained by the turning of a dial, Thereminists act as censors, giving the public those sounds they think the public will like. We are shielded from new sound experiences.[7]

While Clara Rockmore was responsible for greatly advancing the artistry of Theremin performance, we can thank one of her contemporaries for expanding the original repertoire of the instrument into new musical territory. Lucie Bigelow Rosen (1890–1968), wife of prominent lawyer, banker, and art patron Walter Rosen, befriended Theremin around 1930. Theremin hand-built two instruments for her, and she took lessons from him. Under his tutelage, she joined Clara Rockmore as one of the most skilled thereminists ever to play the original instrument. She performed many concerts, including one at Carnegie Hall with the Philadelphia Orchestra.[8]

Rosen was interested in exploring the new musical possibilities of the Theremin. She commissioned several prominent composers, including Bohuslav Martinu (1890–1959) and Isidor Achron (1892–1948), to write original works for her.[9] These pieces explore the outer ranges of the Theremin's pitches, dynamics, and timbres. Martinu's work, the *Fantasia for Theremin, Oboe, Piano and Strings* (1944), uses his characteristic long melodic lines, and both blends and contrasts the tonalities of the Theremin with the strings and oboe. The fifteen-minute piece is beyond the skills of the average thereminist, which is undoubtedly another tribute to Lucie Rosen's virtuosity on the instrument. She premiered this work at Town Hall in New York in November 1945, along with the shorter work *Improvisation* (1945) for piano and Theremin, by Achron.

Although one would by no means call these works avant-garde, Rosen successfully coaxed many listeners into enjoying the new and different sounds made possible by the Theremin. Other composers soon followed in creating works with the unique tonalities of the instrument specifically in mind, among them Edgard Varèse, Joseph Schillinger (1895–1943), and Andrei Pashchenko (1883–1972).

Rosen was a remarkable woman with a tireless passion for the arts. Her devotion to the Theremin encompassed both technical and artistic aspects of the instrument. She compiled a series of technical notes for its care and maintenance, including troubleshooting tips from the inventor himself—which showed that she was more than a mere music parlor enthusiast. She clearly understood the circuitry and principles underlying the operation of the instrument. But it was her passion for the musical potential of the Theremin that set her apart from other thereminists. She made her intentions clear in the printed notes that she wrote to accompany her recitals at her Caramoor estate:

Lucie Bigelow Rosen performing on the Theremin (late 1930s). Photo courtesy of the Caramoor Center for Music and the Arts.

It is the earnest desire of those who are working with this instrument that it shall cease to be a novelty. One does not bring out a new violin or piano every year, though these have undergone great changes, as anyone familiar with the history of instruments knows. We should never again hear the foolish remark, "Oh yes, I heard a Theremin ten years ago, it is not new." We would be surprised if anyone said they did not need to hear Gieseking because they had seen a piano in school, or Toscanini because they had already heard a band. The relative difference is the same, between what was possible ten years ago on the electrical instruments and now, and no one can predict what will be possible in the future, except that as we study them, more and more possibilities appear.

The only impossible thing to imagine is that these new resources should not be irresistibly fascinating to a real musician, or that one example of them should not be heard where any audience for living music is found.[10]

Lucie Rosen and her husband became Theremin's chief benefactors while he lived in New York. During the 1930s, they provided a town house for him at a low monthly rent next to their own on West 54th Street. Theremin had several productive years at this location as he took on commissions to construct a variety of electronic musical instruments.

During this time he invented the Rhythmicon, an early form of drum machine using photoelectric principles and a keyboard (see below); the keyboard Theremin, a primitive synthesizer designed to emulate other musical instruments; and the Terpsitone, a small space-controlled dance platform upon which the foot movements of a dancer would trigger the sounds of the Theremin. The Terpsitone also provides evidence for Theremin's interest in the association of colored light with electronic sounds. An often-ignored aspect of the foot-controlled instrument was a bank of colored lights mounted on the wall behind it. Each was wired to correspond to a given pitch.[11]

Theremin and others—most notably Martin Taubmann with his Electronde in 1933—introduced several variations of the original instrument to make it easier to play for the space-control-challenged. These included key and foot controls to switch the sound on and off so that the Theremin could play individual notes without causing unwanted glissandi.

Theremin had ample room in his town house for entertaining guests, staging demonstrations, and constructing instruments. His space became a popular hangout for composers and artists. Through the Rosens, he was also rubbing elbows with high society and becoming acquainted with leading composers, conductors, and musicians of the day.

Several composers were so fascinated by the Theremin that they approached the inventor directly with some of their own ideas for electronic musical instruments. Two of Leon Theremin's most notable collaborations were with Henry Cowell and Edgard Varèse.

In 1931, Cowell asked Theremin to make a special keyboard instrument that came to be known as the Rhythmicon. Depressing one of the keys resulted in a pitched rhythm that could be repeated automatically. It was possible to play multiple notes and rhythms by depressing more than one key at a time. The Rhythmicon worked on the principle of light beams being cast upon photoelectric cells to produce its electronic frequencies. Cowell used this device in a number of compositions during the 1930s.

Varèse (1883–1965) was another composer who felt a natural affinity for Theremin's work. By the 1930s, he had already staked out his territory as an adventurous, highly original experimenter. Although he composed primarily for traditional instruments, he derived perverse pleasure in the deconstruction of counterpoint. Harmony and melody were subjugated in Varèse's music to dominating rhythms and ripping planes of sound. As early as 1917 he had called for new instruments that were obedient to his thought and that could summon forth all manner of unsuspected sounds. He found a kindred spirit in Leon Theremin and his electronic music instrument.

Varèse was working on *Ecuatorial* in 1933, a piece for a small ensemble consisting of a baritone voice, organ, brasses, and percussion. To this mix, he wanted to add an electronic instrument with a pitch range that exceeded the high C on the normal piano by an octave and a fifth, something akin to the upper register of the violin. He had previously worked with the Ondes Martenot when his massive orchestral work *Amériques* (1918–1921) was staged in France in 1929, and was familiar with the limitations of that instrument. The Ondes Martenot was really just a Theremin-like device with a fingerboard—and it did not have the required range for Varèse's new work. He asked Theremin to construct two instruments to meet his precise tonal and dynamic specifications. The instruments had to be able to play high, sliding pitches and sustain them for a long time.

Theremin responded by resurrecting the "cello" or "fingerboard" Theremin he had first conceived in 1922. Using the same beat frequency principle as the space-controlled model, this Theremin was controlled by sliding the finger up and down a cylindrical fretboard about the size of that found on a cello. It was played upright, resting on the floor and positioned between the legs like a stringed instrument. The left hand picked the notes on the fretboard while the right hand controlled the volume with a lever.

Upon the world premiere of *Ecuatorial* in New York in 1934, favorable reviews in both the *New York Times* and *New York Herald Tribune* remarked on the power and expressiveness of the music. They also described the sound of the fingerboard Theremin variously as "mere caterwauling" and "piercingly shrieking."[12] Although the original score called for the specially designed Theremins, Varèse substituted two Ondes Martenot for the fingerboard Theremins when he revised it in 1961,[13] possibly because fingerboard Theremins were no longer available and the inventor, having disappeared into Russia, was not around to resurrect them.

Interest in Theremin's work quieted as the '30s unfolded and the depression took hold. Despite his fortunate association with the Rosens, Theremin was constantly in a state of debt and trying to find additional work to remain solvent. Complicating matters even more was a secret that even his beloved Rosens did not know. Theremin was a Russian spy and had been passing American technological secrets to the Soviet Union since his arrival in America in 1927.[14] As 1938 arrived, he had been living in the States for ten years on a long-since-expired visa. Time was running out on him. As the intoxicating excitement of living and working in New York City was gradually supplanted by fewer and fewer projects and less and less income, he must have felt increasingly like a man in self-exile. When he became unable to pay his rent, Lucie Rosen's husband was finally forced to threaten the inventor with eviction. Before that could happen, Theremin suddenly left the country—some say under Soviet arrest—and was not heard from again for almost thirty years.[15] His parting gesture before disappearing was to finish the second of two custom-made Theremins that he had agreed to make for Lucie. One of his assignments back in the mother country was to create a new type of electronic surveillance device: the wireless bug.

The last instrument that Theremin constructed for Rosen was befitting of his wealthy patron. It was a somewhat smaller "traveling" model with a lustrous finish of lacquered ebony in the style of Chinese cabinetry. The speaker cabinet matched the instrument and they both had black velvet dust covers. The top of the instrument was less severely angled than the RCA model and had a music stand built in. There was also a means of visually previewing the pitch in the form of a neon tube, which could be viewed through a small hole in the top of the cabinet. A well-trained performer such as Rosen could associate the glowing color of this tube with a pitch range, presumably silencing the instrument with the left hand until the right hand found its mark.

Although its inventor was nowhere to be found, his famous instrument lived on.

After twenty-five years of concert-hall appearances, the Theremin next made a sidelong leap into the public consciousness through its use in motion picture soundtracks. Composer Miklós Rózsa (1907–1995) wanted to use a Theremin in his soundtrack for Alfred Hitchcock's *Spellbound*, released in 1945. He first offered the job to Clara Rockmore, but the Theremin virtuoso declined the offer, in part because she was already committed to a concert tour, but also because she steadfastly refused to use her talents on the instrument for making "spooky noises."[16] Rockmore's refusal became the chance of a lifetime for a foot doctor from Hollywood named Dr. Samuel J. Hoffman (1904–1968).

Trained as a violinist, Hoffman had continued to be active as a nightclub musician in a dance band even after opening his medical practice. In the mid-1930s, while living in New York, he acquired a Theremin in payment for a bad debt owed to him. He soon made the electronic instrument a part of his repertoire. Upon moving to Hollywood in 1941 he registered with the local musicians' union and, as a lark, listed the Theremin as one of his instruments. As he recalled later:

> When Miklós Rózsa thought of using a Theremin in his score for *Spellbound* he called the union to see if any Theremin players were available. I was the only one listed at that time who could read music.
>
> He came out to see me with a sketch of the part he wanted to write

and was delighted when he discovered I could sight-read it. So the Theremin part went into the *Spellbound* score; the score won an Academy Award.[17]

This stroke of luck led to a long association of the Theremin with motion pictures, primarily through the inspired "spooky noises" that Hoffman was so masterful at creating. His respectable list of movie credits is spread equally among hit movies, near misses, and low-budget exploitation films. In addition to *Spellbound*, they include such diverse accomplishments as *The Lost Weekend* (1945), *Lady in the Dark* (1946), *The Fountainhead* (1949), *Rocketship X-M* (1950), *The Thing* (1951), *The Day the Earth Stood Still* (1951), *The Ten Commandments* (1956), and *Billy the Kid vs. Dracula* (1966).[18] I guess you could say that there's no going up after you receive the Oscar on your very first project.

In 1962 in Ithaca, New York, about the time that Dr. Hoffman's film music career was winding down, a graduate student in physics named Robert Moog was quietly beginning a revolution in the development of electronic musical instruments. An electronics hobbyist since his youth, Moog had learned how to build transistorized Theremins while still in high school. Now a married graduate student at Cornell, he rekindled his hobby for the purpose of making some extra money:

> The height of my Theremin building was in college. We had a three-room apartment on the top floor of a house. For $10 a month, the landlord let me have the furnace room to build Theremins in. So, all through graduate school I had a 10' x 11' furnace room as my shop. I built quite a few Theremins there.[19]

"Quite a few" translated to about 1,000 Theremin kits sold during the height of Moog's little business. Moog's love for the Theremin and the mysterious Russian inventor whom he had never met set him squarely on the path to the invention of his groundbreaking Moog synthesizer several years later. Moog continued to have a soft spot for the Theremin, however, and to this day his company, Big Briar Inc., continues to manufacturer high-quality, solid-state Theremins for adventurous musicians.

Moog's Theremin kits circulated for several years. It was only a matter of time before the sound of this electronic instrument would catch the attention of a new generation of musicians. This time around, following a long stint during which the Theremin had become a staple of horror and science-fiction movie soundtracks, an instrument sounding peculiarly like a Theremin surfaced as the signature sound of the 1966 hit song *Good Vibrations* by the Beach Boys. This story has a Moog connection, but it wasn't a Theremin that we heard on that recording.

Paul Tanner (b. 1917) was a top-notch trombonist in Hollywood working in movies and television. He was in great demand as a session man. About 1958, Tanner sat in as a musician on the rerecording sessions for the *Spellbound* soundtrack, which was being updated to produce a stereophonic version of the music. It was during these sessions that he first observed Dr. Hoffman coaxing his mesmerizing electronic sounds from the Theremin. Tanner could relate the space-controlled nature of Theremin performance to the inexact science of moving the slide on a trombone. This motivated him to go into competition with Hoffman as another provider of spooky musical effects.

Tanner turned to a local actor, Robert Whitsell, for help in making a Theremin. Whitsell had made a few of the instruments as a teenager. But as the two of them discussed the project further, it was clear that Tanner wanted an instrument that could be controlled more easily than the traditional space-controlled Theremin used by Hoffman. Although they originally had a Theremin in mind, what Whitsell built was something else entirely. The device was no more than two off-the-shelf components from Heathkit: an oscillator and an amplifier. The clever part of the design came in the controller that Whitsell devised. On top of the instrument was a strip of paper with a fifteen-inch image of a keyboard. A sliding handle could be moved along the length of the paper keyboard. The handle itself was attached though a pulley-and-cable mechanism to the rotary dial of the oscillator hidden inside the box. Moving the sliding handle turned the dial in one direction or another, changing the pitch. Volume was controlled simply by turning the volume control of the amplifier component.[20] This design offered Tanner the control he needed to repeatedly play the same notes.

Tanner had apparently offered his services as a "Theremin" player prior even to having an electronic music instrument in hand. Whitsell's "instrument with no name" was finished in the early morning hours of the day of their first gig: a recording session in 1958 for an album that would be called *Music for Heavenly Bodies* (1958) with an orchestra conducted by Andre Montero and arrangements by Warren Baker. Both Tanner and Whitsell took part, with Tanner doing the playing.[21] Whitsell was on hand in case the instrument broke.

The nameless instrument was apparently christened the "electro-Theremin" by the producer of the recording or by Cy Schneider, the author of the liner notes.[22] Schneider's words were chosen carefully to distinguish the instrument from its Russian-born relative:

> Its eerie sound is not unlike Dr. Samuel Hoffman's famous Theremin, but it is easily distinguishable to those who have heard both. Tanner's instrument is mechanically controlled, while Hoffman's is played by moving the hands in front of it without touching the instrument.

It operates on a slide, and those who know about electronics will guess immediately that the sound is being created by a variable oscillator.

The audio range of the electro-Theremin covers the complete sound spectrum, from 0 to over 20,000 cycles per second. Its high and lows can only be measured on an oscilloscope. Its sounds are pure sine waves without any harmonics, making it an ideal instrument with which to test your audio equipment.[23]

Tanner and his electro-Theremin were an instant hit with Hollywood music producers. After making some adjustments to the design—specifically to improve the manual articulation of the notes—Whitsell stepped out of the picture and Tanner was off and running with the novel new instrument. He went on to do sound effects for several Warner Brothers movies and ABC television shows in the late '50s and early '60s. He also did work for the other television networks, CBS and NBC.[24] The electro-Theremin can be heard in films including *The Giant Gila Monster* (1959) and *Straight-Jacket* (1964). The instrument was often used for sound effects for the TV shows *I Love Lucy* and *My Favorite Martian*. In the latter, the electro-Theremin was heard every time Uncle Martin's antennae popped up. Tanner also played on the theme music for the shows *Dark Shadows* and *Lost in Space*.[25]

Tanner's most famous electro-Theremin job came when Brian Wilson (b. 1942) of the Beach Boys asked him to join their 1966 recording sessions. These were the sessions leading up to the album *Pet Sounds* and the single *Good Vibrations*. The first piece on which Tanner played was *I Just Wasn't Made for These Times*. It was followed a few days later by the first of many sessions for the landmark *Good Vibrations*.

When it came time to take the show on the road, the Beach Boys asked Tanner to come along, but he declined. He was a busy musician and instructor in California and couldn't take time out to join them. The group had by this time heard of Robert Moog and his Theremins. They called him and asked if he would construct a portable instrument that could be used in concerts. It is a popular misconception that what Moog built for them was a Theremin. What he actually provided was a transistorized audio oscillator housed in a slim walnut box about two feet long and six inches wide that was played by sliding the finger along a ribbon controller: "a thin metal band, covered with Teflon-impregnated cloth."[26] It was handheld, had a volume control, and was powered by being plugged into the wall. It could be marked at the places where the finger had to stop to play the notes of a song.

By 1970, the resilient Theremin had prospered though nearly fifty years of music-making, having been invented for classical music, unleashed upon movie soundtracks, and reborn as an expressive voice in rock music and even jazz. But its story was not over.

A few stalwart thereminists kept the tradition going in both classical and jazz music. American composer Eric Ross (b. 1929) is both a classical music composer and freestyle Theremin player. He has composed more than fifteen works for the Theremin since 1982, including one for fourteen instruments. Jazz trumpeter and thereminist Youseff Yancy, born in Belgium, has been playing the Theremin since the late '60s and often teams up with Ross.

In 1989, after having disappeared back into the Soviety Union for more than fifty years, Leon Theremin returned to the West. With his reemergence, the ninty-three-year-old inventor once again became the center of attention in the music world as tributes and concerts were held in his honor. An award-winning documentary about his life was also produced by Steven Martin (*Theremin: An Electronic Odyssey*, 1993). He died in 1993, but not before having a brief reunion with his old protégée Clara Rockmore.

The Theremin lives on today. It has been used by numerous rock groups over the years, not the least of which being Led Zeppelin (*Whole Lotta Love*, 1969), the Pixies (*Velouria*, 1990), Portishead (*Humming*, 1997), and the Kurstins (*Gymnopédie*, 2000). Furthermore, the classical tradition of Theremin performance is once again alive and well in the capable hands of Lydia Kavina, (b. 1967), the granddaughter of Leon Theremin's first cousin, and his final protégée. In 1999, Kavina released the first album consisting only of works composed expressly for the Theremin (*Music from the Ether: Original Works for the Theremin*, 1999).

The design of electronic musical instruments began to liven up after the initial success of the Theremin in the 1920s. Many of these devices could rightfully be considered offspring of the Theremin, since the basic principles underlying them were borrowed from Leon Theremin.

German inventor Jörg Mager (1880–1939) saw in the technology the potential for further subdividing the chromatic scale into additional pitches. He was interested in microtonal music, which separates the scale into more notes than are found on the conventional piano keyboard. The first instrument he designed was called the Sphaerophon and could play quarter tones. Mager described his invention in a pamphlet in 1924 and demonstrated it publicly during 1925 and 1926. It produced sound using radio components and a beat frequency principle similar to the Theremin. The Sphaerophon was monophonic, like the Theremin, and was played from a keyboard rather than being space-controlled, thus eliminating a reliance on sweeping glissando tones. Mager was an early evangelist of quarter-tone music and had great faith in its future. Unfortunately for him, most of the congregation wasn't listening, and the Sphaerophon sank into oblivion. One of its rare shining moments came in 1931 when

Winifred Wagner, daughter-in-law of Richard Wagner, commissioned Mager to produce electronic bell sounds for a production of the opera *Parsifal* at the Bayreuth festival. In 1935, Mager successfully reengineered the Sphaerophon as a polyphonic instrument that could play normal keyboard music written for the chromatic scale. This device was called the Partiturophon, but it was quickly eclipsed in the marketplace by the recently introduced Hammond electric organ. All of Mager's instruments were destroyed during World War II.

The Ondes Martenot

The most successful offspring of the Theremin was the French-made Ondes Martenot, originally called the Ondes Musicales ("musical waves"). This device was designed by musician Maurice Martenot (1898–1980). He wanted to invent an electronic musical instrument that could join the ranks of traditional symphonic instruments and be the focus of works written by leading composers. To accomplish this, he had to address two major obstacles that hindered the Theremin from becoming more widely accepted by musicians and composers. First, the Theremin didn't look like a musical instrument, but more like a radio; and second, its space-controlled design was difficult, if not impossible, for most people to master.

Martenot borrowed Theremin's principles for generating musical tones, but provided an entirely different instrument design that was pleasing to the eye and looked at home in the orchestra. It was the size of a small, upright keyboard instrument such as the clavichord. Its elegant wooden cabinet and matching loudspeakers were fashionably tailored using an art deco motif.

Having an instrument that looked the role was only half the battle. The Theremin had existed in the public eye as a scientific curiosity before it was generally accepted as a serious musical instrument. This probably diminished its chances for taking the musical world by storm. Martenot wanted his invention to find a place alongside other symphonic instruments from the start. To ensure this, he carefully packaged the introduction of the Ondes Martenot by commissioning an orchestral work to spotlight its musical qualities. The instrument was introduced to the world in Paris when Martenot himself played the solo part in the world premiere of Dimitri Levidis's (1886–1951) *Symphonic Poem for Solo Ondes Musicales and Orchestra* in May 1928. It was a dramatic way for the Ondes Martenot to enter the public consciousness. This very first piece used microtonal elements including quarter and eighth tones, an impressive beginning for an instrument that is still in active, albeit limited, use today.

The Ondes Martenot was more than a Theremin hidden inside a fancy cabinet. Although it used the same beat frequency technology as the Theremin, Martenot designed it expressly for playing parts that could be transcribed for a keyboard. The Ondes Martenot was monophonic and thus was restricted to the playing of melodies, but it triggered notes in such a way that the musician could relate them to the chromatic scale. The original instrument played by Martenot at its Paris premiere controlled pitch by the lateral movement of a finger ring that was attached to a metal wire. The ring was moved using the index finger of the right hand. This in turn adjusted a variable capacitor on the ribbon that changed the frequency of the tone over a seven-octave range. Sliding the ring to the left played lower notes, sliding it to the right played higher notes. The ribbon was ingeniously superimposed over a picture of a piano keyboard, and movements of the ring corresponded to notes of the scale and gradations in between.

By 1932, Martenot had made several improvements to the Ondes Martenot and introduced the instrument with which we are most familiar.[27] Foremost among these changes was the addition of an organ-style keyboard, early versions of which Martenot had been using since 1929.[28] The instrument could be played using either the keyboard or the finger ring slide control—which now used a metal ribbon in place of the wire and was positioned in front of the keyboard—but not both at once. Five- and seven-octave versions were available. An intriguing feature of the keyboard was that any individual key could be jiggled laterally back and forth to produce minute fluctuations in pitch for vibrato effects. These effects could also be created on the ribbon-controlled model by moving the finger back and forth ever so slightly. The slide control ran parallel to the keyboard so that the musician could relate the position of the finger ring to notes on the keyboard. The surface over which the slide control was moved was also marked off by small metal bumps corresponding to notes on the scale.

The left hand controlled volume with a pressure-sensitive key. This was unique in that when the key was fully released no sound was heard. As the player gradually depressed it, the volume increased. A knee lever was also provided to regulate this volume key. Using the knee lever to vary volume would free the left hand so that it could control a small bank of expression keys to filter the tones. Finally, there was a foot volume control with a unique pressure-sensitive mechanism. David Kean, president and founder of the Audities Foundation, described this feature of the model in his collection:

> It is a small "bag" with carbon-impregnated pellets. As one pushes on the
> pedal and compresses the bag, the density increases, the resistance goes

A keyboard model of the Ondes Martenot. The left hand is positioned on the expression controls. The index finger of the right hand is inserted into the finger ring. Any individual key could be jiggled laterally to produce vibrato. Photo by Thom Holmes (2000).

down, and the volume goes up. Amazing. It feels wonderful to have that kind of proportional, physical feedback in conjunction with an impetus to increase volume. Very sensual; how French![29]

The improved Ondes Martenot was not a difficult instrument to learn and thus appealed to the musician more than the theatrical gymnastics required to perform on the Theremin.

Martenot took special care in designing several ways to project the sound of his invention. Four basic loudspeakers, or "diffusers," were offered. The first, called the *haut-parleur* ("loud speaker"), was a standard loudspeaker and was the loudest of the four varieties. The *Resonance* was a unique speaker for creating reverberation. It had an upright rectangular wood cabinet and in addition to a conventional speaker cone could pass the electrical sound output through a vertically oriented veil of clear plastic strips resembling venetian blinds. This produced haunting, resonating tonalities that were startlingly fresh at the time. A third speaker system, called the *métallique*, was shorter and reproduced sound by means of a metal gong. Tone signals were run through a transducer directly into the gong, using the sympathetic vibrations of the metal body to resonate an audible pitch. The resonating properties of the gong further modulated the sound and offered striking, bell-like metallic sounds reminiscent of ring modulation. The fourth loudspeaker, called the *palm*, had a resonating body shaped somewhat like that of an inverted cello. Twelve strings were stretched over the front and back of the speaker. The electrical tone signals were converted by a transducer and played directly through the strings themselves, which vibrated to reproduce the pitch. The combination of the vibrating strings and resonating cello-like body cavity produced the eerie bowed-string sounds of the palm.

Even though some of the instruments were able to connect more than one loudspeaker at a time, this was not advised because the volume would be significantly diminished. Compared with the output level of the *haut-parleur*, "the *Palm* or *Métallique* would be lost in a performance of *Turangalila*," even without splitting the signal.[30]

The musician used keys on the left-hand controller to choose which speaker to play. When combined with the filter controls, the four kinds of loudspeakers gave the musician and composer an extraordinary range of timbral effects. The ability to mute the sound of the Ondes Martenot by releasing the volume key allowed the performer to dampen the glissando sounds created by moving the ribbon from note to note, thus eliminating one of the primary challenges of playing the Theremin. The volume control allowed the use of glissando when desired and also permitted the manual shaping of the envelope of the sound. Furthermore, because the finger ring slide control version of the Ondes Martenot could play the twelve notes of the chromatic scale and everything in between, it was possible to use the instrument for performing microtonal music. One way to do this was by replacing the picture strip of the conventional piano keyboard with another modeled to show quarter tones or any other division of the scale desired by the composer.

Maurice Martenot did indeed inspire leading composers to write music for his instrument, and the Ondes Martenot met with unprecedented success. Following its impressive debut in 1928, the conductor Leopold Stokowski (1882–1977) brought Martenot to the United States to perform the Levidis work with the Philadelphia Orchestra. This led to a tremendous flurry of composition for the device and the creation of a formalized training program and school for the instrument under the direction of Martenot in Paris. During the 1930s, well-known composers such as Darius Milhaud (1892–1974), Arthur Honegger (1892–1955), and Olivier Messiaen (1908–1992) wrote serious music for the instrument. Composers were attracted to different attributes of the Ondes Martenot. Some used it to produce ethereal effects as an atmospheric accompaniment to an orchestra, as in Marcel Landowski's (b. 1915) *Jean de la peur*. Some were drawn to its ability to create special effects, such as bell sounds or birdsong (e.g., Messiaen's *Turangalîla-Symphonie*, 1948, and *Le Merle noir*, 1951). It was often used effectively as an ensemble instrument (e.g., Milhaud, *Suite for Martenot and Piano*, 1933; Jacques Charpentier (b. 1933), *Lalita for Ondes Martenot and Percussion*). Still other composers experimented with ensembles of Ondes Martenot (works for 2, 4, 5, 6, 8, and 12 instruments: André Jolivet (1905–1974), *Danse Incantatoire for Two Ondes Martenot*, 1936; Messiaen, *Fête des Belles Eaux for Sextet of Ondes Martenot*, 1937). More recently, composer Toshi Ichiyanagi (b. 1933) added yet another work to the repertoire of the instrument when he wrote *Troposphere* in 1990, a duet for Ondes Martenot and marimba. To date, more than 300 composers have contributed to this repertoire, which includes no fewer than 100 chamber works, 50 operas, 100 symphonic works, numerous ballets, and over 500 incidental scores for films and theater.[31]

Like the Theremin, the Ondes Martenot has been associated with several virtuosi performers. The first was Martenot's sister, Ginette Martenot. Perhaps the best-known Ondes Martenot performer is Jeanne Loriod (1928–2001), who from the age of eighteen dedicated her career to the mastery of the instrument and the documentation of its written repertory. She studied with Martenot himself, and recordings of her performances are commercially available. One of Loriod's most noted protégées is Valérie Hartmann-Claverie, who has been playing the Ondes Martenot with orchestras around the world since 1973.

The Trautonium and Mixturtrautonium

The Trautonium of Dr. Friedrich Trautwein (1888–1956) was developed in Germany between 1928 and 1930. It represented yet another distinctive electronic voice to rise from the din of experimentation that was taking place at the time.

The early evolution of the Trautonium was the result of a collaboration between the engineer Trautwein and composer Paul Hindemith (1895–1963). Oskar Sala (1910–2002), a composition student of Hindemith's at the time, recalled how the idea came about:

> It began in 1930 with the meeting of engineer Dr. Friedrich Trautwein and Paul Hindemith in the experimental radio station at the Berlin Academy of Music. The experimental engineer's first plan of developing the electronic organ was refused due to a lack of money. So, when he met the prominent musician, Paul Hindemith, who did not look at music from the perspective of the electronic organ but rather from string instruments and

LIVERPOOL JOHN MOORES UNIVERSITY
LEARNING & INFORMATION SERVICES

their orchestral neighbors, the inventive engineer went in a totally different direction with this ideas. . . . I have no doubts now that he, the engineer [Trautwein], took the idea of an electrical string manual from the
great composer and viola virtuoso not only because he wanted to show
the experimentally interested professor that his could be done electronically, but also because the enlightening idea of an electronic string instrument had so far not been heard of. . . . So, the idea of a keyboard was out![32]

What Sala meant by an "electronic string instrument" was not an electric version of a cello, viola, or other familiar string instrument. The
"string" was a wire that was pressed by the finger to play a sound. The
instrument had a fingerboard consisting of a metal plate about the width
of a medium-sized keyboard instrument. Stretched only a few centimeters
above the plate was a wire. Pressing the wire with a finger so that it touched
the plate closed a circuit and sent electricity to a neon-tube oscillator, producing a tone. The monophonic instrument spanned three octaves, with the
pitch going up from left to right along the fingerboard. Volume was controlled by a foot pedal. The fingerboard was marked with the position of
notes on the chromatic scale to make it easier for a musician to play.

By 1934, Trautwein had added a second fingerboard so that two
notes could be played at once. At the same time, he introduced an ingenious feature for manually presetting notes to be played. A rail was
mounted just a few centimeters above and running parallel to each of the
two resistor wires. To this were attached ten to fifteen springy metal
strips covered in leather, which is nonconductive. These "tongues," as
they were sometimes called, could be slid to any position along the
length of the wire. This enabled the musician to preset the location of
notes to be played. Pressing a tongue was like pressing a key: it pushed
the wire down so that it contacted the metal plate.[33]

The oscillator produced a sawtooth waveform that was rich in harmonic sidebands. This distinguished the sound of the trautonium from
that of the Theremin and Ondes Martenot, both of which used a beat
frequency technology that produced waveforms with fewer harmonics.
To take advantage of this unique characteristic of the neon-tube oscillators, Trautwein devised a set of filters, controlled by rotary dials, to
adjust the amplitude of the harmonics in relation to the fundamental
tone being played. This was the beginning of subtractive synthesis—the
careful manipulation of sidebands to produce timbral changes in tone
color. This schema for shaping sound led to further improvements,
including the addition of more sawtooth oscillators and more rotary
dials for fine-tuning the presence of harmonics. One of the early problems of the instrument was that the attack of the tones could not be
adjusted; they were consistently sharp and loud. To remedy this,

Trautwein devised a way to make the fingerboard touch-sensitive, using mercury-filled resistors beneath the wire mechanism. The harder one pressed the wire with the finger, the louder or sharper the attack of the sound would be.[34] Trautwein thus joined Thaddeus Cahill before him as one of the first to experiment with a touch-sensitive controller for an electronic musical instrument.

The first concert of Trautonium music came about because of a deal struck with Paul Hindemith. The composer had become a frequent visitor to Trautwein's lab and was anxious to get a project under way. He agreed to compose some music for the instrument if Trautwein would promise to build three of them by June 1930.[35] This was all the incentive that the engineer needed.

Hindemith volunteered his composition students to assist with the construction of the three instruments. Sala was the only one who jumped at the chance. "I had become a virtuoso on the soldering iron before becoming a virtuoso on the instrument," he recalled.[36] The job was done and on June 20, 1930, an "Electric Concert" was given at the Berlin Academy of Music featuring the premiere of 7 Trio Pieces for Three Trautonien (1930).[37] The three instruments were played by Hindemith himself, his student Oskar Sala, and a piano instructor at the academy named Rudolph Schmidt.

The reaction to the concert was so encouraging that the German electronics firm Telefunken, the maker of the neon-tube oscillators used in the instrument, decided to manufacture and market a Trautonium for home use. The model featured a single fingerboard and a single pedal. Only a hundred were built and even fewer sold between 1932 and 1935.[38]

Hindemith composed a few more pieces for the instrument, most notably the Concertino for Trautonium and String Orchestra in 1931. But it was his student Oskar Sala who has been most closely associated with the instrument over the years both as a composer and performer.

Trautwein, who sympathized with the Nazis during World War II, was summarily cast out of favor by society and the arts in the years after it. It is ironic that, prior to the war, he was instrumental in preserving the Trautonium project during a fitful time for the arts in Germany. The Nazi Party made life difficult for many progressive and experimental writers, artists, and composers. They had the power to ban one's work and forced many artists to leave the country in self-exile. If nothing else, Trautwein's Nazi affiliation had trained him well in playing the game of favor. Sala recalled:

> Luckily, Trautwein knew a general who was on our side and arranged
> that we could demonstrate the instrument to the minister of propaganda,

Joseph Goebbels—Hitler's right hand man. I played something by
Paganini, and of course he liked it. After that they left us in peace.[39]

After the war, Trautwein dabbled with the instrument some more,
but he was already years behind Sala in making engineering improvements to his namesake. In 1952, he built a specialized instrument called
the Monochord, based on the same technology, for the electronic music
studio of West German Radio in Cologne. By the time of Trautwein's
death in 1956, Sala had assumed the roles of the Trautonium's chief
engineer, inventor, composer, and performer.

Sala had been making incremental enhancements to the instrument
for many years. In 1952, he packaged it all together in a new version,
which he introduced as the Mixtur trautonium.[40] This was during the
same period that electronic music studios were springing up across
Europe, including the studio of Herbert Eimert and young Karlheinz
Stockhausen in Cologne. Rather than join a host of composers dabbling
in musique concrète, Sala was content to work alone with the instrument he knew best.

His primary improvement to the Trautonium was the expansion of
harmonics available for the tones and improved controls. Sala's definition
of a "mixtur" was a combination of four "subharmonics" or harmonics
for a given master frequency. The Mixturtrautonium had two fingerboards
so that two oscillators—master frequencies—could be played at once. His
circuitry would then allow up to three mixtures of four harmonics each to
be played for each of the two master frequencies—twelve harmonics for
each of the two fingerboards, making twenty-four in all. The harmonic
mixtures were controlled by two foot pedals with side switches, one for
each fingerboard. The player triggered notes with the right and left hands
on the fingerboards, then used both feet to control the volume and harmonic mixtures.[41] To this, Sala added a white noise generator, reverberation, and a power regulator to produce rhythmic sequences.[42]

During the '60s, Sala formed his own studio and took on commissions for stage, screen, and television. His instrument was at times called
the Mixturtrautonium or the studio-Trautonium. In 1961, composer
Remi Gassman (b. 1908) collaborated with him to produce the striking
score for the George Balanchine (1904–1983) ballet *Electronics*.
Gassman was particularly attracted to the tonal qualities of the instrument. His comments from the time reveal an obvious distaste for much
of the electronic music being produced by his contemporaries:

> In the music of *Electronics*, I chose to return to sounds of electronic ori-
> gin, since I had at my disposal an electronic instrument of kaleidoscopic
> and practically limitless tonal possibilities. The Studio Trautonium, as

designed and developed by Oskar Sala, made it possible to use this particular electronic instrument as an exclusive source of basic musical sound.
Besides, its recent development incorporates the complete resources of the
electronic sound studio as well. Hence, in this work, electronic sound, the
virtuoso possibilities of the electronic instrument, and the further manipulations and techniques of the electronic sound studio, are for the first time
inextricably bound together. They have been united so firmly that any
penurious derivations of sound from a tonal world free of overtones, or
from electronically ingenious manipulations of traditional sound material,
became, for my purposes, unnecessary and certainly musically inadequate.
...There was now no reason to burn all bridges on our former musical
paths, as some had thought. The electronic emancipation of sound need
not become a dehumanized bedlam of sirens and tonal equations.[43]

Soon after this project, Sala was asked by Alfred Hitchcock to produce a totally electronic score for his 1963 horror film *The Birds*. Sala
created the score using the Mixturtrautonium and magnetic tape. Even
the sounds of the birds themselves were created using his instrument. It
was a highly effective technique that further reinforced the surreal elements of the film's plot.

Music continues to be made for this distinctive instrument thanks to
the continuing work of Oskar Sala and his recent collaborator, ambi-
ent/electronic composer Pete Namlook. The instrument itself has not
changed at all, according to Namlook, except for perhaps the way in
which the two have been applying it:

It has stayed the same with the exception of me using it in connection
with other sound sources, chords that consist of six instead of four subharmonic tones, and thirty-two instead of Oskar Sala's twenty-four partials of the subharmonic row. Which makes a difference but not a big one.
Oskar Sala remains the master of the subharmonic row with his
Mixturtrautonium.[44]

There are only two Mixturtrautoniums in existence. One is in the
Deutsches Museum in Bonn, the other in Sala's private studio. He is the
only person who knows how to play it with a master's touch. He has
amassed over six-hundred works, which are neatly filed on magnetic
tape in his studio. The German manufacturer Doepfer Musikelectronik
has recently worked with Sala to design and produce a semiconductor
version of the Mixturtrautonium as well as component modules for
reproducing the "subharmonic" filtering and controls associated with
the original analog instrument. Perhaps an heir to the Sala legacy will
step forward one day soon, while there is still time for the grand master
to mentor a new student in the fine art of subharmonic music.

The Electronic Organ

During the early 1930s, the family tree of electronic musical instruments developed a separate branch devoted to the creation of electronic organs. Originally designed to replace the traditional pipe organ, electronic organs had to be, above all else, easy to learn and play. The challenge in engineering them was not to produce wild new sounds but to create an instrument that would simply stay in tune, appeal to the conservative tastes of the masses, and not require an electrician to keep it going.

Many inventors experimented with vacuum tubes and other electronics to produce organ sounds, but it was the old tone wheel principle perfected by Thaddeus Cahill in 1900 that proved to be the winning formula for the first successful electronic organ. It resurfaced in 1929 in the developmental work of Chicagoan Laurens Hammond (1895–1973).

Hammond's electromechanical method for generating musical tones was identical to that used in the Telharmonium. The instrument used ninety-one metal tone wheels each about the size of a quarter, all driven on a common rotating shaft.[45] Although he didn't use vacuum-tube oscillators to generate tones, Hammond did take advantage of tubes for other components of his instrument, including power control, sound mixing, and amplification. This allowed him to house in a small cabinet what required an entire basement for Cahill's instrument. This was in stark contrast to the machine room required to make the Telharmonium work. Hammond's design proved to be stable and produced a warm, instantly recognizable sound. It was built to mimic the functions of a pipe organ and had sliding tone filters, reminiscent of organ stops, to remove partials from the sound.

While Hammond's organ was on its way to New York for its world premiere at the Industrial Arts Exposition of 1935, a stop was made in Detroit to demonstrate it for a curious Henry Ford, who was so impressed that he purchased the first available unit. Some 5,000 Hammond electric organs were sold before 1940, with more than a third going right into churches.[46] Even though the Hammond organ was not the first electronic organ to hit the market (the Rangertone, for example, which also used an updated version of Cahill's tone wheel principle, was introduced in 1931), it became very popular because of its excellent design. The Hammond model B3—introduced during the 1950s—remains one of the most sought-after older organs on the market and is highly prized by rock, rhythm-and-blues, and jazz musicians.

The next generation of electronic organ designers began to explore totally electronic means to produce music through the use of vacuum-tube oscillators. In 1939 the Hammond organization introduced two additional models, the monophonic Solovox and the polyphonic Novachord. The Solovox was a soloing instrument that was customarily used in combination with a piano or other organ.

The Novachord was a much more ambitious creation than the original Hammond organ. It had sophisticated attack and decay characteristics, tone-color controls, sustain controls, percussion sounds, and a six-octave keyboard instead of the five-octave model associated with most other organs.[47] All seventy-two keys on its keyboard could be played at once (if you had enough fingers)! The instrument was totally electronic, using twelve triode-tube oscillators to generate the upper octave of the keyboard. A complicated network of additional vacuum tubes was needed to divide these upper frequencies into lower pitches for the other octaves. The instrument had numerous tone controls available to the performer, including "deep," "brilliant," and "full"; "normal" and "small" vibrato; and "strong" and "soft" bass and percussion. Using combinations of these controls made it possible to imitate various orchestral instruments, an unusual feat in those days and one that amazed many listeners. The Novachord was one of the few electronic organs that featured extraordinary timbre controls; in its way, it was the forerunner of the modern synthesizer tuned with "presets" for orchestral effects. Unfortunately, Hammond's ambitious design overstepped the capabilities of technology as it existed in 1939. Using more than a hundred vacuum tubes and related circuitry, the Novachord proved to be unstable and unreliable in performance. Hammond ceased manufacturing it before the end of World War II.

Other "pipeless" organs using audio-frequency oscillators of various types included one employing no fewer than seven hundred vacuum tubes, produced by Edouard Coupleaux and Joseph Givelet during the 1930s; the Clavioline by Selmer; the Electrone by John Compton; and organs that were introduced by the Allen, Baldwin, Connsonata, and Miller companies. In addition, various instruments appeared using techniques such as vibrating reeds combined with electromagnetic pickups (including the Orgatron, invented by F. A. Hoschke in 1935, later sold by Wurlitzer) and photoelectric means (such as the Photona of Ivan Eremeef, 1935).

For every success story such as those of Theremin, Martenot, and Trautwein, the Jazz Age seemingly had dozens more tales of experiments that went largely unrecognized. Before the Trautonium, there was the Hellertion of Bruno Helberger and Peter Lertes from which Trautwein borrowed his basic principles. First built in 1928, the Hellertion, like the Trautonium, also used the neon-tube method of generating oscillation and was played by pressing a leather-covered metal ribbon against a resistance plate to change the pitch. The earliest versions featured one monophonic ribbon board. A later version demonstrated in 1936 had four separate monophonic fingering ribbons so that four notes could be played simultaneously if you had enough hands.

Like many other early electronic musical instruments, the Hellertion faded quietly into the pages of history, a history that is rich in experiments and inventions with quaint, faintly scientific names: the Croix Sonore, Dynaphone, Emicon, Magnetton, Mellertion, Melodium, Ondioline, Oscillion, Photophone, Pianorad, Univox, and the Warbo Formant Organ.

Chapter 5

MUSIQUE CONCRÈTE AND THE ANCIENT ART OF TAPE COMPOSITION

The next era of electronic music development was ushered in by the humble tape recorder. Composers had been waiting for a device that would allow them to store and manipulate sounds better than the acetate disc. When the magnetic tape recorder came out of postwar Germany, they knew exactly what to do with it.

The influence of the tape recorder on the very nature and definition of "music" was profound. On one hand, it led to the creation of a new kind of music that existed *only* as a recording. On the other, it jump-started an obsessive quest for new and different electronic music technology, leading directly to the conception of the modern synthesizer.

Until the arrival of the magnetic tape recorder, electronic music had only been a live performance medium. It was stage music, recital music, requiring a social event with an audience. It employed exotic instruments, but there was little that could be called avant-garde about the majority of works written for these instruments. They were viewed by the world as sonic novelties.

The tape recorder transformed the field of electronic music overnight by making it a composer's medium. The fact that the earliest practitioners of tape composition rarely used any of the performance instruments such as the Theremin is a testament to their vision. They sought other sounds, other structures, other tonalities and worked directly with the raw materials of sound to find them.

Composing with Tape

For the early adapters of magnetic tape composition—Cage, Schaeffer, Henry, and Varèse—the medium had the liberating effect of separating the creation of music from the traditional practice of scoring and notating parts. John Cage put it very plainly when he told me:

> It made one aware that there was an equivalence between space and time, because the tape you could see existed in space, whereas the sounds existed in time. That immediately changed the notation of music. We didn't have to bother with counting one-two-three-four anymore. We could if we wanted to, but we didn't have to. We could put a sound at any point in time.[1]

To understand what he meant you may have had to visit an electronic music studio. There was usually a rack from which hung pieces of tape that had not yet been spliced together. Holding a strip of tape in your hand was like seeing and touching sound. You could manipulate this normally elusive phenomenon in ways that were previously unavailable to composers. It was a technological, psychological, and social breakthrough without parallel for music.

Karlheinz Stockhausen (b. 1928) also had a revelation about the materiality of time as a result of working with magnetic tape. By speeding up or slowing down a sound—even a classically musical sound—all of the formal elements that went into composing that sound are leveled by the hammer of technology. Rhythm once organized in meters can be sped up or slowed down to the point of obliteration. The timbre of chosen instruments, harmony, melody—all of these separately formulated components of a piece of music are transformed uniformly and unequivocally by so many inches per second of tape running on a variable-speed tape recorder. Chords can be sped up to become beats and rhythms. Rhythms can be slowed down to become chords. The components of a musical work are all reduced to the common denominator of *vibration*. This was the unified field theory of serialism "in which duration, pitch and color were aspects of the same thing."[2] Stockhausen called it the "unified time domain."[3]

Even though the practice of composing with magnetic tape is obsolete today, many of the most fundamental effects associated with electronic music originated with the pioneers who learned how to push the limitations of this fragile medium. The state of the art may have shifted from magnetic tape to magnetic discs, CD-ROMs, CD-Rs, minidiscs, and other digital media, but the basic concepts of sound manipulation born over fifty years ago still apply.

Here are some of the magnetic tape editing techniques that shaped the music of early electronic music composers. Most of these ideas are still relevant even when transcribed to the digital editing medium.

Tape Splicing

The cutting and splicing of magnetic tape is, in effect, no different from moving sound around in time and space. You take a sound that occurred at one time and move it to another. Every sound has a given length. The art of sound splicing owes its beginnings to the motion picture industry, where optical sound had been previously used to match up the sound of a movie with its picture. Some limited musical experiments with the direct creation of sounds using optical film recording had been done by John Whitney (1917–1995) and James Whitney (b. 1922) for their experimental films in 1940, but electronic music did not blossom as a force to be reckoned with until magnetic tape became commercially available in the late 1940s.

The mechanics of magnetic tape splicing are simple. Tape is placed on open reels, mounted on a tape recorder, and manually moved across the playback head to locate a precise sound. The composer's only other tools are a ruler to "measure" time in inches or centimeters of tape, a razor blade, and a *splicing block*. The splicing block is a small metal fixture with a channel running through it into which the magnetic tape is laid. It has at least two slots, through which the composer slides a razor blade to cut the tape. The slot on the right is angled as if it were pointing at 10 o'clock, and the one to the left at a right angle to the direction of the tape (12 o'clock high). The ends of the two pieces of tape to be joined are overlapped slightly and then sliced with a razor blade through one of the slots. This cuts them in a complementary fashion. The ends of tape are then butted up against one another in the track of the splicing block and fastened together with a piece of editing tape.

From this limited technology arose various philosophies about splicing tape. The object was first and foremost to create an absolutely silent cut. The slightest misadventure with matching up the two ends of tape, a bubble in the splicing tape, or dust in the adhesive of the splicing tape could result in an audible pop in the edited sound. Various tricks of the trade came about because of this, including the "hourglass" splice that reduced the width of the tape at the point of a splice, providing less surface area for noise during the transition from one piece of tape to the next. Unfortunately, this method could momentarily reduce the amplitude of the signal at the point of the splice, an effect that was sometimes audible.

Splicing could be used in a limited way to change the attack and decay patterns of recorded sounds. A long, angled splice of several inches would create a perceptible dissolve from one sound to the next. Cutting periodic segments of blank tape (or "leader tape," the nonmagnetic protective tape at the beginning or end of a reel) into a block of continuous sound could induce a rhythmic or pulsing effect. Cuts made at right angles instead of the normal 10 o'clock angle created a sharper, percussive jump from sound to sound.

Degeneration of a Recorded Signal

A sound will degenerate over time when it is played back, rerecorded, and played back over and over again. This effect was the underlying idea behind Brian Eno's *Discreet Music* and his collaborations with guitarist Robert Fripp (b. 1946) during the 1970s. But the idea goes back to the '60s. When I was studying composition with Paul Epstein (b. 1938) at Temple University in 1971, he told me about his friend Alvin Lucier (b. 1931) and a piece that Lucier composed exploiting the phenomenon of tape signal degeneration. It was years before I actually heard the piece, but the concept was so compellingly original that it stuck in my mind as a conceptual keystone for "process" composing.

Lucier's music is often strikingly simple in concept and surprisingly rich in execution. He is fascinated with acoustics and ways to use the performance space as a natural acoustic filter. The piece in question was *I Am Sitting in a Room* (1970). It consisted of several sentences of text spoken by the composer and then rerecorded over and over again on tape using a microphone. The acoustics of the room provided a natural filter for the sound that was being "heard" by the microphone, accentuating certain parts of it and deemphasizing others. After many repeated rerecordings, with each successive taping emphasizing the strongest characteristics of the previous, the sound eventually disintegrates into unintelligible, pulsating modulations. It is the aural equivalent of the degeneration that takes place when you make successive photocopies of photocopies. Lucier explained how this piece came to be:

> I had heard that Bose had tested his loudspeakers by doing some kind of a cycling process to see where the frequencies were. I tried it out in *I Am Sitting in a Room*. I did it one night in an apartment that I was in. I made that piece in real time there. I thought up that text right there that night. I wrote it down, without much editing, and then with a pair of tape recorders, a KLH loudspeaker, and some amplifier I just made that piece. I set up the two tape recorders outside the apartment so there wouldn't be any noise from the machinery. I sat inside with a microphone and spoke the text two or three times to get the volume right. Then I put the loudspeaker up where I had been sitting so that the speaker became my voice. The evening was spent with these machines and I would play back the original text recording through the speaker into the microphone to a second machine. I would check that to make sure that the volume was all right. Then I rewound that, spliced it onto the first machine, and played

that back. I spliced it sixteen times. It took me all night. You would think that's not going to take long. But there were noises. There were cars going by, things like that. So the final product is that tape.[4]

Tape Echo, Delay, and Looping

The tape recorder makes possible several basic techniques for repeating sounds that have been popular since the earliest experiments with tape composition. The idea of taking a piece of magnetic audiotape, splicing it end-to-end to form a loop, and then playing it back on a tape recorder so it constantly repeats itself is as old as the field of recorded electronic music and continues to be popular with composers. Unlike echo, in which each repetition of the trigger sound becomes weaker until it diminishes entirely, the sound repeated by a tape loop does not weaken.

Echo is the repetition of a single sound that gradually decays in amplitude and clarity. This was first achieved using tape recorders equipped with three "heads"—the erase, recording, and playback elements, across which the reel of tape passed to record, play, and delete sounds.

To create echo with a tape recorder, the playback output signal of the machine is fed back into the input, or record head, of the same machine. When this connection is made and the tape recorder is simultaneously recording and playing back, the sound being played is immediately rerecorded by the record head. The distance that the tape must travel from the record head to the playback head determines the length of the delay. Continuing in this manner without interruption creates the echo effect. The signal degrades slightly with each successive playback. The strength or persistence of the echo—how many repeats you hear— is determined by the amplitude of the playback signal being fed back into the recorder. The stronger the signal, the longer the sequence of repeats. Turning up the playback to the point of overload produces echo "frizz," or repeating waves of white noise that eventually overpower the original input signal.

Echo and *reverberation* should not be confused. Echo is the periodic repetition of the same sound signal, whereas reverberation is the modulation of a single sound signal to produce weaker ghost frequencies, or depth. Reverberation is used, for example, to replicate the ambience of a large room or space.

Echo became a staple effect of electronic music composition as soon as the first tape recorders were being used by composers. French composers Pierre Schaeffer (1910–1995) and Pierre Henry (b. 1927) can be credited with adding tape echo to the repertoire of the electronic music composer following World War II. By the 1960s, a variety of specialized tape machines were being manufactured for making echo effects. They have since been replaced by software programs and digital effects units modeled after the most familiar and interesting tape echo boxes of the past.

Before the appearance of digital echo effects using computer gear, a variety of special tape echo "boxes" were manufactured to allow the musician to create echo. They usually operated by using an internally mounted loop of magnetic tape along with the requisite erase, record, and playback heads. One advantage of these dedicated devices was that the distance between the record and playback heads could be adjusted to increase the length of time between echoes.

Composer Pauline Oliveros (b. 1932) has used tape echo not just as a recorded effect but as the fundamental structural process behind some of her groundbreaking works. In *Beautiful Soop* (1967), she used three different brands of tape recorders to create multiple echo effects simultaneously from the same input signal, exploiting the different distances between the record and playback heads of the different machines. She describes this complex circuit:

> With all the feedback loops in operation there is a shimmering effect on attacks, and interesting timbre changes on sustained sounds. Because every delay line was controlled by a separate mixing pot, as much or as little feedback [echo] as designed was introduced, and each delay line could be treated as a separate source. By sending delay lines to various modifying devices, a large number of variations could occur.[5]

A length of tape can be spliced end-to-end to form a *tape loop*. When played, a loop continuously repeats a recorded sound without decay. The periodicity of the repeated sound is determined by the length of the tape loop and the playback speed of the tape machine. Digital sampling essentially mimics the creation of a loop, resulting in a sound that can be played by itself or "looped" in a repeating pattern. Samplers now blur the line between what was once defined as echo and looping. Samplers can be set to repeat a sound at the same volume in a looping cycle or allow it to diminish for an echo effect.

Tape delay combines the recording and rerecording of a sound using a tape loop or combination of tape recorders. The most interesting approach used two or more widely spaced tape recorders through which a single length of magnetic tape was threaded. A sound was recorded on the first machine and played back on the second, creating a long delay between the first occurance of the sound and its repetition on the second machine. If the sound being played back on the second machine was simultaneously recorded by the first machine, an extended echo effect was created with long delays between successive, degenerating repetitions.

Tape delay has been used extensively by several composers, most notably Pauline Oliveros. Its origins go back to the people associated with the San Francisco Tape Music Center in 1960.[6] Terry Riley (b. 1935) may have been the very first to compose a piece using this technique when he created *Music for the Gift* in 1963, possibly the first work to use the accumulating technique of feeding the signal back to the record head of the first tape machine. Riley was in Paris working with jazz musician Chet Baker's group when he got the idea:

> Well, the accumulation technique hadn't been invented yet and it got invented during this session. I was asking the engineer, describing to him the kind of sound I had worked with in *Mescalin Mix* [an earlier tape composition]. I wanted this kind of long, repeated loop and I said "can you create something like that?" He got it by stringing the tape between two tape recorders and feeding the signal from the second machine back to the first to recycle along with the new incoming signals. By varying the intensity of the feedback you could form the sound either into a single image without delay or increase the intensity until it became a dense chaotic kind of sound. . . . The engineer was the first to create this technique that I know of. This began my obsession with time-lag accumulation feed-back.[7]

Oliveros's piece *I of IV* (1966) made extensive use of accumulative tape delay degeneration of the repeating signal. She too did this by threading one reel of tape through two tape recorders. The sound was recorded on the first machine and played back on the second. The distance between the two machines caused a lag of about eight seconds, a fairly long delay. The music was further layered by playing the signal directly, without delay, and also by using shorter echo effects.

It was a widely heard recording of *I of IV* in 1967—occupying the entire side of a CBS-Odyssey record album of electronic music—that seeded the musical world with the idea of tape delay. This was the very same technique used in 1975 by Brian Eno (b. 1948) for his piece *Discreet Music*.

> I of IV was made in July 1966, at the University of Toronto Electronic Music Studio. It is a real time studio performance composition (no editing or tape splicing), utilizing the techniques of amplifying combination tones and tape repetition. The combination tone technique was one which I developed in 1965 at the San Francisco Tape Music Center. The equipment consisted of 12 sine tone square wave generators connected to an organ keyboard, 2 line amplifiers, mixer, Hammond spring type reverb

and 2 stereo tape recorders. 11 generators were set to operate above 20,000 Hz, and one generator at below 1 Hz. The keyboard output was routed to the line amplifiers, reverb, and then to channel A of recorder 1. The tape was threaded from recorder 1 to recorder 2. Recorder 2 was on playback only. Recorder 2 provided playback repetition approximately 8 seconds later. Recorder 1 channel A was routed to recorder 1 channel B and recorder 1 channel B to recorder 1 channel A in a double feedback loop. Recorder 2 channel A was routed to recorder 1 channel A, and recorder 2 channel B was routed to recorder 1 channel B. The tape repetition contributed timbre and dynamic changes to seated state sounds. The combination tones produced by the 11 generators and the bias frequencies of the tape recorders were pulse modulated by the sub-audio generator.[8]

Yet another Oliveros piece—*C(s) for Once* (1966)—used three tape recorders with one tape threaded through all three to affect the sounds being played of live voices, flutes, trumpets, and organ. An equally compelling piece that used tape recorders in the performance situation is *Mugic* (1973), by Charles Amirkhanian. In this work, the composer threaded a single reel of magnetic tape through the record and playback heads of three tape recorders. Spoken words were recorded on tape machine 1 and played back as a delayed signal on machines 2 and 3. Then, taking a page from Lucier's book, Amirkhanian also used a microphone to pick up the acoustic resonance of the sounds being played in the room so that the clarity of the dialogue and playback signal gradually deteriorated as the piece continued.

Tape Reversal: Playing Sounds Backwards

The idea of playing recorded sounds in reverse had crude beginnings with the turntablism of primordial musique concrète. With tape composition, the effect came into its own as an essential ingredient of the electronic music repertoire.

Tape reversal is created by literally snipping out a length of recorded tape and splicing it back into the reel backwards, or, on a tape that has only been recorded on one side, turning it over and running it backwards past the playback head. The playing of sounds backwards as part of a piece of music was a radical statement during the '50s. It was a declaration of independence for the sound itself, freeing it from the earthly means that created it. Composers just couldn't get enough of tape reversal. For a time, it became overused to the point of becoming trite. Yet the resource of playing sounds backwards has persisted as an important technique in electronic music through the evolution from tubes and transistors to microprocessors and software.

Pauline Oliveros in the San Francisco Tape Music Center, mid-1960s. Photo courtesy of John Bischoff, Mills College Center for Contemporary Music.

Pierre Henry, Pierre Schaeffer, and the Institutionalization of Sound

Early electronic music was institutionalized from the very moment of its birth. It was subject to the taste, and pocketbooks, of those running the institutions. Music produced by these studios was viewed as somehow more legitimate than music produced by outsiders. There was nothing liberal about the social context of electronic music. It was only liberated by those who cast off the institutions and produced it themselves.

The coming of the tape recorder gave composers another choice. The head and ears of the listener became the performing stage had. The walls of oscillators, filter banks, reel-to-reel tape recorders, and other gadgets that adorned the shiny confines of the studio became the orchestra. It was a liberating period for those who had facilities at their disposal. It was also a period of the haves and the have-nots; those who had equipment and those who did not. Electronic music became largely institutionalized because of the economics of producing in the medium.

During the '50s and '60s, electronic music equipment was so expensive to own and operate that only large organizations or institutions could afford to sponsor studios. In the United States, these studios usually belonged to universities or to private, commercial recording companies serving the entertainment industry. In most other countries, studios were subsidized by governments as part of a research program or nationalized project in radio experimentation. The field of electronic music also became increasingly technical. Composers were pressed to become familiar with the operation of machines and the principles of acoustics that governed the electrical generation of sound. Some embraced it and some didn't, but nearly every young composer during the early '50s wanted to get their hands on a tape recorder and try their hand at producing a masterpiece for the radical new medium.

By 1966, only eighteen years after the establishment of the first major electronic music studio—the Groupe de Recherches Musicales in Paris—there were about 560 known institutional and private studios in the world.[9] Of these, approximately 40 percent were sponsored by an institution of some type. In the United States and England, where government sponsorship was virtually nonexistent, many composers aligned themselves with universities or corporations that could afford to underwrite studios. Others formed their own private studios as needed.

There is an impression that between the years 1948 and 1966 electronic music composers in the United States had little institutional support. This is not entirely true. If one defines the top fifteen studios in the world by the number of tape compositions they produced—with the exception of strictly private studios that were used by fewer than five people—the United States accounts for five of these, and four were institutionally supported. But for a country that had the greatest number of studios overall, far fewer of the electronic music facilities in the United States were supported by parent organizations than in other countries. The hotbed of activity was in Europe, where government funds were available in most countries to underwrite these studios. The money was not only used for equipment but for publicity and performances as well. Most of the leading government-sponsored programs were associated with state-run radio stations. One part of the working arrangement with composers was that their music would be featured regularly in nationally broadcast concerts. It was a time of unprecedented exposure for electronic music in Europe. Various schools and styles took shape, and there was a healthy rivalry among European factions in this emerging art.

American composers were often hard-pressed to compete on a technological basis with their peers in other countries. It was perhaps even worse in England, where there was even less institutional sponsorship of electronic music than in the United States. This is not to say that composers without an institutional connection were unable to compose elec-

Key Electronic Music Studios around the World: 1948–67

Location/Name	Affiliation	Established	Representative works
Buenos Aires, Argentina: Laboratorio de Musica Electronica	Instituto Torcuato di Tella, Centro Latinoamericana de Altos Estudios Musicales (CLAEM)	1962	*Lutero* (Bolaños, 1965), *Dos en el mundo* (Bolaños, 1965), *Dance bouquet* (Rondano, 1965), *Las paredes* (Bolaños, 1966), *La fiesta hoy* (Rondano, 1966)
Gent, Belgium: Institut voor Psychoakoestiek en Elektronische Muziek (IPEM)	IPEM	1962	*Escurial* (de Meester, 1963, for television), *Endomorfie I* (Goethals, 1964), *Votre Faust* (Pousseur, 1965–66), *Ouverture* (Buckinxc, 1966)
Toronto, Canada: University of Toronto Electronic Music Studio	University of Toronto	1959	*Etude No. 1* (Schaeffer, 1959), *Composition for Flute and Tape Recorder* (Aitken, 1963), *Sequence Arrangement No. 1* (Hassell, 1964), Three Etudes for Hugh Le Caine (Cross, 1965), *Pictures from the Old Testament* (Pederson, 1965), *Alchemy* (Charpentier, 1966), *I of IV* (Oliveros, 1966)
Santiago, Chile: Laboratorio de Acústica	Catholic University	1958	*Variaciónes espectrales* (Asuar, 1959)
London, England: Radiophonic Workshop	British Broadcasting Corporation (BBC)	1956	*The Disagreeable Oyster* (Briscoe, 1959), *Opium* (Almuro, 1959), *Anathema, for Reciter and Tape* (Wilkinson, 1962), *A Round of Silence* (Smalley, 1963)
Paris, France: Groupe de Recherches Musicales (GRM)	French National Radio-Television (RTF)	1948	*See text*
Berlin, Germany: Experimentalistudio für Künstliche Klang und Gerauscherzeugung, Laboratorium für Akustisch-Musikalische Grenzprobleme	RFZ (East German Radio)	1962	*Der faule Zauberer* (Kurth, 1963), *Amarillo luna* (Kubiczek, 1963), *Quartet für elektronische Klänge* (Wehding, 1963), *Variationen* (Hohensee, 1965), *Zoologischer Garten* (Rzewski, 1965)

Location/Name	Affiliation	Established	Representative works
Cologne, Germany: Studio für Elektronische Musik	West German National Radio (WDR)	1951	*See text*
Munich, Germany: Studio für Elektronische Musik	Siemens Corporation	1957	*Studie für elektronische Klänge* (Riedl, 1959), *Klänge unterwegs* (Brün, 1961), *Antithese* (Kagel, 1962), *Rota II* (Hambraeus, 1963), *Imaginary Landscape No. 3* (Cage, realized by Kagel, 1964), *Heterophony* (Antoniou, 1966)
Milan, Italy: Studio di Fonologia	RAI (Italian Radio)	1953	*Mimusique n. 1* (Berio, 1953), *Notturno* (Maderna, 1955), *Etude 1* (Boucourechliev, 1956), *Scambi* (Pousseur, 1957), *Thema–Omaggio a Joyce* (Berio, 1958), *Continuo* (Maderna, 1958), *Fontana Mix* (Cage, 1958–59), *Momenti* (Berio, 1960), *Intolleranza* (Nono,1960), *Visage* (Berio, 1961), *Music for Vibraphones* (Hassell, 1965)
Tokyo, Japan: Electronic Music Studio	NHK (Japan Radio)	1953	*Music for Sine Wave Selected on a Ration Principle of Prime Numbers* (Mayuzumi, 1955), *Ondine* (Miyoshi, 1959), *A Red Cocoon* (Moroi, 1960), *Phonogène* (Takahashi, 1962), *Parallel Music* (Ichiyanagi, 1962), *Telemusik* (Stockhausen, 1966), *Comet Ikeya* (Yuasa, 1966)
Eindhoven, The Netherlands: Center for Electronic Music (Philips Research Laboratories)	Philips Gloeilampenfabrieken	1956	*Poéme électronique* (Varèse, 1958), *Variations électronique* (Badings, 1957), *Whirling* (Dissevelt, 1958), *Electronic Ballet Music III* (Badings, 1959), *Contrasts* (Raaijmakers, 1959), *Pianoforte* (Raaijmakers, 1960)

Location/Name	Affiliation	Established	Representative works
Oslo, Norway: Norsk Rikskringkasting	NRK (Norse Radio	1961	*Epitaffio* (Nordheim, 1963), *Response I* (Nordheim, 1966)
Warsaw, Poland: Studio Eksperymentalne	Polish National Radio	1957	*Campi integrati* (Evangelisti, 1959), *Passacalia na 40 z 5* (Dobrowalski, 1960*), Brygaa smierci* (Penderecki, 1963), *Assemblage I-III* (B. Schaeffer, 1966).
Murray Hill, N.J.: Bell Telephone Laboratories	Bell Telephone	1957	*In the Silver Scale* (Guttman, 1957), *Pitch Variations* (Guttman, 1957), *Stochatta* (Pierce, 1959), *May Carl I* (Mathews, 1959), *Five Stochastic Studies* (Tenney, 1962), *Composition No. 3– Music for the IBM 7090* (Strang, 1963), *Composition* (Risset, 1965), *Swansong* (Mathews, 1966).
New York, N.Y.: Columbia-Princeton Electronic Music Center	Columbia and Princeton Universities	Tape Center, 1951; Music Center, 1959	*See text*
San Francisco, Calif: San Francisco Tape Music Center	Private until 1966; later, Mills College	1961	*See text*
Waltham, Mass: Brandeis University Electronic Music Studio	Brandeis University	1961	*Perspectives* (Shirley, 1962*), Etude No. 1* (Hughes, 1962), *UCLA* (Subotnick, 1964), *Piece One* (Adamis, 1964), *Milwaukee Combination* (Behrman, 1964), *Mix No. 2* (Gnazzo, 1964), *Rozart Mix for Magnetic Tape* (Cage, 1965), *Elegy for Albert Anastasia* (Lucier, 1965), *Quintona* (Krenek, 1965), *Music for Solo Performer* (Lucier, 1965), *Tonegroups I* (Epstein, 1965), *Medeighnia's* (Lentz, 1965), *From My First Book of Dreams—live electronic music* (Lucier, 1965), *Whistlers* (Lucier, 1966–1967)

Location/Name	Affiliation	Established	Representative works
Urbana, Ill.: University of Illinois Experimental Music Studio	University of Illinois	1959	*Three Electronic Studies* (Hoffman and Shallenberg, 1959), *Collage No. 1* (Tenney, 1961), *Amplification* (Hiller, 1962), *Seven Electronic Studies* (Hiller, 1962–1963), *Computer Cantata* (Baker and Hiller, 1963), *Antiphone* (Gaburo, 1963), *Futility* (Brün, 1964), *Machine Music* (Hiller, 1964), *27'10.554" for a percussionist* (Cage, realized by Neuhaus, 1965), *Tape Piece Using Trombone Sounds* (Lewis and Powell, 1965), *Adjacencies* (Amacher, 1965), *Algorithms I and II* (Hiller, 1966)

tronic music. Many independent composers across the world successfully amassed their own private stockpiles of oscillators and tape recorders.

Studios ran the gamut from being highly organized, "clean-room" environments with people running around in lab coats to setups consisting of nothing more than a room under a stairwell with a haphazardly patched-together collection of hustled audio gear. Yet every studio, no matter how professionally equipped or operated, bristled with the enthusiasm that something extraordinarily new and different was happening to music.

Origins in France

Pierre Schaeffer was a radio engineer, broadcaster, writer, and biographer. Pierre Henry was a classically trained composer. Together, these two French collaborators instigated a revolution in music that brought electronic technology into the mainstream of classical music. The art form they released on the world was musique concrète: recorded electronic music that could contain any and all sounds. The institution they founded was the electronic music studio.

Schaeffer graduated from the Ecole Polytechnique in Paris in 1931 and continued his studies in the field of electricity and telecommunications. He later accepted an apprenticeship as an engineer at the Paris facilities of French National Radio and Radiodiffusion-Television Françaises (RTF), which led to a full-time job as a technician and broadcaster.

RTF was at that time under the control of the German occupying forces. During World War II, Schaeffer led two lives. By day he worked as the director of a branch of RTF called the Studio d'Essai of the Radiodiffusion Nationale, which he had organized in 1943. His work there was devoted to experiments in radio production and musical acoustics. He also led a shadow life during the war as a member of the French resistance.

His job at RTF gave him access to a wealth of radio broadcasting equipment, including phonograph turntables, mixers, microphones, and a direct-to-disc cutting lathe. He also had at his disposal a large archive of sound effects records owned by the studio and routinely used for radio productions. During 1944, he immersed himself in the production of an eight-part radio opera series called *La Coquille à planètes*.[10] Although an audio engineer by trade, Schaeffer had been raised in a musical family and was becoming acutely aware of the musical possibilities of audio recording techniques. For the opera production, he used a variety of nonmusical sounds as part of the audio montage being broadcast over the radio. He undertook most of the technical work himself, learning how to work with turntable technology. In one part of the opera, Schaeffer combined noise and music in a more overt manner. He later explained that this experience in manipulating recorded sounds revealed "preoccupations which led to musique concrète."[11]

On another occasion, he remarked about the sense of discovery that enveloped him during the production of *La Coquille à planètes*:

> I was suddenly aware that the only mystery worthy of interest is concealed in the familiar trappings of triviality. And I noticed without surprise by recording the noise of things one could perceive beyond sounds, the daily metaphors that they suggest to us.[12]

After the war, in 1947, Schaeffer met the audio engineer Jacques Poullin, who became his close collaborator on the design of specialized audio equipment for the radio studio. By January 1948, Schaeffer was ready to stretch the limitations of turntable technology for a series of five compositions collectively known as the *Etudes de bruits*. He worked on them all year and premiered them on the radio on October 5, 1948.[13] These were the first completed works of *musique concrète*, a term that Schaeffer coined to denote the use of sound objects from nature, "concrete" sounds of the real world. These were opposed to the "musical objects" of tonal music, whose source was the abstract value system of the mind.

Five pieces were presented during the October "concert of noises":

1. *Etude aux chemins de fer* (a montage of locomotive sounds recorded at a train depot);

2. *Etude aux tourniquets* (for xylophone, bells, and whistling toy tops called tourniquets or whirligigs);

3 and 4. *Etude au piano I* and *II* (both using piano material recorded for Schaeffer by Pierre Boulez);

5. *Etude aux casseroles* (using the sounds of spinning saucepan lids, boats, human voices, and other instruments).

The *Études de bruits* were composed using only turntable technology. Schaeffer used the following equipment to fashion them:

- A disc-cutting lathe for making recordings of the final mixes
- Four turntables
- A four-channel mixer
- Microphones
- Audio filters
- A reverberation chamber
- A portable recording unit
- Sound effects records from the radio station library and newly recorded sounds

Schaeffer's list of recording and editing techniques for the *Etudes* reads like a glossary for an electronic music clinic. Remember that the year was 1948 and that the tape recorder was not yet in general use. Think about what it would be like to make a motion picture without the benefit of editing what comes out of the camera, and you have an idea of how monumentally complicated and difficult it was for Schaeffer to fashion the five *Etudes*. He edited different sounds together by playing them back and rerecording them directly onto the disc masters. He played sounds in reverse. He created lock grooves—endless loops—with the disc cutter so that sounds would repeat. He played the sounds back at different speeds. He used volume control to create fade-in and fade-out effects. He took some of the equipment outside of the studio to record natural sounds, including locomotives at the Batignolles train depot, amateur musicians, voices of friends, spinning saucepan lids, and piano music played for him by friends, including Pierre Boulez. He combined these sounds in various ways with stock sounds from sound effects records and recorded music from Bali and America.[14] The result was a tour de force of technical ingenuity and resourcefulness.

Historically, the *Etudes de bruits* introduced the world to the abstract plasticism of sounds plucked from the real world and woven together like so many swatches of multicolored linen. Schaeffer did not merely offer a montage of sounds as if taken from a documentary film. He modified and structured them rhythmically and sonically as musical resources. Although Cage had been the first to compose a piece of music for a recorded medium (*Imaginary Landscape No. 1* for turntable and recorded sounds, 1939), it is Schaeffer who generally gets credit for laying the groundwork for the emergence of electronic music composition—well-deserved praise for a man who could sometimes be guilty of talking too much and composing less.

The significance of the *Etudes* rests on four principles:

- The act of composing music was accomplished by technological means; the way in which the organization of sounds was created was as important to the outcome as the sounds themselves.
- Many of the sound materials were of natural, not musical, origin.
- The work could be replayed identically over and over again.
- Presentation of the work did not require human performers.

Composing a work of musique concrète began with the sound material itself rather than with a mental schema laid out by the composer beforehand, such as a score. The *material* preceded the *structure*. Sounds were then processed and edited by the composer until they were recorded in their final structure. This approach to composition was nearly the opposite of that of traditional music, which begins with a predefined structure that is then completed by the composer. Not all tape composition was composed in this manner, but it was the approach preferred by Schaeffer in his work.

Schaeffer created the field of musique concrète and tape composition by sheer force of mind. In elevating the stature of "noise" sounds to that of raw material for the making of music, his objective was not unlike that of Russolo and the Futurists some thirty years before. Why Schaeffer found success and Russolo did not is a good question. After all, Russolo theoretically could have had access to the same disc-cutting and radio broadcasting technology as Schaeffer. Unlike Schaeffer, who was virtually unknown until his broadcast concert in 1948, Russolo was attached to a group of artists and poets that was highly visible prior to his manifesto on noise music. There is every reason to believe that Russolo could have received funding and access to technology to promulgate his music, but that never happened. The reason would seem to be that society was simply not ready for Russolo's ideas. It took thirty intervening years of the development of new musical resources in classical, jazz, and popular music to prepare listeners for a music of technology in which noise was an essential part.

The success of the *Etudes* attracted composer Pierre Henry to the studio; he joined Schaeffer and Poullin in their work in 1949. In 1951, after several more successful experimental works and broadcasts, the RTF provided funds for the creation of the first audio studio in the world devoted exclusively to the production of electronic music. This was the Groupe de Recherches Musicales (GRM).

Now that magnetic tape recorders were available, Schaeffer and Poullin set to work on the design of several ingenious new tools for audio recording and editing. By 1951, in addition to the requisite audio signal generators and filters, they had equipped their studio with:

- A three-track tape recorder.
- The Morphophone, a tape machine with ten heads for the playback of loops and the creation of echo effects.
- The Tolana Phonogène, a keyboard-operated tape machine designed to play loops. It had twenty-four preset speeds that could be triggered by the keyboard.
- The Sareg Phonogène, a variable-speed version of the Tolana Phonogène tape loop machine.
- The Potentiomètre d'Espace, a playback controller for distributing sound to four loudspeakers.[15]

Although Schaeffer and Poullin remained fascinated with electronic gadgetry, Henry's presence at the studio brought an immediate sense of musicality to the work that had been lacking in Schaeffer's collages. At the same time, Schaeffer's engineering mind was compelled to devise an empirical approach to making music from noise. Much like Russolo had done before him, he classified sound "objects" into several categories:

- Living elements (including voices, animal sounds)
- Noises
- Modified or "prepared" instruments
- Conventional instruments

Symphonie pour un homme seul (Symphony for a Man Alone, 1949–50) was the first major collaboration between Schaeffer and Henry. Although the twelve-movement work underwent many revisions over the years, the original recording, composed using phonograph machines, was a striking and ambitious piece, even by today's standards. It was based primarily on two categories of sounds as defined by the composers:

1. Human sounds (breathing, vocal fragments, shouting, humming, whistling)
2. Nonhuman sounds (footsteps, knocking on doors, percussion, prepared piano, orchestral instruments)

As an approach to composing the work, these sounds were either modified using the technical resources that were at the composers' command or left alone and simply edited into intriguing patterns. The work freely employed spoken voice, broadcast music, prepared piano, and various mechanical or natural noises. Disc loops (repeating grooves) were effectively used to create rhythmic passages of spoken words. The piece was originally structured as a series of twenty-two movements or expositions on certain combinations of sounds. It grew in complexity from movement to movement, creating greater and greater abstractions of recorded sounds, until a finale of booming instrumental sounds brought it to a thundering close. It was highly charged and fraught with tension, a trademark of early musique concrète.

The success of Schaeffer and Henry's turntable experiments and broadcasts led to the founding of the Groupe de Recherches Musicales in 1951. Tape recorders, audio signal generators, filters, and other audio equipment were assembled to replace the disc lathe and turntables.

The studio attracted much attention through its ambitious productions of electronic music and collaborations with performance troupes. In 1953, Schaeffer and Henry collaborated on *Voile d'Orphée,* a "concrete opera." The work combined traditionally sung arias with musique concrète blaring from loudspeakers. The tape sounds of sweeping electronic tones and distorted human voices were mixed with scored music being played by a live orchestra. The performance created an uproar at the annual Donaueschingen festival in Germany. A new version of *Symphonie pour un homme seul* was produced in 1955 as the basis for a ballet by the choreographer Maurice Béjart. Béjart and Henry continued to collaborate for many years afterward.

In the early '50s, Schaeffer began to present lecture-demonstrations of the group's work, and during the next few years many composers visited to try their hand at tape composition. Among these were Pierre Boulez (who had already assisted Schaeffer by providing piano fragments for two works), Karlheinz Stockhausen, Marius Constant, Darius Milhaud, and Olivier Messiaen. A research assistant named Abraham A. Moles also joined the group in 1951. Schaeffer and Moles developed one of the first formal aesthetic handbooks for electronic music. In it, they catalogued sounds, described the various tape-editing techniques that formed the basis of musique concrète, and tried to establish a philosophical basis for the new medium. They touched upon the major themes that continue to underlie the existence of electronic music: the permanency of recorded work; the ability to reproduce music without the participation of performers; and the ability to manipulate the space and time components of the material.

Pierre Henry became the most prolific composer associated with the studio. By 1954 he had composed no fewer than forty-four pieces, most as solo works. He worked at the RTF studios until 1958, when he left to start his own studio, the Studio Apsome, with Maurice Béjart. He continued in the tradition of musique concrète but gradually began to bring more lyricism and dynamic variety to the medium, which had always been characterized by extremities, contrasts, and choppy effects. Two of his best-known works, *Le Voyage* (1961–62), consisting largely of processed feedback, and *Variations pour une porte et un soupir* (Variations for a Door and a Sigh, 1963), are among the most mature pieces of musique concrète ever realized.

Henry was not an engineer like Schaeffer: He was a composer. Unlike his colleague, he did not rely on the phenomenological analysis of sound for motivation. He worked with the emotional content of music, composing with an acute instinct for the communicating power of musical and nonmusical sounds. Whereas the sounds themselves were the starting point for Schaeffer, Henry's compositions began with a structure or form:

> One of course has to compose with a direction, a lucid idea. One has to have in mind a certain construction, a form. But that form differs according to the theme, to the character of the work and of course according to the material. A work like *Le Voyage* has a form, another like *La Porte* another one. And another work that requires a voice or chanting . . . every work has its form, but this form is there in the art of creation. I think that from the beginning of my work I have been more original in my form than in my material.[16]

Propelled by a modicum of commercial success during the '60s, Henry has remained a vital composer of electronic music for over thirty years. Many of his tape pieces have been written for live performance with singers, orchestras, or dance ensembles. In 1975 he composed a work called *Futuriste* (1975) to honor Luigi Russolo, for which a new set of mechanical *intonarumori* were built and accompanied by a montage of recorded noises.

Henry's colleague Maurice Béjart choreographed a ballet for a performance version of *Variations pour une porte et un soupir*. He described the music and the dance as "a cyclical work which closes in on itself; unfolding, development, exhaustion and destruction, evoking the rhythm of a day or of a life."[17] For each of the twenty-five parts of the dance version, the dancers drew lots prior to each performance to determine who will dance which parts. A certain number of dancers was prescribed for each part. The dancing was improvised but inspired by the names of the different parts of the work: Slumber, Hesitation, Awakening, Yawning, Gymnastics, Waves, Snoring, Death, and so forth.

A blackboard was used to inform the audience ahead of time as to which dancers had drawn which parts for a given performance. Béjart explained his rationale for working this way:

> The dancers draw lots for their numbers on stage, in front of the audience, thus renewing each evening the cyclical ritual of life with its arbitrary course in which the human being and anguish swirl around in the multiple stages of an absurd theater.[18]

During the '90s, Henry returned to some of the ideas that he first explored while at the RTF studio. Looking back, he underscores the emotional and symbolic nature of the sounds with which he works:

> My sounds are sometimes ideograms. The sounds need to disclose an idea, a symbol. . . . I often very much like a psychological approach in my work, I want it to be a psychological action, with a dramatic or poetic construction or association of timbre or, in relation to painting, of color. Sounds are everywhere. They do not have to come from a library, a museum. The grand richness of a sound palette basically determines the atmosphere. At the moment I try to manufacture a certain "tablature de serie." I won't talk about it. I almost become a late serialist. After a big vehement expressive period, post-romantic, I think that now I'm going into a period of pure ideas. It all reminds me very much of my work of the '50s.[19]

Pierre Schaeffer decreased his activity as a composer as "trained" composers spent more time in the RTF studio. Instead, he found himself in a pitched philosophical battle with the Cologne electronic music studio where Eimert and Meyer-Eppler were lecturing about the purity of their serial approach to composing music using only electronic signals. Schaeffer responded in 1952 with a treatise on the treatment of "sound objects," classifying them according to seven values of sounds that govern the creation of electronic music:

- Mass: organization of the sound in a spectral dimension.
- Dynamics: measurable values of the various components of the sound.
- Tone quality/timbre: particular qualities and "color " of the sound.
- Melodic profile: temporal evolution of the total spectrum of the sound.
- Profile of mass: temporal evolution of the spectral components of the sound mass.
- Grain: analysis of the irregularities of surface of the sound.
- Pace: analysis of amplitude dynamics of the sound.[20]

Schaeffer further divided these characteristics into about fifty "points of morphological description," approaching his own form of serialism for noise sounds that might also include musical tones. However, it was the composers themselves who eventually left the theories of Schaeffer, Eimert, and Meyer-Eppler behind. There was no acceptable doctrine for creating electronic music that made one piece of greater intrinsic value than any other.

Interestingly, Schaeffer questioned whether much of his own musique concrète work should have been accepted as music at all:

> I fought like a demon throughout all the years of discovery and exploration in musique concrète. I fought against electronic music, which was another approach, a systemic approach, when I preferred an experimental approach actually working directly, empirically with sound. But at the same time, as I defended the music I was working on, I was personally horrified at what I was doing. I felt extremely guilty. As my father, the violinist, used to say, indulgently, "What are you up to, my little boy? When are you going to make music?" And I used to say, "I'm doing what I can, but I can't do that." I was always deeply unhappy at what I was doing. I was happy at overcoming great difficulties—my first difficulties with the turntables when I was working on *Symphonie pour un homme seul*, my first difficulties with the tape recorders when I was doing *Etude aux objets*—that was good work, I did what I set out to do. My work on the *Solfège*—it's not that I disown everything I did—it was a lot of hard work. But each time I was to experience the disappointment of not arriving at music. I couldn't get to music, what I call music. I think of myself as an explorer struggling to find a way through in the far north, but I wasn't finding a way through.[21]

After kick-starting the RTF studio, Schaeffer pulled back from composition and was content to observe the development of the medium at arm's length while he served as a guiding influence. One of his achievements was bringing several noted composers to the studio, including Luc Ferrari (b. 1929), Iannis Xenakis (1922–2001), and Edgard Varèse. There, these composers created some of the most influential tape compositions of all time.

Computer Musique Concrète

The hammering of sounds from the natural world into new structures continues to this day in the spirit of musique concrète. The only difference is that it is now being done largely with computers and software.

Tetsu Inoue (b. 1969) is a contemporary composer who constructs short, micro-forms of music in a painstakingly detailed manner that is reminiscent of the conceptual challenges that faced the earliest composers of tape music. Working with a combination of sampled sounds and synthesized tonalities of his own design, he carefully architects his music moment by moment. The works are short and disciplined, and although they do not sound much like classic musique concrète, they were created with a sensibility that is not too far afield from that of the early French and German schools. Inoue explains his technique:

> I have been working with more two-minute, three-minute short pieces. I like the short sound. Compressed information and compressed emotion. Putting lots of information in short pieces. A few years ago when I was doing ambient my songs were more like forty minutes.
>
> First I make an interesting sound. Then through that sound I get an idea. It is like an oil painter placing color onto an image. First I experiment with sound. If I like a sound, I save it. I use several programs. I use MIDI as well.
>
> I don't like randomness so much. I like to control the randomness. That is my goal. My pieces do have a certain rule.[22]

There is something utterly visual about Inoue's music. After first hearing some of his recent "computer musique concrète," I remarked that his music reminded me of a Jackson Pollock painting. He strongly disagreed, saying that his music was much more organized than that. Upon another listen I understood what he meant, but the visual images still kept coming. This time I told him that his music sounded like a Sol Lewitt pencil wall drawing with all of its intricately intersecting matrices of lines. "Ah, I can see that. Yes, maybe that is better." Tetsu works with sound like an artist does with paint, creating libraries of tones and textures and carefully—meticulously—organizing them into startling, explosive works of crystal clarity.

The works on one of his CDs, *Fragment Dot*, are a good example of this approach. "The idea behind *Fragment Dot* is that I wanted to cut and paste," he explained. "It took one month to finish the first song. I was cutting micro-seconds and then pasting together those kinds of things. It is time-consuming."[23]

The German School

The French jumped into electronic music headfirst. The Germans went in one toe at a time, writing about it first, acting it out later. In 1949, Dr. Werner Meyer-Eppler (1913–1955), a distinguished German physicist and theorist, published an important paper, "Elektrische Klangerzeugung," outlining the development of electronic music technology. At the same time, the composer and musicologist Herbert Eimert (1897–1972) became interested in electronic music instruments as a means of extending the compositional theories of Anton Webern and other serialists. The link between these two men was a sound engineer named Robert Beyer (b. 1901), who collaborated with Meyer-Eppler in 1950 to present a series of lectures on the possibilities of what they termed "elektronische Musik," or electronic music. These demonstrations resulted in a program that Meyer-Eppler, Beyer, and Eimert organized for West German Radio (NWDR, now WDR) in Cologne on October 18, 1951. That event marked the broadcasting system's commitment to sponsor an electronic music studio under the direction of Eimert.

The intellectual animosity that existed between the WDR studio in Cologne and the RTF in Paris was tangible. Composer Konrad Boehmer (b. 1941) worked in the German studio at the time. "You could say that in the '50s, you had two types of Cold War," explained Boehmer. "One between the Soviet Union and the United States and one between the Cologne studio and the French studio. They disgusted each other. The aesthetic starting points of Schaeffer were *completely* different from Eimert's views."[24]

The roots of this dislike first sprung from the French, with memories of World War II still fresh in their minds. Pierre Schaeffer poignantly recalled that "after the war, in the '45 to '48 period, we had driven back the German invasion but we hadn't driven back the invasion of Austrian music, 12–tone music. We had liberated ourselves politically, but music was still under an occupying foreign power, the music of the Vienna school."[25]

Schaeffer was reacting to the potent drawing power of serialism following World War II. The new generation of young German composers were not the only advocates of serialism; Pierre Boulez and Milton Babbitt were two notable non-German composers working in this form. But having originated with the techniques of Webern, the serialist approach to composition was taken up by young German composers with a passionate conviction. It represented in some ways their own protest against the Third Reich that had left Germany in ruins. Webern, of course, was a victim of the Reich as well.

Pierre Boulez and Karlheinz Stockhausen were the most vocal forces behind the "total serialization" of a piece of music. They extended Webern's rules for pitches, timbres, and rhythms in twelve-tone composition to dynamics, densities, and amplitude as well. The period during which total serialism reigned was brief. It preceded the establishment of the Cologne studio by two years and only lasted about four, from 1949 to 1953.[26] Why it was a short-lived trend is best expressed by a witness to many of the premieres of serialist music at the time:

> The impression made by all these works, even on a listener who had read the commentaries beforehand, was one of chaos. They reminded one of multi-colored oscillograms in which the traditional categories of melody and harmony had been suppressed in favor of shock effects of dynamics and timbre. The fact that these shock effects were organized according to pre-chosen series was only of theoretical interest.[27]

One of the objectives of total serialism was the removal of sentimentality and programmatic aspects from music, a reaction against French impressionism and German romanticism before it. In America, John Cage had already begun his experiments with chance operations to effect the same results by different means.

Eimert viewed pure, electronically generated sound as a wholly new resource at the disposal of the composer. He and his colleagues had little respect for French musique concrète. They considered Schaeffer's work to be nothing more than mere dawdling, a scatter-shot concoction of freewheeling natural sound and noise: a novel accident. Like Schaeffer in Paris, Eimert had the resources to piece together a state-of-the-art electronic music studio. He did so, however, not with the intent of producing musique concrète in the style of the French. Because the early emphasis of Eimert, Beyer, and Meyer-Eppler was on the physics of purely "electronic music," Eimert equipped the studio with tone-generating instruments and filters rather than specialized tape machines for embellishing sounds of the real world.

The German studio had a predisposition for electronic musical instruments. It had a Monochord, an updated version of the monophonic Trautonium built especially for it by Friedrich Trautwein. It also had a Melochord, originally built by Harald Bode (1909–1987) in 1947 for Meyer-Eppler to use during his physics lectures and demonstrations. The Melochord had two monophonic tone-generating systems that were separately controlled using a split, five-octave keyboard, for which the upper three octaves could be assigned to one tone generator and the lower two octaves to another. Two notes could be played at a time. It also had controls for shaping the attack, sustain, and decay envelopes of

A section of the WDR Studio for Electronic Music, Cologne, in 1966 when Stockhausen was composing *Hymnen*. From left: corner of a 4–track tape recorder; mixing console; mono tape recorder; Springer (in front of the mono tape recorder) with rotating head for suspending sounds; board with 6 roller guides for long tape loops; switching board with 3 sliding faders; sound meter; large stop watch; second mono tape recorder; 9–octave filter; 2 Albis filters; portable Telefunken M5 tape recorder. Photo courtesy Stockhausen-Verlag.

the sound. In 1953, the WDR studio commissioned Bode to build yet another Melochord for them. The new model had two separate keyboards. Another new feature was the ability to control the filter from the keyboard, "tuning" the timbre of the sound. One could, for example, maintain a steady pitch and only change the tone color.[28]

Engineers were the unheralded geniuses behind most of the classic electronic music studios: GRM had Jacques Poullin, the WDR Fritz Enkel (1908–1959). In addition to the electronic musical instruments just mentioned, Enkel was challenged to make a control console for mixing and recording other numerous sound sources and audio gadgets, including:

- Audio oscillators for generating sine and sawtooth waveforms.
- A variable-speed tape recorder.
- A four-track tape recorder. The WDR studio was using four-channel tape recorders long before the rest of the world. Most

studios were still adopting to two-channel tape machines around 1957.

- Audio filters, including band-pass filters.
- A ring modulator.
- A white noise generator.

The first musical output of the Cologne studio was by Eimert and Beyer. They were preoccupied with the physics of sound and theories about musical structure that bordered on mathematics. The studio itself had little resemblance to a place to create music: "The equipment with its arrangement of different electroacoustic procedures outwardly resembles more a research laboratory."[29] There was nothing accidental about the first electronic music compositions made at the WDR studio. Eimert demanded discipline and control of anyone he invited to join his circle of experimenters. Viewing electronic music as the means of exercising control over every structural aspect of a piece, they constructed their earliest works by additive and subtractive synthesis, using sine waves as their primary tonal constituent. Eimert likened his group to visual artists who had to first learn the traditional techniques of oil painting before breaking the rules: "The work of composition begins first with the mastering of the 'material,' in other words, the given material itself must suggest a suitable and direct method of erecting and working on it."[30]

The first work of the studio used precious little instrumentation other than sine waves. It is safe to assume that the sonorous overtones of Trautwein's Monochord were of little use to the first Cologne composers. Harald Bode's Melochord, however, with its fairly pure sine tones, served them well. Composer Konrad Boehmer, who was invited by Eimert to join the studio in the late '50s, recalled that in order to use the Melochord for their additive synthesis pieces they "had to take every sound from the keyboard, put it on a tape and then start the synchronization and the montage work."[31]

The purely serialist electronic music compositions of the WDR studio did not occupy these composers for long. Within a year, those working at the studio were already straying away from tone exercises and experimenting with other aspects of the wonderfully rich palette offered by electronic music. While most of the work in Cologne continued to be made with purely electronic sounds, the use of echo, reverberation, and more conventionally musical organization of sound belied the strictly serialist intent of its creators. Konrad Boehmer notes:

> Though is may be true that the (self-nominated) "spokesman" of the Cologne School tried to give the impression of an absolute homogeneous

stylistic and technical evolution within the WDR studio, the compositions which were realized between 1952 and about 1958 manifest considerable aesthetic and methodical differences.[32]

While calling the music of the Cologne studio "musique concrète" would have been blasphemous in 1954, there were actually great similarities in the structural and editing approaches used by both studios by that time. The piece *Klang im unbegrenzten Raum* (1952) by Eimert and Beyer sounds very "acoustic" in its spatial movement of sound, reverberating depths, and fuzzy tones. Eimert's *Klangstudie I* (1952) bears little resemblance to serialism, with its repeating sweeps of the sound spectra and dramatic subplots of clangorous noises that appear and disappear into washes of echoing sonorities.

The equipment available to the WDR composers during the '50s did not change much. By about 1960, the composers were still using the same basic sine wave and noise generators and primitive filters that were in place when the studio began. This was equipment designed for making scientific measurements, not for composing music. As Stockhausen and other composers—including guests Henri Pousseur (b. 1929), Györgi Ligeti (b. 1923), Cornelius Cardew (1936–1981), Maricio Kagel (b. 1931), and others during the '50s—began to push the technical limits of the studio, they devised an engineering bag of tricks to realize their musical ideas. Stockhausen was clearly at the forefront of this innovation, inspired, and propelled, by the competitive nature of the field at the time.

The electronic music studio of the WDR has had a long history. Over the years it has been moved and upgraded with new equipment, particularly synthesizers. During the '70s, a British-made EMS Synthi 100 analog modular synthesizer with a digital sequencer was added to the studio along with an EMS vocoder and E-mu Emulator digital sampler. Other composers who have realized works there include Krenek (*Pfingstoratorium-Spiritus Intelligentiae* 1956), Ligeti (*Glissandi*, 1957; *Artikulation*, 1958), Cardew (*1st* and *2nd Exercises*, 1958), Kagel (*Transición I*, 1958–1960; *Acoustica*, 1969), and Gehlhaar (*Tanz I-V*, 1975). Stockhausen himself was artistic director after Eimert from 1963 until 1977. From 1977 to 1990, he served as the permanent artistic director, using the studio from time to time to compose new electronic works. As of this writing, however, the fate of the studio is uncertain. Stockhausen was informed in 2000 that the building housing the studio had been sold and that the studio was going to be closed down. Much of its equipment would be scrapped. When asked most recently about whether he had met with any success in keeping the WDR open, the composer simply told me, "No progress. It will be closed!"[33]

Otto Luening, Vladimir Ussachevsky, and the Columbia Tape Music Center

Electronic music activity in the United States during the early '50s was neither organized nor institutional. Experimentation with tape composition *was* taking place, but it was mostly by individual composers who threw together whatever equipment they could lay their hands on. The first institutional electronic music studio in America—the Columbia Tape Music Center—arose from these very first makeshift efforts.

The story begins in 1951. American composers Otto Luening (1900–1996) and Vladimir Ussachevsky (1911–1990) were both music instructors at Columbia University in New York City. The music department had acquired some tape equipment so that music programs could be recorded, including a dual-speed Ampex 400 tape recorder that could run at 7.5 and 15 inches per second, a Magnachord tape recorder borrowed from a radio store, and a Western Electric 369 microphone. A young engineer at the school named Peter Mauzey (b. 1930), who provided the composers with technical help, also built a circuit for creating reverberation. Ussachevsky was anxious to experiment and began piecing together tape music during the fall and winter of 1951–52. The first public recital of this tape music took place at Ussachevsky's Composers Forum on May 9, 1952.[34] Ussachevsky's *Sonic Contours* was played, among other works. This raised some eyebrows, and the word began to spread about tape music coming out of Columbia.

Luening and Ussachevsky began a long-standing partnership as collaborators and caretakers of Columbia's Tape Music Center. There was no permanent studio at first; the two men moved the portable equipment from one location to another in the trunk of Ussachevsky's car. There had been enough interest in their experiments to generate several commissions during 1952 and 1953, and during August of 1952, they set up shop in the corner of a renovated carriage barn at Bennington College in Vermont. That fall, they moved for two weeks into Henry Cowell's cottage in Shady, New York, to complete several short works for a Leopold Stokowski concert to be held at the Museum of Modern Art in Manhattan. From there the portable studio landed for a short time in the Ussachevsky living room in New York and then the sound studio in the basement of conductor Arturo Toscanini's (1867–1957) posh Riverdale home. Luening even mixed his work *Invention* in twelve notes using the far superior collection of tape recorders at the Union Theological Seminary in New York.[35] Finally, after many months of traveling around, the tape center landed in a room in the Columbia Music department.

Luening's and Ussachevsky's earliest experiments, like those of the Paris studio, did not make use of any electronically produced sounds.

They had no oscillators or other signal-generating equipment. Instead, Luening and Ussachevsky turned to the manipulation of recorded instrumental sounds. This was an important choice for them to make. Luening explained their decision: "We had a choice of working with natural and 'nonmusical' sounds like subway noise and sneezes and coughs, or widening the sound spectrum of existing instruments and bringing out new resonances from the existing world of instruments and voices. We chose the latter."[36] They composed their first pieces using only tape manipulations (speed changes, reverse sounds, splicing) and reverb using Mauzey's black box.

Luening used the flute as his sound source and Ussachevsky the piano. Their first exercises were all composed on tape. When invited to present some electronic music at the Museum of Modern Art, the pair hastily gathered their resources and set to work on their first electronic masterworks. These included *Fantasy in Space* (1952), *Low Speed* (1952), and *Invention in Twelve Notes* (1952) for Luening's flute, and *Sonic Contours* by Ussachevsky using the piano. Both composers experimented with altering the nature of the sounds through tape speed changes. Luening also employed some twelve-tone composition techniques in his work and used multiple tracking to superimpose separate tracks of flute sounds that were played with slight differences in pitch. *Low Speed* used these techniques to synthesize overtones in much the same manner as that used with sine wave oscillators.

The museum concert catapulted Luening and Ussachevsky into the public eye. They were featured on television, including a live appearance on NBC's *Today* show. The two men became America's spokesmen for electronic-music. After three more years of composing, lecturing, demonstrating, and performing their work, they received a grant from the Rockefeller Foundation to study the field of electronic music in both Europe and America and to respond with a plan for establishing an electronic music center in the United States.

In their travels in Europe, Luening and Ussachevsky visited Schaeffer and the GRM studio in Paris, WDR in Cologne, and several others. They hadn't seen so much audio equipment before and sought technical advice from anyone who would give it. They endured Schaeffer's intellectual browbeating about a new aesthetic, which Luening later called the "aesthetic of an engineer."[37] Eimert proselytized about the purity of German electronic music, and Stockhausen decided against letting them look over his shoulder while he worked, because, he said, any fool could make electronic music; it was just a matter of knowing the electrical permutations and algorithms.[38]

Luening and Ussachevsky were intellectually and physically

The RCA Mark II music synthesizer in 1959 after having been installed at the Columbia-Princeton Electronic Music Center in New York City. This photo shows a composer working at one of the punched paper-tape input stations. Photo courtesy of RCA.

exhausted after their trip. Not only was postwar Europe a completely changed place from the Europe that the two of them had previously known, but now the rise of electronic technology was beckoning a radical new stage in the history of music. On the flight home, their minds darted back to the sophisticated tape machines, audio generators, filters, and other gear that they had seen in European studios. They were already making a wish list when they arrived back in the States.

Upon their return, they were pleasantly surprised to hear about a new electronic music "synthesizer" that had been developed at RCA's David Sarnoff Laboratories in Princeton, New Jersey. This most propitious announcement couldn't have been better timed. They immediately arranged for a demonstration, and seized the opportunity as the means to establish a modern, fully equipped electronic music studio at Columbia University.

The device that brought Luening and Ussachevsky to Princeton was called the Olson-Belar Sound Synthesizer. It was named after its inventors, Harry F. Olson (1902–1982) and Herbert F. Belar, senior engineers at RCA. Introduced to the public in July 1955, the device was the first sound synthesizer in the modern sense. It was comprised of integrated components that could generate, modify, process, record, and present complex sonorities intended for musical applications.

Early hopes for the device focused on the ability to imitate and play the sounds of existing musical instruments—without needing musicians:

> If a composer has in mind what he wants to achieve, the effects can be obtained by means of the electronic music synthesizer, regardless of whether he can play a musical instrument or not. The composer or musician can produce the sound of any existing musical instrument as well as other sounds, regardless of whether they have ever existed.[39]

Years later, in 1967, Olson qualified that statement about replacing musicians, because it had become increasingly unfashionable: "Electronic music does not displace or supplant anything or anyone," he said. "The idea is to supplement conventional music."[40]

Another suggested application of the synthesizer was the automated composition of pop tunes and music for commercials. For these pedestrian applications, Olson developed the Electronic Music Composing Machine, which could be programmed to compose music in any style that could be defined in binary code: "The electronic music composing machine, which has been developed as an aid to music composition, depends upon a random selection of notes weighed by a probability based upon preceding events."[41] In other words, in certain styles of music that can be defined, there are only certain notes that are likely to follow certain other notes; the machine used random probability calculations to pick them. There was clearly a hope at RCA that, by coupling the RCA Music Synthesizer with the Electronic Music Composing Machine, the equipment could be commanded at the push of a button to churn out song after song like a sonic sausage factory. None of that ever left the lab.

Luening and Ussachevsky immediately saw through the haze of publicity surrounding the RCA music synthesizer to focus on its inherent value as a tool for the serious composer. They also realized that this one synthesizer could singlehandedly take care of most of the tone-generating needs that they envisioned for their studio. If they could acquire this machine for their studio, they could trash the wish list they had developed while in Europe. This was their future.

Discovering that composer Milton Babbitt, then at Princeton University, was also interested in experimenting with the synthesizer, Luening and Ussachevsky joined forces with him to lobby for some time on the machine. For the next three years the trio made regular trips to the Sarnoff labs to develop new musical material.

Luening and Ussachevsky became well-known for their experiments with tape composition. Together with Milton Babbitt and Roger Sessions (1896–1985) of Princeton University, they were the guiding lights behind the Columbia-Princeton Electronic Music Center and continued their work using equipment such as the RCA Mark I and II synthesizers. Sticking close to the classical tradition, these men often explored modern elements of music using electronics in combination with traditional instruments. Some of their most important achievements centered on the synchronization of live performers with electronic music played on tape. In 1954, Luening and Ussachevsky composed *A Poem in Cycles and Bells* (1954) for tape recorder and orchestra, which was, along with Varèse's *Déserts* of the same year, among the first works to synchronize the live performance of a symphony orchestra with tape music. This approach became the standard operating procedure for combining the live performance of an ensemble of musicians with electronic music, only supplanted by the use of portable synthesizers in the late '60s. Recorded accompaniment, usually in the form of a laptop hard disk or CD player, is still used today, particularly by academic practitioners.

In 1957, Luening and Ussachevsky completed a 155-page report for the Rockefeller Foundation on their findings in the electronic music field. In it they recommended the establishment of the Columbia-Princeton Electronic Music Center, the first institutionally sponsored studio in the United States. The result was an additional grant from the foundation for $175,000 to be paid to both Columbia and Princeton universities over a five-year period. In cooperation, RCA first rented their synthesizer to them, and in 1959 gave an improved version (then called the RCA Mark II) to the center on permanent loan. The operational committee of the center included Luening and Ussachevsky from Columbia and Milton Babbitt and Roger Sessions from Princeton; Ussachevsky was the chairman. The center was established in New York City and consisted of three studios: one for the RCA Mark II and related recording equipment, and two other studios equipped in a more traditional manner with audio oscillators, mixers, reverberation, and other familiar tape composition tools.

The RCA synthesizer was a large device that occupied the better part of the studio in which it stood. This was not surprising, because its electronics consisted of vacuum-tube components. It did not resemble a musical instrument in any way. It had seven racks of gear dedicated to the following functions:

- Frequency/tone generation provided by twelve tuning-fork oscillators and white noise
- Glider and vibrato generator
- Envelope and volume controller

- Timbre controller, including filters
- Program relay for octave settings
- Program relay for frequency settings
- Amplifiers and mixers

The synthesizer generated sound using simple tuning-fork oscillators. It was conceived to produce music using the twelve-tone chromatic scale, but its rich set of controls over the timbre, envelope, and pitches of sounds provided many options for those who were more experimentally inclined.

One additional feature of the RCA Mark II set an important technical precedent. It could process input from a microphone. This was probably the first electronic musical instrument with this capability, foreshadowing the synthetic sampling and processing of natural sounds by ten or more years.

The RCA Music Synthesizer was not a computer in the sense that we currently define them, but it did provide a binary, mechanically programmable means for specifying and changing sound parameters including pitch, volume, duration, and timbre. The ability to store instructions was perhaps the greatest innovation of the device. Sounds were preset using a roll of punched paper and a typewriter-style keyboard. When a roll was run through the input device on the synthesizer, it passed over a line of metal brushes, one for each row of instructions on the paper. When there was a hole in the paper, the brush made contact with a drum on the other side, closed an actuating circuit, and sent the electrical instructions to the other components of the synthesizer through a series of relays. Only two channels of sound could be programmed or played at the same time when using the paper roll. The roll itself contained up to thirty-six columns of possible instructions in binary code, eighteen for each of the two notes. These codes could set the timbre, pitch, duration, and pattern of the notes. The system was later modified to accept tab-card input as well. The synthesizer was designed to construct a piece of music layer by layer, requiring the composer to assemble it using a recording medium such as magnetic tape.

The RCA Music Synthesizer that Luening, Ussachevsky, and Babbitt saw in 1955 did not have a magnetic tape recorder attached to it. Instead, Belar and Olson had connected it to an elaborate disc-cutting lathe and playback turntable for recording purposes. Using this system, the composer could record any paper-roll sequence on a disc and then combine it with other sequences being played in real time onto a new disc. Milton Babbitt worked closely with RCA to attach a tape recording system to the synthesizer by 1959 when the device was installed at the Columbia-Princeton Center.

Using the magnetic tape recorder, multitrack tape works could be built up in successive steps, so that as many as 343 individual tones or "voices" could be recorded onto one seven-channel tape. Seven tones at a time could be mixed down to one track on the tape recorder. Seven passes could be made to record 49 separate tones, seven per track. This production step could be repeated one more time for all seven channels, resulting in 49 voices per channel for a grand total of 343. *Composition for Synthesizer* (1964) by Milton Babbitt is a good example of a work that uses the multitracking capabilities of the RCA synthesizer.

This grand combination of the computer and the player piano gave the composer excellent control over the construction and editing of a piece of music even before it was played on the synthesizer. When their German colleagues heard about this device, Luening and Ussachevsky were immediately elevated to the status of computer music pioneers. The good fortune of having the RCA Music Synthesizer fall into their possession had instantly vaulted the Columbia-Princeton Electronic Music Center to the forefront of the world's leading studios.

Internationally known composers were often invited to use the Columbia-Princeton Center. In the first two years, it sponsored work by such composers as Mishiko Toyama (b. 1913) from Japan, Mario Davidovsky (b. 1934) from Argentina, Halim El-Dabh (b. 1921) from Egypt, Bulent Arel (1919–1990) from Turkey, and Charles Wuorinen (b. 1938) from the United States. The center drew on this body of work when it presented its first public concerts on May 10, 1961, in the McMillan Theatre of Columbia University. The program consisted of seven works, six of which were later released on a Columbia record album (the missing piece was Wuorinen's *Symphonia Sacra* for chamber ensemble, three voices, and synthesized sound on tape). These works were tape pieces alone or involved the interaction of live musicians with tapes of synthesized sounds. Among the other people associated with the studio in later years were Edgard Varèse (who completed a second version of *Déserts* at the studio in 1961), Luciano Berio, Ilhan Mimaroglu (b. 1926), Wendy Carlos, Jon Appleton (b. 1939), Pauline Oliveros, and Jacob Druckman (1928–1996).

Many composers associated with the Columbia-Princeton Electronic Music Center were swept up in American serialism during the '50s and '60s. The RCA synthesizer was, after all, designed as a programmable twelve-tone music machine. This is not to say, however, that others kinds of work did not emerge from the studio. The influence of Varèse and Stockhausen was apparent in the works composed when the center opened its doors to the world in 1959. Many prominent and up-and-coming composers contributed to a growing repertoire of adventurous works arising from Columbia-Princeton. Varèse himself used the studio in 1960 and 1961 to revise the tape parts to *Déserts* with the assistance of Max Mathews and Bulent Arel.[42] In addition to Ussachevsky, Babbitt, Luening, Varèse, Arel, and Mathews, other noted composers who used the center include Tzvi Avni, Luciano Berio, Wendy Carlos, Mario Davidovsky, Charles Dodge (b. 1942), Jacob Druckman (1928–1996), Halim El-Dabh, Ross Lee Finney (b. 1906–1997), Malcolm Goldstein (b. 1936), Andres Lewin-Richter (b. 1937), Ilhan Mimaroglu (b. 1926), Jon Appleton (b. 1939), Pauline Oliveros, Alwin Nikolais (1910–1993), Mel Powell (1923–1998), William Overton Smith (b. 1926), and Charles Wuorinen. More electronic music from this single studio was released on record than from any other in North America.

The styles and compositional approaches used at Columbia covered the gamut. Babbitt's *Ensembles for Synthesizer* (1961–63) and *Philomel* (for soprano, recorded soprano, and synthesized accompaniment, 1963–64) remain two of the most appealing electronic serial compositions ever composed. Wendy Carlos, a graduate student at Columbia at the time, ran tape machines for the premiere of *Philomel* in 1964.[43] Carlos's own *Variations for Flute and Electronic Sound* (1964) was written for a flutist accompanied by magnetic tape. The work consisted of a "strictly organized set of six variations on an eleven bar theme stated at the outset by the flute."[44] Mimaroglu's *Le Tombeau d'Edgar Poe* (1964) used as its only sound source a recorded reading of the Mallarmé poem, utilizing the full spectrum of studio editing techniques and effects to modify and transform the sound. Davidovsky's *Electronic Study No. 1* (1960) used the purely electronic sound sources of sine waves, square waves, and white noise modified through the use of filters and reverberation, then layered five times, inverted, and transposed to change its amplitude and density. *Animus I* (1966) by Jacob Druckman employs a live trombonist who spars with a tape of electronic sounds, eventually being driven off of the stage by the ensuing pandemonium, and concludes with the musician returning for an uneasy truce with the tape recorder. *Time's Encomium* (1968–69), by Charles Wuorinen, was a thirty-two-minute masterpiece, perhaps the last great work composed with the RCA synthesizer just prior to the emergence of computer music in the '70s. It used the twelve-tone tempered scale and was structured to explore variations in passing time—first between the notes themselves and then for larger parts of the whole. Wuorinen's own comments underscored the consequence of the composer's temporal experiments: "Those who like relatively severe and slowly-unfolding music should listen first to Side One. Those who like complex and rapidly unfolding music should listen first to Side Two. Eventually, both parts should be listened to in succession, with a break between."[45]

Chapter 6

THREE PIONEERS: JOHN CAGE, EDGARD VARÈSE, AND KARLHEINZ STOCKHAUSEN

John Cage and the Advocacy of Chance

John Cage wrote his first piece for recorded medium in 1939. *Imaginary Landscape No. 1* was conceived for turntables and test records and was produced long before magnetic tape composition was available to the composer. Cage recalled, "*Imaginary Landscapes No. 1* used records of constant or variable frequency. We had clutches on those machines that allowed us to produce slides. You didn't shift from 33⅓ to 45 rpm, for instance, but you could go gradually through the whole thing."[1] This work preceded Schaeffer's musique concrète by nine years, again showing how prophetic Cage's musical vision had been.

While many of his contemporaries, particularly in Europe, were seeking serial approaches to control every aspect of written music, Cage was exploring the assembly of musical material using composition techniques for which the outcome was not preconceived: composition that was "indeterminate of its performance." The serialist game was aimed at a total democratization of tones, replacing the composer's instincts for making "pretty" music by an elaborate set of rules for choosing which notes and dynamics could come next in a series. Philosophically, Cage's chance methods began with a similar intent: he wanted to remove in entirety the composer's taste from the process of composition. This is also where the similarities between serialism and chance music end. Cage did not restrict his sound palette to a certain number of tones, but instead opened his ears to any and all possible sounds, pitched and unpitched. His method of composing removed not only his taste from the outcome, but also the minutest degree of control or personal choice that one might want over the musical result. About 1950, he established

John Cage and David Tudor, 1962. Used with permission of the John Cage Trust.

his own rules for doing so based on chance operations derived from the *I Ching*, the ancient Chinese *Book of Changes* that provided a methodology for choosing random number sequences.

A common way that Cage worked was as follows. He might choose the instrumentation for a piece ahead of time—prepared piano, strings, radio sounds, etc.—although some works were also written for any number and kind of instruments. He would then use random numbers to denote choices for any decision that had to be made regarding the characteristics of the sound, such as pitch, amplitude, duration, timbre, and envelope. Individual performances might also vary because he might make the parts or choices interchangeable.

In 1951, Cage organized the Project of Music for Magnetic Tape. He, Earle Brown (b. 1926), Morton Feldman (1926–1987), Christian Wolff (b. 1934), and David Tudor all began to explore the tape medium with the technical assistance and studio facilities of Louis (1920–1989) and Bebe Barron (b. 1927) in New York. The Project of Music for Magnetic Tape came at an auspicious time for new music. David Tudor, Cage's longtime collaborator, later recalled:

In those days one did not have easy access to electronics, so John Cage tried to find something like we now would call a grant situation and a friend of ours [Paul Williams] gave us $5,000 to start experimenting with magnetic tape so we could use an electronic studio and pay an engineer [the Barrons].

John Cage started the project and I helped him as much as I could and after a few weeks he made an assessment of how much money was left and what could be spent and he decided he had to immediately make the composition [*Williams Mix*] because all the time had to be spent on realizing one single thing. And it was clear that experimentation takes a great deal of money, so he decided that in order to have a result, they should make a project which would enable one to experience things to the greatest depth possible.[2]

The idea of using tape splicing techniques as a major compositional element of a piece of music, rather than as a device for hiding transitions from one recorded sound to another, had come to Cage as early as 1952, when he composed *Williams Mix*. This was his first composition using magnetic tape recordings as source material. His first tape piece, completed in January of the same year, was his fifth *Imaginary Landscape* No. 1 and was scored for "any forty-two records" that were subsequently "realized as a magnetic tape."[3] *Williams Mix* consisted of hundreds of taped sounds edited together using unusual splices to change the envelope of the sounds. The piece lasted only four and a quarter minutes but was created from a daunting 192-page graphical score, which was in chart style and consisted largely of editing instructions for the piece. *Williams Mix* was created primarily by Cage, Brown, and Tudor, with the technical and creative assistance of Louis and Bebe Barron. Cage had no ready access to professional tape recording equipment and was anxious to find allies who might help him in this regard.

The Barrons had met Cage at a monthly gathering of the Artists' Club on 8th Street in New York City, where participants took turns explaining their work and projects to others. Cage had in mind the creation of eight tapes that could be played simultaneously. The Barrons were given the daunting assignment of recording literally hundreds of sounds in the six categories required by the score: city sounds, country sounds, electronic sounds, manually produced sounds (including musical instruments), wind-produced sounds, and small sounds requiring amplification to be heard. They met so often that they soon formed an informal lunch club at the Barrons' studio, where the team took turns providing lunch.

The experience revealed much to the Barron's about Cage's music and methods:

John was simply spectacular to work with. Mostly he would ask us to somehow record sounds from the various categories. It sounds like an easy assignment. But in those days, to record country sounds, small sounds, and so forth, it was a major assignment because we were in no way prepared to go out into the country. We did a couple of times and we took a little of our most portable equipment with us, which was in no way portable.

For the editing, I think that we did work with the score. I don't know how else we would have done it. I mean, we cut the tape into wild shapes. It was a tremendous editing job. We were obviously shaping the envelopes and we were putting tapes together so you could not discern where one piece of tape ended and the next one began, even though it may have been a totally different category. It was very interesting. We were using yarrow sticks to see what the next step would be in the editing.[4]

By Cage's account, the Barrons recorded between five hundred and six hundred sounds, although Bebe Barron's recollection is that it was somewhat fewer than that.[5] The resulting eight tapes were assembled over a nine-month period by a team consisting at times of Cage, Tudor, and the Barrons at their Greenwich Village studio, but also at various other places, including Cage's apartment. The splicing job was so laborious that anyone who happened to be in town or visiting would be recruited to make a contribution. It required hundreds of *I Ching* coin tossings to determine the various parameters that governed the assembly. The nature of each splice was determined by chance from a number of predetermined choices. However, one choice required the editor to freely make a splice in whatever pattern he or she wished, however irregular or unconventional.[6] The piece received its first public performance in 1953 at the Festival of Contemporary Arts, University of Illinois.

Like his work for the prepared piano, Cage had taken a familiar tool, the tape recorder, and found a way to creatively subvert its conventional use for his own ends. He was not unaware of the impact of his unconventional approach to splicing. In 1958, he wrote:

The chief technical contribution of my work with tape is in the method of splicing, that is, of cutting the material in a way that affects the attack and decay of sounds recorded. By this method, I have attempted to mitigate the purely mechanical effect of electronic vibration in order to heighten the unique element of individual sounds, releasing their delicacy, strength, and special characteristics, and also to introduce at times complete transformation of the original materials to create new ones.[7]

While many composers found Cage's compositional methods a bit too radical for their taste, the influence of *Williams Mix* and other Cage works nonetheless began to broaden their opinions about what was or was not musical. The concertgoing public was even further divided on the use of chance and noise in music, as a recorded performance of *Williams Mix* at Town Hall in New York in 1958 plainly reveals. As the piece drew to a close, it was met with equal amounts of applause, booing, and verbal invective.

By 1954 the Project of Music for Magnetic Tape had run its course, largely because the participants became disenchanted with the restrictions of formal tape composition. Under the umbrella of the project, Cage and Tudor had produced *Williams Mix,* as well as *Imaginary Landscape No. 5* (1952) for any forty-two recordings (they used jazz records as source material); Brown had created *Octet I* (1953); Feldman had composed *Intersection* (1953); and Wolff had created *For Magnetic Tape* (1953).[8] After this, Brown, Feldman, and Wolff returned to experimental music using acoustic instruments, while Cage and Tudor extended their interest into the use of electronics in live settings.

Electronic Music Pioneers: Louis and Bebe Barron

The first piece of electronic music for magnetic tape composed in America was not by John Cage, Edgard Varèse, Otto Luening, Vladimir Ussachevsky, or any other of the "name" composers of the day. It was a little work called *Heavenly Menagerie* by Louis (1920–1989) and Bebe Barron (b. 1927). Bebe dates the work to 1950, about the time that she and her husband acquired their first tape recording equipment.[9]

The Barrons were musically inclined and creatively blessed. She had studied music with Wallingford Rieger and Henry Cowell. He had studied music at the University of Chicago and also had a knack for working with a soldering gun and electrical gear. Having just married and moved to New York in 1948, the couple decided to try their hand at the business of music recording. They started their enterprise mostly because it seemed like an interesting thing to do. They didn't really expect great success:

> We had to earn a living somehow so we opened a recording studio that catered to the avant-garde. We had some pretty good equipment, considering. A lot of it we built ourselves. Then the commercial equipment began to come onto the market. We were able to purchase some of it. We had a really thriving recording business. There was nobody who was competition. So, we did all right.[10]

Louis and Bebe Barron in their Greenwich Village electronic music studio, 1956. They were equipped to record electronic sounds onto magnetic tape and synchronize them to motion picture images using 16mm magnetic film recorders. Photo courtesy of Bebe Barron.

Heavenly Menagerie was a purely electronic work. It grew out of the Barrons' interest in avant-garde music. New York City in the early '50s was the base of operations for everything experimental in American culture—avant-garde music, film, and writing all thrived in the growing bohemian atmosphere of Greenwich Village. The Barrons were at the epicenter of the postwar cultural revolution and were soon collaborating with many of these artists. They were in a unique position to do so, explains Bebe, because "I believe we had the first electronic music studio in America. The only people that I knew who were working before us were Schaeffer and Henry in France."

One reason for the Barrons' success with their electronic music studio was that they had a short-lived monopoly on tape recording equipment. Just after World War II, when the secrets of the tape recorder were just being distributed in the United States, Bebe and Louis had two family connections that proved to be instrumental in getting them into the business of electronic music. The first was a link to the man who invented the Stancil-Hoffman tape recorder in Germany; the other was a cousin working for the Minnesota Mining and Manufacturing Company (3M). They managed to have a Stancil-Hoffman custom-made specifically for them.

Through their cousin, they were able to obtain some of the earliest batches of magnetic tape that 3M was developing.

Providing music and sound effects for art films and experimental cinema was one of the Barrons' mainstays. Beginning in 1950, and lasting through most of the decades they collaborated with such celebrated filmmakers as Maya Deren and Ian Hugo, who was married to the writer Anaïs Nin. The Barrons scored three of Hugo's films based on Nin's writings, including *Bells of Atlantis* (1952). For Deren, they assisted in the audio production of the soundtrack for *The Very Eye of Night* (1959), which featured music by Teiji Ito. A few years later, when Madison Avenue became interested in using electronic music in commercial advertisements, the Barrons were one of the only options in town. They were competing with other private New York studios, particularly those of Raymond Scott (1908–1994) and Eric Siday (1905–1976).

By the early '50s, the Barrons' studio at 9 West 8th Street in Greenwich Village was a well-equipped, if not entirely orthodox, hub of electronic music gear. Bebe recalls:

> We were using the same equipment that the classic electronic music studios were using, although we were more limited because, number one, we were considerably earlier than most of them and we had to make a lot—in fact almost all—of our own equipment. We were also limited financially because we were trying to support ourselves. We didn't have an institution behind us.
>
> We built this monstrous big speaker and it sounded wonderful. It had a very heavy bass, which I always loved. That was the speaker we worked with. I believe it was one of those big old theater speakers. We built the encasing out of fiberglass. We had electronic oscillators that we built ourselves. We had one that produced sine and sawtooth waves and one that produced sine and square waves. We had a filter that we built; a spring reverberator; several tape recorders. The Stancil-Hoffmann was built primarily for playing loops, which we had just discovered and were wildly excited about. We had a setting on the front of the machine that enabled us to play loops very easily. We would build up the capstan to change its speed.
>
> We had two 16 mm projectors that were tied into a 16 mm tape recorder. They always ran at the same speed, so we didn't have that problem to worry about. We used amplitude modulation, frequency modulation.[11]

In their partnership Louis did most of the circuitry design and Bebe did much of the composing and production. Both became adept at soldering circuits and editing tape. They were both influenced by mathematician Norbert Weiner's book *Cybernetics: Or, Control and Communication in the Animal and the Machine* (1948), and this carried over into their approach to circuit design:

> We never considered what we did at that point [to be], composing music. It really wasn't at all like music because we were not concerned with note-by-note composition. What we did was build certain kinds of simple circuits that had a peculiar sort of nervous system, shall we say. They had characteristics that would keep repeating themselves. With *Forbidden Planet*, for instance, we built a circuit for every character. Then we would vary these circuits accordingly. We would consider them as actors. They were like leitmotifs. Whenever one character was on screen and another would appear, you would get the motif of both characters working. Of course, the form of the music was dictated by the film.[12]

The Barrons' electronic music score for the film *Forbidden Planet* (1956) was a watershed event. It was the first major motion picture score that was dominated by purely electronic music. The producers of the film had not originally intended to use so much electronic music. They had been considering hiring Harry Partch (1901–1974) to do most of the score. "We were hired originally to do twenty minutes of scoring," explains Barron. "After they heard the twenty minutes of sample scoring that we did they got very enthusiastic about it. We were then assigned about an hour and ten minutes of scoring. They gave us a work print of the film. We took it to New York and worked there." This in itself was unheard of, because most film scores were made in Hollywood at the time. The studio had wanted to move the Barrons and their equipment to the West Coast, but the couple would not be uprooted.[13]

The circuits they built to make their sounds tended to burn out eventually, never to be revived. They never knew how long one might persist, so they made a habit of recording everything and then piecing it together using their tape recorders. About the life of their circuits, Barron recalls:

> Some of them would go on and on . . . in the same kind of way for a long time and then they would reach a kind of climax and then

die. No matter what we did, we could never reconstruct them. They just seemed to have a life span of their own.

With some of them, like the monster circuit [the Id monster from *Forbidden Planet*], we had hours of things that came out of that circuit. With some of them they were very short. There was just no predicting. We could predict a little bit whether the tone of the circuit would be something pleasant to listen to or something horrible; something active or passive. That's about as far as it went. We never could predict the movement of them, the patterns of them. It really wasn't like composing music at all.[14]

The Barrons developed a method of working that was the organic equivalent of the simple circuits that they were building. Mixdowns of multiple tracks were accomplished using multiple tape recorders. They would manually synchronize the starting points of the two tapes that were to be mixed, count "one-two-three-go," and then push the playback buttons simultaneously. The output of each machine was fed into a third tape recorder that would record the two tracks as a mix onto one tape. Precise synchronization was not vital for their style of atmospheric music: "That was close enough sync for us. If it was a little bit out of sync, it usually enhanced the music. We were loose in our requirements."[15]

A good example of the Barrons' working methods is revealed by the way in which they arrived at the pulsing, rhythmic tones for the Id monster in *Forbidden Planet*, Bebe's favorite "circuit" from the film:

We wanted to make the monster come off as lovable. So we would start out with horrible-sounding monster music, typical of what you might expect. Really frightening, horrible stuff. I just didn't really like that approach. We were working with our circuits and out came some very high-pitched tinkly stuff. It was barely audible because it was so high-pitched. I was listening to that at length—I would go through all of the existing tapes and listen for what might have possibilities with further processing—and when I heard this, the tones were so pure and high that I said, this has got to be slowed down. We started slowing it down and with each generation out would emerge things that you couldn't hear when it was going faster. It became more and more beautiful.[16]

The Barrons edited the entire score themselves. The music and sound effects were so stunning that during a preview of the movie, the audience broke out in spontaneous applause after the energizing sounds of the spaceship landing on Altair IV. An interesting bit of trivia involves the screen credit for the Barrons. It was originally to read, "Electronic Music by Louis and Bebe Barron." At the last minute, a contract lawyer became fearful that the musicians' union would be in an uproar if they called the score "music." The "lawsuit proof" credit that was finally used boldly declared, "Electronic Tonalities by Louis and Bebe Barron."[17]

Louis died in 1989, and Bebe did not do any further composing until 2000, when she was invited to be artist-in-residence at the music department of the University of California at Santa Barbara. "I was as analog as you could be," she freely admits, but now speaks the language of SuperCollider and other computer-based synthesis tools that were at her disposal. She completed he first work in over ten years, a five-minute, forty-four-second work called *Mixed Emotions* (2000).

Cage himself composed only a few pieces for magnetic tape alone. Another one of these was *Fontana Mix,* reportedly named after his landlady in Milan, and completed in 1958 at the Studio di Fonologia in Milan. It was actually conceived for any kind of instrument, but Cage (like several other Americans) was invited to do some work in the friendly confines of the Milan studio. Because the results of each studio "performance" of *Fontana Mix* were unknown ahead of time—indeed unknown even during the act of creating it—committing the piece to tape seemed to defeat the purpose of creating indeterminate or chance music. Thereafter, Cage rarely dealt with the tape medium in isolation, although he frequently used it as a source for sounds in live performance situations.

Fontana Mix represented a milestone of another sort for Cage as well:

> After the work in Milan, where I won the "Lascia o Raddoppia" prize, that was the first time I had any money to speak of. Otherwise I was as poor as a churchmouse and I was nearly fifty years old. Through the money I made there, and then through the invitation from Richard Winslow to become a fellow in the Center for Advanced Studies at Wesleyan, everything began to change and it was at that moment that Peters decided to be the exclusive publisher of my music. So everything

came together at that point. I used the fellowship at Wesleyan to prepare
fair copies of much of the music that I didn't have good copies of.
Everything began to change. People, for instance, who didn't like my
music could say they liked my writing (*Silence* was published in 1961)—
and vice versa.[18]

The "Lascia o Raddoppia" prize Cage refers to was not a presti-
gious Italian music award but the name of a popular television quiz
show. Cage appeared as a mushroom expert, and during five appearances on the program won the equivalent of $6,000 by correctly answer-
ing the questions put before him. (He also supported himself by selling
mushrooms to fancy New York restaurants, and was quite active in the
New York Mycological Society.)

Fontana Mix was eleven minutes and thirty-nine seconds of total
surprise. Like *Williams Mix* before it, it used many tapes of found
sounds—traffic, radio voices, recorded music, room sounds, etc.—lovingly pieced together using chance operations to determine how to edit
and combine them. Cage also used electronic sounds, speed shifts, and
liberal patches of silence as part of the mix. The score for *Fontana Mix*
was itself an experiment. It consisted of several transparent plastic sheets
that were imprinted with geometric images. One sheet included a grid
upon which the other transparencies were laid according to Cage's
instructions. There were ten transparencies with points, ten with curves
(six each), and a transparency with an even line. The parameters of the
sound events were determined by laying these sheets on top of one
another and interpreting the intersection of the graphic elements. For
example, the height of a curve on the grid determined the amplitude of
the sound. The duration of a sound would be determined by the point
at which a curve first touched the grid and then left it. Spaces in between
the intersection would mark silence. The relationship of sound and
silence was thus spatially defined.

Cage understood that magnetic tape composition, no matter how
the material was conceived, forever fixed a performance in time. He was
conflicted over this, because chance music should be just that: indeterminate of its performance. Cage expressed his dilemma in this way:

Everyone now knows that there's a contradiction between the use of
chance operations and the making of a record. I mean not only myself,
but I see no reason for living without contradictions. But I *do* think that
one can live without recordings. And I do that. I don't play them, except
when I use them in a live performance. Just the other day I was asked to
read for a radio program that text where I say, "They'll have music in
Texas if they take out all the recordings from Texas because someone will

learn to sing." I still believe that that's true; that if you want music to come alive, that you must not can it.[19]

Cage later found a more productive way of deriving lists of random numbers through the use of computers. In the late '60s, a friend of his at Bell Labs wrote a program that printed out a long list of randomly generated numbers. The printout was several inches thick and was produced using a large IBM computer that was programmed using keypunch cards. Cage used this list for several years. He kept the edge-worn printout on his work table, consulting it regularly, crossing off numbers as he used them, continuing page after page. He told me that when the list began to run short, he asked his friend Paul Zukofsky, who had connections at Bell Labs, if they could replenish his supply of numbers by having the program run again. That was so many years later that the keypunch-card computer had since become obsolete and was no longer in service. After some scrambling around in Bell Labs, they eventually found one old machine that was still working and made a new printout. Cage had a million new numbers again. But the new printout came with the implicit warning that he had better find another source of random numbers for the next time around. He was able to do this with microcomputers by about 1984. He also found that the computers at IRCAM (Institut de Recherche et Coordination Acoustique/Musique)—a noted French research institute dedicated to the application of computers in new media and music—could assist him in this way: "I was delighted when I got to IRCAM to discover that I didn't need my printout because they have it in their computer there. You can have the *I Ching* whenever you want it!"[20]

Cage's Live Performance Works

The mid-'60s were a time of enormous experimentation with the staging of live performances. Elements of theater, dance, film, and music were often combined to create new and unexpected performance situations. John Cage was, as usual, right in the thick of the revolution. His works involving electronic music during this period—*Variations I–VI* (1958–66) for any number of players and instruments; *Rozart Mix* (1965) for twelve tape recorders, performers, and eighty-eight tape loops; *Assemblage* (1968); and HPSCHD (1967–69) for harpsichords and computer-generated sound tapes—were always produced and performed in collaboration with other musicians. Cage, the dancer and choreographer Merce Cunningham, and their numerous collaborators pushed the concept of performance art to its most absurd and thought-provoking outer reaches.

Live Electronic Music

One of the appeals of all music is the magic of performance in real time with live musicians. Whether you are the performer or a member of the audience, live performance requires an alertness of mind, an awareness of the acoustic space, and the psychological interplay of people in a social situation.

The early history of electronic music had a tradition of live performance. The predecessors of synthesizers were all performance instruments—the Theremin, Ondes Martenot, and Trautonium, to name a few. The prevailing approach was to bring those instruments into the fold of classical music, giving them solo parts and featuring them within larger ensembles of musicians playing traditional instruments. With few exceptions, that music was not considered to be avant-garde or even electronic. Varèse and Sala stand out as the exceptions to the rule. Those two pioneering composers successfully injected experimental electronic tonalities into music using the earliest technology.

The modern history of electronic music—music composed for electronic media—begins with the widespread availability of the tape recorder in the '50s. The first of these works only existed in the form of tape recordings. Musique concrète and other tape composition first went public over the airwaves in Europe in 1948. It soon graduated to the concert stage in both Europe and the United States, but only as *loudspeaker* music: magnetic tape played over loudspeakers. Putting a tape recorder on stage and playing the music through loudspeakers is *not* equivalent to live performance. Tape music is oblivious to the presence of human beings until someone pushes the off button on the tape recorder.

By the mid-'50s, recognizing that the novelty of playing a tape to a live audience had limited appeal, enterprising composers including Varèse, Luening, and Ussachevsky considered ways of bringing the human element into a performance of electronic music. Their first solution was to write instrumental music with tape accompaniment. The "concrète opera" *Voile d'Orphée* (1953) by Schaeffer and Henry, and Varèse's *Déserts* (1954) both rank as masterworks of this idiom. Yet even these remarkable pieces were exceptions to the rule; live performers plus prerecorded accompaniment usually resulted in a restrained, if not utterly predictable, performance. The idea of "interplay" had no meaning if the performers were forced to move in lockstep with a preprogrammed tape. Neither they nor the audience enjoyed being dragged along by the scruff of the neck by a tape recorder. It is amazing that imitators still use this approach today, only having replaced the analog tape recorder with digital recording gear. The technique is an inbred one that has flourished only in academia, where the intended audience is the composition professor.

As intimidating and pretentious as loudspeaker music could be, the Cologne artists were quite at home with it. They developed lectures about electronic music, armed themselves with a chalkboard and a tape recorder, and faced off with the audience. Eimert and Stockhausen both took their shows on the road for many years. They sermonized about total serialism and the serial perfection of the electronic music medium.

It all began with the work that Cage did for the Merce Cunningham Dance Company. Cage and Cunningham had already been working together since the early '40s. Until about 1950, when David Tudor joined the company to work with Cage, all of the musical accompaniment had been acoustic. With the coming of the tape recorder in the early '50s, they shifted their attention from acoustic to electroacoustic music for Cunningham's choreography. Their first efforts were dance performances set to prerecorded loudspeaker music: *Symphonie pour un homme seule* by Schaeffer and Henry in 1952, and Christian Wolff's *For Magnetic Tape* in 1953.[21] It wasn't long, however, until Cage realized the chief liability of relying on prerecorded tape music:

> I was at a concert of electronic music in Cologne and I noticed that even though it was the most recent electronic music, the audience was all falling asleep. No matter how interesting the music was, the audience couldn't stay awake. That was because the music was coming out of loudspeakers. Then, in 1958—the Town Hall program of mine—we were rehearsing the *Williams Mix*, which is not an uninteresting piece, and the piano tuner came in to tune the piano. Everyone's attention went away from the *Williams Mix* to the piano tuner because he was *live*.[22]

The artistic backlash to loudspeaker music began with Cage and Tudor. By this time, they had begun to use rudimentary electronics while working with the Cunningham Dance Company. The necessity of creating interesting electronic music for Cunningham "stimulated us very much, and it led to the use of microphones for purposes other than to amplify."[23] Some of their earliest experiments were merely to move the sound around in the performance space. This led directly to works such as *Cartridge Music* (1960), in which phono cartridges were plugged with different styli and scraped against objects to magnify their sounds. This seminal work resulted in electronic music conceived primarily for live performance, a critical stage in the evolution of avant-garde music.

Cage's growing interest in chance music paralleled his first electronic works for the Cunningham Dance Company. The abstract and untested potential of electronic music was a natural complement to Cunningham's equally original choreographic vision. While the two had sometimes composed the music first and then the dance, or the other way around, they came to the realization that the two were coequal partners, unified by the element of time: "The relationship between the dance and music is one of co-existence, that is, being related simply because they exist at the same time."[24]

The company soon became Cage's laboratory for experimenting with live electronic music, a tradition that he oversaw with help primarily from David Tudor, Alvin Lucier, David Behrman, and Gordon Mumma for thirty years.[25] This was the mountain spring from which all live electronic performance music eventually flowed.

The reason that Cage got involved with dance in the first place was another motivating factor leading to the development of live electronic music. As a composer working in the '40s, he found it increasingly difficult to find large ensembles of musicians willing to learn and play his music: "I soon learned that if you were writing music that orchestras just weren't interested in—or string quartets, I made several attempts, I didn't give up immediately—that you could get things done very easily by modern dance groups."[26] After establishing a base of operations with the Cunningham Dance Company, and having brought David Tudor on board as his chief musical collaborator, the two began to take their live electroacoustic performances on the road in the early '60s. These performances throughout the United States and Europe defied all conventional wisdom in the field of classical music. Rather than sitting around writing instrumental music and waiting for someone to perform it, these classically trained composer-musicians took control of their careers by packing up their own gear and doing it all themselves. Theirs was the antithesis of the Cologne loudspeaker roadshow: no theory, no proselytizing, just performers making live electronic music.

In 1958, Cage composed the first in a series of *Variations* for any number and combination of instruments. The works were improvisatory in the sense that performers were allowed to make "immediate but disciplined decisions, and within specific structural boundaries," a mode of composing used at the time by composers including Cage, Earle Brown, and Christian Wolff.[27] Wolff himself notes that the *Variations* were most significant because they

> really pushed the notion of what constituted a piece of music, because nothing was said about anything except you had to make yourself something out of these lines and dots and things that were on plastic sheets. And that seemed to be about as far away from a musical identity as possible. But what always struck me as so mysterious was that what people did with those things almost all the time would come out sounding like John's work. . . . There's this mysterious thing that in those days people would try some of John's chance techniques, but their music wouldn't come out sounding like John's.[28]

Variations V (1965) was certainly the most ambitious of these pieces. The "score" was written after the first performance, and, as Cage has said, it merely consists of "remarks that would enable one to perform *Variations V*."[29] The piece sprang from the idea of electrically triggering sounds through the physical movement of people. Preparation for the first performance at Lincoln Center in New York (July 23, 1965) became something of a Manhattan Project for new-music technology. The performance featured the Cunningham dancers on stage and an assemblage of musicians and electronic gear on a raised platform at the rear of the stage. Experimental film by Stan Vanderbeek and video images by Nam June Paik were also featured.[30]

Some of the sounds were triggered by movements of the dancers on stage; others were controlled and mixed by the musicians. Audio sources included continuously operating tape machines (at least six) playing sounds composed by Cage, Tudor, and Mumma; shortwave receivers (at least six); audio oscillators; electronically generated sounds triggered by proximity-sensing antennae (similar in principal to the Theremin); light beams aimed at photocells that could be interrupted to generate sounds; contact microphones attached to objects on stage (e.g., chairs and a table) that could be used by the dancers; and other homebrewed electronic sound generators that were manually adjusted as needed. Cage recruited several engineers to fabricate the equipment he needed to produce the music. Max Mathews from Bell Labs built a ninety-six-input mixer into which all of the sound sources were fed. Robert Moog was retained to make the proximity-sensing antennae that were triggered when a dancer came near them. The light beams were in the base of the antennae and aimed at photocells to close a sound-generating circuit; when a dancer broke one of the beams by stepping into it, whatever sound being fed by that circuit was interrupted.

As one might imagine, the performances resulting from this assem-

John Cage, David Tudor, and Gordon Mumma with the Merce Cunningham Dance Company performing *Variations V* at Lincoln Center, 1965. "There were so many cables and what-not that it was like walking on a forest floor." —Robert Moog, who acted as an audio engineer for the performance. Used with permission of the John Cage Trust.

blage of interactive gear were remarkably chaotic. Moog was somewhat puzzled by the whole plan, but knew that he was taking part in a legendary event:

> John Cage retained us to build some equipment for the first production of *Variations V*. It was done but it didn't work all that well. Sometimes, I had a hard time understanding why it *had* to work. There were six Theremin-like antennas that the Merce Cunningham dancers would dance around and they would turn on different sounds. That was our part of *Variations V*. We had the antennae tuned so that if a dancer came within four feet of one it would set something off. They were scattered around the stage. There was so much stuff. . . . I can't remember all that there was, but there was just a lot going on. It was an experience for me. All these wires at the edge of the dance area, where all of the technicians like me were set up, there were so many cables and whatnot that it was like walking on a forest floor. You couldn't determine whether something was

working or not. I think John Cage knew. But I don't think anybody else knew. It was serious business, though.[31]

Composer Ron Kuivila became acquainted with the history of this event while working with David Tudor, acknowledging that Moog was not alone in being puzzled by the piece's technological complexity. The proximity-sensing antennae apparently did not work as they had hoped during the Lincoln Center premiere. One had to get very close to them to get a respone. The idea had been for the dancers to trigger them by moving about more freely on the stage.[32] But the show did indeed go on the road with more success. According to Mumma, "we always used the proximity antennae and the photo cell emitters, though we cut back on the number (about one half) of them because of the logistic challenges in touring performances."[33] Mumma also made some modifications to the equipment so that it worked better.

Another performance that must go down in history as one of the most complex multimedia events ever staged occurred in 1969 at the University of Illinois. John Cage and Lejaren Hiller (1924–1994) teamed up to present a joint composition called *HPSCHD*. Using a computer-derived extrapolation of the *I Ching* developed for Cage, the two assembled fifty-one sound tapes generated by computer and combined them in a live setting with the activities of seven harpsichordists. The work was presented in a sports arena, with the electronic sounds amplified by fifty-one individual speakers mounted along the ceiling. Seven additional speakers were also used to amplify the harpsichords. Fifty-two slide projectors provided streams of unrelated imagery, which was projected onto a large hanging screen measuring 100 feet by 160 feet as well as a semi-circular screen that ran 340 feet around the inside rim of the ceiling. For five hours, hundreds of people sat in the bleachers and milled around on the main floor of the arena immersed in this sensory bath. It was big and absorbing and live. The commercial recording of *HPSCHD* released by Nonesuch Records (H-71224) in 1969 included a computer printout (individualized for each copy of the record) with a randomly generated set of instructions for controlling the volume, treble, and bass knobs on one's stereo while listening to the music. Each printout was individually numbered. Mine happens to be "Output Sheet No. 374."

Cage's Influence

John Cage was without question one of the most important and influential composers of the twentieth century. His work had a ripple effect that permeated not only the fields of classical music, but also jazz, rock, dance, and other performance art. The fact that he often used electronics in his work was only secondarily important. The true impact of his music was in changing people's expectations about what was musical and what was not. In 1937, he said, "Wherever we are, what we hear is mostly noise. When we ignore it, it disturbs us. When we listen to it, we find it fascinating."[34]

His dissatisfaction with tape composition was amplified by his thoughts about musical indeterminacy delivered in a lecture entitled "Composition as Process":

> An experimental action is one the outcome of which is not foreseen. Being unforeseen, this action is not concerned with its excuse. Like the land, like the air, it needs none. A performance of a composition which is indeterminate of its performance is necessarily unique. It cannot be repeated. When performed for a second time, the outcome is other than it was. Nothing therefore is accomplished by such a performance, since that performance cannot be grasped as an object in time. A recording of such a work has no more value than a postcard; it provides a knowledge of something that happened, whereas the action was a non-knowledge of something that had not yet happened.[35]

In a conversation with the author, Cage characterized his experience with chance music:

> I think the thing that underlies my works since the use of chance operations—whether it's determinate or indeterminate—is the absence of *intention*. I've used the chance operations as a discipline to free the music precisely from my taste, memory, and any intentions that I might have. It's a discipline equivalent, I think, to that of sitting cross-legged, but the cross-leggedness would carry one, so to speak, in toward the world of dreams, the subconscious and so forth, whereas this discipline of chance operations carries one out to the world of relativity.[36]

Varèse and the Listener's Experiment

Like John Cage, Edgard Varèse (1883–1965) is one of those seminal figures in twentieth-century music whose name comes up no matter what period you are discussing. Varèse went from his native France to live in New York City in 1915. He was the first composer to recognize that the natural extension of avant-garde music was into the use of electronics. Although his most respected and experimental work still lay before him, he showed an uncanny sense for the future of music when in 1916 he made the following statement in the *New York Morning Telegraph*: "Our musical alphabet must be enriched. We also need new instruments very badly. . . . In my own works I have always felt the need for new mediums of expression . . . which can lend themselves to every expression of thought and can keep up with thought." In 1917 Varèse wrote in the periodical *391*, "I dream of instruments obedient to my thought and which with their contribution of a whole new world of unsuspected sounds, will lend themselves to the exigencies of my inner rhythm."

Varèse's greatest output as a composer was during the '20s and '30s. Unlike most of his contemporaries, he did not prefer to work in either twelve-tone or neoclassic music. It wasn't that he disdained tonality; instead, he shaped his music around rhythms and timbres, a move that instantly branded his approach as radical. He used unabated dissonance and energized his music with striking rhythms, clashes of timbres, and unusual combinations of instruments. If it weren't for the generous support of conductor Leopold Stokowski, many of Varèse's works would never have been heard.

Responding to critics in 1940, Varèse defended his work by saying, "I prefer to use the expression 'organized sound' and avoid the monotonous question: 'But is it music?' 'Organized sound' seems better to take in the dual aspect of music as an art-science, with all the recent laboratory discoveries which permit us to hope for the unconditional liberation of music, as well as covering, without dispute, my own music in progress and its requirements."[37] This statement came ten years before the availability of the tape recorder made electronic music a reality.

When musique concrète came into its own around 1950, Varèse was already sixty-five years old. The explosion in electronic music, however, was vaunted by a new generation of experimental composers who held him in high regard. He was their vanguard of new music.

Varèse's first work of tape composition was *Déserts* (1954), realized at the Paris studios of GRM. The work consists of seven parts—four instrumental and three for magnetic tape. They play one after the other but not at the same time. Varèse scored the instrumental parts as was his normal practice and left places where the electronic tape would be played. The instrumental parts of the work underscore his use of rhythm, tone color, and radical dynamic changes, techniques that he perfected long before the advent of tape composition. The tape part did much the same, but with concrete and electronic sounds. Varése composed it in this way as if to demonstrate that all music—instrumental or electronic—shared many of the same experimental resources. The piece was performed live several times using stereo loudspeakers to project the sound. A young Stockhausen was proud to man the volume controls for one of the early performances.

If it can be said that Stockhausen's *Gesang der Jünglinge* marked the beginning of the end of classic musique concrète, then Varèse's *Poème electronique* (1958) must be considered its final, brilliant flame.

The architect Le Corbusier (1887–1965) was contracted to build a pavilion for the Philips Radio Corporation at the Brussels World's Fair in 1958. Philips also asked Varèse to provide some music on tape. Along with Iannis Xenakis, Le Corbusier's architect assistant at the time, Varése and Le Corbusier conceived a union of architecture and electronic music that has seldom been matched. The Philips Pavilion was designed for the express purpose of presenting Varèse's tape piece. It was built in the shape of a circus tent with three peaks, a shape that was also likened to that of a sheep's stomach. Inside were four hundred loudspeakers to broadcast the sound in sweeping arcs throughout the pavilion. The music was accompanied by visual projections selected by Le Corbusier.

The directors of Philips did not understand the music of Varèse and for several weeks tried to remove him from the project. Le Corbusier had gone off to India to supervise another project, leaving Xenakis to fill in for him. He reported the open hostility of the Philips executives to Le Corbusier in writing, and Le Corbusier's reply was as bold an endorsement as Varèse could hope for: "The *Poème electronique* cannot be carried out except by Varèse's strange music. There cannot for a moment be a question of giving up Varèse. If that should happen, I will withdraw from the project entirely." The Philips people bothered Varèse no more.[38]

A little-known sidenote to the Philips Pavilion story is that Xenakis, too, contributed a piece of electronic music to the project. His *Concret PH* (1958) was played after every two performances of *Poème electronique*. The short work, only two and three-quarter minutes in length, was composed by modifying the amplified sounds of burning embers. Xenakis spliced the sounds into one-second lengths, modified their speeds, filtered them to give the crackling sound a metallic effect, then layered the result into a thick, continuous rain of drifting sound-specks in space. Like *Poème electronique*, *Concret PH* had been composed with the design of the pavilion in mind and was an equally compelling work, if not as melodramatic in its exposition as Varèse's piece.

Varèse composed *Poème electronique* as a work of "organized sound." This was, in effect, his version of musique concrète, and he worked with many classic editing techniques and tape effects first developed by Schaeffer and Henry. The work was one of the first completed at the Center for Electronic Music of the Philips Research Laboratories in Eindhoven. The eight-minute piece combined passages of familiar sounds with starkly electronic effects and treatments. Church bells tolled and metallic scrapes cut the space in shreds. Organlike tones droned quietly as ominous electronic sounds built a threatening crescendo. A voice moaned, thunderous crashes interrupted, and dark sonorities lurked in the background. All of this was contrasted by the brilliant use of pauses and silence, ever increasing the tension of the work. The lights were dimmed for each performance and the music was accompanied by a light show of projected colors. *Poème electronique* was a dramatic and fitting closure to an episode in the history of electronic music composition, and was heard by five hundred people at a time who stood inside the pavilion during the summer of 1958.

Poème Électronique was also, in modern parlance, a crossover work that revealed some of the pleasures of electronic music to the general public. It was premiered in America at the Village Gate, a club in Greenwich Village, Varèse's bohemian stomping grounds in New York City. In the view of one bold critic, the piece deserved a spot alongside Cage's *Williams Mix* as a milestone in the young history of electronic music. *Williams Mix* had been premiered in New York in May 1958 and was the object of much derision at the time. It was as if Cage had cleared the palate of the listening public, preparing it for the tamer experiment of Varèse. The critic noted:

> The focus of the concert . . . was on Edgard Varèse. Samuel Baron conducted his *Octandre*, which is now 34 years old. In this piece Varèse demonstrates his peculiarly architectural sense of space, combined with extremely idiomatic writing for the eight instruments. Varèse then spoke, saying among other things that an artist was never ahead of his time, but most people were behind it. . . . Then came the major event—the United States premiere of Varèse's *Poème electronique*. There were loudspeakers all over the large hall, and fragments of sirens, drums, choirs, solo voices, and many electronically derived sounds poured from them, in new and almost frightening counterpoint. Alone with John Cage's *Williams Mix*, this is one of the most impressive electronic compositions to date. And wild as the sounds seem to us now, it is hard to doubt a future for such means of composition. In a world of jet planes, man-made moons, atomic submarines, and hydrogen bombs, who is to say this music does not have a place?[39]

Varèse, who often answered questions with his own brand of reverse logic, probably said it best when he stated, "My experimenting is done before I make the music. Afterwards, it is the listener who must experiment." With *Poème Électronique*, Varèse succeeded in bringing many a new listener into the experiment.

Stockhausen's Journey

Buried in the visitors' log of Schaeffer's French GRM studio for 1952 are several entries for a twenty-four-year-old composer from Germany. The young man was living in Paris while studying with Olivier Messiaen.

After meeting Pierre Schaeffer, he was granted a few hours of supervised studio time each week at the GRM. This was young Karlheinz Stockhausen's first experience with tape editing and electronic music:

> First, I recorded six sounds of variously prepared low piano strings struck with an iron beater, using a tape speed of 76.2 centimeters per second. After that, I copied each sound many times and, with scissors, cut off the attack of each sound. A few centimeters of the continuation [remaining sound], which was, briefly, quite steady dynamically, were used. Several of these pieces were spliced together to form a tape loop, which was then transposed to certain pitches using a transposition machine [one of the Phonogènes]. A few minutes of each transposition were then recorded on separate tapes.[40]

Next, the composer wanted to splice in sections of silent leader tape periodically throughout the piece. This would transform the once-continuous sounds into a rhythmic pattern. The few hours of supervised studio time that he had each week would not be enough to finish editing the work. Realizing this, Stockhausen created a makeshift editing bench at his student hostel by pounding several nails into the top of his desk. These served as spokes for the tape reels containing his raw sound files. He edited without being able to listen to the result, calculating the length of his leader insertions down to the millimeter. This was done on two separate reels of tape. Back in the studio, he synchronized the start of the tapes and played them back so that he could mix the result onto a third tape to create the final mix. The result was not what he had expected. As he listened to the juxtaposed tracks, he became "increasingly pale and helpless. I had imagined something completely different! On the following day, the sorcery despairingly continued. I changed my series, chose other sequences, cut other lengths, spliced different progressions, and hoped afresh for a miracle in sound."[41]

The result was a striking little one-track piece called *Etude*, a progression of atomized bursts of sound. It was not much more than an exercise and lasted a slight three minutes and fifteen seconds. But Stockhausen was affected for life by the creation of this simple tape piece. He found that it galvanized his most creative and obsessive forces, taking him inside the molecular structure of sound. It was a place he liked to be, in a zone of his own. This is what he would come to call the "unified time domain,"[42] a personal realization inspired by his experience with tape composition. In this domain, space and time became equivalent forces to be worked like any other material substances of music. The technical instrumentation and editing techniques of electronic music permitted him to gain control over all of the constituent parts of musical sound. This appealed to his fascination with Webern's serialism, which he and his German colleagues had been extending.

Stockhausen's unified time domain in music has many similarities with the unified field theory of physics; it was his attempt to find an underlying controlling element over all of the parameters of sound:

> The ranges of perception are ranges of time, and the time is subdivided by us, by the construction of our bodies and by our organs of perception. And since these modern means have become available, to change the time of perception continuously, from one range to another, from a rhythm into a pitch, or a tone or noise into a formal structure, the composer can now work within a unified time domain. And that completely changes the traditional concept of how to compose and think music, because previously they were all in separate boxes: harmony and melody in one box, rhythm and meter in another, then periods, phrasing, larger formal entities in another, while in the timbre field we had only names of instruments, no unity of reference at all.[43]

This attempt to exercise precise control over all the elements of sound is an obsession that permeates all of Stockhausen's most spectacular works. He returned to Germany fortified by these personal discoveries in music and sound.

The first live concert of tape music from the Cologne studio was given on October 19, 1954, in a small transmission hall of the radio station. The works were played over loudspeakers. Among the pieces played were Stockhausen's *Studie I* and *Studie II*. *Studie I* (1953) was the purest example of serial music among these early works. It was composed using sine waves, without overtones, through a process of additive synthesis. *Studie II* (1954) also used pure sine tones, but with an added twist: they were run through a reverberation unit and re-recorded, adding bands of distortion similar to white noise. It was also the first electronic work for which a score had been written. The score graphically depicted the placement of five groups of overlapping frequency bands in time, along with envelope characteristics.

Stockhausen's earliest electronic music compositions were based on his analysis of sound phenomena. Like other composers, he soon found himself immersed in a medium so rich with sonic possibilities that it was difficult to limit himself to the expressions of pure serialism. Instead, his analytical nature led him to establish several rules—conditions, really—that governed the practice of composing electronic music. All of these ideas were forming around 1957 when he wrote an influential article called ". . . how time passes . . ." for the new music journal *Die Reihe*.[44] In this article, he speaks about the need to move beyond the limitations imposed on music by total serialism, no doubt having in mind the new sonic vistas he had lately discovered by composing electronic music.

Years later, in 1971, he reviewed the way in which he had distilled the composition of electronic music into four guiding principles:

Unified time structuring. Stockhausen noticed how the mechanics of the electronic music medium could be used to transform a sound by temporal modification. A sharp pulse, if repeated continuously and speeded up enough, eventually becomes a pitch. A recording of a symphony, if speeded up enough, eventually becomes a blip

Splitting of the sound. This term refers to the ways in which the smaller elements of a synthetically produced sound can be manipulated independently. This is literally a way of composing the sounds themselves. For example, think of a sound consisting of six sine waves played at the same time but being generated by different oscillators. The unification of the separate sounds has a given character. One can change any of the individual tones independently of the others, however, to hear the sound "gradually revealing itself to be made up of a number of components which one by one, very slowly leave the original frequency and glissando up and down." The theme or aspiration behind some electronic works, including Stockhausen's own *Kontakte* (1959–60) and parts of *Hymnen* (1966–67), is this very idea of "composing the sound." Such music may lack melody, rhythm, and every other normally regulated dynamic in exchange for a unifying motif that explores the composition and decomposition of sound itself.

Multi-layered spatial composition. Stockhausen ranks the spatial projection of electronic music as one of its most endearing attributes. By this he means the control of amplitude and the placement of sounds (using loudspeakers) in the listening hall. So important to him is this element of his work that he usually stations himself in the middle section of an auditorium—having several seats removed if necessary—so that he can have a good vantage point from which to control the mixing, volume control, and spatial projection of music coming from the loudspeakers. He imparts on the placement of sound in space the same importance as any other "composed" element of the music. One technique of his is to juxtapose two sounds of different amplitudes. The louder one masks the quieter one, but when the louder one dissipates, the quieter one is revealed. This occurs in *Kontakte* about twenty-four minutes into the work.

Equality of tone and noise. On the surface, this idea is reminiscent of Cage. However, Stockhausen's definition of noise is far from Cage's. Stockhausen attributes electronic music with providing the means to control the continuum between tone and noise. While he claims on one hand that "any noise is musical material," on the other he says that "you cannot just use any tone in any interval relationship." Considered from the standpoint of electronic music composition, he prefers the *construction* of noise—controlled sounds—over letting all natural sounds just be themselves.[45]

Around the time that Stockhausen was formulating these criteria for electronic music, the nature of his work began to change dramatically. After completing the two electronic *Studien*, he returned to instrumental writing for about a year, completing several atonal works for piano and woodwinds, as well as the ambitious orchestral work *Gruppen*. *Gruppen*, written for three complete orchestral groups, each with its own conductor, marked Stockhausen's first major experiment with the spatial deployment of sound. He positioned the separate orchestras at three posts around the audience so that their sounds were physically segregated in the listening space. The groups called to each other with their instruments, echoed back and forth, sometimes played in unity, and sometimes took turns playing alone so as to move the sound around the audience. Gruppen and his other instrumental experiments of that time were Stockhausen's bridge to his next electronic work. By the time he embarked on the creation of *Gesang der Jünglinge* (Song of the Youths, 1955–56), his views on the control of dynamic elements of electronic music had broadened considerably.

Gesang der Jünglinge is perhaps the most significant work of electronic music of the '50s because it broke from the aesthetic dogma that had preoccupied the heads of the Paris and Cologne studios. It was a work of artistic détente, a conscious break from the purely electronically generated music of WDR, in which Stockhausen dared to include acoustic sounds, as had composers of musique concrète in France. Yet the piece is entirely unlike anything that preceded it. Stockhausen's objective was to fuse the sonic components of recorded passages of a youth choir with equivalent tones and timbres produced electronically. He wanted to bring these two different sources of sound together into a single, fluid musical element, interlaced and dissolved into one another rather than contrasted, as had been the tendency of most musique concrète. He practiced his newly formed principles of electronic music composition, setting forth a plan that required the modification of the "speed, length, loudness, softness, density and complexity, the width and narrowness of pitch intervals and differentiations of timbre" in an exact and precise manner.[46] There was nothing accidental about this combination of voices and electronic sounds. At thirteen minutes and fourteen seconds, *Gesang der Jünglinge* was longer than any previous worked realized at the Cologne studio. It was a "composed" work, painstakingly drawn out using a visual score showing the placement of

sounds and their dynamic elements over the course of the work. The
result was an astonishingly beautiful and haunting work of sweeping,
moving tones and voices. The text, taken from the Book of Daniel, was
sung by a boys' choir as single syllables and whole words. The words
were sometimes revealed as comprehensible sounds, and at other times
merely as "pure sound values."[47]

Stockhausen's assimilation of a boy's singing voice into the work was
the result of painstaking preparation on his part. He wanted the sung
parts to closely match the electronically produced tones of the piece. His
composition notes from the time explain how he made this happen:

> Fifty-two pieces of paper with graphically notated melodies which were
> sung by the boy, Josef Protschka, during the recording of the individual
> layers. Stockhausen also produced these melodies as sine tones on tape
> loops for the circa 3-hour recording sessions. The boy listened to these
> melodies over earphones and then tried to sing them. Stockhausen chose
> the best result from each series of attempts for the subsequent synchro-
> nization of the layers.[48]

Gesang der Jünglinge is historically important for several reasons. It
represented the beginning of the end of the first period of tape composition, which had been sharply divided aesthetically between the Paris and
Cologne schools of thought. The maturity of Stockhausen's approach to
composing the work, blending acoustic and electronic sounds as equiv-
ocal raw materials, signified a maturing of the medium. The work successfully cast off the cloak of novelty and audio experiments that had
preoccupied so many tape compositions until that time. Stockhausen's
concept of "composing the sound"—splitting it, making the changing
parameters of sound part of the theme of the work—was first exercised
in *Gesang der Jünglinge*. Rhythmic structures were only nominally present, no formal repetition of motifs existed in the work, and its theme
was the continuous evolution of sound shapes and dynamics rather than
a pattern of developing tones.

The composer's newly formed interest in the spatial deployment of
sound, as nurtured during the production of *Gruppen* the year before,
was another important milestone for this work:

> This is a new way of experiencing musical speech, but another feature of
> the composition is equally essential: here for the first time the direction
> and movement of sounds in space was shaped by the composer and made
> available as a new dimension in musical experience.[49]

Gesang der Jünglinge was composed on five tracks. During its performance, five loudspeakers were placed so that they surrounded the

audience. The listener was in the eye of the sonic storm, with music emanating from every side, moving clockwise and counterclockwise, moving and not moving in space.

Stockhausen became increasingly fascinated during the late '50s with the spatial projection of music in the performance space. For *Kontakte* in 1958, using four-track tape, he devised a clever way make the sound of his tape music spin around the audience at various speeds. He did this in the studio using a rotating platform with a loudspeaker mounted on top. He could manually rotate the speaker up to four times a second. By setting up four microphones around the speaker platform, each plugged into one track of a four-track tape recorder, he would play a tape through the loudspeaker and rerecord the sound onto a four-track tape through the microphones. Each microphone would catch the sound slightly behind the one before it. When the resulting four-track tape was played in an auditorium—with a speaker for each channel positioned in the corners of the space—the sound would spin from speaker to speaker around the audience. This dizzying effect only worked, of course, if the speakers were hooked up in the same order as the microphones that recorded the sound. This was a favorite technique of Stockhausen's, who personally manned the mixing board during his live performances. He was still using this technique in compositions during the late '60s. An interesting sidenote is that New York–based electronic improviser Lary Seven has recently revived this idea for live performance. He uses an ordinary phonograph turntable to rotate a small loudspeaker. Sound from the rotating loudspeaker is directed into four microphones positioned around the turntable with the aid of a paper funnel. The mikes, in turn, feed a set of four loudspeakers arranged around the performance space to produce the effect of rotating sound.

Stockhausen also used a specialized tape recorder called the Springer. Originally developed to lengthen or shorten radio broadcasts, it used a rotating matrix of four to six playback heads that spun in the opposite direction as the tape transport. As the tape passed the rotating playback array, one of the playback heads was in contact with it at all times. The output was equal to the sum of the rotating heads. The speed of the rotating heads could be adjusted within a variable playback speed range from –30% to +50%.[50] Stockhausen employed a Springer with a rotating six-part playback head, using it to provide the disorienting effect of gradually speeding up or slowing down the tempo of a recorded sound without changing its pitch. He frequently used this technique in his major works of the mid-'60s, especially *Hymnen* (1966–67).

Stockhausen succeeded Eimert as director of the Cologne studio in 1963. As closely as he became associated with electronic music, he continued to apply himself to a wide variety of projects and musical for-

Stockhausen built this rotating speaker table in 1958 to record the effect of a spinning loudspeaker onto different tracks of tape. In a multitrack surround sound performance, the resulting sounds would rotate around the audience. Photo courtesy of Stockhausen-Verlag.

mats. He kept developing his postserialist techniques with orchestras, producing such works as *Momente* (1962–64), for soprano, four choral groups, and thirteen instrumentalists spatially deployed around an auditorium; *Stop* (1965) for orchestra; and *Adieu* (1966) for wind quintet. In the field of electronic music, his work in the '60s can be roughly divided into two categories: tape composition, and live performance for electronics and other instruments.

Stockhausen's tape works during the '60s were few in number but highly influential. *Telemusik* (1966), which he composed in the studio of Radio Nippon Hoso Kyokai (NHK) in Tokyo, can legitimately be called the first recording of global or world music in the modern sense—a work that weaves influences from various cultures into one musical entity. Like *Gesang der Jünglinge*, it consisted of a seamless contour of electronic and acoustic sounds. The acoustic sounds in this case were drawn from recordings of indigenous music of Japan, Bali, China, Spain, North Africa, Hungary, and the Amazon. Stockhausen called it his first step in composing a "music of the whole world, of all countries and all races."[51]

Stockhausen's most influential piece of electronic music was *Hymnen*. It remains the finest example of formal tape composition of the '60s. The word *Hymnen* means "anthems." The piece was 113 minutes long and occupied four album sides when it was originally released. Each side, or "region," used a number of national anthems as source material. Most of the anthems were taken from commercial recordings, which Stockhausen then modified and processed as part of his overall sound design. At least one anthem, the Russian, was beautifully realized in a stripped-down form using purely electronic means. The work had the unpredictable atmosphere of a collage, but moved in precise, well-planned stages that unfolded musically through changing sounds and textures. It was replete with broadcast sounds, miscellaneous noises, shortwave radio interference, crowd sounds, Stockhausen's breathing—which inspired the eerie breathing sequence in the movie *2001: A Space Odyssey* (1968) when HAL the computer is being shut down—and brilliant moments of pure electronic bliss. He used the Springer to suspend sounds in time, allowing him to freeze a moment of music and further transform it in real time as it floated, seemingly weightless and detached from the way that sounds are expected to behave. It was a central audio theme of the work.

Stockhausen underscored his personal indebtedness to the composers Pierre Boulez, Henri Pousseur, John Cage, and Luciano Berio by dedicating each of the four regions to one of them. *Hymnen* was presented many times using a quadraphonic sound setup, and Stockhausen also composed a concert version that included parts for six soloists. All in all, *Hymnen* is one of the few authentic electronic masterworks, a piece that continues to inspire new composers. It has an undeniable humanity that launched an entire generation of imitators in what might be called electronic space music.

Aus den sieben Tagen (From the Seven Days, 1968) is a cycle of works representing, perhaps, the least obsessive side of Stockhausen's personality. Drawn up as a series of twelve compositions, each for different instrumentation, the score for each merely consists of a simple, interpretive text instruction. The performers of *Es* (It) were asked to play:

> . . . only when one has achieved the state of **non thinking**, and to stop whenever one begins to think. . . . As soon as a player thinks of something (e.g., **that** he is playing; **what** he is playing; **what** someone else is playing or has played; **how** he should react; that a car is driving past outside etc.) he should stop, and only start again when he is **just listening,** and at one with what is heard.[52]

The instructions were even more abstract for *Aufwärts* (Upwards):

Play a vibration in the rhythm of your smallest particles.
Play a vibration in the rhythm of the universe.
Play all the rhythms that you can distinguish today between the rhythms
of your smallest particles and the rhythm of the universe, one after
another and each one for so long, until the air carries it on.[53]

There is an unintentionally amusing footnote on the liner sleeve of
the original recording bearing the above instructions for *Aufwärts*: "It
should be mentioned here, that the musicians had previously interpreted
several other texts in which rhythms of the limbs, cells, molecules,
atoms, or rhythms of the body, heart, breathing, thinking, intuition etc.
occur." This note was added to explain that by the time the performers
had recorded *Aufwärts*, they had already gone through several earlier
pieces in the cycle under Stockhausen's coaching to fine-tune their meditative skills. Stockhausen is not at all comfortable with spontaneity, but
this was not readily apparent to anyone who just listened to the seemingly formless, sonic beauty of these recordings.

About this time, I was composing music scored for small ensembles
of electronic musicians, each of whom was required to wear headphones
connected to one of the other players. They were instructed to play in
response to what they were hearing, but they could not hear the sounds
of their own playing because of the headphones. I shared this piece with
Cage and naively suggested that I was attempting to produce a form of
improvisation like Stockhausen's *Aus den sieben Tagen*. He said, "I
think it is different from Stockhausen. He lets people play freely, but
before the audience hears it he controls it from a master panel."[54]

Stockhausen's output of magnetic tape compositions diminished
during the '60s as be became increasingly interested in working with
electronic music in a live setting. In 1964, he began to tour extensively
with a group of players and set out to compose works involving the electronic modification and accompaniment of music being played by
instrumentalists. He called this music "intuitive," a term that suggests
free improvisation, but it was not. His intuitive music was scored, albeit
minimally or graphically in many cases, providing great freedom for the
individual performers within the boundary lines established by the composer. This set of works consisted largely of the amplification and modulation of the sounds of acoustic instruments with electronic effects.
Mixtur (1964) and *Mikrophonie I* (1964) were the first of these.

Mixtur was scored for an ensemble consisting of woodwinds,
brass, cymbals, and tam tams, plus four ring modulators and four sine
wave generators. Microphones picked up the sounds of the instruments
and fed them into the ring modulators. Four musicians played sine
wave oscillators to modulate the ring modulators, changing the texture

and width of the sidebands being triggered by the processed sounds of the instruments. The smallest, inaudible sounds of the cymbals and tam-tams were amplified using contact microphones and modified in the same manner. All of this was played and mixed according to Stockhausen's instructions, and he controlled the final blend that was amplified and projected by loudspeakers. It was music of timbres and textures and amplified small sounds, a blast of continuously changing, seemingly formless playing. Stockhausen also composed a version of *Mixtur* for a smaller ensemble and, taking a page out of Cage's book, gave the conductor the freedom to vary the number of players in any way.

Stockhausen's passion for live performance led to many pieces following the same general approach: instruments played live and modified by electronics in real time. What differed from work to work were the instrumental timbres he chose, the changes to filtering, volume, duration, spatial projection, and other dynamics that he controlled as the "mixer," and the nature of his instructions to the musicians. *Mikrophonie I* fully exploited the amplification of the small sounds of the tam-tam. *Mikrophonie II* (1965) used twelve singers, four ring modulators, a Hammond organ, and tape. *Solo* (1965–66) was for any solo melody instrument and tape, wherein the musician's playing was amplified and mixed with the sounds of a prerecorded tape. The frequently performed *Prozession* (1967) was written for his five touring players, including Fred Alings and Rolf Gehlhaar (tam-tam), Johannes Fritsch (viola), Harald Bojé (Electronium), and Aloys Kontarsky (piano). In this work, the musicians' previous experience with earlier Stockhausen works forms the basis for their parts. Stockhausen explained, "The musical events are not individually notated, but are variants of parts of my earlier compositions played from memory by the performers."[55] The tam-tam players and the "microphonist" used *Mikrophonie I* as their reference point, the viola player referred to *Gesang der Jünglinge*, *Kontakte*, and *Momente*, the Electronium player referred to *Telemusik* and *Solo*, and the pianist to *Klavierstücke I-XI* (1952–56) and *Kontakte*. All the time, Stockhausen manned the "monitoring desk," where he mixed and controlled the spatial projection of the sound through loudspeakers. He also frequently recycled tape music from previous compositions as material to be mixed with the live performances.

Even the most astute listener of Stockhausen's live electronic works will have trouble understanding what was "composed" and what was not in this music. Yet underlying all of this so-called spontaneity is the mind of Stockhausen. In *Kurzwellen* (1968), six players reacted spontaneously to the sounds being broadcast over six shortwave radios. The

Experiencing Electronic Music from the Inside Out

In 1967, just following the world premiere of *Hymnen*, Stockhausen said this about the electronic music experience:

> Recently during a conversation I suddenly realized that musicians, through that new music which they have created since 1951, have given rise to widespread perplexity, and that this perplexedness has not at all led to a nihilistic resignation; on the contrary, it has enormously cultivated the fantasy of the individual. Many listeners have projected that strange new music which they experienced—especially in the realm of electronic music—into extraterrestrial space. Even though they are not familiar with it through human experience, they identify it with the fantastic dream world. Several have commented that my electronic music sounds "like on a different star," or "like in outer space." Many have said that when hearing this music, they have sensations as if flying at an infinitely high speed, and then again, as if immobile in an immense space. Thus, extreme words are employed to describe such experiences, which are not "objectively" communicable in the sense of an object description, but rather which exist in the subjective fantasy and which are projected into the extraterrestrial space.[56]

composer himself asked the performers to react "on the spur of the moment," yet he defined the processes and rules by which they reacted:

> What I have composed is the process of transforming: *how* they react to what they hear on the radio; *how* they imitate it and then modulate or transpose it in time—longer or shorter, with greater or lesser rhythmic articulation—and in space—higher or lower, louder or softer; *when* and *how* and *how often* they are to play together or alternately in duos, trios or quartets; *how* they call out to each other, issue invitations, so that together they can observe a single event passing amongst them for a stretch of time, letting it shrink and grow, bundling it up and spreading it out, darkening it and brightening it, condensing it and losing it in embellishments.[57]

The crowning technical achievement of Stockhausen's concertizing days were the performances given at the 1970 World's Fair in Osaka Japan. He was asked to collaborate with an architect in designing a performance space for his electronic music. Like Varèse before him, Stockhausen was able to design an auditorium from scratch conceived only for the purpose of listening to electronic music. It was the perfect opportunity to fully explore his interest in the spatial deployment of sounds. The resulting hall was a huge globe that could seat six hundred people on a metal platform in the middle, which consisted of a grid so that sound could travel through it. Loudspeakers were organized in circles to surround the audience by sound, and there were seven circles of speakers from the bottom of the globe to its top—three below the audience and four above. The music consisted of various Stockhausen works played on tape, sung, or performed by live musicians perched in six balconies around and above the audience. All of the sound was piped into a mixer ("soundmill") controlled by Stockhausen or one of his assistants. The mixer had two pods for directing the sound to any vertical or horizontal configuration of speakers. The sound could be manually rotated at speeds up to five revolutions per second in any direction.

Stockhausen described how he could control the sound:

> I could decide to make a voice go in an upward spiral movement for two or three minutes, either clockwise or anti-clockwise, while at the same time another player's sound moved in a circle using the other soundmill, and a third crossed in a straight line, using just two potentiometers.[58]

This was the composer's ultimate experiment in spatial composition. The troupe of twenty musicians from five countries worked for six and a half hours every day for 183 days. Over a million visitors experienced the spectacle in Osaka during the World's Fair.

For the past thirty years, Stockhausen has largely turned his attention back to instrumental and orchestral works, and also opera. The criteria he developed for composing electronic music have continued to serve him well, and he has often found ways to integrate electronic elements into his work, even to this day. The addition of the EMS Synthi 100 analog synthesizer to the Cologne studio in the early '70s gave the composer greater control over musical scales, the recorded sequencing of notes, and the manipulation of all dynamic parameters of the sound in real time. The first piece on which he used the Synthi 100 to full effect was *Sirius* (1975–77) for electronic music, trumpet, soprano, bass clarinet, and bass. Stockhausen's comments about the electronic music for *Sirius* show us that he has come to view electronic music as a means for experiencing a unification with natural forces in the universe:

> By listening to this music . . . one perceives how the newly discovered means and structural possibilities of electronic music can awaken in us a completely new consciousness for revelations, transformations and fusions of forms, which would never have been possible with the old musical means, and become increasingly similar to art of the metamorphosis in nature.[59]

Chapter 7

A RENAISSANCE OF INVENTING: THE 1950s

Electronic music studios were born during a dramatic time of transition in the field of electronics. During the '50s, electrical components became less expensive as the reign of the vacuum tube slowly gave way to the transistor. Hobbyists took up electrical projects in increasing numbers as Radio Shack, Lafayette and Heathkit competed vigorously for their business. Magazines such a *Popular Electronics* were brimming with projects for budding self-taught gadget makers. One of the consequences was a new generation of young people interested in all things electrical. It was inevitable that some of these wunderkinds of the '40s and '50s would turn their attention to improving the state of electronic music instruments. Robert Moog, Donald Buchla, and Hugh Le Caine (1914–1977) were all a part of this new wave of inventors.

Studios needed equipment. They had outgrown the capabilities of the electronic performance instruments that were rooted in technology of the 1920s. A new generation of inventors responded with a dizzying portfolio of electronic musical instruments and gizmos. Some of the braver souls even ventured into the commercial marketing of these instruments. The results of their efforts extended the life cycle of the major electronic music studios and also led to an eventual migration away from centralized studios as technology became less and less expensive.

Here are the stories of some of the most influential and remarkable achievements during the period leading up to yet another paradigm shift from transistors to semiconductors and microcomputers.

Raymond Scott in his home music "laboratory," 1959. Photo courtesy The Raymond Scott Archives, Manhattan Research Inc.

Raymond Scott: Designer of Plastic Sounds and Electronic Music Devices

You can look in nearly every book written about electronic music in the past fifty years and never see the name of Raymond Scott (1908–1994).[1] Titles published as recently as 2000 make no mention of him. Yet anyone who grew up in the '50s or '60s heard his electronic music at one time or another. Scott was the composer and electronic architect of a myriad of jingles, special effects, mood pieces, and other commercial applications of electronic music for radio, television, and industrial films. His specialty was the snappy tune, space-age sounds, and joyful electronic abstractions—all for hire.

Scott had two different lives in music. He was most visible as a renowned bandleader during the '30s, '40s, and '50s. Many of his catchy melodies—*Powerhouse, Twilight in Turkey, Dinner Music for a Pack of Hungry Cannibals*—were adapted for use in cartoons by legendary Warner Brothers music director Carl Stalling (1888–1974).[2]

The other side of this man was little known to the public. Scott was at heart an inventor and a self-trained electronics wizard, and spent many of his early years soldering, tinkering, and inventing musically oriented contraptions. By the late '40s, he had accumulated enough wealth from his work as a bandleader and composer to purchase a mansion in North Hills, Long Island. In it were eight rooms devoted to his electronic experiments. He had a professionally outfitted machine shop for making his electronic gear, one room set aside for nothing but spare parts, and a spacious razzle-dazzle recording studio with a disc lathe, reel-to-reel tape recorders, and a wide assortment of wall-mounted instruments, mixers, and controls that grew more complex from year to year as he continued to invent new gizmos.[3] If you wanted to read about *this* side of Raymond Scott, you had to flip open a copy of the trade magazine *Advertising Age*, which reported on his innovative electronic music for commercials. There was also the latest edition of *Popular Electronics*, which might feature an article about Scott's unrelenting perfectionism as an electronics hobbyist—and a rich one at that—making him the envy of every American male who ever dreamed of building something from Heathkit.

Scott occasionally reached out to other engineers to obtain gear. Bob Moog recalls a visit he and his father made to Scott's home around 1955. Scott was interested in using one of the younger Moog's Theremin circuits. Bob Moog later remarked:

> I can't remember the first time I saw that much stuff. But you don't go
> from having nothing one day to having thirty feet of equipment the next.
> Scott probably was fooling with that kind of stuff for years and years.[4]

What was Scott doing in his basement all that time? He was inventing electronic music instruments and other devices that would put him at the top of the field in the business of writing music for commercials. New York was the hotbed of advertising production at the time, and Scott and Eric Siday—Bob Moog's second customer—were the two most sought-after composers of commercial music.[5] Scott formed Manhattan Research Inc. in 1946 as an outlet for his commercial electronic music production. By about 1960, he was offering a grab bag of gadgets for various musical applications, including four models of electronic doorbells, an electronic music box, and three models of an instrument he called the Electronium.[6] By the mid-'60s, his advertising billed Manhattan Research Inc. as "Designers and Manufacturers of Electronic Music and Musique Concrète Devices and Systems."[7] His most original inventions included a variety of keyboard instruments, multi-track recording machines, and automatic composing instruments. They included:

Multitrack tape recorder (1953). Scott invented two of the earliest multi-track magnetic tape recorders. His patented machines could record seven and fourteen tracks on a single reel of tape. Les Paul (b. 1915) had previously used the technique of recording sound-on-sound in the early '40s, but that method only involved recording from one mono tape recorder to another while playing along. Scott's multitrack machines recorded seven or fourteen parallel audio tracks on the same reel of tape. Paul made a prototype of an eight-track machine in 1954,[8] and in 1955 Hugh Le Caine invented a machine that mixed six separate but synchronized tapes down to one track, but nobody came close to matching Scott's early achievement.

Clavivox (1959). This was a form of keyboard instrument about the size of a combo organ. It used the beat frequency principles of the Theremin but had the unique ability to glide the notes from key to key at adjustable rates of portamento. It also had left-hand controls for vibrato, hard attack, soft attack, and a kind of mute button that allowed you to abruptly silence a note while it was on the rise.[9] The instrument was one of the few products that Scott marketed commercially, although relatively few were made.

Electronium (1959–72). No one has successfully described the Electronium. Scott once remarked that "the Electronium is not played, it is guided."[10] The basic idea underlying it was that the composer could interact with the instrument to create music—in a collaboration of sorts. One set it in motion and it took on decisions of its own. It also used "processes based on controlled randomness to generate rhythms, melodies, and timbres."[11] How the Electronium would respond to the composer's guidance could not be predicted. Scott's hope was that the device, once set into motion, could produce in hours what would have normally taken days or weeks for composers to fashion on their own. He envisioned it as a cost-saving innovation for the production of television and motion picture music.

Scott used many of his other sound-generating inventions to feed the Electronium. For a time, the wall of equipment in his basement represented the ever-evolving array of gadgets he had interconnected to complement the machine. Perhaps its most impressive and innovative feature was its sequencer, an early electronic version of which was in operation by about 1960.[12] In one version of the device, it could produce rhythmically uniform sequences "in which 200 elements can be combined in infinite permutations of pitch, tempo, meter, timbre, or special mood."[13] The Electronium was an instrument that took Scott ten years to perfect. When he began publicizing it in 1970, Motown Music Inc. immediately expressed an interest in buying one. They actually hired Scott to be their technology consultant for several years. His one and only Electronium was delivered to Motown in the early '70s and now resides in the

Hollywood-based studio of former Devo member Mark Mothersbaugh who hopes to one day restore it to operating condition.

Scott was, by all accounts, paranoid that others would steal his trade secrets. One reason he never gained the recognition he deserved was that he failed to publicize the technology behind most of his achievements. In the world of engineering, like science, one can only build a reputation by gaining peer acceptance. But Scott was unwilling to do so except in the form of public relations talks. Rather than speak at a conference of audio engineers, he would do self-promotional show-and-tell sessions about writing jingles at advertising conventions. Even those who supplied him with components had no idea what they were going to be used for. "He never bought our stuff with the idea that he would plug it in and use it," recalled Bob Moog. "He was developing his own instrumentation. During the early days of us making synthesizers, Scott wanted us to make little things that he would then incorporate into instruments he was working on."[14] As a result, Raymond Scott had minimal influence on the field of music technology.

Space Age Electronic Pop Music

Avant-garde experiments in electronic music naturally spawned many commercial applications of the same techniques. Raymond Scott is most notable because he was a knowledgeable tinkerer and inventor in the field. But several other composers and musicians became better known than Scott by composing electronic pop music for the masses.

Two of the earliest composers to create purely electronic pop music were Tom Dissevelt and Dick Raaijmakers from the Netherlands. Working in various studios including the Philips Eindhoven Research Laboratories and the University of Utrecht, they crafted short, syncopated melodies with instrumental voices synthesized from the most basic of tools: oscillators, filters, and tape recorders. Both composers had one foot in the camp of avant-garde compostion and one in pop music. Perhaps it was to protect his standing as a serious composer that Raaijmakers used the pseudonym of Kid Baltan when he released his pop tunes on several recordings issued by Philips in the early '60s. *Song of the Second Moon* (1957), a pleasant little song lasting only two minutes and forty-nine seconds, was composed the same year and in the same studio as Varèse's *Poème electronique*. Philips also altered the titles of Dissevelt's and Baltan's works when they packaged them for

North America, giving them such kitschy titles as *Moon Maid* (formerly *Drifting*), *The Visitor from Inner Space* (formerly *Vibration*), *Sonik Re-entry* (formerly *Whirling*) and *Twilight Ozone* (formerly *Intersection*). The following endorsement graced the American release:

> Never before has electronic music been so melodic, so fully arranged, and such pleasant listening. Tom Dissevelt and Kid Baltan have created groovy vibrations and singing sounds to delight the ears of all who hear.[15]

Jean-Jacques Perrey (b. 1929) and Gershon Kingsley (b. 1925) teamed up for two whimsical works of electronic pop music. They purchased their first Moog synthesizer in 1966, the same year that they released their first album, entitled *The In Sounds from Way Out* (Vanguard VSD-79222; 1966), but this record did not feature the Moog. It was composed using tape loops and classic tape composition techniques, Frenchman Perrey having learned about loops and editing from Pierre Schaeffer. He also played the Ondioline, a compact French electronic keyboard instrument invented by Georges Jenny and dating from 1941. The composers became fast friends with Robert Moog and received personal assistance from the inventor in learning the new instrument.[16] Perrey's first album featuring the Moog was *Amazing Electronic Pop Sounds of Jean-Jacques Perrey* (Vanguard, 1968). After their collaboration of several years, both went on to work separately in the field of popular electronic music stylings, and continue to do so today. Perrey released several other pop albums. Kingsley organized a Moog quartet for a Carnegie Hall performance in 1970. Speaking about their interest in making electronic music fun and accessible to the public, Perrey remarked:

> Technology gives technical progress but forsakes other emotions. We have to rediscover the sensibility that makes the instruments speak to the heart and to the soul of the listeners. That's why I advise the new generation of electronic musicians to work hard and not to be ruled by the sound capacities of the machines.[17]

When the age of stereo was first upon us, producer Enoch Light (1907–1978) and his Command label were there to fill our walnut-veneered record cabinets with exciting new sounds. He employed an eclectic stable of studio musicians who could adapt their stylings to whatever turn popular music was taking. One of his more venerable performers was keyboardist Dick Hyman (b. 1927). This most versatile of musicians could be relied upon to take a turn at whatever keyboard instrument or musical style was popular at the moment. His list of album credits is nearly countless, and he played everything from jazz piano to funky organ and "happening" harpsichord. He was one of the first artists to release a Moog album following the overnight success of Wendy Carlos's *Switched-On Bach* in late 1968: *The Electric Eclectics of Dick Hyman* and *The Age of Electronicus*, both released in 1969. His songs had fun titles such as *Topless Dancers of Corfu Hyman, The Moog and Me*, and *Tap Dance in the Memory Banks*, belying how truly tedious and not-fun it was for a skilled keyboard player to piece together music layer by layer using the monophonic Moog. Hyman recently recalled his days with the Moog in this way:

> I got started on the Moog at the urging of the Command people, Enoch Light and Bobby Byrne, and learned what the basics were from Walter Sear. I eased out of the field when it became more specialized and I felt I had reached the limits of my interest. Still, I used the Minimoog as an occasional double on various recording sessions. I last tried Walter Sear's equipment as an overdub for a sequence in Woody Allen's *Everyone Says I Love You* around 1998, but we rejected the effect.[18]

A veritable blizzard of Moog recordings from many artists stormed the market in the years immediately following *Switched-On Bach*. Most are collector's items today, although at the time they were written off by most people as genuinely uninspired imitations designed to make a quick buck. But they didn't, and it wasn't long before those expensive synthesizers were collecting cobwebs in some of the busiest commercial recording studios in the business.

One composer-performer who had a chance to peek into Raymond Scott's private studio was Bruce Haack (1931–1988). Haack was a musician and television performer with his own history of making homemade analog musical gizmos. He was in no way as sophisticated about electronics as Scott, but he produced many interesting, highly original recordings incorporating electronic music in the '60s, '70s, and '80s. Primarily known as a composer of children's songs, he had a wacky sense of humor that Scott appreciated. It was reportedly Haack's album *Electric Lucifer* (1970) that caught Scott's ear. For a time, Haack became a familiar face at the Scott studio and may have collaborated with him on some music. But evidently Scott wouldn't let Haack touch the toys, recalls longtime Haack friend Harry Spiridakis:

> There was a little static in the connection between him and Scott. Bruce was quite in awe of Scott and the really professional, expensive dream machine he had produced. But I think Bruce was like a kid in a way, jealous that he couldn't fly it on his own, so to speak. He did rave about the Electronium and was very enthusiastic about it. The future had arrived as far as he was concerned—including using brainwaves to transfer musical thought onto circuits and tape.[19]

Many of Scott's electronic works are now available on CD. In addition to examples of his commercial work on the Manhattan Research Inc. CD, there have been reissues of his highly quirky three-album series *Soothing Sounds for Baby* (1964), a collection of bizarre and amusing electronic music vignettes originally produced by the Gesell Institute of Child Development.

Hugh Le Caine and the Sackbut Blues

- *Sackbut*: the name given to the trombone until the eighteenth century, when it came to England.
- *Electronic Sackbut*: the first voltage-controlled electronic music synthesizer, invented by Hugh Le Caine between 1945 and 1948.[20]

One supposes that Hugh Le Caine (1914–1977) called his electronic musical instrument the Electronic Sackbut to acknowledge the colorfully brassy sound of its sawtooth oscillator. The name was a quaint blend of the modern and the arcane and itself symbolized the time during which Le Caine was actively inventing. Beginning in the vacuum-tube years just following World War II, this Canadian audio engineering genius always seemed to be redefining the outer limits of musical technology.

Whereas Raymond Scott declined to share his musical inventions with the rest of the world, Le Caine was a product of academia and made his work known as a matter of course. He frequently contributed to the engineering literature, and by 1954 was employed full-time by Canada's National Research Center to work on his electronic music inventions. This was a privileged position seldom afforded to an engineer of music technology in any country. For twenty years, this gifted and affable inventor and instructor proved time and time again that nobody was better suited to the job than he.

Le Caine is acknowledged as a major influence both by electronic music composers and engineers. Robert Moog, who became known as the inventor of the first commercially successful voltage-controlled synthesizer in the mid-'60s, recalls Le Caine as a "profound influence."[21] An entire generation of electronic music composers can thank Le Caine for providing them with state-of-the-art equipment in the early days of North American electronic music studios. Le Caine's biographer, Gayle Young, reminds us that he almost "single-handedly equipped electronic music studios at the University of Toronto (opened in 1959) and at McGill University in Montreal (opened in 1964)."[22]

In 1966, Pauline Oliveros had been working with tape delay techniques in the San Francisco area, where she lived. The equipment at the San Francisco Tape Music Center consisted largely of a cleverly patched-together amalgam of tape recorders, oscillators, and filter banks. That summer, she went to Toronto to study circuit-making with Le Caine for two months, and while working there she suddenly found that she had access to some of the most innovative and sophisticated electronic sound-processing and recording equipment available anywhere. "The techniques that I had invented for myself were very well supported by the studio set up at UT," explains Oliveros today about Le Caine. "He was a very generous man and wished to share his knowledge. I worked with some of his devices there—like the twenty-channel loop machine. But most of my work was done with my own system."[23]

Not surprisingly, Oliveros responded with a deluge of output; some ten tape compositions and another six ultrasonic tape studies in just a few short weeks.[24] Among these was one of her best-known electronic works, the twenty-one-minute *I of IV*, featuring tape delay and twelve tone generators connected to an organ keyboard. The keyboard and oscillators were already set up that way in the Toronto studio and were evidently one of the versions of Le Caine's various "oscillator bank" permutations, this one having been installed in 1961. Oliveros did what came naturally to her: she pushed "the edges as far as possible."[25] Le Caine's studio gadgets and instruments were invented with the sound sculptor in mind.

Many other budding electronic music composers also came under Le Caine's mentorship during that period. Le Caine did not consider himself to be a composer, despite the fact that he composed one of the most famous examples of musique concrète, the two-minute *Dripsody* (mono 1955, stereo 1957). His "etude for variable speed tape recorder" consisted of tape manipulations of a single sound: a drop of water falling into a bucket. He transformed the sound of the drip into a series of pitched notes by adjusting its playback speed and rerecording it. For many years, *Dripsody* was undoubtedly the most often-played tape composition in any college music course.[26]

Like his other works, *Dripsody* was primarily a demonstration of one of Le Caine's latest electronic music inventions, his Special Purpose Tape Recorder, which he prototyped in 1955. Also called the "Multi-Track," this customized tape recorder consisted of six independently running magnetic tapes that could be mixed down to a single channel. A special feature of the Multi-Track was that the speed of each of the six reels of tape could be adjusted independently. Le Caine was using the raw material of simple recorded sounds, changing the pitch and timbre through speed adjustments and juxtaposition, and creating rhythmic patterns by selectively rerecording and repeating patterns. The Multi-Track continued to evolve and became a fixture in the Toronto and McGill electronic music studios.

Electronic Sackbut (1945–73). The Electronic Sackbut was Le Caine's longest-running project. He began working on it in 1945, and the instrument continued to evolve along with parallel advances in electronics for more than twenty years. The final model, dubbed the Sackbut Synthesizer, was an unsuccessful attempt to introduce a commercial version of the instrument. It was completed around 1971. Tragically, Le Caine died in 1977, at the age of sixty-three, from injuries suffered in a motorcycle accident. It is probably safe to say that the world had not yet seen the end of the Sackbut, had he only lived to continue his work.

The Electronic Sackbut was the embodiment of Le Caine's theories about the effective design of electronic musical instruments. It was conceived to give the performer unprecedented touch-sensitive control over the elements of pitch, timbre, and volume. He viewed the spectrum of sound as having many more tonal and pitch possibilities than the ones that could be hardwired to the keys of an electronic organ. His opinion was that polyphonic instruments were merely "an expedient necessity," built for those who wished to perform conventional music. In response, he designed the Electronic Sackbut as a monophonic instrument with the synthesizing flexibility to serve as "the starting point of all musical thinking."[27]

The Electronic Sackbut used voltage-control techniques to trigger and modify sounds. In this regard it anticipated the work of Robert Moog—and the entire synthesizer market that grew from Moog's success—by twenty years. Equally significant were Le Caine's radical design ideas. In his effort to give the composer more freedom to experiment with sound, he devised several touch-sensitive controls that could be easily manipulated without the necessity of learning extraordinary techniques like those necessary to play the Theremin or Trautonium.

Control over pitch was achieved through a familiar-looking keyboard, but its operation was anything but conventional. Its keys were spring-mounted and pressure-sensitive so that the volume of the sound would increase with the force being applied on them. You could also make a smooth glide from one note to another by pressing a key sideways toward the next higher or lower key. With a little practice, this effect could be accentuated to take on a portamento glide by releasing the first key and then quickly pressing the destination key.

The keyboard was but one controller for Le Caine's instrument. Waveform and timbre could be modified using a touch-sensitive pad for the left hand, which had individual controllers for each finger. Because the hand could remain in a stationary position, the dexterity and practice needed to effectively play the controls was greatly minimized. All you needed to do was move the fingers and thumb. The thumb had two pads for controlling the balance of overtones in a tone: one controlled the dominating frequencies, or "main formant," of the waveform, and the other controlled the "auxiliary formant." The index finger rested on a movable circular pad that could be pressed in any direction to continuously change the waveform and timbre of the sound. This deceptively simple controller provided the player with extraordinarily fluid manipulation of the waveform. The oscillator provided sawtooth and pulse waveshapes. The pad was marked so that the musician could equate locations on the disc to various approximations of tonal quality, such as the reedy timbre of an oboe, the brassy sound of a trumpet, or the more purely abstract "foundation tones" of the oscillator. The remaining three fingers of the hand each had a pressure pad that could be pressed to modify the strict "periodicity" or regularity of the waveform, resulting in surprising and sometimes unpredictable changes to the tone.

The final version of the Sackbut that Le Caine had developed by 1971 continued to improve on these basic techniques for providing continuously variable touch-sensitive control of the waveform.

Touch-Sensitive Organ (1952–57). Le Caine considered polyphonic organs to be inflexible instruments from the standpoint of electronic music composition. In his opinion, their fixed pitches and hardwired timbres did not give the composer adequate freedom. This is not to say that he wasn't fascinated by the challenge of designing a better organ, and he did so for several years as he came on board with the National Research Center. His improvement? He made the keyboard touch-sensitive for volume levels. Once again, he was well ahead of the time when this feature would become standard fare on commercially sold synthesizers about twenty years later. A commercial prototype was made of this organ, and the rights to the patent were acquired by the Baldwin

Organ Company in 1955, although they never exercised its use to man-ufacture a version of their own.[28] Le Caine himself sometimes used the Touch-Sensitive Organ as an audio source for his own tape composi-tions, as in his piece *Ninety-Nine Generators* (1957).

Special Purpose Tape Recorder (1955–67). Otherwise known as the "Multi-Track," this was Le Caine's early version of a tape recorder capable of recording and mixing multiple individual tracks. Monophonic recording was still the industry standard when he first pro-duced a six-track version of the machine. Unlike later multitrack recorders—and Raymond Scott's invention from two years earlier—the Multi-Track did not record its sound using multiple tape heads and a single reel of tape. Instead, Le Caine's device synchronized the playback and recording of six individual tape reels. The sound from all six was mixed down into a single track. It was possible to control the variable speed of each of the six tapes independently of one another, making the reader ideally suited for tape composition of electronic music. The speed of each tape was controlled by a touch-sensitive, three-octave keyboard. This allowed Le Caine to associate the drip he recorded for *Dripsody* to notes of the musical scale. This tape recorder was the key component of the University of Toronto Electronic Music Studio when it opened in 1959.[29] Le Caine refined the device over the years, eventually making a more compact, solid-state version in 1967.

Oscillator banks (1959–61) and the Spectrogram (1959). Le Caine built several versions of a device for controlling and experimenting with multiple audio oscillators. Each had a touch-sensitive keyboard for trig-gering the individual oscillators, which could be individually tuned and switched to play sine, pulse, and sawtooth waves. He built versions with 12, 16, 24, and 108 oscillators. In addition to the touch-sensitive key-board controller, the oscillator bank could be programmed using an optical reader called the Spectrogram. Le Caine invented the Spectrogram to enable the graphical input of program instructions, a uniquely artistic method of sound programming even to this day. Images were fed to the Spectrogram using a roll of paper and scanned using an array of one hundred photocells.

Serial Sound Generator (1966–70). This forerunner of sequencers used analog switches to program a series of tones and related effects. Essentially, it was an analog computer dedicated to the programming of musical sequences. It gave the composer control over the pitch, dura-tion, timbre and repetition of sounds, and used a voltage-controlled oscillator as its sound source.

Sonde (1968). The Sonde was yet another instrument dedicated to controlling a large number of sine wave generators. In this case, it had two hundred signals available, controlled by a panel of slide controls, one for each tone. Transistorized circuits greatly reduced the space needed to house all of this gear; the Sonde stood four feet high and two feet wide and was smaller than Le Caine's earlier oscillator banks that had many fewer audio generators available.

Polyphone synthesizer (1970). At the height of the monophonic Moog craze, Le Caine sat down to design what would become one of the most powerful and least-known analog synthesizers of all time. The voltage-controlled instrument was built for the McGill University Electronic Music Studio and was fully polyphonic, a feature that other makers of voltage-controlled synthesizers would not introduce for several more years. Like the Minimoog that also appeared in 1970, the instrument provided a compact unit with many sound-shaping modules built-in. Unlike any other synthesizers available at the time, however, the Polyphone had touch-sensitive keys and individual pitch and waveform controls for each key. Le Caine was able to build in these capabilities by giving each of the thirty-seven keys its own dedicated oscillator.

Even though Le Caine's inventions were never mass-marketed like those of Moog and others, his influence was nonetheless significant because his ideas and equipment were used every day by a host of composers and technicians who frequented the Toronto and McGill electronic music studios. However, he is often overlooked because he was content to be a behind-the-scenes person, allowing the spotlight to fall on the musicians with whom his work was associated. He refused to take himself too seriously. This comes through loud and clear in his recorded demonstrations of several of his inventions, including the Electronic Sackbut:

> When a composer writes a piece of music, he attempts to induce in the listener a specific mood or feeling. Here it is a mood best characterized as "low down." I think you will agree that a new peak in "low downness" has been achieved. The title is "The Sackbut Blues."[20]

Chapter 8

ROBERT MOOG, WENDY CARLOS, AND THE BIRTH OF THE COMMERCIAL SYNTHESIZER

Hugh Le Caine invented the voltage-controlled synthesizer in 1945 but was never able to successfully market one as a commercial product. That distinction goes to American engineer Robert Moog, whose finely crafted solid-state synthesizer modules, introduced during the mid-'60s, were the first to be sold with any success. His instruments are classics in the same way as the Hammond organ and Rhodes electric piano. Moog synthesizers represent the gold standard of the electronic music industry.

The idea of the "synthesizer" is as old as Cahill's Telharmonium, and the term was first used by him in 1896, to describe that power-hungry dynamo. Cahill's idea was virtually the same as Moog's: use a combination of tone-generating and modulating devices to build sounds from their component parts. Moog was not the first person to build a synthesizer, but he has become the most recognized. The Moog synthesizer in any one of its many manifestations became the most commonly used instrument in electronic music studios during the late '60s and '70s.

The secret of Moog's success was that he listened to musicians and solved the three biggest issues plaguing the use of synthesizers at that time: size, stability, and control. Transistorized and solid-state components solved the first two problems by reducing the size of the sound-generating components and producing stable oscillators. Providing controls over the myriad possible sounds that could be made with the synthesizer was the bigger challenge.

Earlier electronic music "performance" instruments were controlled through the manual adjustment of dials that would directly affect the AC output of the device. This method was difficult to control, because each separate component of a system, from the multiple oscillators to filters and other special devices, required precise manual adjustments to duplicate any given effect. Moog became the first synthesizer designer to popularize the technique of *voltage control* in analog electronic musical instruments. Donald Buchla in the United States and Paul Ketoff in Italy had been developing commercial synthesizers using the same principle at about the same time, but their equipment never reached the level of public acceptance of Moog's products.

In a voltage-controlled device, a small amount of current is applied to the control input of a given component to modify the output signal. This voltage signal is preset, precise, and quick, and can be activated by such easy-to-use voltage-control components as the synthesizer keyboard, thus making the analog synthesizer much easier to manage. What the keyboard was actually doing was sending a voltage signal of a particular amount to the sound-generating oscillator of the synthesizer and telling it to produce a note of a certain pitch. Moog's synthesizer was designed as a modular device with self-contained but connectable components to generate, modify, modulate, and output sounds. Moog succeeded in creating a product that could be manufactured with consistent high-quality results.

Moog's success encouraged many manufacturers to enter the market for commercial synthesizers. Collectively, these companies revolutionized the design of synthesizing equipment by employing the latest in integrated circuitry to produce entirely self-contained electronic music machines. As the instruments became more affordable, they began to migrate from institutional electronic music studios into the homes of composers and musicians. Desktop music systems can now be put together for the cost of a personal computer. The possibility now exists for anyone to produce electronic music using inexpensive, sophisticated, and easy-to-use instruments, software, and digital recording systems.

If a definition of a synthesizer is in order, let's try this one. A synthesizer is a self-contained electronic music system for the generation, modification, and playing of electronically produced sounds. The original Moog Modular Synthesizer was designed primarily as a way to create sounds to be used during tape composition. Much like the Barrons and the composers at GRM and WDR, a composer could use the Moog to collect interesting sound material on tape and then use mixing, multitracking, and splicing to "realize" a musical composition moment by moment. By the '70s, synthesizers began to include preset "libraries" of sounds, programmable note patterns, and highly portable designs, making them well-suited for live, real-time performances. Microcomputers, inexpensive mass storage and RAM, and software for synthesizing, mixing, sequencing, composing, and recording sound are now the composer's most familiar tools.

Synthesizers can now be grouped into three configurations:

- Keyboard instruments for live performance and studio composition.
- "Slave" modules without keyboards that are controlled by other MIDI keyboards or a personal computer.
- Virtual synthesizers that only exist in the form of sound modeling software. These can be controlled by the computer or an external MIDI keyboard.

Whether using analog or digital synthesis, all synthesizers have the same basic components:

- Two or more oscillators for generating raw sound material. The waveforms normally offered include sine, sawtooth, square, and sometimes triangle. These can be combined to create variations on the default waveshapes.
- Preset sounds, or instrumental "voices," are provided on all synthesizers. Many allow you to create new sounds and save them as new "presets."
- A noise generator.
- Amplitude modulation of waveforms.
- Frequency modulation of waveforms.
- Envelope controllers for modifying the way a sound starts, continues, and ends.
- A sequencer or other means for recording note sequences.
- High- and low-pass filters for selectively adding and removing frequency ranges from a complex sound.
- MIDI in/out/thru for controlling one of more keyboards or interfacing a synthesizer with a computer in real time.

The Moog Synthesizer

The Moog synthesizer was not invented overnight, but it did grow out of a meeting that Robert Moog had with Hofstra professor Herbert Deutsch (b. 1932), an electronic music composer. Interestingly, Moog can thank his Theremin kits for having made this relationship possible. He recalls:

Many people had those Theremins, including Herb Deutsch, a music instructor at Hofstra University on Long Island. He was also an experimental music composer. It was in the winter of 1963 that I was at a music teachers' conference—the New York State School Music Association—in the Catskills. I was demonstrating the Theremin. I didn't even have my own booth. I was at a friend of mine's booth. Herb Deutsch came along and he started a conversation off by saying that he had one of my Theremin kits and that he used it for sight-singing and ear-training exercises in the classroom, which was interesting. Then at one point he said, "Do you know anything about electronic music?" At that point I really didn't. I had never heard any. I only had the vaguest idea of what people like Ussachevsky were doing. Even though my undergraduate work was at Columbia, I never met Ussachevsky while I was there or heard any of his music. He said he was looking for equipment to compose electronic music.[1]

Deutsch invited Moog to attend a concert of his music in New York City in January 1964, just a few days after New Year's. The performance was at the studio of sculptor Jason Ceely, who was known for making sculptures out of automobile bumpers. Deutsch had composed a piece for magnetic tape using the sounds of a percussionist playing traditional instruments as well as Ceely's sculptures. Moog recalled, "He had composed this using the crudest possible equipment. The tape recorders were one or two Sony home tape recorders that one could buy for a couple of hundred dollars. I was completely hooked. I was very excited by it."[2] Moog knew from that moment that he wanted to get involved with electronic music.

After a few more conversations, the two men arranged to get together for some constructive brainstorming and tinkering. In the summer of 1964, Deutsch brought his whole family up for a vacation in the Finger Lakes region of New York state, near where Moog lived in Trumansburg. Moog continues the story:

> The vacation consisted of his family hanging out at the local state park while Herb and I worked together. That was about two or three weeks, a relatively short time. But I built stuff and he tried it out and at the end of that period he had a couple of tapes of interesting stuff and the two of us together had the basic ideas for a modular analog synthesizer. What I'm sure I came up with for Herb at that time were two voltage-controlled oscillators and one voltage-controlled amplifier. As for controls, I'm not sure. Maybe we used doorbells. I don't think we even had a keyboard at that time. He was perfectly content to set this thing up to make a sound, record that sound, and then splice it into his tape music. That's how everyone else was making tape music at that time.[3]

The result was a piece of music for demonstration purposes (*Jazz Images* by Deutsch) but no real system to play it on. Moog continued his work, and by the end of the summer he had his first complete prototype ready. He wrote a paper entitled "Voltage-Controlled Electronic Music Modules" and was invited to present it at a convention of the

The earliest commercially available Moog Modular Synthesizer, 1965. Photo courtesy of Roger Luther, Moog Archives.

Audio Engineering Society (AES) that fall. The prototype that Moog eventually provided Deutsch consisted of a module with two voltage-controlled oscillators and two voltage-controlled amplifiers triggered by two keyboards.

After Moog took his "little box of stuff" to the AES in October 1964, the secret was out of the bag. He accepted his first orders at that convention and things began to move ahead gradually. The early adopters were individual composers who wanted to have the synthesizer for their personal use. Moog's first production model was sold in the spring of 1966 to Alwin Nikolais, director of the Nikolais Dance Theatre, who composed many of his own scores on tape. His next model went to Eric Siday, a New York composer of music for radio and television commercials and a competitor of Raymond Scott. In 1967, Moog officially christened his product the "Moog Modular Synthesizer."

The earliest Moogs consisted primarily of oscillators and amplifiers. The design was still in flux, and after another year or so Moog began to incorporate other kinds of audio modulators. Many of these devices were developed in response to requests from interested composers. Vladimir Ussachevsky of the Columbia-Princeton Electronic Music Center contacted Moog very early on with a specific request:

I still remember the letter, asking us to build what amounted to two volt-age-controlled amplifiers, two envelope generators, and two envelope fol-lowers. He gave the specifications for all of these things. The specifications for the envelope generator called for a four-part envelope. Attack, initial decay, sustain, and release. That way of specifying an enve-lope is absolutely standard in today's electronic music. That came from Ussachevsky's specification. Ussachevsky wasn't interested in a keyboard. He had this rack with the six modules that I just mentioned and for a long time that's how the Columbia-Princeton Electronic Music Center did their envelope shaping. In some of the pictures taken in the late '60s you can see that piece of equipment right in the middle right above the mixing console.[4]

Keyboards were not the only controller developed by Moog at the time. He also designed a ribbon controller consisting of a teflon-coated thin metal band that was played by touching the finger up and down its length. By sliding the finger, you could create glissando effects not unlike those of the Theremin, except of course you might have an entire bank of oscillators at your command instead of just a single, relatively pure waveform.

Another composer who provided Moog with many suggestions was Wendy Carlos. Carlos was already a veteran of the Columbia-Princeton Electronic Music Center that Ussachevsky managed, but her musical interests were not in the experimental sounds that represented most of the output of the studio. She later recalled, "I thought what ought to be done was obvious, to use the new technology for appealing music you could really listen to. Why wasn't it being used for anything but the academy approved 'ugly' music."[5]

Carlos had experimented with tape and instrumental pieces much in the manner of Otto Luening, but ultimately became interested in explor-ing the electronic realization of traditional musical forms. Having worked at the Columbia-Princeton tape music studio, she became prac-ticed in the traditional methods of constructing music track by track, using tape recorders, oscillators, and tape splicing. She was not a fan of the RCA synthesizer and did not use it to compose her electronic music of that time. Carlos explains, "I didn't care for it as an approach for doing my music any more than the punch cards that you had to use on the earliest computer music, which I also played with. That was before the days that computers were tied to controllers of any kind. You had to type a note list, a timbre list, an envelope list, a conducting list, and then all of those things got ground together into very mechanized, stilted, pseudo-performances that just drove me up the wall. It seemed that both of those techniques were sadly lacking."[6] She saw in Robert Moog an attentive inventor whose synthesizer had the potential of greatly simplifying the entire process. Moog remembers that "every time we visited her there was not one but a whole handful of ideas."[7]

During the period from 1966 to 1968, Moog pounded the pavement to get the word out about his new instrument. As an engineer, he frequented professional conferences and gave demonstrations of his equipment. He only had three salespeople, stationed in New York, Los Angeles, and London. The Moog synthesizer had begun to appear on commercial records, but trying to pinpoint which album was released first is not easy. Less puzzling is knowing *who* played the instrument on these first recordings. Musician Paul Beaver was Moog's West Coast sales representative. Being one of the only people who knew how to set up and perform on the Moog meant that he was often recruited to sit in on recording sessions for other people.

Because of Beaver, the very first commercial recording featuring the Moog synthesizer appears to be *Zodiac Cosmic Sounds* by Mort Garson (Elektra EK 4009, mono, EKS 74009, stereo, 1967). It came about in a most serendipitous way. Moog recalls:

> We went out to California to the Audio Engineering Society convention in April 1967. It was at the Hollywood Roosevelt Hotel. It was the first time we had ever been out to the West Coast. At that time, believe it or not, the Audio Engineering Society in Los Angeles was a very small show. Hollywood was sort of a backwater of New York. How things have changed. This was the very first synthesizer we had shipped west of the Rockies. We had arranged for a representative to sell these things on our behalf out there. He invited all of the session musicians that he knew to come down to see this thing. That began a whole wave of interest out on the West Coast. One night during that show, we took the modular synthesizer to the recording studio where they were working on *Zodiac Cosmic Sounds*. Our representative, Paul Beaver, produced the sounds, turning the knobs and hitting the keys. If you can get a hold of that album the very first sound on it is ooooaaaahhh—a big slow glissando.[8]

Apparently every strange instrument found within a fifty-mile radius of Los Angeles was used in the same recording session. With the release of *Zodiac Cosmic Sounds*, the Moog entered the pantheon of exotic instruments being plundered to make "head music," a commercial vein of mondo-exotica from the psychedelic '60s.

Beaver was also recruited later in the year for a couple of other albums. The first was by percussionist Hal Blaine for a wild album that he produced called *Psychedelic Percussion*. Beaver played the Moog and the "Beaver Electronics System" on this psychedelic exotica album. He also contributed Moog and Clavinet sounds to an album by vibraphonist Emil Richards called *Stones*.

Few people understood how the sounds on *Zodiac Cosmic Sounds* were being made. It was more than a year later that a curious little classical music record released by Columbia Records resulted in the smash success needed to propel the Moog synthesizer into the public's consciousness. The album was Wendy Carlos's *Switched-On Bach*.

Wendy Carlos and the Exploration of Musical Consonance

Her name is forever linked with the early Moog synthesizer. Her album *Switched-On Bach*, released in late 1968, became the top-selling classical music album at that time. Her warm and sparkling electronic interpretations of Bach's keyboard music singlehandedly inspired such interest in music synthesizers that a new industry was launched overnight. She dragged the synthesizer by its patch cords out of the chilly atmosphere of academic electronic music studios into the spotlight of public awareness. It was exciting, it was fun, it was hard work, and it was trend-setting. Yet Carlos would probably trade that notoriety in a minute for a different place in music history—to be remembered as the consummate composer that she is. Wendy Carlos brought *consonance* back to electronic music. "I tried to avoid gratuitous obsession with only dissonance. I tried to make music that was not ugly."[9] Many other composers were avoiding consonance at any cost, along with the regularity of rhythm, melody, and counterpoint that came with it. For them, atonality had a strong bias toward dissonance.

Carlos is part physicist, part musician, part composer, part philosopher, and part stargazer. While an undergraduate at Brown University, she pursued a crossover major that integrated music and physics. Her interest in astronomy has never waned, and for many years she has traveled the world photographing total eclipses of the sun.[10] As a graduate student, she studied music at Columbia during the heyday of the Columbia-Princeton Electronic Music Center, circa early-to-mid-'60s. But she was a harmonic composer trying to survive in a dissonant world. Serialism was the rage at Columbia and most other university music schools, and she found it difficult to focus on what she liked best: music with classical elements of melody, harmony, structure, and rhythm. She recently recalled:

> When anything I tried to do had anything like a melody or a recognizable
> chord progression or the same meter in three measures in a row, it was all
> considered demeaning and laughable and not nearly serious enough
> because it wasn't designed to be profound and befuddling to the average

Wendy Carlos, October 1986, with her two Synergy keyboards. Her left hand is operating the instrument's fader knob, which she uses to shape the notes being played by the right hand. Photo by Vernon L. Smith © Copyright 2001 Serendip. Used with permission.

person. I tried to follow Debussy who said, "I do what pleases my ear." Rules be damned, effectively. I think the established composers were just too much in love with their abstract systems to consider that the music coming out of it was, by and large, fairly forgettable and kind of hateful. That music was created with a lot of arrogance and pomposity. And this attitude pretty much wrecked my ability to have a serious music career.[11]

That such a talent could be so stifled is not unusual in the high-pressure, ego-driven halls of academia. Rather than be subsumed by the system, however, Carlos struck out on her own. She sensed an opportunity for someone with her musical imagination and know-how in the then-emerging field of electronic music. Having heard of Robert Moog's early synthesizer work, she got in touch with him and quickly became one of his more ardent and collaborative customers. She created an electronic music studio in her New York City apartment and outfitted it with early Moog Modular components, many of which were built or modified according to her specifications. She has always been technically skilled with electronics and has designed and soldered her own circuits and equipment as needed. She built her own eight-track tape recorder, a radical piece of hardware at the time considering that even the Beatles were still using four-track machines in 1967. She is a composer-inventor in the most modern and generous sense, seeking technology to play the music she hears in her head. If the appropriate technology has not yet been invented, she is not opposed to designing it herself or working with others who can.

For many months, Carlos had been working steadfastly with Moog's equipment to lay down her interpretations of Bach's keyboard music. The process was complicated by the fact that the Moog was a monophonic instrument. Playing two or more notes at the same time to construct even the simplest chords required multitracking, synchronization, and impeccable timing. The original Moog keyboard was not touch-sensitive, which would have made her performance of Bach that much more difficult to assemble. A little-known fact is that Carlos commissioned Moog to build two touch-sensitive keyboards for her. Each key rocked mechanically on a small vane and optical sensors to detect the velocity and depth of a key being depressed.[12] According to Carlos, the keyboards were impossible to play rapidly. "I had to clatter away slower than [at] actual speed. You could never play faster than moderato. Sixteenth notes at a good clip? Forget it!"[13]

It was no accident that Carlos chose to interpret Bach on her landmark album. Knowing the limitations of the synthesizer, she chose a body of classical music that seemed ideally suited to the new instrument. Bach's keyboard music is highly structured and rhythmic, mathematical in its complex of interweaving, contrapuntal lines of notes. The music was originally intended for the organ and harpsichord, two instruments for which touch-sensitivity on the keyboard was nonexistent. Not involving any other orchestration, the Bach keyboard works could be transcribed "as is" directly to the voltage-controlled synthesizer. But many timbral decisions were made. Carlos added expression to her performance by using the touch-sensitive keyboard, but also through the judicious application of timbre and modulation changes.

She explained her basic approach to transcribing Bach keyboard music:

> The Moog wasn't all that elaborate. There were three to six oscillators,
> and you adjusted them to track the octaves. You would pick a wave shape
> from the four available: sine, triangle, pulse wave, and sawtooth. There
> was a white noise source, and a filter to reduce the high end of the wave
> to make it sound more mellow, to add resonance, or take out the bottom.

Wendy Carlos' Custom Moog Synthesizer, late 1968. Patch cords in abundance, this is what Carlos' Moog looked like at the end of the *Switched-On Bach* sessions. This photo shows the two custom-made touch-sensitive keyboards as well as her home-made pullout mixing board postioned below them. Tape recorders are to the left of the instrument, including an 8–track Ampex machine that she assembled from an assortment of used parts and home-built components. Photo © Copyright 2001 Serendip. Used with permission.

> Then there were envelopers that came from Ussachevsky's ideas: attack time, decay, sustain, and release [abbreviated as ADSR]. Set the thing to ramp up at some rate: slow for an organ or fast for a plucked string. Make it decay immediately for a harpsichord, or sustain for a piano. Have the final release-time based on the need; short and dry, or longer for the vibrating body of a cello or drum. Easy.[14]

In addition to her custom-built Moog, Carlos used a stereo Ampex 440B tape recorder, a homemade eight-track tape recorder,[15] a homemade varispeed box, a homemade voltage-controlled oscillator, and a homemade mixing panel. The equipment was all housed in her downtown apartment studio in New York City.

The Moog was sensitive to temperature fluctuations and frequently went out of tune during Carloss' *Switched-On Bach* sessions. This made the multitracking process of recording anything tedious. "You would adjust the tuning, play a phrase, then check the tuning again. If OK, continue. Otherwise, go back and do it again."[16] Chords were created by recording one part per track and synchronizing them, "which was particularly challenging." For contrapuntal melodies, a slight error was allowable in the Sel-Synching (synchronization) of individual lines.

Columbia Records didn't expect much from *Switched-On Bach*. It was good timing in that it fit with Columbia's "Bach to Rock" sales campaign at the time. At the time of its release, the record was one of three new Columbia albums being promoted. Another was *In C* by Terry Riley, which was part of the Columbia Masterworks, Music of Our Time series produced, interestingly enough, by electronic music composer David Behrman. The third album was the one that was expected to be the biggest commercial success of the three, a rock album called *Rock and Other Four Letter Words,* by two rock journalists, J. Marks and Shipen Lebzelter. The latter featured a collage of free jazz and psychedelic music intermixed with snippets of interviews with rock notables including Brian Wilson, Jefferson Airplane, Tim Buckley, Ginger Baker, and a host of others.

It was one of those legendary press parties that people still talk about, held at Columbia's famous 30th Street studio in New York. Carlos dropped in to make a brief appearance, "grabbed a press kit and snuck back out."[18] Robert Moog was asked to demonstrate the synthesizer:

> I remember there was a nice big bowl of joints on top of the mixing console, and Terry Riley was there in his white Jesus suit, up on a pedestal, playing live on a Farfisa organ against a backdrop of tape delays. *Rock and Other Four Letter Words* went on to sell a few thousand records. *In C* sold a few tens of thousands. *Switched-On Bach* sold over a million and just keeps going on and on.[19]

Working completely outside of the institutional world of electronic music, Carlos first made her mark in the upper echelons of commercial music, creating several albums for which she transcribed and reorchestrated keyboard and orchestral music of Bach and Beethoven and others. She also composed exquisite original movie music for Stanley Kubrick's *A Clockwork Orange* (1971) and *The Shining* (1980), and then Disney's computer-animated *Tron* (1982). By 1980, following the completion of *Switched-On Brandenburgs* (1979), Carlos was beginning to move from the Moog to other synthesizers, particularly digital instruments. After ten intensive years of analog synthesizer experience coaxing sounds out of the Moog, she and her producer, Rachel Elkind, did some serious homework before considering digital synthesis. They

Wendy Carlos on Technology and Composing Music

I don't feel that a great art can really be approached *only* intuitively or only by being synthesized directly by rule. I think it's both the left and right hemispheres—I'm being a little stereotypic. Both of those sides of one's mind have to be brought together in a kind of a truce for really in-depth art to come out of a human being.

It's a combination of those two things, and the interface has to reflect that and the technology that you use has to reflect that—just as they reflected it with the traditional symphony orchestra. I come from that background. I trained as a classical composer for symphony orchestra and I know that whole world very well. I am comfortable notating, and notating is an excellent tool for making larger pieces of music that are bigger and more intricate than you can hold in your head as if you were just writing a song. In the end, it is going to be a combination of different modes of thinking and working that will come together in the particular piece that you are doing. Hopefully, each time you set out again you will shake the contents up and try not to just fall back into duplicating the same path that you took the last few times so that your music will have something original as much as the originality is in you. I don't think you can pretend originality. Either you tend to be a fairly original person or a fairly nonoriginal person. But let's try to be good first and not worry about the *original* or *different* or *new*. I think too many people are tied up with those terms. They are the buzz words that seem to have the commerce behind them. But "good" is really the word that will make your career have any longevity. You should try to be as good as you possibly can be with the instruments you use, whether they are an orchestra or string quartet, pianist, or singer, or some variation of synthesizers, and it doesn't matter whether it's digital or analog.

Digital does make it a little easier to dig a little deeper with precision that an analog might not have. With the ability to save things—and while I work I do save a great many of my steps along the way—you can almost always go back and reconstruct at least the general drift of what was happening while producing these steps. That includes the timbres. It includes the rhythmic patterns and melodies and harmonies and interesting tunings and orchestrational ideas. It's the whole gamut. All of those things come together. It isn't only one. There are clusters of many parts.[17]

visited Bell Labs in the mid-'70s. They tried the Fairlight CMI, which Carlos described as being "sample-playback-oriented, quite limited at the time. It was only playing back a single sample at a time. You couldn't filter it. You couldn't merge samples. You couldn't put them together in a key-map. It was very limited."[20] At Dartmouth, they played with the early Synclavier. Carlos thought it was too expensive and "architecturally kind of thin." She explained, "What was thin wasn't the sound. The distinction here is that you could sample with it and get very rich timbres if they were rich samples. Architecturally, it just had four layers that could either be an oscillator pair or a sample. That's not enough. It did not have much meat on the bones for advanced synthesis, additive and complex."[21] An engineer was hired to build a digital synthesizer to her specifications, but that experiment became too expensive to continue: "It was an amusing, deep device, but we didn't have the money or the staff to develop it further, or market it. It's foolish for a composer to try to do that on his or her own."[22]

Of all the digital synthesizers being developed at the time, she took a liking to the one made by Digital Keyboards Inc. Their first model was the General Development System (GDS), then came the less-expensive Synergy. In evaluating musical technology, Carlos's standards are high:

> The GDS/Synergy was a machine I got very deeply involved with in 1981, my first significant involvement with a digital machine. It is still superior in certain areas to the machines that have come out since. . . . No one else has bothered to do some of the things the Synergy could do. Yes, others have done it quieter, with greater fidelity, better high frequencies, and less hiss. But they have not developed the real difficult tasks, like full additive synthesis with complex modulation.[23]

Some of the "other" brands that also took up residence in her studio included the Yamaha DX models and later SY77, the Kurzweil K2000/2500/2600 digital keyboards, and the Korg Z1 for modeling several acoustic sounds. Carlos is apt to use any and all of these instruments in her current work, along with Digital Performer MIDI software from Mark of the Unicorn to orchestrate the many instrumental and purely electronic timbres of her music.

Carlos wants to get inside the sound when she composes. Much like Stockhausen, she *composes the sound itself*, often transforming it into rich "Klangfarbenmelodie"—a melody of changing timbres. Because of this, she is more interested in the precision controls of a synthesizer than the bells and whistles:

> You can't have a synthesizer that purports to be a great musical instrument if basically all it has are a few canned sounds. You try to find an instrument

that is fairly open-ended—like the old first synthesizers from the days of the RCA and eventually the Moog and the Buchla synthesizers—that they have enough things that you can control with enough degree of precision so you can begin to shape even a small palette according to your own taste and the desires of what you need for a particular context.

You are looking for a device that is of high quality—like a Steinway is an excellent-sounding piano and the Stradivarius is an excellent-sounding violin—but you need more than that. You also need it to be responsive to a human being's performance touch, to an orchestrator or instrument designer's needs on variations of timbre and have enough subtleties that the things that are weak about the instrument can be overridden by dint of willpower when you sit down to come up with a sound that might not be the easiest kind of sound for this device to make. There should be enough supersets of things you can get at that can allow one to come pretty close to the sound that's in your head, that you are going to look for. That's how I approach things. I usually have some pretty good ideas in my head of what I'm looking for and try to have enough versatility under the hood to let me get at it.

Finally, you need a good interface. You need something which is a little less tedious to get at all of those parameters than some of the early-'80s devices. There were some instruments that made it really very painful to get at a few basic properties. Manufacturers made it too difficult to bother with. I think that if you put too many hurdles in the way it ceases to be of much use.[24]

Carlos's major works over the years cover a lot of musical territory. What unifies them all is a remarkable sense of wonder, and joy. Even *Tales of Heaven and Hell*—with its dark sound palette and sense of foreboding—manages to emote a kind of unearthly mystery for its disembodied souls. She uses less-common tonal scales and often microtonal scales of her own invention. Timbre and tone color are constructed with the same care as a melody or counterpoint. It is music that springs from the intuition of a gifted composer.

The *Switched-On* series established a rut for Carlos that was difficult to escape from. After creating two albums of Bach interpretations, she was recruited by Stanley Kubrick to do much of the same for Beethoven in the soundtrack of *A Clockwork Orange*. The challenge facing Carlos in this case was monumental—creating convincing orchestrations of Beethoven's Ninth Symphony and other symphonic music. It was far different from transcribing small-ensemble music, and required a seriously altered palette of new sounds, which immersed her for the first time in one of her lifelong passions: the modeling and synthesis of acoustic orchestral instruments. Adding to the multilayered arrangements was the sound of a synthesized choir created by Carlos using a vocoder and many vocal performances by Elkind. This deft touch added a haunting humanity to the music that any first-time listener can attest to.

The soundtrack to *A Clockwork Orange* also gave Carlos a chance to leave the idiom of classical interpretation and compose some new music of her own. Most notable were two lissome works that were only sparingly used in the movie: *Timesteps* and *Country Lane*. These works established her as a composer with a new voice in electronic music. This was music of rhythm, harmony, melody, and a rich timbral palette: an exposé of movement and emotion. Put another way, it was highly classical in its roots but modern in its execution and imagination. It was approachable by the average person who might have previously been turned off by the always dissonant abstract sounds of most serious electronic music of the time.

Carlos's work immediately following *A Clockwork Orange* was yet another dramatic departure from Bach and Beethoven. *Sonic Seasonings* (1972), originally released as a double album, was nothing less than the record that started the movement in new age music that persists today: soothing harmonies, electronic meditations, and blends of music with the sounds of nature. It was Carlos's version of musique concrète without all of the melodramatic edits. She and Elkind combined electronic simulations of natural sounds created on the Moog with actual recordings of outdoor environments and quietly strung it together with musical themes that dissolved in and out of the sonic whole.

Several years after *Sonic Seasonings*, in 1980, Carlos embarked on a mission to upgrade her equipment so that she could more easily endeavor to create the music she was imagining. The digital technology provided by the Crumar GDS and Synergy instruments gave her the tools she needed to perfect synthesized replicas of orchestral sounds, putting the entire orchestra and many extrapolations at her fingertips. This required many months of methodical work with the programming of this digital synthesizer, but the results were stunningly robust and have been of use to her for many years.

Digital Moonscapes (1984) was completed using what Carlos dubbed the "LSI Philharmonic"—programs using Large Scale Integration circuits to churn out realistic-sounding orchestral instruments. This was the first digitally synthesized orchestra of any significance that a single composer could command.

When faced by critics who only view her achievement as that of replacing the human musician with a digital one, she scoffed by focusing rightfully on the promise of the resulting music:

But why do all this? Do we now have the "orchestra in a box"? Not really, considering the time and effort required to produce an orchestral recording in this manner. Rather, we should consider the reality of replication as only a measure of the quality of the synthesis, not as the ultimate goal. The goal ought to be providing the base on which to build new sounds with orchestral qualities that have not been heard before but are equally satisfying to the ear . . . look for the next steps using the experimental hybrid and imaginary sounds which have grown out of this work.[25]

Carlos's successive works have delivered on her promise of creating new and unimagined sounds that can be managed and played within the context of an orchestra. *Beauty in the Beast* (1986) and *Tales of Heaven and Hell* (1998) are two of the most fully realized works of electronic music ever to apply the discipline of the traditional symphonic composer.

Even though Carlos has been the consummate electronic tinkerer throughout her career, she has now reached a point where she is more interested in composing than finding yet another new big technology to embrace. "I don't think that any of the technologies have done anything but to tap the surface of a very rich vein that still lies, for the most part, buried. It will be explored in time, but not in my lifetime. That's fine. You would expect this to go on for decades, probably even a few centuries."[26] The dream of the general-purpose, do-anything synthesizer has never arrived.

Which brings us back to the way that one composes. Carlos composes instinctively, but with the know-how of a symphonic artist. She trusts her inner rhythms to sculpt a progression of sounds that moves ahead with energy and purpose.

Hers is a music of diatonic consonance, a welcomed concept that almost seems new amid the blare of field recordings, ear-splitting drones, and recontextualized sounds that make up so much of the universe of electronic music. The music of Wendy Carlos is experimental in its redrafting of scales and digital abstraction of acoustic sounds, yet familiar at its core of human sentiment and intellect. Synthesist Larry Fast, a collaborator of Carlos's, encapsulated her achievement: "By the time *Switched-On Bach* came out in 1968, Wendy Carlos proved to me that one person could use electronics to express a personal sonic vision."[28]

The ability to put it all in perspective is a defining force behind Carlos's career:

Music is something you are very lucky to be able to do. You are lucky to have this time in history when the field is morphing into something new and maybe a few of the little tidbits that you've been able to scratch out of the clay and the mud will have lasting effect. . . . You can laugh at those who call you a nerd or laugh at those who say you're obsessive because that's how it's done. There's no way to get around that without doing a poor or clichéd job of it. You have to know what you're doing. Feeling and thinking.[29]

Moog Goes Mainstream

Wendy Carlos was recognized as the first virtuoso player of the Moog. Her record had unusual appeal because, despite being electronic music, the album was palatable to nonclassicists and classicists alike. The public wanted to like electronic music. "We tried to do something with the medium that was musical and likable," says Carlos.[30] The genius of her musical performance far exceeded any curiosity about the instrument. In 1969, *Switched-On Bach* sold so many copies that it began to climb the industry sales charts for popular as well as classical music. It received a gold record in August 1969 from the Recording Industry Association of America (RIAA) for having sold more than 500,000 copies. In November 1986 it became the first classical music album to ever sell more than a million copies, giving it RIAA certification as a platinum record. *Switched-On Bach* also received three Grammies in 1969, for Best Classical Performance, Instrumental Soloist; Best Engineered Classical Recording; and Classical Album of the Year.

Glenn Gould plainly called Carlos's interpretation of Bach's Brandenburg Concerto No. 4 (included on the second Carlos album, *The Well-Tempered Synthesizer,* 1969) "the finest performance of any of the Brandenburgs—live, canned, or intuited—I've ever heard."[31] Because of the album's popularity, "synthesizer" suddenly became a household word. The interest generated by this one record was responsible for the burgeoning use of synthesizers in all music genres, from rock and jazz to classical and the avant-garde. The Moog was much in demand and every hip musician and commercial recording studio wanted one. "It was largely the musicians who were going crazy over it. A lot of rock people and jazz people wanted it. The commercial studios, therefore, jumped in as well."[32]

The basic studio model of the Moog Modular Synthesizer was assembled from a variety of independent components that could all be interconnected. The customer ordered whatever components they wanted. The modules were neatly mounted in walnut-framed racks that gave each a superbly professional and finished appearance. But it was conceivable that every model could have been different than the one ordered before it, because Moog's company was intent on keeping the system design as flexible and modular as the varied needs of his customers. For Ussachevsky at the Columbia-Princeton studio, a method of controlling envelopes was most appropriate. Another early Moog customer was composer Joel Chadabe (b. 1938) at the State University of New York at Albany. In 1965, Chadabe received a small grant to create an electronic music studio. He bought a small synthesizer, but, as he explains:

> We didn't have enough money for a power supply so the first year we ran it on a car battery. It wasn't really strong enough to make a lot of interesting electronic sounds, but I could make collages and automate the collages in different ways. In fact, I asked Bob to make a kind of keyboard-mixer for me. It was actually a series of gates. It had about eight keys. As I pressed each key the sound could pass through a gate that was controlled by that particular key.[33]

Two years later, in 1967, Chadabe received a larger grant and hand a much more ambitious dream:

> Then, I remember, one night about two in the morning, I got an idea. It was for a completely programmable studio. Now, at that time—it was about 1967—to have something "programmable" could barely have meant a computer. . . . I thought if we bought a computer to control this analog synthesizer it would probably take us a couple of years to develop software and learn about it and get it up and running. I wanted to be making music faster. So, I thought of an analog programmable studio and was lucky enough, in fact, to raise the money at the State University. . . . So, I got a grant for about $18,000 and ordered a synthesizer from the R. A. Moog Company. We went back and forth a little bit about the design of it and the specific design of the sequencers. This was doubtless the single largest installation of the Moog sequencers in the world. The whole studio was controlled by a digital clock. It was delivered in 1969. I worked with it pretty intensively for the better part of a year to figure out the best way of using it. In the course of that, I started to work with different kinds of automated procedures. From an analog studio point of view, this was a serious deviation from the norm. Normally people were playing it as a musical instrument with a keyboard. It was about that time that Wendy Carlos came out with *Switched-On Bach*, for example, where she was playing it like an organ or harpsichord. This was a different matter altogether. It was a question of setting up automatic procedures and then guiding them.[244]

Customizations aside, the basic components that could be ordered as part of the Moog Modular Synthesizer included:

- **A five-octave, monophonic keyboard for triggering voltage-control signals.** This could be set to operate like a chromatic keyboard using the twelve-tone scale or adjusted for alternate pitch scales and microtonal systems. Only one pitch could be played at a time, represented by the highest voltage (highest key) being depressed on the keyboard at any given time.
- **High-range voltage-controlled oscillators (VCO).** These had a frequency range of .01 to 40,000 Hz. The range of human hearing is only about 20 to 20,000 Hz. The Moog provided frequencies above (ultrasonic) and below (subaudio) this range that could be used as control voltages to modulate audible tones. The original Moog contained two VCOs as sound sources. Larger studio models such as the Moog 55 had up to seven VCOs. Each VCO was switch-selectable for sine, sawtooth, triangular, and rectangular (square/pulse) waves.
- **A voltage-controlled amplifier (VCA).** The VCA can be used to amplify any voltage. It was most often used in conjunction with an envelope generator to change the loudness of a waveform during an attack-sustain-decay sequence.
- **A voltage-controlled filter (VCF).** The voltage-controlled filter was one of the most cleverly engineered components of the system. Its design was so unique that several other synthesizer manufacturers copied it until Moog's company forced them to cease and desist. The ARP 2600 used this filter, as did synthesizers made by Crumar. Moog calls the filter "the only patent I ever got that is worth anything."[35]
- **An envelope generator.** It controlled the duration of rise, sustain, initial decay, and final decay of the output signal.
- **A ribbon controller.** This was available as an optional triggering device. It consisted of a Teflon ribbon with a wire on its underside, suspended slightly above a contact strip. Pressing the ribbon against the contact strip at any point along its length would close a circuit and producer a corresponding voltage. This voltage was used to drive oscillators. A dial was used to adjust the frequency range of the ribbon controller.
- **Patch cords, used to make connections between the different modules.** All of this was done using RCA phono jacks on the front panel of the instrument, resulting in a dizzying tangle of cables required to set up patches for the creation of a desired sound or modulation pattern.
- Popular accessories, included **spring reverberation,** a **ring modulator, pink** and **white noise generators,** a **vocoder** (analog voice processor), and **frequency shifters.**

The studio model of the Moog was not an easy instrument to learn. Using it required some fundamental knowledge of wave physics and the way in which voltage-controlled components behaved. Notating electronic music was itself impractical, and composers turned to patch-cord setups and diagrams of control-panel settings to document the often bewildering matrix of cable connections required to produce a set of sounds. Composers were sometimes given patch-panel diagrams, not unlike pages from a coloring book, upon which they could draw the various connections for any given setup of patch cords and dial settings. Using these drawings, a performer could reconstruct, sound by sound, the various steps needed to recreate whatever effects had been discovered. The safest bet for most composers, however, was to simply record everything that was happening on tape, then return later to assemble the finished work as a composite of prerecorded sounds.

Standardized operating instructions for patch-cord setups were not generally available, because each installation of a Moog system could have been configured differently. Composers worked by trial and error to explore the potential of the synthesizer. The composer's bible was the textbook *Electronic Music: Systems, Techniques, and Controls* by Allen Strange. This softcover manual was the first successful attempt to structure information about the newly evolving field of electronic music instruments with "pedagogical sensibility."[36] Strange was a practiced composer, musician, and electronic musician. Thirty years later, the first and second editions of his book are still highly valued as exquisitely detailed documents of the analog past.

While the Moog Modular Synthesizer was best suited for studio use, there was increasing demand for a portable version that could be easily taken on the road. In 1969, Moog's company set another precedent by introducing the Minimoog, a simple, compact monophonic synthesizer designed for live performance situations. With sales of about 12,000 units, this model became the most popular and widely used synthesizer of all time. Most of the patching between modules was preset (read "hardwired") and controlled by rocker switches and dials. The keyboard featured two unique performance controls that were widely imitated: the "pitch wheel" for bending notes, and the "mod wheel" for adjusting the degree of modulation of the output signal. The original Minimoog was in production until the late 1980s.

Robert Moog's original company went through several periods of transition, during which it was acquired twice by larger companies. Moog himself left Moog Music in 1977 to pursue his engineering interests independently. Working as a much sought-after consultant for many years, Moog eventually started up a new instrument-manufacturing

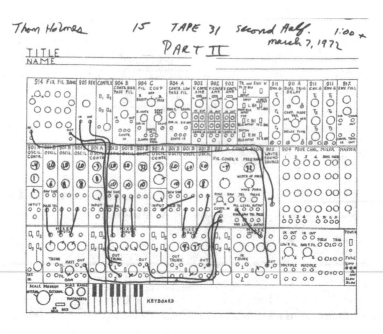

Moog patch diagram once used by the author for composing music on the Moog Modular Synthesizer. Worksheets like this were essential for documenting one's patch setup on the instrument. Photo by Thom Holmes.

company called Big Briar Inc., located in North Carolina. Big Briar is currently the maker of Moog-designed Theremins and a series of high-quality analog sound-processing modules called Moogerfoogers, comprising filters, ring modulators, and digital delay "stomp boxes." As of this writing, Moog's company had just completed the design of a new analog performance synthesizer—an updated version of the Minimoog.

The Buchla Synthesizer
In 1965, Morton Subotnick and Ramón Sender of the San Francisco Tape Music Center put out the word that they were looking for an audio engineer to help them design an instrument that could help them create electronic music. The studio at the time barely had more than half a dozen oscillators, filters, and tape recorders at its disposal. Engineer Donald Buchla came calling and the three of them set to work on the design of an innovative analog synthesizer.

Like Robert Moog and Hugh Le Caine, Buchla was onto the idea of voltage control as the most practical approach for producing a synthesizer that could be managed effectively by a composer. Unlike Moog, Buchla was a musician and had a strong, natural affinity to the needs of the composer. Moog's original synthesizer was designed strictly as a stu-

Buchla 100 synthesizer at the Mills College Center for Contemporary Music, early 1970s. Photo courtesy of John Bischoff, Mills College Center for Contemporary Music.

dio tool. "There was never a notion that a synthesizer would be used by itself for anything."[37] In contrast, Buchla, Subotnick, and Sender envisioned an instrument that could be used in live performance.

In 1963, at about the same time that Moog was also working on voltage control synthesizer design, Buchla created the basic parts for what would become the 100 series Modular Electronic Music System (MEMS). He used this work as a foundation for the instrument that he built for Subotnick and Sender at the SFTMC, which was then sold in 1966 as a commercial product.

Buchla emphasized two aspects of synthesizer design to accommodate the needs of composers. First, he offered great flexibility in the modification of tone color. Next, he provided a way to "program" a series of repeatable sounds using a pattern of repeating control voltages. This was the first sequencer available on a commercial synthesizer. Moog admired Buchla's work, recently stating that Buchla designed a system not only for "making new sounds but of making textures out of these sounds by specifying when these sounds could change and how regular those changes would be."[38]

Buchla began delivering prototype components of the synthesizer modules to the SFTMC "one by one as they were developed."[41] William Maginnis was one of the first people to compose a piece of music on the

Morton Subotnick and the Buchla Synthesizer

Subotnick's early electronic music recordings were the first to feature a voltage-controlled synthesizer, an instrument made by Donald Buchla. Subotnick's colleague Pauline Oliveros also used the Buchla Box, but she was a real-time composer working with whatever she could adjust on the synthesizer during the course of a piece. In contrast Subotnick worked meticulously with the sequencing features that he had helped Don Buchla design. His early recordings are primordial examples of sequencing. Oliveros recently made the following observation about Subotnick's work at that time: "Sequencing now is something anyone can do anytime, anywhere. But this was the first time that you could do it in this way. He certainly made a great use of it and advised Don in that direction, I'm sure. Because before, he was cutting and splicing tape."[39]

The release of Subotnick's *Silver Apples of the Moon* in 1967 pre-dated recordings featuring the Moog synthesizer by about a year. Subotnick was the acknowledged master of Buchla's fascinating, performance-oriented instruments, several of which were at the heart of many of Subotnick's most important works:

> The most important thing about these [Buchla's] instruments is that there is a kind of neutrality about the way things are designed and laid out, so that a composer can impose his or her own personality on the mechanism. For example, Don always disassociated a voltage-controlled amplifier from its control voltage source. That meant that the voltage source could be used for controlling anything.[40]

system. Called *Flight*, it was realized on the first night that the initial components arrived in 1965.

The solid-state MEMS was outfitted similarly to the Moog in its use of voltage-controlled oscillators, amplifiers, and filters. Instead of a keyboard, the Buchla employed various arrays of touch-sensitive plates. These capacitance-sensitive plates could each trigger sounds that had been manually programmed using patch cords on the control panel, or they could be set to emulate an actual keyboard tuned to the chromatic scale. The SFTMC instrument had two sets of touch-sensitive plates. Subotnick explains how they were used:

> One had 12 keys and you could tune it straight across the board. You could get a chromatic scale if you chose to. It had three control voltages

per position. The other one had ten keys and one output per key. We often used this one to control the amplitudes of concrète tapes during playback. You could literally play ten loops with your fingers.[42]

Subotnick became the foremost virtuoso of Buchla's synthesizer. Although the instrument was suited for real-time performance and improvisation, Subotnick's tendencies have always been toward more highly composed works. He is genuinely the composer's composer of electronic music. His pioneering work with the Buchla MEMS resulted in a series of landmark realizations that were released by Nonesuch Records: *Silver Apples of the Moon* and *The Wild Bull* (1968) were the first works of electronic music commissioned solely for release as long-playing record albums.

Buchla's instruments never experienced the runaway popularity that Moog enjoyed. Yet, by retaining control over his products and only manufacturing them in limited numbers, Buchla was able to remain independent and relatively unaffected by the synthesizer marketing wars that came and went along with many companies and products during the '70s and '80s. He is recognized today as a kind of musical engineering guru, manufacturing highly individualized and personal instruments that are dearly valued by their owners. Philadelphia composer Charles Cohen (b. 1945) is an original owner of a Buchla Music Easel, only about twenty-five of which were manufactured in 1971. He still uses it for live performance, remarking:

> The instantaneous and very light touch of the keyboard is part of what I like. The ability to smoothly and/or rapidly move around amongst and between all the basic electronic sound textures is the other big plus. While I no doubt could replicate the sounds with modern instruments, its playability and stability in the free-flowing, wide-ranging, and fast-moving genre of live performance group improvisation is very satisfying.[43]

The Buchla synthesizer has gone through several developments over the years. In 1970, he introduced the 200 series Electric Music Box, which became one of the centerpieces of the studios of the Mills Center for Contemporary Music. A year later, he built the first hybrid, digitally controlled analog synthesizer, the 500 series. In 1972, he introduced the Music Easel performance synthesizer, about twenty-five of which were made. During the mid-'70s, Buchla built several analog/digital hybrid instruments and a model with a keyboard (the Touché, 1978). By the mid-'80s, MIDI was so prevalent that Buchla shifted his attention from designing synthesizers to making unique MIDI-compatible controllers for musicians other than keyboardists. Then, in 1987, he introduced the model 700 with MIDI controls.

During the mid-'80s, Buchla turned his attention to new electronic instruments, the Thunder and Lightning, light-controlled wands for triggering MIDI signals using any MIDI-compatible synthesizer. He upgraded these in 1996 with the improved Lightning II. Then, in 1999–2000, he introduced the Marimba Lumina, a mallet-style MIDI controller with an onboard synthesizer. The mallets were programmable and triggered tones and control signals when they were "played" on a flat, touch-sensitive matrix of tiles configured like a marimba.

Other Commercial Synthesizers

Following the success of the Moog and Buchla systems by the late 1960s, many new manufacturers entered the market with variations on the modular voltage-controlled synthesizer. Japanese manufacturers in particular designed innovative and less costly technology. Among the instrument makers to join the synthesizer wars were ARP, Oberheim, Korg, Yamaha, Roland, EMS, and Crumar, some of which continue to make electronic music products to this day. Over the years, analog technology evolved into hybrid analog/digital technology, then to microcomputers with sound cards, and finally to purely digital performance instruments. One predominant trend at the time of this writing is the "virtual analog" instrument: digital keyboards using sound-generating algorithms and controls that emulate the manual control and tone color of classic analog instruments. Another is the popularity of software synthesizers and music created using only laptop computers.

Chapter 9

ONCE AND FUTURE INNOVATORS:
ROBERT ASHLEY AND GORDON MUMMA

In 1947, when he was just twelve years old, Gordon Mumma (b. 1935) took apart one of his father's record players and rebuilt it "so that it played records both forwards and backwards, and by attaching a rubber band around one of the gears I could vary the speed of playback." In 1949, he learned about the latest audio recording technology of the time from a neighbor who had in his basement a large studio for making 78 rpm records. While studying at the University of Michigan in Ann Arbor, in 1953, he was asked to compose music for the theater department. They had some of the first tape recorders Mumma had seen, and he proceeded to take them apart to see how they worked. Around 1955, after he'd dropped out of college, he had learned enough about electronics to begin designing his own circuits for making electronic music. "Motivated further by broadcasts of musique concrète from France and the early recordings of Les Paul and Mary Ford,"[1] making circuits and exploring electronic music became a "nonstop activity."[2] These were his first steps toward a long and distinguished career as a composer, performer, and circuit designer in the field of experimental music.

Robert Ashley was born in Ann Arbor, Michigan, in 1930 and was educated at the University of Michigan and the Manhattan School of Music. As a graduate music student in Ann Arbor, he also took some courses and worked for three years at the university's Speech Research Laboratories, where he could get access to the latest audio technology: "The materials of that science were the same materials that I was interested in in music. The technology of that science was the same technology that you would find inside the electronic music studio." Although Ashley was not formally enrolled in the acoustic-research program, the

187

head of the department offered him a doctorate if Ashley would stay on. He declined because he was most interested in music.[3]

Mumma and Ashley knew each other from their student years, both having been a part of Ross Lee Finney's graduate composition seminars. But it was through a sculptor named Milton Cohen that the two began working together. In 1957, Cohen had constructed his "Space Theater," a loft designed for performances of projected images and music. He asked Ashley and Mumma to produce electronic music for the events.

This collaboration between Ashley and Mumma led to the creation of the Cooperative Studio for Electronic Music in 1958. The "studio" consisted of rooms set aside for electronic music equipment in each of their two homes. Ashley's room was about as big as a bathroom. Each composer had his own equipment but shared resources as needed. They had about a half-dozen tape recorders between them, as well as oscillators, filters, mixers, and other audio processing circuits, many devised and built by the two. They were serious tinkerers in electronics.

The Space Theater was a loft converted by architect Harold Borkin (b. 1934) so that it could serve as a multimedia performance space. Borkin created a domelike effect in the loft by covering the corners of the ceiling with white reflective panels. People sat on the floor or lay down on pillows to experience the performances. Ashley explained:

> It basically consisted of a huge pile of various kinds of projection equipment and mirrors and things that rotated and did all that kind of stuff that put the light projections all around the room. Milton wanted to have live electronic music with those performances. He asked Gordon and me to work with him. We transformed his loft, the Space Theater, into a light projection and electronic music theater.[4]

The group produced live multimedia performances twice a week for seven years, from 1957 to 1964, always to capacity audiences of about forty people. Because it was before the time of commercial electronic music instruments and synthesizers, the music was created using instruments and equipment designed and built by Ashley and Mumma.

The following "script" was typical of the "simple, but dramatic" performance pieces presented at the Space Theater, this one being conceived by Ashley:

- Milton and his wife entered in white formal dress, as if at a wedding.
- There was an extended rubbing together of stones.
- A man was dragged on his back (by a rope) through the performance space.

Gordon Mumma and Robert Ashley, in Ashley's home where his half of the Cooperative Studio for Electronic Music was located. Ann Arbor, Michigan, 1960. Photo courtesy of Gordon Mumma.

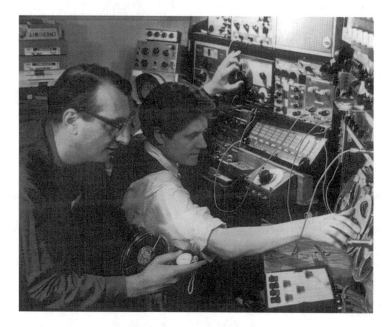

George Cacioppo and Gordon Mumma, at Mumma's part of the Cooperative Studio for Electronic Music, Washtenaw Ave, Ann Arbor, Michigan. 1963. Photo courtesy of Gordon Mumma.

- There were four steel wires drawn from the four lower corners of the space, meeting at its apex, with steel rings to be "thrown" on the wires toward the apex. All of this was treated with "enormous amplification of the wires—a kind of thunder and lightning effect."[5]

Mumma's effect of the amplified wires was later used in one section of his electronic theater composition *Megaton for William Burroughs*, and his film score *Truro Synodicle* of 1962. Mumma and Ashley were two of the earliest composers to thoroughly explore the creation of live music using amplified small sounds, an idea that began with Cage.

In the world of the Space Theater, every theatrical piece was also conceived with an electronic music component. Every performance was live. The two composers would make use of tapes they had composed in their home studios, but these were always combined with live electronics. Most of the performances were about an hour and a half in duration, much longer than most tape compositions at the time.

Aside from Cage and Tudor and the Ann Arbor group, the only other performances of live electronic music in the United States at the time were the "Sonics" events produced by the founders of the San Francisco Tape Music Center beginning in 1961. These were held in a small electronic music studio in the attic above the San Francisco Conservatory of Music and attracted a loyal following who came to hear the early works of Riley, Subotnick, Sender, Oliveros, and Talbot. Many of their works involved the experimental use of tape delay and loops (see Chapter 5).

The swan song for the Space Theater came in 1964, although the group didn't realize it until after the fact. Italian composer Luigi Nono (1924–1990) invited Milton Cohen and the Space Theater troupe to perform during the music portion of the annual Venice Biennale performing arts festival. Ashley designed four pieces in the four-part manner of the Space Theater performances, and a number of Ann Arbor people came along to help out. Their performance space was a loft above the old La Fenice opera house. They did daily shows for five days. The event was a great success, except that they had trouble getting paid. The growing differences between the American and European avant-garde were punctuated one day by a conversation over lunch, which Ashley recalled:

> We were taken to lunch by Nono in a beautiful restaurant on the Grand Canal (where Nono was addressed by the restaurant workers as "Maestro"). It was the best lunch anyone had ever had. After the lunch, over coffee, Nono said to me, "May I ask you an important question?" Of course. "Is John Cage serious?" I said I thought so.[6]

Before they left Venice, Cohen quietly announced to his friends that he was done with the Space Theater and was going to return to sculpture. "Who could blame him?" says Ashley.

At the time of this writing, the only commercially available recording of music composed for the Space Theater is one of Gordon Mumma's compositions, an excerpt from the Venice production called *Music from the Venezia Space Theater* (1964).

The success of the Space Theater and a burgeoning community of performing artists in Ann Arbor provided the momentum to take their efforts to the next level. Beginning in 1961, composers Ashley, Mumma, Roger Reynolds (b. 1934), George Cacioppo (1927–1984), Bruce Wise, and Donald Scavarda (b. 1928) joined forces with the local Dramatic Arts Center of Wilfrid Kaplan to produce the first ONCE festival of contemporary music. They were joined by artists in other disciplines, including architects Harold Borkin and Joseph Wehrer, filmmaker George Manupelli, and painter-sculptors Mary Ashley and Milton Cohen.[7] Prior to the ONCE festivals, the only periodic showcase for new music had been in Darmstadt, Germany, and by the early '60s, those had become more of an aesthetic battleground than a showcase. Darmstadt was also institutional in its backing and those who managed it exercised judgmental control over the selection—and censorship—of works to be featured.

The ONCE festival, on the other hand, grew out of the devotion of its artist-performers and was sustained both by the efforts of Kaplan as the initial patron and by the tremendous public support that the series gained. Gordon Mumma explained:

> The ONCE festival happened because a community of artists took matters into their own hands. They extended their responsibilities beyond the limits of producing their art into the organization and promotion of their art before the public. In this process they simultaneously took advantage of the means of commerce, private and public patronage, and pedagogy. But for the most part they did this outside of the established avenues of artistic commerce, pedagogy and patronage.[8]

Even though the ONCE festivals took place in Ann Arbor, they existed without any support from the University of Michigan. Being outside of the normal avenues of commerce for the arts, it was difficult finding financial and other support for the festivals. Despite the fact that some of the participants were employed by the university, Mumma noted, "virtually all efforts at enlisting support from this institution precipitated resistance and animosity to the project. Applications and contacts with numerous foundations, continuously for more than six years, produced no responses beyond a growing file of polite, through some-times enthusiastic, fine-bond, raised-letterhead replies."[9]

Ashley recalled that one of their principal benefactors withdrew his support in 1965 because the festivals were getting too far-out: "He and his wife were amateur musicians who had friends in the University of Michigan music department, which I think it is fair to say was fero-ciously jealous of our success. I think his departure was under their influence."[10]

Contrary to its name, the festival did occur more than once and con-tinued to grow year by year, filling successively larger auditoriums. There were six ONCE festivals in all between 1961 and 1965 (two occurred in 1965, the final one being called ONCE AGAIN).

From the start, Ashley, Mumma, and Reynolds made an effort to attract European composers and conductors to the festival. They also opened their arms to influential jazz musicians who were exploring the outer reaches of that idiom. The concerts were an immediate interna-tional success, and a potent antidote to the musical dogma associated with Darmstadt.

The first ONCE festival took place in a two-hundred-seat Unitarian church in Ann Arbor and consisted of four concerts. The subsequent fes-tivals comprised four to eight performances spread out over a week or two, usually in February and March. According to Ashley, only one per-formance during the entire eight years had less than standing-room-only attendance. Apart from the festivals themselves, there were also year-round concerts and performances given by individual members of the collective, which came to be known as the ONCE group. The fame of the concerts eventually inspired similar events around the country, par-ticularly on college campuses.

The programs of the ONCE festivals featured the hottest new-music performers and musicians. Live and taped electronic music was at the heart of many performances. Twenty-nine concerts of new music were offered during the six ONCE festivals, including 67 premiere perform-ances out of a total of 215 works by 88 contemporary composers.[11]

The fourth festival was preceded by a publicity controversy that enraged the critics almost as much as the music itself did. Mumma recalled:

> Mary Ashley designed an accordion-folded, purple and white flyer that featured on one side the enormously detailed programs. On the other side was a photograph of the composers Ashley, Cacioppo, Scavarda, and myself, looking like the Mafia in drag, standing behind a voluptuous nude reclining on the lunch counter of a well-known local eatery called "Red's Rite Spot."

The appearance of this flyer created a small hysteria, and the Dramatic Arts Center called an emergency meeting. Suggestions that the flyer be withdrawn were overcome: the ultimate problem was obtaining further funds for reprinting it to meet the demand for souvenir copies. The extent of this flyer's success was indicated to me dramatically in New York City the following April. At the seminar following one of Max Polikoff's "Music in our Time" concerts, on which Ashley and I had just performed, the first question from the audience concerned the availability of autographed copies of the purple ONCE flyer.[12]

A list of the programs themselves shows that the history of the ONCE festivals evolved from that of mostly musical performances in a normal proscenium setting to more open-ended stagings including dancers, multimedia, and lighting effects. By the time Alvin Lucier took part in 1965, the musicians were beginning to mingle with the audience in the performance space for some pieces, as was the case with the first performances of Lucier's *Vespers* for an ensemble using small echo-location (pulse wave oscillators) devices called Sondols (*son*ar *dol*phin):

> I first did the piece called *Vespers* in Ann Arbor at the ONCE festival[13] in the ballroom at the graduate center. I wasn't anxious about it. I didn't know how it was going to play out. I needed to see the space and the performers. I had all these ideas. It was just a question about who was going to play the Sondols and what they would do. So, I designed the performance that afternoon for the space: "You go there"; "Somebody start here"; "Don't do this—do this." And so you make the piece. In all honesty to the music, you couldn't really plan it in advance because that was not the way it was. I don't know if I blindfolded them or not on this occasion. I actually made up some of the performance during the performance, if you can imagine. I had leather shoes on and the floor was made of wood. The lights went down and I walked around the space and you could hear echoes from my feet. Now most people wouldn't pay attention to that because it was just walking. I opened the drapes on the windows to get a more reverberant space. I was *preparing* the space, actually. I was giving the audience clues as to what might be going on. Everybody knows if you open the drapes there's more reverberation. Then I had stacked some chairs up. I deployed some of those as obstacles. I think there were even potted plants that I put as obstacles. It was kind of like someone preparing for a dinner party. I went around and rearranged some of the furniture.
>
> I had four players. They were in four parts of the room. I instructed them to try, by means of hearing the echoes that came back to them, to move as if they were blind. And that they should only play when it made

sense to. To hear the echoes. That they shouldn't just play the instruments as instruments, they shouldn't decide to speed up or slow down for musical effect. That kills the performance immediately. It had to be based on survival and task. That was my score. This built the task into the performance. It was in the dark.[14] [Gordon Mumma adds that the performers were also blindfolded for this performance.][15]

In spite of the perennial ribbing of media music critics—many of whom enjoyed beginning reviews, as Robert Ashley recalls, with a line such as "Once is enough"—the ONCE festivals served as a major influence on the contemporary-music scene. Their successful run had a galvanizing effect on the experimental music community, bringing together American composers from both coasts and ensuring that the spirit of radical experimentation of Cage and Tudor would continue into the next generation. While it would be contrary to its spirit to suggest that all of this experimental activity formed a cohesive school, it did indeed propel several movements in new American music. Many of these artists from New York, San Francisco, and Ann Arbor shared similar challenges and a common purpose: to create something new and original in contemporary music that was a reaction against what had come before and what was being lauded by the European avant-garde. As Gordon Mumma reflects, "The origins of the jazz traditions occurred in the same way—collaborative and interactive. While the Darmstadt model established fences on musical creativity, jazz traditions and the ONCE festival example let things grow, without putting limits on creative innovation"[16]

The Cooperative Studio for Electronic Music came to an end in 1967 when both Mumma and Ashley moved on from Ann Arbor to continue their musical work elsewhere. In the nine years that they maintained their home studios, they completed more than seventy-five tape compositions.

The work of the SFTMC continued to evolve during this time as well, including instrumental and electronic performances using tape and live electronic music, theater and dance pieces, and visual projections. The ONCE and SFTMC groups developed an ongoing correspondence and shared many ideas related to their common experiences. Oliveros was invited to perform at the ONCE festival in 1965. In 1966 she returned to Ann Arbor with a new work written for the ONCE group called *C(s) for Once*. It was scored for trumpets, flutes, voices, organ, and three tape recorders, with one tape threaded through all three to modify the sounds of the live performers. This work led to some interesting collaborations in later years between veterans of both groups, including Oliveros's production of *Valentine* (1968), which was commissioned by the Sonic Arts Union of Ashley, Mumma, Behrman, and Lucier.

Leading Indicators for the Future: The Sonic Arts Union (Ashley, Behrman, Lucier, Mumma)

By 1966, Robert Ashley, Gordon Mumma, David Behrman, and Alvin Lucier had become well-acquainted because of their mutual collaborations and performances with John Cage, David Tudor, the Cunningham Dance Company (after 1966), and the instrumental performances of the ONCE festivals. With the festivals coming to an end, the four of them decided to join forces as a touring group, the Sonic Arts Group, later known as the Sonic Arts Union (1966–76).

The inspiration for doing this was clearly the success that Cage and Tudor had experienced by taking their music on the road. Lucier explained, "David Tudor really freed a lot of us. . . . That was a great stimulation—that you could design your own equipment, that you could find it at Radio Shack. You could configure it in certain ways and you could make your own work. That was very important."[17] What the world received as a part of this union were four very individual voices ready to break another set of sound barriers.

Each of the members of the Sonic Arts Union is still active in music today. In speaking to them individually about their work, it is clear that the Sonic Arts Union was an especially bright period in each of their remarkable histories. Behrman thinks that the unifying element behind their individual work was an interest in doing pieces "in which established techniques were thrown away and the nature of sound was dealt with from scratch."[18]

Forming the group was largely a matter of practicality. Some of the members had been receiving invitations to perform in Europe and elsewhere, but the expense of producing a concert on one's own would have made it economically impractical to accept such offers. By teaming up, they could pool their equipment and eliminate other costs by serving as both technicians and musicians. Because there was often little or no payment for such performances, the union served as a hedge against unnecessary expenses.

The Sonic Arts Union toured North America and Europe into the early '70s. Even though they pooled their equipment, they didn't often collaborate on compositions except by helping each other out during performances. Each composer would bring a piece to a concert and the others would act as musicians by manning the equipment. "A Sonic Arts Union concert was about 1,000 miles of wire and all these little boxes that plugged into each other," recalls Ashley.[19]

Sonic Arts Union performance, Sveriges Radio, Stockholm, 1971 May 4. From left: Gordon Mumma, Alvin Lucier, Robert Ashley, David Behrman. Photo courtesy of Gordon Mumma.

The Sonic Arts Union was happening during a period of transition for each of its members. Behrman was nearing the end of a successful period of record producing for Columbia Records, during which he added the names of Cage, Oliveros, Babbitt, Lucier, Reich, Riley, Pousseur, and other avant-garde composers to the repertoire of artists represented on the Columbia Masterworks label of classical music recordings. Even as he worked with the Sonic Arts Union, he was busy touring with the Cunningham Dance Company and assisting John Cage on several projects. By the end of the union's run, he had become codirector of the Center for Contemporary Music at Mills College with Ashley.

At the time of the formation of the Sonic Arts Union, Lucier had been teaching at Brandeis University (1962–69), where he conducted the Brandeis University Chamber Chorus, devoting much of its time to new music. His own work was commissioned by the Cunningham Dance Company in 1970. During his stint with the Sonic Arts Union, he took a teaching post at Wesleyan (1970), where he continues to work today.

Ashley and Mumma had concluded the ONCE festivals in 1966 in Ann Arbor and were moving on to wider vistas. Mumma became increasingly active as a musician for the Cunningham Dance Company, working closely in the design and performance of electronic music with David Tudor. In 1970 he collaborated with Tudor on the design of the audio system for the Pepsi pavilion at the World's Fair in Osaka, Japan. Mumma calls his association with the Sonic Arts Union as "one of the two most nourishing artistic situations I've ever been in," the other being the Cunningham Dance Company.[20]

Ashley took an entirely unexpected turn. One morning in April 1968, he decided to stop composing. He made this decision as if it were going to last forever. His reasons were many, including the economic pressures of trying to produce concerts while eking out a living with day jobs. With little money available for composers, he began to believe that "there was no *reality*" to his dreams.[21] He had also been deeply discouraged by one of the last performances of the touring ONCE group, an event during which the audience physically assaulted the musicians:

> The performance we did at Brandeis was a beautiful piece called *Night Train*. It involved, among a lot of other things, giving the audience something when they came in. The idea of the piece was that we were aliens and trying to make friends with the Earth people. So, everybody who came in along with their ticket got something edible, like an apple or an onion or a fish or a loaf of bread or something like that. Somehow in the middle of the performance the audience kind of lost it and started attacking us. Of course, the way humans would attack aliens. They literally attacked us. They were throwing things. The main problem that I had was that they were throwing things at the performers on stage and a lot of the things were dangerous to throw. Besides the hard pieces of vegetable, like an onion, we were passing out lights. Harold Borkin had a group of ten or so students there who were soldering one end of a flashlight bulb to one end of a battery and then soldering a wire to the other end of the battery. When the audience started throwing those I knew we were in deep trouble. We got through the performance but it was very ugly. I didn't like it at all. It was 1967 or '68. That's the only time we ever performed the piece. It was very discouraging and I stopped composing soon after that. I had had enough. And I didn't compose music for another five years or something like that. It was really extremely discouraging.[22]

Ashley didn't want his music to only "end up in his filing cabinet." He stopped composing, but was determined to stay involved in music and find a way to further the cause. The Sonic Arts Union gave him the chance to continue performing with like-minded individuals. He also took the job of director of the Center for Contemporary Music at Mills College in 1969 and revitalized one of the most influential music programs in the country during a time when several of its founding members—most notably Subotnick and Oliveros—had left for other opportunities.

Ashley, of course, returned to composing after about five years, the discouragement of audience attacks behind him and several fulfilling years with the Sonic Arts Union and Mills College under his belt. Ultimately, it was Mimi Johnson who challenged him by saying, "Well, if you are a famous composer you've got to compose music." Which is what he did by inventing the field of contemporary opera for television with *Music with Roots in the Aether* (1975).

One can only describe the music of the Sonic Arts Union by understanding the interests and tendencies of its four composers. If Cage represented the first wave of live electronic music production—the use of magnetic tape and the amplification of small sounds—then Ashley, Behrman, Lucier, and Mumma surely represented four important extensions of that early electronic music. There is no greater testament to the gravity of their work than to realize that the four paths explored by these innovators were the leading indicators of musical practices that are still with us today. Witness, if you will, their chosen specialties in new music, and you will have no difficulty relating them to the current state of new music performance.

Gordon Mumma (b. 1935). Extended Cage's use of tape and amplification of small sounds to the real-time, adaptive electronic processing of sounds using acoustic and electronic sources. Most of this work has been done with circuits that he builds himself. He and Tudor were responsible for creating the performing culture of a table full of black boxes and wires, of interconnected components that can be mixed and modulated at will. Mumma says, "In spite of my fairly solid education in the 'Euro-American traditions,' I found no conflicts or contradictions in my developing work with electronic music, though most of my teachers, and a good number my 'traditional' peers, thought I was 'off the track' or downright crazy."[23]

Robert Ashley (b. 1930). Explored narrative music—storytelling music—for new media, including television and live performance with multimedia elements. In his words: "I thought and still think that television is an ideal place for music. Especially for opera. It hasn't happened in my lifetime except in my work. But I think it will eventually happen. I think that it is inevitable that there will be operas for television. . . . The television medium allows for a new kind of opera because it eliminates all of that machinery of the opera stage that slows an opera down. You can write an opera that goes as fast as any sitcom."[24]

Alvin Lucier (b. 1931). Advocated music designed around simple acoustic processes, exploring the real-time processing of sounds in resonant environments. Lucier notes, "So often, when I'm in school and teaching, I try to get students just to think clearly about something. . . . The first papers they write are very confusing. They hear this, their opinions are confusing. Then I say that I'm not interested in your opinions. I say that you've got to have perceptions, not opinions. Everyone's got opinions. But perceptions. What are you hearing? So that is why my work is simple."[25]

David Behrman (b. 1937). One of the earliest adapters of semiconductors and then microcomputers and software in the creation of interactive, responsive computer music systems. Behrman says, "When I think back, I don't know, there hasn't been any generation of artists who have lived through an experience like this. Going from tubes to transistors to chips to microcomputers to very, very, powerful, tiny computers. It's never happened before. God knows what the future holds."[26]

The following works are representative of the composing tendencies of these four individuals, especially during their years together as the Sonic Arts Union.

Adaptive radiance: *Hornpipe* **(1967) by Gordon Mumma.** *Hornpipe* is a solo work in which Mumma played the waldhorn and French horn, at first unmodified, working from four predetermined types of sound materials: sustained tones; natural reed horn; articulated reed horn; and staccato reed horn. On his belt was a "cybersonic console," a black box containing adaptive resonant circuitry of his own design. Mumma noted, "The cybersonic console monitors the resonances of the horn in the performance space and adjusts its electronic circuits to complement these resonances."[27] This can be likened to controlled feedback, but the feedback was first run through additional circuitry where it was further modulated and articulated prior to being made audible through loudspeakers.

Because of its dependence on the resonant behavior of the performance space, each rendering of *Hornpipe* is different. It is improvisatory in that the musician must concentrate on what is happening and react to the electronic sounds being triggered by his own playing. The first part of the piece allows the player and cybersonic console to "train the space," so to speak, learning how sounds made with the horn will be electronically modified. Mumma then provides guidelines for what should follow this learning stage: horn playing with electronic sounds; long unmodified sequences of unmodified cybersonic replies; and electronic sounds "articulated directly by horn sounds."

Robert Ashley: Assembling Stories and Music for Media

About *Dust* (1998), one of his recent multimedia opera pieces for voice, electronic music, video projections, and lighting effects:

By the time we got to *Dust* I had been working with the same ensemble—Jackie Humbert, Sam Ashley, Joan LaBarbara, Tom Buckner, and Tom Hamilton—for ten years. I knew them so intimately as musicians that it was very easy for me to imagine what it would sound like.

Technically, the way I do it is to compose the various sections. Then I send a rehearsal tape, which has just the basic orchestra elements in it, and the text to each of the performers before we all get together to rehearse. Then everybody comes right here to the sixth floor and we discuss the piece. We discuss all the aspects of how to do it and how to perform it and that kind of thing. By that time, Tom Hamilton and I have made the realization of the opera. Sometimes, I think probably even with *Dust*, I had the rehearsal tapes done before I had actually finished the orchestration. While the singers are rehearsing their parts at home with this rehearsal tape then Tom and I finish the orchestra here with the synthesizers and computers and computer programs that I use. So, when everybody gets together, we have everything except that we really haven't done it yet. Then we rehearse for a week or so and then do a performance.

The speed of English with music, to my taste, is so fast that the pitch range is usually not more than an octave. And the inflections, or the embellishments that we rehearse, are a hundred times as fast as in conventional opera. Those are all developed by the singers themselves. I send them the song with the harmonies and the rhythms and I send them a demonstration of how I do it. Then, when we get together, then I get the four different interpretations of my imagination based on what the four singers can do. It's a nice way of working for me because I get that personal quality of each singer in each song as opposed to the traditional way of doing opera.

The recording of *Dust* is made up of different parts of performances that we did at the Kitchen [a performance venue in New York]. When we performed at the Kitchen, we recorded the two so-called dress rehearsals. Then we recorded the five performances. We recorded those on eight-track tape. When we finished at the Kitchen I went through all of the performances and I picked the best performance for each of the sections. Then I processed each of the voices in addition to what was on the tape. Then Tom Hamilton came in and we made an assembly on the computer. He put a process on the whole thing, the orchestra and the voices, so that what's on the CD now are basically the performances at the Kitchen with the additional processes that were required to make it more like a studio version.

After listening to it a couple of times through, I finally narrowed it down to the last three performances. You know, the more we did it the better we got. So, it turned out that almost all the takes are from the last three performances. I think there is one exception.

I've always been interested in opera and I think that an opera should be as interesting as an Emmylou Harris CD. It should bring just as much pleasure as listening to a Marc Anthony CD. It should be the same experience of liking it and understanding the words and the words mean something. It doesn't change your life but it's a pleasant experience.[28]

Hot and cold running circuits: *Runthrough* (1967–68) by David Behrman. Long before the word "computer" became associated with any music by David Behrman, he was creating works that provided interactivity between the performers and the electronics. Behrman describes *Runthrough* as a piece that required no special performance skills other than the ability to turn knobs and aim flashlights, making this early work of interactive live electronic music as playable by non-musicians as musicians. It was one of Behrman's earliest experiments in electronic interactivity, pre-dating his landmark work with computer circuits by nearly ten years.

The piece required two to four players and was often performed by the Sonic Arts Union. Sound was generated and modified using home-made synthesizers that were manually controlled by dials and switches. One or two of the people would play those. Behrman described this equipment: "The homemade synthesizers, built into small aluminum boxes and powered by batteries, consisted of various devices that were not too difficult or expensive to build at that time—sine, triangle, and ramp wave generators, voltage-controlled amplifiers, frequency and ring modulators."[29]

Homemade "photocell mixers" were used to direct the sound to four or eight loudspeakers that were normally set up surrounding the audience. The light-sensitive mixers consisted of a flat panel with several rows of photocells. Aiming a flashlight at a photocell would pipe the sound of the synthesizers to one of the speakers. The two players assigned to the photocell mixer each used two flashlights. The mixer required a darkened hall, which added yet another dramatic touch to what must have seemed like a work of magic to some members of the audience.

Sounds would result from any combination of dials being turned, switches being flipped, and photocells being activated. Players generally felt their way along on this sonic beachfront, learning to work together to produce astonishing effects. The more practiced players, including the Sonic Arts Union members themselves, could propel the work along, "riding a sound" they liked in a kind of wavy unison.

The work had no score. It only consists of some circuit diagrams. But that hasn't deterred a couple of recent attempts to realize *Runthrough* with digital technology. Composer Mark Trayle, who is currently chair of the composition program at the California Institute of the Arts, was able to recreate the piece using digital audio software. His students worked on it and played it for Behrman while he was there for a residency. This encouraged Behrman to revive some of his other earlier interactive pieces: "I just did a revival of homemade synthesizer music with sliding pitches running in MAX MSP on a PowerBook. It sounds sort of the same. It's very easy to do. I mean it's not exactly the same. Then, of course, it can do a million other things that you couldn't do in those days."[30]

Ambience deflected: *Automatic Writing* **(1974–79) by Robert Ashley.** *Automatic Writing* was much talked about when it was released on record by Lovely Music Ltd. in 1979. Ashley wrote it over a five-year period after having just come back from his self-imposed exile from composing in the early '70s. He performed it many times in various formative stages with the Sonic Arts Union before finally committing it to disc.

Automatic Writing was frequently lauded as an early work of ambient music because of its quiet, tinkling sound. It consisted of forty-six minutes of music that was so quiet that you would miss most of it if you left your volume control at its normal setting. The underlying keyboard music that makes up a layer of the work's texture was so muted that it sounded like it was coming from another room. *Automatic Writing* was compared to minimalism because it was sparse and repetitive and had some of those other characteristics that are often thought to be minimalist. It was also called "text sound" composition because it included spoken dialogue. While all of those descriptions were superficially accurate, most attempts to assign *Automatic Writing* to a genre were unhelpful. They failed to notice that Ashley was pointing to a place up the road ahead. The piece was Ashley's first extended attempt to find a new form of musical storytelling using the English language. It was *opera* in the Robert Ashley way.

The basic musical material of *Automatic Writing* was the spoken voice, closely miked, uttering what Ashley characterized as "involuntary speech": random, seemingly rational comments that might not make sense at all, depending on the context in which they were heard. He was searching for the essence of character and narrative, of human emotion translated through language and sound into performance. This essence, this emotion, was not always communicated by words. The shape and quality of the voices, the level of amplification, and the musical accompaniment were all potent musical resources in *Automatic Writing*. Ashley was very aware of what he was up to.

Not long after the release of the first recording, he told me:

> In *Automatic Writing* I had become interested in the idea of characters in an operatic or dramatic sense. Of characters actually being manifested through a particular sound. I was fumbling around looking for ways I could work in an operatic sense that would be practical. I didn't want to start writing things that wouldn't be performed for twenty-five years without forming a group. So, I went toward the idea of sounds having a kind of magical function. Of being able to actually conjure characters. It's sort of complicated for me to think about it because I don't entirely understand it. It seemed to me that in a sort of psychophysical sense sounds can actually make you see things, can give you images that are quite specific.[31]

The piece evolved slowly over a number of years. All along, Ashley was aiming for four characters, four personalities to weave a sense of story and interaction. Two of these ended up being vocal, two instrumental. He first used some tape materials for the character part that was later replaced by the organ. Then he added the second speaker in the guise of Mimi Johnson, who acted like a "shadow talker." They staged it using live electronics and some reactive computer circuitry by Paul DeMarinis (b. 1948) so that they could interact electronically in real time. The idea to add the French-language reading came to him when he went to Paris for the premiere of *Music with Roots in the Aether*: "I felt this weird desire, which was totally unwarranted, to put a French translation along with the monologue. You can hardly understand the English, so to put a French translation—I don't know what made me do it. But I did it, and as soon as I heard that sound of the French translation I realized that I had three of the four characters."[32] That became the part read by Johnson in the final version.

After several years of development, Ashley was ready to produce a definitive recording of *Automatic Writing*. He set up the recording studio at Mills College one summer while everyone was on vacation so he could work totally alone. He recorded his own vocal part by himself, adjusting the recording level for the microphone just at the point of feedback: "The microphone was probably not more than an inch from my mouth. It was about as close as it could be. That was the core of the piece, that sound of the close miking."[33] He added the subtle and eerie modulations of the voice to complete the track for the first character, rendering most of the words he read incomprehensible. The other three characters were added later to complete the recording, with the help of Mimi Johnson and Paul DeMarinis. This brought the life cycle of *Automatic Writing* to a natural conclusion:

> I had the monologue itself with the electronics. I had the synthesizer accompaniment to that, the inversion of that. I had the sound of the French language. Then, I realized that I just needed a fourth character and finally I found it in that Polymoog part. So, those four characters had been performed in various different manifestations for a couple of years before I did the record. Then when I did the record the piece was over and I never wanted to perform it after that. I had finished it—I had found the four characters.[287]

Brainwave music and the chicken doctor: *Music for Solo Performer* (1964–65) by Alvin Lucier. This was the first piece of music composed for amplified brainwaves—and not the last, I might add. Lucier got the idea from research being done by physicist Edmond Dewan at the Air Force Research Labs in Cambridge, Massachusetts. With the aid of an electroencephalograph (EEG), Dewan's subjects were able to control the amplitude of their brains' alpha rhythms and transmit them to a teleprinter in the form of Morse code. In his adaptation of this idea, Lucier skipped the Morse code and worked directly with amplified brainwaves as a musical resource.

Music for Solo Performer was first performed on May 5, 1965, at Brandeis University. "The brainwave piece is as much about resonance as it is about brainwaves. In fact, it isn't very much about brainwaves," admits Lucier.[35] It was really about using the room as an acoustic filter, one of his earliest experiments in this area that has occupied his projects for many years.

At the time of this work, the phenomenon of high-fidelity stereo was making a big splash. Bose and KLH had just introduced high-quality suspension loudspeakers for the home. Loudspeakers were a critical element in the success of any work of electronic music. Lucier recalls, "When you think about the violin makers in Italy in the early eighteenth century—Amati and Stradivari—all the composers made pieces for those violins. We were making pieces for loudspeakers."[36] His idea was not only to generate sounds by amplifying the brainwaves, but to place the vibrating surfaces of the loudspeakers in contact with percussion instruments that would, in turn, make sounds of their own. Snare drums, gongs, and other small objects were used. They were placed underneath, on top of, or against the loudspeakers:

> For the snare drums, I put little loudspeakers right on the skins of the snare drums. For the gongs, I put the gongs mostly touching the edge of the speakers, either near or almost touching. I'm trying to make the connection between sympathetic vibration, which is a physical thing, and the next idea is the room as a speaker.[37]

The intensity of the brainwaves would increase as one attained an alpha state. The different percussion instruments responded to differing levels of intensity in the brainwaves. The vibrating, rattling, chiming, and buzzing sounds changed with the flow of the performer's mental state. A performance of *Music for Solo Performer* was a captivating experience. When performing it himself, Lucier generally sat at the center of the stage, alone in a chair, with electrodes attached to his head by a headband. Loudspeakers flanked him on either side, arranged within proximity of a multitude of percussion instruments. Except for his facial expressions, and the opening and closing of his eyes, there was no visible correspondence between the performer and the sounds being heard on the loudspeakers. Alpha waves became strongest when he closed his eyes and stopped when he opened them. The humming persisted as long as he could concentrate on forming alpha waves.

A radical experiment such as this cannot be without at least one amusing mishap, and *Music for Solo Performer* is no exception. David Tudor was preparing for a performance of the piece at the University of California at Davis in 1967. Lucier was not involved, and when it came time to set up the proper equipment, they realized that they needed a special amplifier, a differential amplifier. It so happened that the veterinary school on campus had such a thing and was more than willing to help. Composer Larry Austin was also taking part and retrieved one of his own loudspeakers and a stereo amplifier to complete the complement of equipment for the test. At the lab, there was a doctor who knew how to place the sensors for the detection of brainwaves, but he had only done it with chickens. He placed the electrodes on David Tudor's forehead. Tudor noted, "And it was fine, but . . . in Alvin's original version, you controlled the sound by closing your eyes. If you opened your eyes, then the sound would stop."[38] In the case of the chicken doctor, just the opposite was true: if you closed your eyes, the sound would stop. This was amusing, but unacceptable, so they repositioned the electrodes to the back of Tudor's head to see what would happen. Suddenly, they had signals of a much greater amplitude. They were so strong, in fact, that before too long the loudspeaker went up in a puff of smoke and caught fire. It was smoking from David Tudor's brainwaves, a backhanded compliment if there ever was one. Larry Austin had sacrificed one of his prized loudspeakers for science, but a successful performance was nonetheless given using other equipment.

The San Francisco Tape Music Center

The San Francisco Tape Music Center (SFTMC) is important not only because of the composers who worked there but also because its early history reflects the dilemmas faced by many American composers of electronic music in the early 1960s. There was no funding or institutional support for their efforts, making it necessary to pool their equipment, locate performance spaces, and raise funds for publicity on their own. The SFTMC is also unique among private American electronic music studios in that its success led directly to a sizable grant to become a part of Mills College. What had begun as a makeshift operation run by a handful of dedicated composers became one of the greatest success stories of any university-based electronic music studio in the world. After thirty-five years, it is still in operation as a vital part of the program of the Center for Contemporary Music at Mills College.

The artistic climate in San Francisco in 1961 was ringing with new ideas. A number of young composers, including Ramón Sender, Pauline Oliveros, and Morton Subotnick, had been experimenting with tape composition. Oliveros completed her first work in 1961. Called *Time Perspectives*, it was a piece of musique concrète using natural sounds that she had recorded with her Sears and Roebuck Silvertone home tape recorder. Without any other equipment at her disposal, she used the natural acoustics of her bathroom and some cardboard tubes to filter and enhance the raw sounds.[39]

Ramón Sender was a student at the San Francisco Conservatory of Music when he met Oliveros. He had received a little financial support from the conservatory to start an electronic music studio, and he and Oliveros teamed up to organize the project, calling it Sonics. "The first program we gave," recalls Oliveros, "included first tape works by Ramón Sender, Terry Riley, Phil Winsor, and me."[40]

Later in 1961, Sender and Morton Subotnick decided to pool their tape recording and audio equipment and founded the San Francisco Tape Music Center. Oliveros soon joined them. The center was first located in a condemned building whose days were numbered. Enough interest was stirred by their first few months of work that Sender and Subotnick worked out a plan to move into new quarters as part of a larger cooperative involving radio station KPFA, Ann Halprin's (b. 1920) Dancer's Workshop (for which Subotnick was musical director), and Canyon Cinema. Their new address on Divisadero Street was spacious and well-organized for their purposes. The Tape Center occupied the upstairs office and shared a large room for performances with Canyon Cinema. The dance workshop occupied another hall, and the radio station set up a remote studio in an adjoining office so that it could broadcast concerts. The cooperative held monthly performances to pay the rent. Terry Riley's *In C* (1965) was premiered in this space.[41] Tony Martin (b. 1936) joined the group as their visual artist in charge of light projections for the performances, and William Maginnis signed on as both engineer and composer from 1964 to 1967.

Maginnis defined the center as a "nonprofit cultural and educational corporation, the aim of which was to present concerts and offer a place to learn about work within the tape music medium." The center itself had little more equipment than six audio oscillators and some tape recorders.[42] This forced the composers to develop some novel approaches to making electronic music, including Oliveros's elaborate tape delay set ups. The composers were also very interested in creating music that could be presented live, which led them to the use of light projections to accompany tape pieces. The collective was highly successful and influential. It undertook regional and national tours during the mid-1960s.

As we have noted, in 1965 Donald Buchla worked with Morton Subotnick and Ramón Sender of the San Francisco Tape Music Center to design an instrument that could create electronic music. The first Buchla synthesizer was installed in the SFTMC at the end of 1965, and Subotnick continued to collaborate with Buchla on the further development of his electronic music synthesizers. The availability of this device rapidly changed the nature of the music that could be produced at the center. No longer dependent only on recorded natural sounds, audio oscillators, and tape manipulation to compose their music, the sound palette of works produced by Subotnick, Sender, and Oliveros began to shift toward new and increasingly complex sonorities.

1965 was a banner year for the SFTMC in more than one way. The Rockefeller Foundation was interested in the operation and granted it

$15,000 in operating funds. In 1966, the center worked with the foundation to secure an even longer-term commitment. An agreement was struck whereby the foundation would grant the center $400,000 for four years under the stipulation that it would agree to move to Mills College. Oliveros explained, "The foundation did not consider the Tape Center capable of administering the funds, so the move was deemed necessary in order to utilize the Mills College administration and to insure continuity when the grant period was over."[43] At Mills, the center was first known as the Mills Tape Music Center, and later, the Center for Contemporary Music (CCM). The new electronic music studio was going to be built from scratch, although some basic equipment—including a Bode frequency shifter, Fairchild compressor, and a Buchla 100 synthesizer—pre-dated its construction.[44]

1966 and 1967 were years of transition for the center. Not only was it moving to a new location, but it was having difficulty finding someone to be its director. Subotnick, who had been teaching at Mills, was the natural choice. He had to decline, however, because he was taking a position at New York University. Another choice would have been Sender, but he was also unavailable. Oliveros was next in line and accepted the position, only to leave the following year after being offered the position of lecturer at the University of California in San Diego. One of her accomplishments while director of the center was to convince the Mills administration that the studios should have a public-access policy.[45]

Changes in leadership at the Mills Tape Music Center delayed plans to complete the new electronic music studio. It wasn't until 1969, when Robert Ashley was appointed director at Mills, that work started in earnest on the new facilities. This was three years after the initial grant. Although prior to Ashley's arrival much work had been initiated by Tony Gnazzo and Lowell Cross to configure existing equipment into a working studio, Ashley was faced with bringing in new gear to realize the ultimate plan of creating a professionally equipped environment. He recalls the state of affairs when he was recruited for the job:

> Part of that grant that Mills got had been designed to build an electronic music facility. It had never really become anything because each person who was supposed to run it left. . . . So, they invited me to come there because apparently I was known for being able to do this stuff. I took a wonderful guy, a friend of mine, Nick Bertoni, as the engineer. We started from scratch and built a really nice studio.
>
> There was a recording studio, a work studio where students could build their own synthesizers and learn electronics, and then there was a Moog synthesizer studio and a Buchla synthesizer studio, and there were a

couple of smaller studios where people could do mixing and those kinds of things. They were all attached to the main studio. We had a four-track in one studio and an eight-track in another studio. We had a very nice mixing board that I designed and Nick Bertoni built. We made something that I was very proud of.[46]

Ashley also managed to keep alive Oliveros's recommendation for a public-access facility:

After we got the studio built—which took a couple of years—we were able to offer anybody in the Bay Area, any band in the Bay Area, access to that studio with an engineer at very low cost. I think the recording studio was like $10 an hour. . . . I think we invented the public-access studio. . . . There were rock bands and rap bands and everything. People coming in to learn the Moog equipment and that kind of thing. There is nothing like it in the world and hasn't been since.[47]

Composer John Bischoff (b. 1949), currently an instructor and studios coordinator at the CCM believes that in 1972 anyone in the neighborhood could rent the Buchla studio for a mere $2.50 an hour or the Moog studio for $5.00 an hour. Composers Maggi Payne (b. 1945), who has been at Mills since 1970, and Robert Sheff (aka Blue Gene Tyranny, b. 1945) "alternated weeks as recording technicians for the community users." Payne is currently an associate professor and co-director of the CCM. About the hourly rates, she added, "If people wanted instruction, I taught Moog and Buchla for an additional $5.00 and hour."[48]

If there was a distinction between Oliveros's original concept of a "public-access" studio and Ashley's, it might have been that Ashley opened the doors to people who were not necessarily associated with the composing community or staff of the college.[302] Ashley was director of the CCM until 1981. He created a master's degree program in "Electronic Music and the Recorded Media," and also received Ford Foundation funding to grant sixteen composers a month's residency in the studio to work with the latest multitrack recording equipment that they had installed. "No composer at that time in 1970 had any experience with a multitrack studio," explains Ashley. "Only the Beatles and the Rolling Stones had multitrack studios. So, we had Alvin [Lucier] and David [Behrman], and Christian Wolff and David Tudor and people like that."[50] The grant program lasted two years.[51]

In the generally underfunded and unsupported world of electronic music development, what Subotnick, Oliveros, Ashley, and others accomplished between 1961 and 1970 was simply astounding. But it also made sense to Mills. Ashley recalls again:

When I proposed this idea to the Rockefeller Foundation and we got the money to do the public access studio, I think Mills was very proud because the campus itself had become very isolated from the city of Oakland. It improved our relationship with the community a lot. I have to say that the people who were responsible for helping me—like Margaret Lyon, who was the head of the music department, who I think is really a total genius—and the dean of faculty, Mary Wood Bennett, equally a genius, they saw the social potential of this in a positive way. They were very supportive. That allowed me to do things that I couldn't have gotten away with in any other institution. Mills was so independent itself that if they decided that something was a good idea they would do it.[52]

Maggi Payne remarks that the studio facilities have since expanded to about double the size of the facilities in the '70s, "although it's still not enough."[53] This is surely a healthy sign for the state of new music at Mills College, and new music culture in general.

Chapter 10

MUSIC FROM MAINFRAMES: THE ORIGINS OF COMPUTER MUSIC

By 1990, the use of analog synthesizers in the tradition of Moog, Buchla, ARP, and others was entirely superseded by the availability of inexpensive, computer-based, digital synthesizing techniques. Computer processors are used in every kind of music equipment imaginable. They are at the core of digital synthesizers, effects boxes, mixers, multitrack recorders, and other basic devices used by the working musician. Most commercial recordings are now recorded, mixed, and mastered using digital means.

The personal computer has become an essential component of the electronic musician's equipment arsenal. It has many applications, including:

Composition and notation. Software can greatly accelerate the process of composing by providing editing, notation, and printing capabilities that are much more time-consuming to do by hand.

MIDI control and sequencing. Computers offer the only practical method of controlling MIDI-compatible electronic music instruments. Sequences of note values can be stored, edited, and readily played in real time using control and sequencing software.

Sound synthesis and modification. Personal computers now contain sound chips that are sophisticated enough to produce a range of electronically generated sounds that are as rich and varied as their standalone synthesizer predecessors. Many software programs are now available for creating digital musical sounds directly on the computer. The sounds can be triggered by the computer keyboard, a MIDI-compatible standalone musical keyboard, or other external control devices connected to the computer.

Digital recording and mixing. All of the steps needed to record, edit, and mix music can now be done digitally on a personal computer with specialized software.

Digital sampling. Sampling is a form of recording that uses software to further manipulate and modify recorded sounds.

Performance and control software. Musicians who wish to add a computer to their list of live performance instruments require software that allows them to create and modify sounds quickly in real time. Computers are also used in a live setting to sample and play back sounds and control the interaction of instruments connected by MIDI cables. There are programs dedicated to making this easier to accomplish.

The phenomenon of digital music systems, like the personal computer itself, has deep roots in general-purpose computing and the development of mainframes reaching back to the '50s. The history of this technology is recounted here.

Computer music was largely institutionalized by the research branches of the companies, universities, or governments that underwrote the research. It is an approach that began with large mainframe computers at places such as the University of Illinois, Bell Labs, and IRCAM. This work was the flip side of the experiments done by the independent solderers and composers discussed later in this chapter. It was most closely associated with research into new and emerging technology, white lab coats, and audio facilities for which the artist had to contend for time.

What Is Digital Synthesis?

Any type of analog system operates through the *measuring* of quantities. In this sense, a bathroom scale is an analog device: it translates a person's weight into a reading by the movement of a needle along a scale of measurement. The degree of movement of the needle is dependent on the amount of weight on the scale, and this movement is said to be *analogous* to the weight.

Analog electronic musical instruments express sounds as measurements of voltage. The sound is represented by electrical vibrations that, when amplified, physically drive the components of a loudspeaker system.

Whereas an analog system operates on the basis of measuring, digital systems operate on the basis of *counting*. Quantities are expressed as numbers. A digital bathroom scale translates one's weight into a number value that is used to display a corresponding number on a digital display.

In a digital music system, quantities representing the frequency, amplitude, timbre, duration, and envelope of a sound are also expressed as numbers. Numbers are input and calculated to produce the desired results, such as increases in volume, or changes in timbre. Instructions for making these changes might be made through software on a computer or directly from physical controls (e.g., dials and switches) on an electronic musical instrument.

Applications of Computers in Music: An Historic View

The development of computer technology historically paralleled the development of the modern electronic music studio and synthesizer, leading to a cross-fertilization of the two fields that greatly benefited electronic music.

Traditionally, the term "computer music" referred to the ways in which large, general-purpose mainframe computers were applied to the making of music.

Computer Composition and Scoring

The computer aids the composer in producing a printed score to be played using traditional musical instruments. When Lejaren Hiller and Leonard Isaacson first attempted to make a computer create a musical score at the University of Illinois in 1955, the computer was allowed to create sequences of notes that were then selected and organized by the composers and transcribed onto sheet music for a string quartet. This wasn't intended as a way to eradicate the human being from the composition process, but rather to enable the traditional composer to harness the power of the computer for organizing and editing a musical composition. Pioneering work in this field was done at the Massachusetts Institute of Technology, and many software packages for home computer systems now provide music-composition aids. The introduction of MIDI in the mid-'80s made it possible for a composer to play notes on a piano-style keyboard and have them automatically transcribed to sheet music.

Computer Synthesis of Sounds

The computer produces tones using solid-state oscillators on integrated circuits. The tones may be triggered directly by playing a MIDI-compatible instrument, or be generated by a software-based synthesizer. A digital-to-analog converter (DAC) is used to convert digital binary codes into analogous electrical waves that can drive a loudspeaker system.

The quality and robustness of digital synthesis depends on the power of the computer being used. Many software programs have been written to control and produce sounds on general-purpose desktop and laptop computers, but they are limited by their processing speed—real-time modeling of digitally produced sound waves is a processor-intensive operation—and the power of their onboard sound chips. Sound cards and chips designed specifically for digital signal processing (DSP) are required for more advanced and responsive real-time sound generation. The most versatile and powerful digital electronic music systems today usually employ two computers: one is a general-purpose laptop or desktop computer used as a controller, sequencer, and mixer; the other contains DSP hardware and is dedicated to processing audio signals under the control of the first computer. The two computers working in tandem are powerful enough to process sounds in real time, even during a performance where interaction is taking place between a computer and live performers.

Composer Joel Chadabe has a long history with the development of electronic music systems. As previously mentioned, he had the distinction in 1969 of having ordered the largest bank of Moog analog sequencers for any single Moog Modular Synthesizer installation. As president of Intelligent Music, he published several innovative controller programs for electronic music including M (1986), and Jam Factory (1986). With the help of programmer David Zicarelli, Chadabe developed a musician-friendly version of MAX, a powerful object-oriented music controller that had been born at IRCAM.[1] He was the first customer of the New England Digital Synclavier and also one of the first to use a Macintosh computer in a live, interactive performance situation.

Chadabe, like David Behrman, was a pioneer in the creation of interactive computer-controlled music systems. About the same time that Behrman was experimenting with homemade pitch-sensing circuits, Chadabe was exploring ways to create interactive performances with larger commercial synthesizers. He was trying to provide a process by which the many daunting features of a synthesizer could be managed during live performance. Chadabe explained:

> I got the idea that one could automate a process but then interact with that process while it was going on. I have since come to think of this as something of a *fly-by-wire* system. For example, it's impossible to fly an Airbus 340 in the way that pilots used to fly World War I type airplanes because there are too many controls and variables affecting the way the plane flies. So, fly-by-wire means that the pilot tells the computer what the pilot wants the plane to do and the computer flies the plane. It's a sophisticated control system in which the controls can be spread out and made context-sensitive and the pilot can interact with it. In 1971 I developed this concept of setting up automatic controls to deal with the huge number of variables that would make a synthesizer produce music, and then to develop controls so that I could guide it and interact with it. The effect was very interesting and very *conversational*. The music grew out of that kind of conversation with the very instrument that I was performing.[2]

One of Chadabe's more recent electronic music tools of choice combines Kyma (Greek for "wave") software running on a desktop computer with a proprietary audio-processing system called Capybara (named after a Patagonian, aquatic guinea pig). In a 2001 performance at Engine 27 in New York of what Chadabe dubbed his "audiomagic interactive environment," several solo musicians took turns interacting with sounds that were triggered by Kyma and generated by Capybara in response to the sounds being made by the performers. Chadabe preset his rules for engagement in Kyma so that the computer would react to the dynamics of the performer-created sounds with a high degree of randomness, making it impossible for the performers to know what the system was going to do from moment to moment. The result in this case was a warm symbiosis between performer and machine.

Computer Control over External Synthesizers

Standalone electronic music instruments may be controlled using MIDI or proprietary computer-interface software. Software on a computer is used to designate the pitch, timbre, amplitude, duration, and envelope of sounds being played on instruments connected to the computer. The computer may act merely as an elaborate sequencer to aid a performing musician, or it may control multiple aspects of the production of a piece of music that are really beyond the control of any single individual in real time. This area of involvement for the computer first blossomed during the late '70s with the availability of inexpensive microprocessors.

Computer Sampling of Audio Input

This is the opposite of digital-to-analog conversion. In an analog-to-digital conversion, input from a microphone, tape recorder, or other analog audio input is converted into binary code, which can then be processed and reorganized at will on a computer. This is the basis for the sound sampling that is such a familiar element of popular music. Conceptually, sound sampling provides a digitized means for creating musique concrète, much as the French were doing in the '40s. Bell Labs was experimenting with the computer digitization of analog sounds as early as 1958.[3]

A Concise History of Computer Music

The following chart presents a brief history of computer music, tracing its general development from the environment of large mainframe computers to the appearance of proprietary computer-based music systems and the integration of personal computers with music software and sound-generating hardware.

Outline of Major Developments in the History of Computer Music

1953–54	Romanian-born Greek composer Iannis Xenakis employs a computer to aid in the calculation of variable-speed glissandi for his orchestral work *Metastasis*.
1955–57	Lejaren Hiller and Leonard Isaacson develop a computer program to generate sequences of data that can be applied as pitches and parameters of a musical score. The two men select portions of this output and assemble it into the first significant piece of music composed with the aid of a computer, the *Illiac Suite* for string quartet (1957).
1956	Two computer engineers at the Burroughs Corporation, Martin L. Klein and Douglas Bolitho, program a Datatron computer to compose popular songs automatically. Affectionately nicknamed "Push-Button Bertha," the unit reportedly composes some 4,000 pop tunes after being fed the characteristics of 100 that are then popular.
1956–62	In Paris, Iannis Xenakis writes some probabilistic computer programs to aid in the composition of music. Rather than having the computer itself compose a piece, Xenakis feeds the processor previously calculated information and employs it to work out complex parameters of scores for various sizes of instrumental groups. Works he composes using this approach include *ST/10–1,080262 for Ten Instruments*, *Atrées (Law of Necessity)*, *Morsima-Amorsima*, and *ST/48–1,240162 for 48 Instruments*.
1957	At Bell Labs, researcher Max Mathews successfully demonstrates the computer generation of sound for the first time using a digital-to-analog converter (DAC). For Mathews, this is the beginning of a long association with computer music.
1959–66	Mathews and his Bell Lab associates experiment widely with computer-synthesized music. Their compositions range from mundane demonstrations (for example, *Pitch Variations* by Newman Guttman, *Sea Sounds* by John Pierce, and *Noise Study* by James Tenney) to simple renditions of familiar tunes and more complex pieces (*Five Stochastic Studies* and *Ergodos* by Tenney). The Bell Labs team develops a series of programs for automating the digital processing and organization of such works. These programs begin with Music I in 1957 and are updated regularly with improved versions. Music IV (1962) is used widely during the 1960s. Many of the pieces using these programs became available in the 1960s on a recording, *Music from Mathematics*.
1965	At Bell Labs, French physicist and composer Jean-Claude Risset employ a program by Max Mathews and Joan Miller to digitize the sound of a trumpet. This experiment in analog-to-digital conversion is particularly important because previous programs have been unsuccessful in faithfully reproducing the sound of a brass instrument.[4]
1966	Mathews and L. Rosler at Bell Labs develop a graphical interface for composing music. It consists of a cathode-ray tube onto which a light-sensitive pen is used to draw parameters of pitch, amplitude, duration, and glissando onto a grid representing the passing of musical notes in time. The output is permanently stored and can be played back using computer synthesis. This is the first successful composer-friendly experi-

ment using software to draw, copy, erase, and edit musical values on a computer.

1967–69	At the University of Illinois, John Cage and Lejaren Hiller collaborate on a massive multimedia piece called *HPSCHD*. The work is scored for seven harpsichords and 51 computer-generated sound tapes. It is prepared by Cage and Hiller using a computer to assemble sound patterns based on calculations derived from *I Ching* chance operations.
1969–74	Max Mathews, F. R. Moore, and Jean-Claude Risset at Bell Labs release their Music V program, an improved version of the earlier Bell programs for developing computer-generated sounds. In response to a call for a computer-music program that can be used in performance situations, the group develops a program called GROOVE, which permits a computer to be used as a voltage-control device for an analog synthesizer.
1971–74	President Georges Pompidou of France appointed Pierre Boulez to establish and direct an institute for musical research. Construction is completed in 1974 for the opening of IRCAM. Boulez brings in Jean-Claude Risset to direct its computer operations. This international center for the exploration of computer music and media has since hosted many projects and developed software tools for the use of composers.
1974–75	The first commercially available portable digital synthesizer is created, developed by the composer Jon Appleton and the engineers Sydney Alonso and Cameron Jones. Called the Synclavier, the instrument is performance-oriented and includes a means to store tracks of sound that could be used interactively with real-time keyboard performance. The Synclavier is a vital contribution to the realm of electronic performance instruments and sets the early standard for computer-based synthesizers. New England Digital Corp. is established to manufacture and sell it.
	Frustrated with the limitations of notational composition and the lack of computer memory, precision control, and logical design of analog electronic music instruments, composer Laurie Spiegel (b. 1945) begins using GROOVE, a "hybrid" computer-controlled analog music system at Bell Labs. GROOVE is a computer music system that is programmed in two languages, FORTRAN IV and DAP. Her compositions with it include *Appalachian Grove* (1974) and *The Expanding Universe* (1975).
1975–82	Mini- and microcomputers begin to be used as control devices for analog synthesizers. Developments in microprocessor technology introduced the use of sound-synthesizing "chips" in consumer musical instruments and professional synthesizers. The first all-digital synthesizers for the commercial market are introduced. Computer-music programs become available for use with personal computers made by such companies as Apple, Commodore, and Atari.
1976	The 4A Digital Sound Processor is completed at IRCAM by a team headed by Giuseppe Di Giugno. Additional versions of this software synthesizer are released between 1976 and 1981 as the 4B, 4C, and collectively as the 4X series.
	In the United States, Joel Chadabe becomes the first paying customer of the Synclavier developed by New England Digital Corp. He doesn't buy

the keyboard. Instead, for his first Synclavier project, he asks Robert Moog to develop some Theremin controllers for the synthesizer. "I used them not to make sounds as the Theremin makes sounds but rather to control the computer. He [Moog] designed frequency voltage converters in the base of the Theremins that I plugged into the synthesizer."[5]

1979	An IRCAM team headed by Xavier Rodet completes the first release of a computer program called Chant that creates synthesized sounds based on computer models of the singing voice.
1979–84	The Fairlight CMI (Computer Music Instrument) digital synthesizer is developed in Australia and introduced in 1979. Providing a full complement of sound-design features, it comes equipped with its own dedicated computer, dual eight-inch disk drives, a six-octave touch-sensitive keyboard, and some software for the creation and manipulation of sounds. Its most innovative feature was an analog-to-digital converter for processing incoming audio signals from analog sources. This is the first commercially available digital sampling instrument. An external audio signal can also be used as a controlling signal, much like earlier voltage-controlled synthesizers. It also features a sequencer, 400 preset sounds, and the ability to create new tonal scales tuned in increments as small as one one-hundredth of a semitone. As a recording device, live tracks can be merged with recorded passages for overdubbing. In the studio, the system can control the synchronization of up to 56 parts on an eight-track tape recorder. The cost of the average Fairlight is $25,000 to $30,000. Another digital synthesizer is introduced by Crumar and called the General Development System. Based on Bell Labs designs, it is designed for additive synthesis and has two eight-inch floppy disk drives, a Z-80 microprocessor, computer terminal, and keyboard controller. It sells for $27,500. It is the first stage of a product line to introduce the lower-priced Synergy in 1982.
1980	Casio introduces the first portable digital electronic music instrument, the Casio VL-Tone. Selling for about $70, this small monophonic instrument with its two-and-a-half-octave mini-keyboard includes presets for rhythms and instrument voices and permits the player to store a sequence of up to 100 notes in memory. It is programmed by entering an eight-digit number to select a waveform (e.g., piano, guitar, fantasy) and envelope. Three waveforms can be modulated by a low-frequency oscillator. It is the first low-priced digital synthesizer.
1981	E-mu introduces the Emulator, a dedicated digital sampling keyboard. Its sample time is short by today's standards: only two seconds. It also has eight-voice polyphony and a real-time looping feature. The Emulator sells for about $8,000. The first computer work composed by Pierre Boulez at IRCAM, *Répons*, is premiered during the Donaueschingen festival. It is created using the 4X software synthesizer developed at the institute. The work is performed by twenty-four musicians, with the sounds of the soloists each being modulated by the synthesizer and distributed to a network of loudspeakers in the concert hall.

1981–83   Personal computers from IBM and Apple Computer begin to dominate the market for home computing. Rudimentary and inexpensive software packages begin to appear for the creation of simple music on these machines.

In 1982, Crumar introduces the Synergy, a lower-cost digital synthesizer with a retail price of about $6,000, a significant price drop at the time from the Fairlights and Synclaviers. Wendy Carlos becomes an avid user of the Synergy, after working with its expensive precursor, the GDS. With her score to *Tron*, she combines original orchestral music with analog Moog sounds and GDS digital synthesis all as part of the same ensemble.

1983   Casio introduces the PT-20, a 31-key monophonic instrument with two and a half octaves. It includes seven preset voices, including piano, organ, violin, and flute, and offers 17 background rhythms. Preset algorithms for chords are played by buttons with designations for chords such as major, minor, and seventh. Using a feature called an "automatic judging chord generator," the keyboard can be played with one finger and the PT-20 will automatically select and play an accompanying chord. The keyboard can also store up to 508 notes for playback. This device is introduced at a retail price under $100. It is a breakthrough not only in terms of price but in the way that Casio engineers use the computer as an interpretive tool and accompanist for the user.

The Synclavier II is introduced. It features the same general capabilities as the Fairlight CMI but is designed more as a musical instrument than as a computer. The control panel features dozens of buttons that are logically arranged by functions such as volume, envelope, recorder control, vibrato, and timbre bank. The instrument features 16 digital oscillator voices and 16–track recording. A digital sampling feature can digitize analog sounds using a higher frequency range than the Fairlight instrument. Its digital memory recorder can store a sequence of 2,000 notes, and can be expanded to record 15,000 notes. The Synclavier II becomes the premiere product in the market for proprietary digital synthesizers. It costs from $28,000 for a basic configuration, up to about $55,000 for a fully equipped system.

Kurzweil Music Systems introduces the K250, the first performance keyboard to use digital samples of acoustic instruments as its sound source. Stored in ROM, the samples faithfully reproduce piano, strings, choirs, drums, and other acoustic instruments with great clarity. It becomes the benchmark for preset digital sampling keyboards.

Syntauri Corporation introduces its alphaSyntauri system, designed to enable a desktop computer to create music. This system uses a 48K Apple II computer as its brain, one or two disk drives for storage, and a video monitor. The digital audio oscillators are contained in a circuit board developed by Mountain Computer. Syntauri provides software, a four- or five-octave piano-type keyboard, interface hardware, and instructions to start creating digital music with its system. Laurie Spiegel, who had previously been working at Bell Labs, was a member of the team that developed the alpha Syntauri music system. Although not as powerful as the Fairlight CMI or Synclavier II, the alphaSyntauri marks the beginning of a trend toward less expensive electronic music systems built around PCs. The most elaborate model, including a five-octave keyboard and 100 preset sounds, costs around $2,000, not including the computer, which costs another $1,500 to $2,000.

1984   MIDI is introduced as a standard interface language for synthesizers and personal computers.

Apple Computer introduces the Macintosh computer, which soon becomes the desktop computer of choice for most musicians. Its graphical user interface and pictorial operating system are better suited for musical software applications than previous PCs.

Roland introduces another way to use an Apple II computer to create music with its Compu Music CMU-800R system. This device is an external add-on to the computer and provides six digital tone generators and seven rhythm sounds. The unit is plugged into the Apple II through an interface circuit board and is "played" or programmed through the computer keyboard. External controls are also provided for the envelope and volume of the melody, chord, and rhythm components of the sound. This $500 contraption is as short-lived as the Apple II after the introduction of the Macintosh, but anticipates by many years the trend toward the use of external slave synthesizers with personal computers.

1981–1985 After working on the alphaSyntauri music system for the low-cost Apple II computer, Laurie Spiegel finds herself consulting next on a the design of a high-end analog music instrument. The Canadian made computer-controlled McLeyvier is a "more general and customizable compositional system." It is built on a hefty DEC LSI 11/23 computer. The 16-voice system has a bank of 16 analog "voice cards," and 50 analog-to-digital converter *per card*. That's an astonishing 800 digital-to-analog converters. It excels in compositional control and notation. The instrument is in development for four years but never comes to market. One of the works Spiegel composes using the McLeyvier, is *Three Modal Pieces* (1983).[6]

1985   Mark of the Unicorn, a software developer, introduces Performer (now Digital Performer), one of the first MIDI sequencing programs for the Macintosh computer.

IRCAM releases its first musical software for personal computers. It is developed by a team led by David Wessel. In addition, a library of computer functions for computer-assisted composition is completed by Claudy Malherbe, Gérard Assayag, and Jean-Baptiste Barrière.

1986   After seven years of work on GROOVE in the rarified atmosphere of Bell Labs, as well as acting as a key consultant on the creation of the alphaSyntauir and McLeyvier systems, Laurie Spiegel is determined to create a computer music system of her own. After the McLeyvier project fell apart in 1985, she oscillates back in the direction of the small, inexpensive desktop computer. her bet known program from this period is *Music Mouse—An Intelligent Instrument for the Macintosh* (Mac 512k onward), Amiga, and Atari computers. *Music Mouse* is an enabler of music making rather than a programming environment. It provides a choice of several possible music scales (e.g., "chromatic, octatonic, middle eastern"), tempos, transposition, and other controls that are all played using a "polyphonic" cursor that is moved with the mouse around on a visual grid representing a two-dimensional pitch range. The simple yet elegant Music Mouse is an example of what Spiegel calls an "intelligent instrument," able to manage some of the basic structural rules of harmonic music making for the user.

1988	Korg introduces the M1 Music Workstation, a dedicated computer-based synthesizer with onboard display, sequencer, drum machine, digitally sampled sounds, and digital effects. About 250,000 units are sold, a breakthrough for a computer-based music system.
	IRCAM releases it first version of MAX, a graphical programming language for music applications, created by Miller Puckette. It is developed to support real-time interaction between the performer and computer and provides a rich array of virtual patches and controllers for the management of audio processing.
1990	A musician-friendly version of MAX is introduced by Opcode, with its design improved by David Zicarelli. This microcomputer program for the Macintosh becomes an instant success and continues to be the most widely used software controller for real-time music synthesis throughout the decade.
	Symbolic Sound introduces a two-processor microcomputer-based electronic music system. The software controller is called Kyma, which works with a proprietary set of sound processors called Capybara. Like MAX, but with its own dedicated audio processing hardware, it is well suited to the real-time processing of audio signals during live performance.
1999	IRCAM, with developmnet led by François Déchelle, completes jMAX, a new real-time version of its performance software for personal computers.

A Brief History of Soldering and Composing

There is a tradition of instrument-making in the field of electronic music. Beginning in the post–World War II years, when vacuum tubes were king, and continuing to the present, there have always been independently operating individuals who took it upon themselves to make their own equipment. These were the persistent soldering composers, the circuit builders who imagined sounds and then found ways to create them. Not content with—and unable to afford—the kinds of synthesizing equipment that only rock stars could buy, they worked with the trickle-down technology of the computer industry, the cheapest chips and mass-produced kits and circuits. They were from the Radio Shack school of electronic music begun by David Tudor and promulgated in successive generations primarily by Gordon Mumma, David Behrman, Pauline Oliveros, Joel Chadabe, Paul DeMarinis, Laurie Spiegel, John

Gallery of Homemade Electronic Instruments

Buchla Controller (Donald Buchla, mid-1960s) "Detail of a fascinating voltage control device. There are four circular pressure sensitive pads in maze patterns, with different voltages assignable to the four quadrants and a center position (set by the knobs above). I have never come across another one of these." —Matt Rogalsky. The controller was used by David Tudor. Photo by Matt Rogalsky, used with permission.

Electronic Music Live Performance System (Gordon Mumma and David Tudor, 1970) Mumma (shown here) collaborated with David Tudor on the design of the audio projection system and music for the Pepsi Pavilion at the 1970 World's Fair in Osaka. Photo courtesy of Gordon Mumma.

The Circon ("Circular Controller," Wendy Carlos, 1978). Carlos created the Circon so that she could pro-duce "connected pitches" for her soundtrack to The Shining. The effect was not unlike the continuous gliding tones produced by a Theremin. The Circon grew out of her experience playing lab-style audio oscillators with their circular dials. It was controlled by a rotary "pitch wand." She added the semi-circular image of a piano keyboard to assist in playing notes with some precision. Photo © Copyright 2001 Serendip. Used with permission.

Clavivox (Raymond Scott, 1959). This early synthesizer could be likened to a Theremin under keyboard control. The unique keyboard allowed one to glide from one note to another whether or not the keys were adjacent. Pitch was triggered by the modification of a light source falling on a photoelectric cell. When a key was depressed, the light beam was filtered through a transparent piece of film shaded to the given pitch. Photo by Thom Holmes.

Trombone-Propelled Electronics (Nicolas Collins). This is "a digital signal processor controlled by a trombone and played back through a speaker affixed to its mouthpiece. I can press any combination of some 28 to 30 switches and push the slide a millimeter out, a millimeter back, and make a miniscule change in some parameter, slowly ramp something up, slowly ramp something down. If I want to make big changes I can do that, too."—Nicolas Collins. Photo by Thom Holmes.

Mbira Board (David Behrman, 1987). A mbira modified with an attached circuit board. "The mbira was bought in a store selling exotic instruments in Greenwich Village in the mid-eighties. The electronics measured the time a finger was in contact with the metal prongs. That turned out to be a pretty good way to measure loudness and attack of the acoustic sound made when the finger left the prong and it bounced back to begin vibrating. The electronics were connected to an Atari computer. This was one of two used for the "Keys to your Music" installation (1987–89). Photo by Thom Holmes.

Feedback Workstation (David Lee Myers, circa 1990). Composer David Lee Myers' most elaborate "feedback workstation." This was one of several pieces of equipment he devised to make music generated entirely by the feedback created by interconnected audio components. Myers explains the setup: "Four Digitec 7.6-second delays seen in the right hand sloping rack are the main deal. Included are custom mixer with feedback matrix, a smaller submixer, two DIY ring modulators, a nutty timeclock generator/enveloper/delay modulator, and various general-use processors like graphic EQ, Alesis reverb unit, patchbay, etc." Photo courtesy David Lee Myers.

Digital Frequency Divider Synthesizer (Laurie Spiegel, 1979). "I built this inside a 7-inch magnetic tape box. The large flat white thing is the battery from an SX-70 Polaroid camera film pack, the only one flat enough to fit in the box and power the audio. This is a self-contained instrument. In the only performance I ever gave with it, I played it into a microphone like any other acoustic instrument and it went through a digital signal processor that David Behrman ran the controls of. It was a lot of fun."— Laurie Spiegel. Photo by Larry Fast, courtesy of Laurie Spiegel.

Electronic Sackbut Prototype (Hugh Le Caine, 1948). This was the first voltage-controlled synthesizer. It was built between 1945 and 1948. ©Copyright Hugh Le Caine Archive, National Research Council Canada

Bischoff, Tim Perkis, Nicolas Collins (b. 1954), Ron Kuivila (b. 1955), and Matt Rogalsky (b. 1966), among others. This is a brief history of their work—the other side of computer music that evolved in the hands of composers, not engineers.

Maybe it's because I grew up in the Ann Arbor area, near Detroit, that I tend to view the evolution of *any* technology from the standpoint of the automobile. My father was an automotive engineer, my brother is an ace diesel mechanic. Even though my aptitudes apparently lay elsewhere, I still tend to view the world from behind the wheel of a metaphorical '65 Ford Falcon. So imagine being an automotive mechanic who knows how to assemble and disassemble a gasoline-powered engine at will. Now, consider what it would be like if the technology of automotive engines changed drastically—fundamentally—every five years. What happens to the auto mechanic in a situation like that? He either learns the new technology and survives, or falls behind and finds other work.

The challenge facing this imaginary auto mechanic is not unlike the actual dilemma faced by electronic musicians over the past forty or fifty years. These were times of unprecedented paradigm shifts in the field of electronics. Even the most persistent and studious electronic musicians were obligated to muddle through several stages of reeducation along the way. The most rapid changes occurred in the '70s with the coming of affordable integrated circuits and microcomputers.

From Transistors to Semiconductors

As the '70s began, the paradigm in the world of electronics began to shift from transistors to computer chips. Integrated circuits were like having micro-collections of transistors in one component; they were much easier to work with than transistors. The first "oscillator-on-a-chip" that was both inexpensive and widely available was the Signetics NE/SE566, designed for use in touch-tone telephones. It was the first audio chip that Nicolas Collins acquired. The year was 1972 and he was in his last year of high school and about to embark on undergraduate study with Alvin Lucier at Wesleyan. Collins taught himself to assemble a little gadget that could make satisfying boops and beeps with the SE566: "It cost $5, which seemed like a lot of money at the time. But, you know, the synthesizer was $5,000."[7] This was several years before the widespread availability of home computers, when chip technology was first being built into appliances, calculators, toys, and other household items.

It turned out that Collins's discovery had also been made by several other soldering composers. A few years later he was able to look "under the hood" of one of David Behrman's early homemade synthesizers. This was not a computer, nor even a synthesizer in the traditional sense, because it had none of the usual paraphernalia found on commercial instruments, such as voltage-controlled filters, envelope generators, and modulation wheels. All Behrman wanted was a lot of oscillators. He soldered them together along with logic circuits and pitch-sensors to create an early logic-based interactive sound synthesizer. It was used for his work for synthesized music with sliding pitches. Tones were triggered by several musicians and sustained by the synthesizer, dying out after a few seconds. As a tone died out, it modulated or deflected the pitches of other tones that were being played and this caused sliding pitches to occur during the attack and decay parts of a tone. The soldering composer had crossed the first line into the digital age. The chips provided him with a sonic wall of wavering, digital bliss. Behrman had become the "Phil Spector of Downtown,"[8] the father figure of a new wave of electronic music tinkering.

Collins calls the Signetics chip the "cultural linchpin for an entire generation" of composer-hackers. A lot of tinkeerrs learned basic IC breadboard design with the SE566. Even more significant was that, before too long, the Signetics chip was already obsolete, only to be replaced by the next generation. Each successive IC was more versatile yet less expensive. The economics of technology were for once working in favor of the electronic musician. Composers Collins and Ron Kuivila had just started taking classes at Wesleyan:

> We were like the idiot twin children of Alvin Lucier. We were desperately trying to learn electronics. I don't think either of us had any real intuition for it. We just forced ourselves to do it. What else could you do? You were a student, you had time and no money, so you were trying stuff.
>
> But here's what happened. Technology got cheaper and more sophisticated and there was a little window generation of composers who taught themselves this stuff. There was Ron, myself, John Bischoff, Tim Perkis, Paul DeMarinis. Those are the names that come to mind offhand. And we're all about the same age. It is 2001 now. We're all essentially between forty-five and fifty-five years old.[9]

Behrman found himself immersed in a new generation of electronics once again, hitting the books, trying to keep up with the changes. "I remember riding on the Cunningham bus in the early '70s with manuals about logic gates," explained Behrman. "There was a period several years before the computer entered the picture where I remember we could do switching networks."[10]

As a new generation of composers was discovering the work of

In the Beginning There Was Gordon Mumma

The name of Gordon Mumma is frequently intoned with great reverence in any discussion about the origin of tinkering-and-soldering composers. Even David Tudor, the elder statesman of the movement and about ten years Mumma's senior, attributed him with opening his eyes to the possibilities of making his own circuits:

> He had been around radio men, broadcast engineers, and electronics
> buffs for years, so his suggestions were always to the point,
> although he never offered any solutions. He didn't say "do this," or
> "do that." He just told me about something that somebody had told
> him or he said, "maybe you should look at the cables," suggestions
> really of practical help.[11]

A few years later, Mumma tutored David Behrman in the making of audio components by writing step-by-step do-it-yourself instructions in the form of electronics experiments:

> I started soldering around 1965. Gordon wrote me. He was in Ann
> Arbor with the ONCE group. We became friends and he started
> writing me letters. I have a collection of letters from him that
> describe these projects, starting with a preamp and a ring modula-
> tor, voltage-controlled amplifiers, and envelope followers and things
> like that. You couldn't buy synthesizers yet.[12]

One factor that enabled them to make their own equipment was the tumbling cost of electronic parts. Mumma began by repurposing war-surplus parts in the vacuum-tube '50s. By the mid-'60s, the transistor had become inexpensive and widely available. Transistors were, in essence, shortcuts for creating circuits. They were more compact than the equivalent amount of hardwired parts required to perform the same functions. They could also be powered by batteries, which improved the portability of electronic music components.

A community of electronic music tinkerers began to grow during the mid-'60s. Oliveros, Mumma, Tudor, and Behrman were trading circuit diagrams. Whenever a composer friend went to a technical conference where people like Robert Moog and Hugh Le Caine were speaking, they would quickly circulate any papers being given out that revealed new and inventive ways of making their own instruments. The era of the voltage-controlled synthesizer was also upon them, making available high-quality modular components with which to experiment.

What were these composers making with these transistorized components? The technology wasn't cheap enough for them to build their own synthesizers. Taking a cue from Mumma's work, they focused on creating black boxes for modulating and processing acoustic or electronic sounds in real time: ring modulators, filters, delay circuits, phase shifters, and the like.

Mumma had by this time graduated to making performance circuits that could actively respond to signals during a live performance. His "cybersonic" components, which date back to as early as 1958, were an example of these. He explains the idea:

> The word "cybersonics" derives from the Greek *kybernan*, meaning to steer or guide. The work "sonics," from the Latin *sonus*, pertains to sound. Cybernetics, the science of control and communication, is concerned with interactions between automatic control and living organisms. The cybersonic sound controls are derived from the sound materials themselves and applied directly to their own musical modification and articulation.[13]

These circuits self-adjusted to the acoustic properties of sounds in a given performance space, generating electronic responses in the form of modulated feedback and control signals that could also trigger other sound-generating circuits. During this adjustment, some circuits would become imbalanced and "attempt to rebalance themselves," which was a key performance variable. For example, "in *Medium Size Mograph* (1963) for piano, four hands, the cybersonic process involved mostly changing the articulation of the piano sounds by an envelope follower—that is, readjusting the natural acoustical envelope of the piano's attack and decay so as to have the attack characteristic occur shortly after the piano sound had already begun. Near the end of the performance an accompaniment was added: a recording of further cybersonic processing of the piano sounds."[14]

Circuits didn't always work as expected, which was a constant source of discovery for these composers. This trial-and-error approach to making circuits sometimes paid unexpected dividends. The sound character of Behrman's *Runthrough* was largely due to imperfections in an off-the-shelf electronics kit that he used to build one of the key circuits:

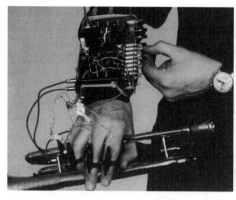

Cybersonic performance by Gordon Mumma during a Sonic Arts Union concert at Brown University in New York City, 1973. The work is Ambivex which uses electronics to modify and generate sounds triggered by a cornet. Left: Closeup of Mumma's equipment for Ambivex. Photo courtesy of Gordon Mumma.

That was a collection of analog homemade circuits that had some components from Lafayette Radio kits that were supposed to make sounds. And sometimes they didn't work properly. I remember one of the components of *Runthrough* was a Lafayette kit for tremolo. It was supposed to make the sound get louder and softer. But somehow because of some feedback or impedance thing it made it go up and down in pitch, which is sort of an accident and the basis for that *Runthrough* sound.[15]

The invention of their own circuits for making music implied a radical shift in the way that music itself was being conceived. In contrast, composers working with mainframe computers were mostly applying new technology to the same old rules of composition. The technical pioneers at Bell Labs "thought that they understood music when in fact they only had a very fuzzy understanding of music."[16] Composers who could afford to use commercially manufactured synthesizers were working with cookie-cutter sounds, rhythms, and preset controls. The tinkerers, on the other hand, were in many ways reinventing music itself. It was a time for violating the first principles of music composition to see where it would lead. Composer Nicolas Collins, a member of the next generation who studied with Lucier in the early '70s, was well aware of the rules that were being broken:

You were not tiptoeing slowly away from tonality through chro-
maticism to serialism. It wasn't like a one-step thing, It was like suddenly wiping the slate clean and starting over again. What if we
violate the first rule and then set off? . . . What if we went back and
stepped on that bug in the year 2 billion B.C. How would life be different? Let's interfere with the past. I think that there was an ethos
at that time about starting over.[17]

Reflecting back on that era in electronic music sometimes
requires a suspension of disbelief. How could all of this really happen? Was the world that receptive at the time? Actually, the world
was a terribly screwed-up place during the '60s and experimental
music just seemed to happen because, well, nobody could stop it.
It had the inertia of change behind it, like so many other aspects of
'60s culture. David Behrman put it in perspective this way:

Thinking about this music that my friends and I were doing in the
'60s, it strikes me that we were not at all concerned with worldly
success. We were intent on pursuing and exploring possibilities
(most of which were very new) and the music scene at that time
allowed us to be booked in halls and galleries, produce a few
records, and travel. Our sponsors were not oppressed by a need to
make big profits and their careers were not compromised if the
events they organized sold only a moderate number of tickets. There
is some quality in hearing this music thirty years later—what is it,
really?—that conveys that situation and those attitudes.[18]

Mumma, Tudor, and Behrman, they began to ask for help in learning
how to build their own instruments. A watershed event for a select
group of these young composers was the "New Music in New
Hampshire" workshop in Chocorua in the summer of 1973. For a little
more than two weeks, more than a dozen students participated, alternately, in classes on composing music and building instruments.

David Behrman and Gordon Mumma both taught courses in building homemade instruments. The classes preceded the final workshop,
which was simply called "Rainforest" and was taught by David Tudor.
His workshop in "sound transformation without modulation" gave
birth to the remarkable installation version of his most famous work,
Rainforest IV (1973), but also brought together a core of young composers—including John Driscoll, Ralph Jones, Bill Viola, and Martin

Kalve—who continued to be Tudor's collaborators in performance for several years. Tudor aptly named the group Composers Inside Electronics because, instead of using electronics as given instruments, they were working with the circuitry, trying to alter it, influence it, discover what it can do.[19]

The purpose of the workshop was for the students to compose and perform live electronic music using only instruments of their own design. Tudor wanted them to learn what it was like to begin with nothing and build something that suited their needs. *Rainforest IV* was an interactive installation of suspended objects that were wired so that sound could be run through them as if they were loudspeakers. The result was reverberant electroacoustic music generated by the vibrating objects, without further electronic modification. It had previously been performed only in a more concertlike version, as Mumma explains:

> This was the first "large-scale" *Rainforest* production. The previous were performances that David Tudor and I did with the Merce Cunningham Dance Company, from the premiere of *Rainforest* [in late 1968] up to the Chocorua project [July 1973]. The MCDC performances were, in character, a special kind of "chamber music," in comparison with the large-scale twelve (or so) performers at Chocorua.[20]

Gordon Mumma and David Behrman next went to California. Mumma had been invited to the University of California at Santa Cruz (in 1973) to establish an electronic music studio there. Behrman joined Robert Ashley at Mills College in northern California in 1975. The Bay Area became the Left Coast's experimental station for soldering composers. Rooted in Silicon Valley and drawing nourishment from the proximity of the first microcomputer manufacturers, the Mills program attracted many young soldering composers, including Paul DeMarinis, Ron Kuivila, Laetitia deCompiegne, and John Bischoff.

Behrman was begrudgingly becoming aware of the advantages offered by microcomputers:

> I remember saying to myself, "No, I'm not going to go down this path into computer software." . . . There were lots of people there who were interested in this new microcomputer thing that was just coming out. Students started coming in with the very first kits.[21]

Up until then, the synthesizers Behrman had been building were hardwired to do only one thing, such as play a defined set of oscillators: "It seemed that this new device called the microcomputer could simulate one of these switching networks for a while and then change, whenever you wanted, to some other one."

The breakthrough in microcomputers came with the arrival of the KIM-1, a predecessor of the Apple computer that used the same chip set. One individual from the Bay Area scene was largely responsible for moving the gadget composers from soldering chips to programming the KIM-1. Jim Horton (1944–1998), by all accounts the leading underground computer evangelist in Berkeley, preached the miracles of the KIM-1 at regular meetings at the Mediterranean Café near UC Berkeley. Collins explained that, "he was the first person to get a single board computer—a KIM—for use for music. This caught on. These computers were made for controlling machines and for learning how a microprocessor worked. They looked like autoharps. They had a little keypad in the corner, a little seven-segment display."[22]

The KIM-1 was a primitive, industrial-strength microcomputer for process-control applications. It could be programmed with coded instructions—machine-language software—but these were entered by pressing keys on a hexadecimal pad. It had no keyboard or computer monitor like microcomputers do today. One entered a sequence of codes and hit the run button. The composer was operating very close to the level of the machinery itself. Behrman, DeMarinis, and other composers found that the KIM-1 was ideal for controlling their primitive, chip-based synthesizers. They built in cable ports, not unlike printer connections, to connect homemade synthesizers to the KIM-1.

Horton's work, dedication, and know-how led to the development of live performances of microcomputer music in the Bay Area during the early '70s. One group founded by Horton was the League of Automatic Music Composers, which also included John Bischoff, Tim Perkis, and Rich Gold. Members of the group have continued to work over the years on the creation of computer music using networked machines, inexpensive technology, and low-level programming languages. One extension of the League of Automatic Music Composers was The Hub, a group of six individual computer composer-performers connected into an interactive network. The Hub took shape around 1989 and included members Mark Trayle (b. 1955), Phil Stone, Scot Gresham-Lancaster (b. 1954), John Bischoff, Chris Brown, and Tim Perkis. Their music is a "kind of enhanced improvisation, wherein players and computers share the responsibility for the music's evolution, with no one able to determine the exact outcome, but everyone having influence in setting the direction."[23]

Then There Was Software

By 1978, microcomputers had advanced to the point where they could accept commands written in coded software languages, such as Forth and Turtle Logo, using some form of alphanumeric display and a keyboard for input. Composers were then faced with learning about software. It was yet another distraction in a series of distractions that conspired to steal away their composing time, and was a growing source of frustration for many. Nicolas Collins was about ready to give up:

> Making the transition was very interesting. I was resistant initially. I had taken a summer course in computers when they were like mainframes and PDP-11 computers and I found them very counterintuitive and, of course, not portable. I was completely committed to live performance and therefore portability was the essential factor. Then, when I was dragging my heels, Paul DeMarinis was thinking about buying a KIM, and he said, "Don't think of it as a computer. Think of it as a big, expensive logic chip." In other words, just think of it as a big chip. It was like a mantra. That got me going.[24]

Moving from soldering circuits to composing with software required a mental adjustment for the composers as well. Composing with circuits in the tradition of Tudor and Mumma was a real-time, action-reaction medium. You turned it on, flipped a switch, and it just happened in parallel with whatever else was going on: another circuit, a circuit affecting another circuit, a musician playing along, a voltage-controlled device modifying the output of the circuit, and so forth. It was *solid state* in the conceptual as well as circuitry sense. It was also transient activity that could not be repeated, because analog systems were more like organisms growing old. Eventually they burned out, fried to a crisp, changing slightly all along the way until total failure. The Barrons had used this characteristic of analog electronics to their advantage when they were composing with tube-based oscillators and circuits in the '50s. Working with analog instruments was more like playing an instrument in real time: a performance existed as a function of human awareness and memory, passing in time, never to be repeated.

Laurie Spiegel: Mousing Around with Microcomputer Software

In 1986, Laurie Spiegel wrote a software program for the early Motorola 6800-based computers that would let the amateur musician—or pro, for that matter—make electronic music painlessly in real time. It was called Music Mouse. At the time of this writing, it could still be downloaded from her website (http:/retiary.org).

About Music Mouse—An Intelligent Instrument:

Laurie Spiegel (circa 1981). Photo by Carlo Carnevali, courtesy of Laurie Spiegel.

"Music Mouse is a software musical instrument that tries to let you interact with musical sound as directly and intuitively as any traditional instrument. It's not an editor, sequencer, or sound processor, nor does it use music notation, Music Mouse provides a real-time interactive human interface to a model of music theory that is optimized for musicality of output in the ear of its creator, a professional composer.

"Like any other musical instrument, its users and uses range widely, from absolute beginners to established professionals. People use Music Mouse for live performances, CD recordings, film soundtracks, dance accompaniment, compositional brain-storming, in music education preschool through postgrad, for music therapy in hospitals and prisons, and for self-expression, relaxation, and pleasure."[25]

About the halcyon days of early microcomputer music, Spiegel remembers:

"There were wonderful electronics parts shops all over this neighborhood [Tribeca, New York City] until gentrification replaced them with expensive restaurants, etc. Especially important was one place on West Broadway just below Chambers that sold little kits they made up with things like buzzers and frequency divider circuits, with a breadboard and all the parts and instructions. I suspect a few of us composers used some of the same kits. I didn't do nearly as much of this as several of my friends, but I kludged up a little synth back in the late 1970s inside a seven-inch tape box that I played live into a microphone like any other acoustic instrument, including through a digital signal processor."[26]

What made microcomputer music different was the concept of computer memory as an adjunct to human memory. Software allowed one to save a control sequence. Actions could be stored and repeated as originally conceived, and repeatedly performed by the computer as often as one liked. The circuits themselves were transitory rather than hardwired. One's actions were reversible, unlike soldering, where you could permanently melt your best work away with one false move of the heating element. Conceptually, the composer could think differently about the organization, variation, and playback of music because there were endless permutations possible through the modification of software controls. Software was also, because of the nature of coding, a linear process consisting of a sequence of instructions to the computer. This departed from the solid-state idea of soldering, in which all things could happen at the same time as long as the switches were flipped on. Whereas it was easy with soldered circuits to run activities at the same time, the linear sequencing of software control was by its very nature stretched out in time.

Soldered systems were *vertical* in conception: stacked and parallel. Software systems were *horizontal* in nature: sequential and time-based. "So you had to stop thinking about parallelism," explained Collins, "and start thinking in sequential terms. It changed the way people worked."[27] When working with computers composers had to adapt their thinking process for creating music.

As microcomputers became more powerful and standardized during the '80s, the emphasis on music for computers shifted mostly to software. Soldering was rendered unnecessary for everyone except those few enlightened tinkerers who understood the richness of circuit sounds and the direct manipulation of electronics without the interloping influence of software. Mumma embraces it all: "I've never left the analog world, because there are processes unique to it that are *not* transferable to the digital world. I use them both."[28]

Software has in many ways equalized the opportunities for electronic music composers. There are MIDI sequencers such as Digital Performer for storing and editing notes played on a keyboard or other instrument. MAX and SuperCollider offer user-programmable controls over the parameters and performance of digital synthesis and audio processing in real time. Software "synthesizers" give the composer the ability to invent their own synthesizer voices. Software samplers capture and edit acoustic or electronic sounds from other sources. You can walk into any home electronics superstore and choose from dozens of programs designed for the digital recording, sampling, downloading, editing, playing, and mixing of music.

The downside of all of this ready-made technology is that it promulgates a homogenized sameness about most music created with it. But this is not a new phenomenon in our culture. The majority of music created with any commonly available instrument—the piano or the electric guitar, for example—is derivative and unoriginal. The uniqueness of new music will always come back to the talents of a special few composers who hear different things than the rest of us.

Whereas Composers Inside Electronics learned how to solder and wire, the new generation is learning to tinker and alter the programs and programming. What MAX and SuperCollider provide are quasi-programming environments in which the user can create a storehouse of predefined connections between the operating components of a virtual synthesizing environment. You can bring in your own sounds, stored as digital information, and control them using patterns and sequences and free-form patch control that is unique to one person's computer. Composers who wish to take an even bolder step—such as Laurie Spiegel, Ron Kuivila, Joel Chadabe, Ikue Mori, and others—can dabble with programming language itself to get totally inside the electronics behind the sound.

Has something been lost by moving away from soldering composing to digital composing? One way to answer this question is by answering another: has the synthesizer made the piano obsolete? Absolutely not. The same will probably be said in ten years' time after the last generation to learn soldering from the masters is persuaded to revive the art of the intuitive circuit for one more curious generation of composers who would rather not stay outside of electronics.

Chapter 11

INSIDE ELECTRONIC MUSIC

Composing Electronic Music

There is no single "best practice" for composing any good music. Unless one is working with a conventional musical scale that can be transcribed to sheet music, the potential sound field associated with electronic music is in many ways beyond the capability of effectively notating it, especially in unusual scales and tunings. Even Wendy Carlos, one of the most practiced composers working with predominantly synthesized tonal music, reaches a point in the creation of each work where fiddling with the physics of the sound is as important as the notes being played. Composing timbres is as important in electronic music as composing pitches.

Just as electronic music altered our concept of music, so too did it change the activity of musical composition. While it is easy to contrast the hyperkinetic nature of total serialism with chance music, who is to say which type of music exercises the least control? Cage remarked that there was no such thing as true randomness, just somebody's *definition* of true randomness.[1] Christian Wolff was well aware that the music from both sides of the Atlantic was similar in its underlying motivations:

> What was so shocking intellectually to everybody was this notion of randomness, that you gave up control. And yet it was clear that control operates at many different levels or angles, and that there was just as much control in John's work as there might be in Stockhausen's or Boulez's. It was just a question of where you applied it and how you focused it.[2]

So with electronic music came just about every method of composing imaginable: graphical scores on paper or transparent sheets of plas-

John Cage on Composing Music

In 1985, I asked John Cage the following question: How do you make music?:

> I have found a variety of ways of making music (and I continue to look for others) in which sounds are free of a theory as to their relationships. I do not hear music before making it, my purpose being to hear as beautiful something I have not before heard. Most of the ways I have found involve the asking of questions rather than the making of choices, and *I Ching* chance operations pinpoint among all the possible answers the natural ones to be used. These questions generally have to do with the writing of music which is later to be practiced and finally performed and heard. Though they sometimes take advantage of technological means (recording means, the activation of electronic sound systems, the programming of computer output of actual sounds), or just acoustic means, instruments over which I have no control (a music of contingency). I hear ambient sound as music. Therefore I have no need to make music, though I continue, as cheerfully as I can, to do so.[3]

tic; computer-generated algorithms; written instructions; oral commands; audible performance cues; and so on. There were no standards other than those for traditional musical notation. Electronic music could not use those rules much of the time, so its very existence as a form of music became a matter of debate. Pauline Oliveros has wrestled with this perception for most of her career:

> My way of composing is seen either as a substantial contribution to the field or it is dismissed as not real music because it is not written in the conventional way and cannot be judged conventionally. It is dismissed because of a lack of written notes, or because participants are asked to invent pitches and rhythms according to recipes or to respond to metaphors. Musicians accustomed to reading notes and rhythms often are shocked by the bareness of the notation compared to familiar conventional scores which direct their attention to specific pitches and rhythms which to them seem predictable and repeatable. What I value is the more unpredictable and unknowable possibilities that can be activated by not specifying pitches and rhythms. I prefer organic rhythms rather than exclusively metrical rhythms. I prefer full spectrum sound rather than a limited scalar system. I sometimes use meter and scales within this fuller context of sound oriented composition.[4]

David Tudor performing on the Buchla 100 during a live concert of electronic music concert at the Mills College Tape Music Center (January 1968). Photo courtesy of John Bischoff, Mills College Center for Contemporary Music.

Time and time again the existence of electronic music has forced us to reassess the very nature of music itself.

Live Electronic Music Improvised

Improvisation is an element of much world music, although it is often most closely associated with American jazz. There is a close affinity between the pioneers of live electronic music and jazz musicians. They often worked together, played to the same audiences, and crossed over as musicians from one idiom to the other. They also share the sociological experience, at least following the '60s, of being cut off from most arts funding because of increasing corporate and institutional pressures to support more mainstream tastes in music.

Improvisation in electronic music is a forty-five-year tradition going back to the late '50s, when the possibilities of live performance in this idiom were first being explored; Cage and Tudor were working with the Merce Cunningham Dance Company about the same time that Mumma and Ashley were giving it a go in Ann Arbor. Its practice has benefited from the evolution of smaller and more compact electronic instruments and computers. The widespread growth of digital sampling, keyboards, turntables, and other real-time audio processing

Zeena Parkins playing her custom-made electric harp. She is in frequent demand as an electronic music improviser. Photo by Thom Holmes (2001).

technology has formed entirely new subcultures of music based on live electronic performance, including hip-hop, techno, and electronica, all of which are sustained by the social settings of raves, clubs, and other performance events.

Improvisation defies clear definition. Even though most musicians have difficulty explaining what it is, many *can* tell you the basic way that they approach it. Unlike jazz, which often deals with improvisatory rules in a kind of gamelike exchange of modes and melodies, electronic music often lacks the qualities of rhythm, harmony, and melody that many jazz musicians rely on. Instead, electronic music improvisation is largely based on the spontaneous modification of nonpitched aspects of sound: the shape of the envelope; timbre; rhythm; layers or filtering; effects (echo, delay, ring modulation, etc.); amplitude; and duration. A seasoned improviser learns how to listen to many layers of sound activity as part of a performance.

When I was a member of Paul Epstein's improvisation ensemble in the mid-'70s, we spent much of our time tuning our senses to the performance space and other musicians with whom we would be working. Most of the work we did was without any instruments at all. We used body movement and vocal sounds as our main musical resource. There were two essential talents necessary to improvise successfully in an environment where any sound, was fair game: *listening* and *patience*. You listened so as to comprehend the dynamics of the sound relationships being explored by other performers, and carefully chose a moment to make a contribution after having been subsumed by the experience.

If I were to try and define this process any further, it would have the following steps:

1. Listening
2. Reacting
3. Augmenting (adding a sound to any fragment of what others were doing)
4. Creating new sounds, or fragments to explore

Those steps in and of themselves might constitute a composition or plan of action for an improvisation using any sound source.

Live, improvised electronic music can be heard downtown in New York City in multiple venues any night of the week. In New York, a number of musicians and composers are in great demand for what they contribute to the improvisational situation. Familiar names include Elliot Sharp, Ikue Mori, John Zorn, Thurston Moore, Christian Marclay, Zeena Parkins, and Charles Cohen. What do these people bring to a performance that their collaborators so admire? Aside from being good listeners, Parkins thinks that it has something to do with the personality of the sound offered by each performer:

> People might be drawn to the personalized sound palette that we have. When you hear the electric harp, it is pretty unlikely that you are going to think of anything else besides what it is. I think the same is true for when you hear Ikue on drum machines. Her sound is pretty unmistakably *her* sound. We have developed this very distinctive language. For those that have imagination to think of situations where that language might be well suited it's a really great thing to have such personalized sounds to work with.[5]

Thurston Moore, Kim Gordon, Lee Ranaldo, and Steve Shelley (Sonic Youth)

The members of the rock group Sonic Youth are an informed bunch when it comes to avant-garde music. While they are mostly known for their inventive, experimental, song-based rock music, members of the group have been active for many years in the performance of freely improvised electronic music. They formed their own record company, SYR, in 1997 for the purpose of distributing this experimental music. I spoke with Thurston Moore (b. 1958) about one of the recordings, *Goodbye 20th Century* (SYR, SYR 4, 1999), which features performances of music by Cage, Wolff, Oliveros, Kosugi, Reich, and others:

Thurston Moore and Kim Gordon of Sonic Youth. Photo by Thom Holmes (2001).

The *Goodbye 20th Century* record was instigated by Willie Winant, the percussionist from the Bay Area. I was really getting interested in the history of twentieth-century composer music and the lineage and the links between the different schools. It was music history that you really had to find. I became fast friends with Willie. He was interested in what we were doing in employing innovations from that music into a rock band context. We started playing together and improvising. He was the one who first said it would be great if Sonic Youth would play some of this music. "You're probably the only band I know where the members of the band have an affinity for this school of music."

So he started collecting scores. Pauline Oliveros said she wanted to write a piece. We discussed different Cage scores we would do. We all got very involved with it. Jim O'Rourke, who was still keeping in contact with us, we knew that he was somebody of our generation—he's actually younger—who was really involved with this music and its history, having studied and played it. He is a scholar of Cage's music as well as a scholar of John Fahey's music, which is really fascinating. So we involved Jim immediately. We decided to contact Kosugi to see if he would be interested [Takehisa Kosugi, music director for the Merce Cunningham Dance Company.]

We involved Christian Marclay for a piece. He had been doing work with Christian Wolff. Willie knew Wolff, so it was nothing for us to just call him up and ask, "Would you like to come down and go over the score with us?" He did and he also performed with us. It was extremely enjoyable. He was really nonjudgmental about the fact that we were a rock band. He didn't really know that much about us, but when he sat down with us and discussed points of the score—it was a typical score that was very visual and very open to interpretation by the musician [the work was *Edges*, 1969]—he was describing certain points on the page and how he felt the musician should interpret it. Kim said, "Oh, that's interesting. I thought it was more along these lines." She described a different approach to it. He said, "Oh no, but in a way maybe you should do that because that's better for you. That would be really great if you do that." Her interpretation was validated by the composer. The way he dealt with that really liberated the musician. I think that was a lot of what the goal was for Cage and Wolff, liberating the musicians but still keeping the composer's role very much active.

We discussed the score of Cage's piece for four players where each musician plays various sound elements based on time and length. Each musician has the same length score but different time intervals. It's a beautiful score.

There were so many musicians now. There was, like, the four of us [SY]. Five of us with Jim. Willie was six. Kosugi was seven. Christian was an eighth at that point. We all wanted to play the piece. So four of us set out and recorded it, and then the other four set out and recorded it. We put each run into the two separate speakers. It ran simultaneously. We were, like, "God this sounds great!" There was some discussion over the validity of doing something like that. What was the proper thing to do? Were we taking liberties with Cage's score with him not being around to say that it was improper? Then there were those who were saying, "No he would have been completely OK with it and would have loved it." So we decided to go with it.

Pauline's [Oliveros] piece was the most difficult because we really had to interpret the score. It was very instructional. It had a certain graphic that was wonderful but we really had to come to terms with "what did she mean here, and here?" We contacted her and she explained it. She had a text in there that was written by another woman that we had to employ. At one point we recorded it without the text because it was a little unwieldy for us. Her immediate response was, "Well, what about the text?" So we tried it again. We put the text in there and it was fine. It was a little strange because her piece had a lot to do with different sorts of velocity. Sometimes we really had to base our decisions on, "Well, does this *sound* good?" We know that we're doing it right but it sounds a little clumsy or a little stiff or a little tentative. So we weren't really happy until we did it until it actually *sounded* good. That one took a little more doing. That's no problem.[6]

Pauline Oliveros has focused on the art of improvisation for many years. Instrumentation is much less important to her than the art of practiced listening:

> The central concern in all my prose or oral instructions is to provide attentional strategies for the participants. Attentional strategies are nothing more than ways of listening and responding in consideration of oneself, others and the environment. The result of using these strategies is listening. If performers are listening then the audience is also likely to listen.[7]

The instructions for one of her works are worth considering within the context of any improvisatory situation:

> My instructions are intended to start an attentional process within a participant and among a group which can deepen gradually with repeated experience. Here is an example of a piece for voices or instruments: *Three Strategic Options*—Listen together. When you are ready to begin choose an option. Return to listening before choosing another option. Options are to be freely chosen throughout the duration of the piece. The piece ends when all return to listening together. 1) Sound before another performer 2) Sound after another performer 3) Sound with another performer. If performing as a soloist substitute sound from the environment for another performer.
>
> In order to perform *Three Strategic Options* all players have to listen to one another. Attention shifts with each option. Sounding before another could have a competitive edge. One has to listen for a silence which is the opportunity. Sounding after another implies patience. One has to listen for the end of a sound. Sounding with another takes intuition—direct knowing of when to start and to end. A definitive performance is not expected as each performance can vary considerably even though the integrity of the guidelines will not be disturbed and the piece could be recognizable each time it is performed by the same group. Style would change according to the performers, instrumentation and environment.[8]

Being aware of these dynamics, even as an audience member, can greatly embellish the experience of listening to live electronic music.

The history of live electronic music is rich. The recordings of two groups that are rooted in the '60s are worth seeking out. MEV (Musica Elettronica Viva) was formed in 1966 by American composers Alan Bryant, Alvin Curran, Jon Phetteplace, and Frederic Rzewski. The members of the group varied, so at times it also included Richard Teitelbaum, Ivan Vandor, Edith Schloss, Carol Plantamura, Steven Lacy and others. They toured heavily during the late '60s, giving more than one hundred concerts in thirty cities in Europe. In addition to their own works, they performed pieces by other composers including Cage, Behrman, Lucier, Cardew, Gelmetti, and Kosugi.

The music of MEV was free-form and radical in the most liberal tradition of Cage and Tudor. Instrumentation varied widely, from the simple amplification of room noise and outside sounds to the inclusion of electronic instruments such as the Moog synthesizer and traditional jazz and rock instruments.

London-based AMM was another touring group of electronic and jazz musicians formed in 1966. Composers Cornelius Cardew and Christopher Hobbs were the only members of the group with formal educations in classical music. The other members included jazz musicians Lou Gare, Edwin Prévost, and Keith Rowe.

Cardew, who was also a member of the musical wing of the Fluxus art movement in England, was the lecturer of the group:

> Written compositions are fired off into the future; even if never performed, the writing remains as a point of reference. Improvisation is in the present, its effect may live on in the souls of the participants, both active and passive (i.e., audience), but in its concrete form it is gone forever from the moment that it occurs, nor did it have any previous existence before the moment that it occurred, so neither is there any historical reference available. . . .
>
> You choose the sound you hear. But listening for effects is only first steps in AMM listening. After a while you stop skimming, start tracking, and go where it takes you.[9]

Ikue Mori (b. 1953) is something of an underground legend in New York. She arrived in the United States in 1977 with a musician friend who was immediately approached to join bands by punk luminaries Lydia Lunch and also by James Chance. Mori, not yet a practiced musician, met guitarist Arto Lindsay, who was looking for a drummer. She gave it a try and they started jamming. The threesome of Ikue Mori, Arto Lindsay, and Tim Wright became the recombinant punk band DNA.

DNA also proved to be Mori's first practice with improvisation. "In the beginning," she recalls, "when we were making pieces out of noise, we were doing a lot of improvisation. We probably made a song list of ten songs. We kept playing the same set for five years. I don't think it was musically developed, but it went beyond. DNA had become something beyond music."

After DNA, John Zorn introduced Mori to other improvisers in town. "Before that," she admits, "I really didn't know how to improvise. I was just playing a beat."

It was about that time that someone gave Mori a drum machine. She fell in love with it. It wasn't long after that, faced with the impracticality of hauling a set of drums up to her tiny new sixth-floor apartment, that she gave up conventional drumming entirely in favor of the drum machine. She has been composing and improvising, most recently with a PowerBook (equipped with MAX software) and two small drum machines. It all fits into a backpack. She is without doubt the most requested PowerBook performer in town. She lays down a backdrop of arrhythmic clangs and clacks to which other performers love to improvise. She has a *sound*, an electronic signature, that is all her own. Her music consists of mutations of signals generated by drum machines and other sources. Some occur in real time during a performance, while others are stored on her PowerBook for recall and modification using MAX. Noise and pitches commingle freely, at her command. They are sometimes rhythmic and structured, but often more amorphous, bounding in an omnidirectional manner about the performing space. She works like a painter, adding colors, depth, and textures to the lines being drawn by other artists.

A performance sometimes becomes an orchestration of people and instincts rather than music. For each production of her *Sheer Frost Orchestra*, Marina Rosenfeld (b. 1968) recruits a new group of seventeen female musicians and performers. The lifeblood of the piece results from the unpredictable interaction of the performers, who are teamed up in various changing combinations as specified by her score. Rosenfeld explains:

> Some of the interests I have as a music composer have crossed over into how I'm dealing with people. I realized that some of the ideas I have about *composing music* are just as relevant to *composing the participation of people* in my music. I'm especially interested in the differences between people and their idiosyncrasies as human beings. This is a feature of *The Sheer Frost Orchestra*, where I am often inviting women to participate based on some ambiance or feeling I get of their personality, as opposed to knowing what kind of musician they are, or might become. Each *Orchestra* performance has been close to an explosion of strong personalities.[10]

The performance of live, improvised electronic music has been with us since the vacuum-tube '50s. The few individual examples noted above barely do justice to a lively idiom that has many practitioners the world over. Improvisation is part of the experimental spirit that makes up the soul of electronic music. It challenges players and listeners alike to discard tradition in assessing improvisation. The criteria for experiencing this kind of electronic music has little to do with traditional music and everything to do with the way in which sounds are constructed and perceived by the whole of the human body and intellect. As Alvin Lucier so aptly puts it, one must be able to, "Go in by yourself and perceive it."[11]

The Art of Drones and Minimalism

Terry Riley and La Monte Young (b. 1935) were classmates at UC Berkeley in 1959. They knew of Cage's work, were immersed in the world of classical music, the German School of serialism, and musique concrète, and were highly aware of the tape music experiments taking place at the Columbia-Princeton Electronic Music Center. Even though they were both rooted in the new-music scene of northern California, both Riley and Young split from the core community of composers at Berkeley and the San Francisco Tape Music Center to pursue their own individual musical missions. Electronic music played a role in the development of their approaches to composition, but the two are most widely recognized as being key influences on a style of music called *minimalism* that has had its own powerful impact on new music.

In 1959, Young attended a summer music course in Darmstadt, Germany, where he studied with Karlheinz Stockhausen. While in Germany he also happened to experience the piano recitals of David Tudor and performances by John Cage, both of which greatly affected his musical direction. Tudor later featured one of Young's compositions—*X for Henry Flynt*—at one of his Darmstadt performances. Terry Riley was impressed by him, later saying, "La Monte was definitely the focal point of the class. He was so radical. I had never come across anyone like that in my life before."[12]

Classmates of Young and Riley included Pauline Oliveros, Paul Epstein, Loren Rush, David Del Tredici, and Doug Lee. While Young and Riley were attending UC Berkeley, they were also working as co-musical directors for Ann Halprin's dance company. There was a healthy rivalry growing between this group of composers. Riley remembers, "Everybody in that class was trying to out-do each other in being far out and seeing what could be the most new and mind-blowing thing that somebody could do in music."[13]

La Monte Young: Musical Reductionist

Prior to Darmstadt, La Monte Young had already begun to explore the possibilities of lengthening the duration of the notes in his music. His *Trio for Strings* (1958) was a serial piece requiring about an hour to perform because it was constructed of lengthy sustained tones and long silences. It has been called the work that established Young as the "father of minimalism."[14]

After experiencing Cage for the first time in Darmstadt, Young boldly began to add chance elements to his work and to strip it of complexity altogether. There was also a touch of Zen, possibly inspired by Cage as well, in his newly developed reductionist point of view. One of his first works following Germany was *Vision* (1959), which Young calls his "assimilation of Darmstadt."[15] It prescribed a time frame of thirteen minutes during which eleven precise sounds were made, the timing and spacing of which were governed by chance operations.[16] Inspired by Cage, Young was clearly conscious of the differences in his work that would set him apart from the elder statesman of experimental music. Cage's work from the early '60s was imbued with a complexity mediated by chance operations. Cage's definition of modernism was that it consisted of "collage and juxtaposition."[17] This was evidenced by works exhibiting an extraordinarily busy mingling of audiovisual events. It was as if Cage were dropping an asteroid in a reflecting pool: ripples became tidal waves that saturated one's perceptions. In contrast, Young submerged himself in a still lake, allowing fewer and fewer ripples to break the surface. His work was about *concentrating on a single thing* very intensely, be it a sound, a process, an action, a thought, an environment, or some other possible element of a performance. His work was equally saturating because of the way it filled the perceptions with the fullness of a simple action.

In 1960, Young moved to New York and worked from a loft in Greenwich Village. He began to explore radical interactions with audiences. Like the Fluxus performers based in England, he became interested in exploring radical aspects of social interaction with the audience. Some of his works from the early '60s were reduced to simple textual instructions, another innovation that followed Cage but also led to similar practices by Oliveros, Stockhausen, and others. *Composition #5 1960* (1960) consisted of a series of instructions, such as:

> Turn a butterfly (or any number of butterflies) loose in the performance area. When the composition is over, be sure to allow the butterfly to fly away outside. The composition may be any length but if an unlimited amount of time is available, the doors and windows may be opened before the butterfly is turned loose and the composition may be considered finished when the butterfly flies away.[18]

Young met Marian Zazeela in the early '60s, and the two have been inseparable ever since. While her expertise has been the creating of light environments for Young's performances, she is also one of the musicians who contributes to his work. From 1962 to 1965, Young's interest in extended sounds and drones led to the formation of a performance group that was eventually called the Theatre of Eternal Music. Members included Young (vocal drone) and Zazeela (vocal drone), Tony Conrad (violin), John Cale (viola), and Angus MacLise (percussion). (Cale and MacLise would go on to be founding members of the Velvet Underground.) Sine wave oscillators were used to create sustained electronic pitches, as was a small aquarium pump that vibrated with an audible hum. One of the extended works that they did was *The Tortoise, His Dreams and Journeys* (1964). Pitches to be performed were determined ahead of time by Young and consisted only of intervals that were multiples of seven, three, two, and one. The group would improvise around this predefined sound palette, mostly holding and permutating the tones for as long as they could. It was played loudly so that the tones would intersect, producing new sidebands and beat frequencies. A performance could last four or five hours.

Young first encountered Indian musician Pandit Pran Nath (1918–1996) in 1970. Learning about the art of the raga reinforced the kind of improvisation he had been practicing in the '60s, but also suggested some subtle changes that became a part of his compositional thinking. Rather than begin a piece with a strong musical statement, as he was apt to do when playing the saxophone, he learned to let a work unfold slowly from the very first note, resulting in a more suspended, organically evolving sound. Around this time, he and Zazeela created the concept of the *Dream House* for expanded musical experiences. The *Dream House* was at once a physical location, a sound and light environment, and a performance that lasted over an extended period of time. The couple did performances in various places. Some were a week long, others two weeks. One performance in Germany was for ninety days, where the performers played the piece every day for a week and then the electronic tones were left to continue sounding for the remaining days.[19] It was performed using voices and electronic drones.

Terry Riley: The Pulse of a New Sound

Riley wrote a *String Quartet* that was influenced in part by Young's *Trio for Strings* with its long sustained tones, but also by the fog horns that he could hear from his home in San Francisco. He then became involved in tape composition for a time with Morton Subotnick at the San Francisco Tape Music Center. As we have noted, he was probably the first composer to experiment with extended tape delay and the accumulating effect of running a single loop of tape through several tape machines, recording and rerecording signals in real time during the course of a performance. Riley came to his music of repeating figures and pulse rhythms largely by way of the tape recorder:

My interest then was to have some good tape recorders and work with tape loops and tape-loop feedback. The electronics were opening up new ideas in music for me. But I had no money to obtain a tape recorder. So I always used my skills as a pianist playing in bars to try to finance that part of my career.[20]

There was an aspect of Young's music that resonated with Riley, waiting to be assimilated into his own work. He recognized it not only as Young's tendency to repeat lines of notes many times, but also to strip the structure of a piece down to its bare essentials. By doing this, Young greatly reduced the motion and tension of a piece of music, so that it did not appear to move. It evolved slowly, through whatever process had been defined ahead of time.

In C, Riley's seminal work from this period, could not have existed without the influence of La Monte Young.[21] Riley knew that the key to In C was its static nature, its motionlessness even in the face of a complex production consisting of many instruments and musicians. Like the complex and machine-made player piano music of Conlon Nancarrow (1912–1997), In C was a conceptual precursor to the idea of programming and sequencing in electronic music. Not surprisingly, Riley went from the acoustic environment of In C to create electronic works for organ and other keyboards, including A Rainbow in Curved Air (1969) and the lovely Shri Camel (1980), which used a Yamaha synthesizer tuned for just intonation. He also became immersed in Indian music and has succeeded for many years in creating music with a tendency toward the transcendental listening experience.

Process Music

One thing I have noticed in speaking with electronic music composers is a fascination with *process*: the steps needed to get from one point to another in the realization of a piece of music. Sometimes the process itself *becomes* the piece of music.

You recognize a piece of process music almost immediately after it begins. In a few minutes you are saying to yourself, "Oh, I get it." You know what's going to happen next: at least you think you do, because the composer has made her or his intentions obvious as the work unfolds. The piece is a kind of game that you can now sit back and enjoy.

Process music does not require electronics. Much of the minimalist instrumental music of Steve Reich and Philip Glass is clearly process music: rules are set up by the composers that the instrumentalists faithfully follow. But I have noticed that many composers associated with this kind of composition—Reich in particular—dabbled first in elec-

Harold Budd: Minimalism Taken to the Extreme

Before he became known, along with Brian Eno, as one of the early progenitors of "ambient music," Harold Budd (b. 1936) was seeing how far the minimalist movement could be taken:

> In the early '70s, I was really searching for my own voice and I had not found it. I knew there was something lurking inside me that had to flower. I had hoped, I had wanted it to, anyway. I was extremely interested in the philosophy of minimalism rather than the actual practitioners. I found myself in a kind of quandary. I was very skillful at being clever without a great deal of exploration and in-depth looking at what I was doing. After I "wrote" *The Candy Apple Revision*, in 1970, which is merely a D-flat major chord, there really was no place to go past that. You could change key, but that was just cynical.
>
> In every sense of the word it was a political statement. Of course it was an artistic statement, but I thought that it was a political statement as well because it was flying in the face of what I thought at the time—still do, actually—was a very moribund practice of avant-garde music which wasn't going anywhere. It had already blown its impact. Nothing was happening. My political statement was to make something short, to the point, no analysis needed, that was absolutely devastatingly lovely, and then walk away from it. That pretty much wiped me out for two and a half years or so. I didn't compose at all. At the time I was teaching at Cal Arts and I had an income. So there were very little prospects beyond that.[22]

tronic music long enough to make the association between the mechanical characteristics of the medium and the possibility of making music based on those characteristics.

So, even though it is correct to say that composing process music does not require electronics, the use of electronic instrumentation often inspires its creation. The very nature of electronic music instruments, old and new, encourages a composer to think in terms of a process, whether that process is a hardwired patch of cables, a virtual patch inside a computer, or the turning of dials to various increments that shape the development of a piece of music.

The tape recorder has inspired process music from the early days of its use. It can be used as a means for recording and composing electronic music, or, in the case of process music, the tape machine itself becomes an integral cog in the process. An early process piece that also served as an installation was *Music for the Stadler Gallery* (1964) by Earle Brown, in which four recordings of the same instrumental piece were continuously replayed, on four separate tape recorders with the four tracks becoming increasingly out of phase with one another. The total duration of this piece was thirty days. An even earlier experiment using tape as the crux of the process was *Improvisation précédée et suive de ses variations* (1954) by Paul Arma, in which a tape recording of an orchestra is played in reverse at the same time as the same orchestra is performing the work live.[23]

Tape composition using tape loops is an example of process music. When Oliveros set up one tape loop running through two tape recorders for *I of IV* (1966), she was taking advantage of the phenomena of tape delays that was made possible by using two tape recorders. This was the defining concept or process behind the piece. Another was that the realization had to be possible in real time—a requirement of much process music. Oliveros was committed to performance pieces that could be engineered in front of an audience. The sounds were recorded on the first tape recorder, and were then played back on the second tape machine after an eight-second delay. Once played, the sound was fed directly back to the record channels of the first tape recorder. With the addition of reverberation, the result was a barrage of slowly unfolding undulations that changed dynamically as sounds continued to be repeated. Every sound that entered the loop was slowly transformed as other sounds were continuously layered on top.

Brian Eno also worked with tape delay much in the manner defined by Oliveros. However, he expressed a somewhat indifferent attitude toward the outcome. He described the realization of *Discreet Music* (1975):

> Since I have always preferred making plans to executing them, I have gravitated towards situations and systems that, once set into operation, could create music with little or no intervention on my part. That is to say, I tend towards the roles of planner and programmer, and then become an audience to the results.[24]

Eno's composition exists as a diagram of the devices used to generate the music. His approach is identical with that of Oliveros except that the sound material was specifically melodic and he did not modify or interact with the sound once the process was set in motion. Oliveros, on the other hand, played an active role during a performance of *I of IV* by continuously triggering new sounds to add to the evolving mix. The result in *Discreet Music* is the gradual transformation of a recognizable musical phrase that starts the process. Along with collaborator Robert Fripp, Eno continued to produce several works and performances using this process technique, but with the increasing involvement of the performer as a real-time wild card for throwing sonic monkey wrenches into the steadily turning wheels of tape-delayed sound.

Steve Reich has composed some of the purest forms of process music. His early tape compositions dating from 1965 and 1966 used tape loops to explore the process of phasing—identical segments of recorded sound were played synchronously using more than one tape recorder and then were allowed to drift out of phase as the speed of one of the players was increased or decreased. As the sounds went in and out of "phase" with one another, they created new combinations of timbres, beats, and harmonics. When the sound material had a natural cadence, the process of phasing often created continuously shifting changes to the rhythm as the sound drifted in and out of phase. Adding additional tracks and loops of the same source sound increased the possibilities for phasing relationships.

Reich's first tape works using this phasing process were based on recordings of the human voice. He discovered the phasing process by accident while playing tape loops of a Pentecostal street preacher he had recorded in San Francisco. The resulting work, *It's Gonna Rain* (1965), began with the simplest demonstration of phasing as two loops began in unison, moved completely out of phase with one another, and then gradually came back together in unison. The same process began again with two longer loops to which Reich added another two and then eventually eight to create a multilayered series of phasing sequences happening in parallel. *Come Out* (1966) was shorter and used a brief tape loop of a young man describing the aftermath of a beating he was given at a police station in New York City. In this case a short phrase of the young man's voice was first played using two loops going gradually out of phase. The natural rhythm and melody of the voice led to a kind of two-voice canon. Reich enriched the canon or "round" effect by then using four and finally eight tracks, the last consisting of a beautifully undulating pulse that sounds more like the reverberating sound of a ticking clock in a tunnel than the human voice.

Reich's use of the human voice as source material was a departure from the norm in electronic music of that time. He recalled why he made that choice in his first electronic music experiments:

> I was interested in real sounds, what was called *musique concrète* in those days, but I wasn't really interested in the pieces that had been done. I thought that they were boring, partly because the composers had tried to

mask the real sounds. I was interested in using understandable sounds, so that the documentary aspect would be a part of the piece.[25]

Reich felt that by not altering the dynamics of the voice—its pitch and tone color—it retained its naturally emotive power. His phasing treatment then magnified the expression of the voice through rhythm and repetition.

After realizing *Come Out*, Reich moved on to compose music for live instrumentalists. His love of the phasing process was so strong that some of his first instrumental works from this period, such as *Piano Phase* (1967), recreated the effect with live musicians. He gradually applied a process approach to an entire canon of works, which placed him on the map as a leading proponent of minimalist music. *Four Organs* (1970), for four electric organs and maracas, is a tour de force of process composition. The piece is based on the augmentation of a single chord of music that is played, note by note, in a slowly unfolding sequence by four organists. Reich described the work in this way:

> *Four Organs* is an example of music that is a "gradual process." By that I do not mean the process of composition, but rather pieces of music that are, literally, processes. The distinctive thing about musical processes is that they determine all the note-to-note (sound-to-sound) details and the overall form simultaneously. (Think of a round or an infinite canon.) I am interested in perceptible processes. I want to be able to hear the process happening throughout the sounding music. To facilitate closely detailed listening, a musical process should happen extremely gradually.[26]

Four Organs is literally a twenty-four-minute piece of music consisting of a single chord. The work has structure only because of the *process* through which the chord is disassembled and recombined.

A conceptual cousin to Reich's *Four Organs* music is *Points* (1973–74) by Ruth Anderson, which used only sine waves as the raw threads of the piece. Individual tones of different frequencies entered at intervals of five seconds, building up a multilayered fabric of sound that gradually began to thin again as the earlier threads of sound were pulled out. The process repeated several times but with different choices of pitches making up the threads.

Composers have developed many clever ways to use the concept of a process in their music. Computer music is a particularly fertile field of possibilities for applying processes. This fact has been recognized by anyone working with any size or vintage of computer.

Figure in a Clearing (1977) by David Behrman used one of his homemade synthesizers based on the KIM-1 microcomputer. The process used in this work consisted of rules being carried out by the

Gen Ken Montgomery and the Packaging of Process

Gen Ken Montgomery (b. 1957) is a sound artist and composer who has been composing and performing in New York City since 1978. He described *DRONESKIPCLICKLOOP* (1997), his work for four compact discs to be played simultaneously:

> The sound source for each of the four programs was created by typing random numbers representing acoustic specifications into a FM synthesis module for the computer. The resulting one or two seconds of sound was offset by random numbers into another channel and repeated for seventeen minutes. (At this time I was almost exclusively using recordings of everyday sounds for my work. No synthesizers or electronics. I used the computer for visuals and communication, not sound. *DRONESKIPCLICKLOOP* was the first piece I created on the computer since the late '80s when I worked with Conrad Schnitzler's Yamaha computer in Berlin).
>
> I have a written score for the performances I made of *DRONE-SKIPCLICKLOOP*. Rather than start the CDs together they overlapped slowly. The first CD (Drone) played for ten minutes before the 2nd CD (Skip) came in, etc. Otherwise, I instruct people to play the four CDs simultaneously.
>
> Phasing is an important element in *DRONESKIPCLICKLOOP*. It was designed from the beginning to create these effects. I had made quite a few random noises and tried phasing them to each other before selecting the four that are used in the piece. The position of the speakers in the room is an important factor in the phasing sound as well. Again making it unique to each performance. And I actively stop and start individual CDs to find the phasing that I like. However, when the four CDs are left to play continuously without my intervention the phasing changes organically as there are microtonal tempo shifts incorporated into the tracks.*

---

* Ken Montgomery, personal communication with Thom Holmes, July 13, 2001.

computer in real time during the performance. A live cellist responded to chord changes played by the computer, which employed sixteen triangle wave oscillators. The computer could also choose those chord changes from any one of several preset tunings. The tempo of the chords was determined by an algorithm modeling the velocity of a satellite in a falling elliptical orbit around a planet. While the computer ran on its own using rules for making chord and tuning changes, the live cellist improvised using six pitches specified by the composer.

Alvin Lucier is the godfather of process music. He is widely known for works that begin with a process or idea that is then carried out according to written guidelines. The process in most of Lucier's works is often a physics lesson of some sort. In *Vespers* (1968), performers walked through a darkened space using handheld echo-location devices to find their way. In a version of *Clocker* (1978) that he produced with Nicolas Collins, Lucier wired himself to a galvanic skin response monitor that could measure the differences in skin resistance caused by mood changes. The electrical signal of the device was amplified and used as a control voltage to modify the speed of a ticking clock. The ticking was amplified and sent through a delay system, creating layers of ticking that Lucier could manipulate, much in the manner of Reich's phasing idea, but in real time rather than on tape: "I wanted to make a work in which a performer could speed up and slow down time, stopping it, if possible, simply by thinking."[27] *Clocker* was the literal implementation of this desire.

Lucier's list of process works is extensive, each one unique. *I Am Sitting in a Room* (1970) explores the process of sound filtering by the natural acoustics of a room by repeated playback and rerecording of successive generations of Lucier's voice reciting a short paragraph. *Music for Piano with One or More Snare Drums* (1990) picks up the sympathetically vibrating sounds of snare drums as "a pianist plays a series of notated pitches in chronological order, repeating them freely in overlapping patterns."[28] In *Music on a Long Thin Wire* (1980), a single piano wire was made to vibrate through the action of a horseshoe magnet and the current from an oscillator. As it vibrated, it began to sound. The acoustics of the room determined how the oscillator would have to be adjusted to get it to work.

The passing of time can be the basis for a process piece. Cage was known for a series of "number" pieces, the titles of which all specified the precise length of the works down to the second. Two of these included *31'57.9864" for a Pianist* (1954), and *27'10.554" for a Percussionist* (1956). A stopwatch was required to perform these.

Composer Laurie Spiegel (b. 1945) has worked with mainframe and microcomputers to compose music. Her approach often integrates a predefined logical process running in real-time on a computer with actions that she can take during the generation of the sound:

> What computers excel at is the manipulation of patterns of information. Music consists of patterns of sound. One of the computer's greatest strengths is the opportunity it presents to integrate direct interaction with an

instrument and its sound with the ability to compose musical experiences much more complex and well designed than can be done live in one take.[29]

Old Wave (1980) was composed using a Bell Labs computer that controlled analog synthesis equipment through a program called GROOVE. With the computer, Spiegel applied weighted mathematical probabilities to develop the pitches and rhythms of melodic lines. The weightings could be made to change "continuously or at given time, so that certain notes would dominate under certain conditions."[30]

In another work, *Pentachrome* (1980), an algorithm is used to continuously accelerate the music, but Spiegel performed the rate and scale of the acceleration by adjusting knobs and dials in real-time. This combination of real-time, almost improvisatory action on the part of a performer who is otherwise following a process is not an uncommon approach to process music when it is performed live. Spiegel always keeps something of the human touch in her music:

> What I could control with the knobs was the apparent rate of acceleration (the amount of time it took to double the tempo), and the overall tempo at which this happened (the extremes of slow and fast that were cycled between). This was only one of the processes going on in the piece. Stereo placement (voicing) was automated, too, except for the percussion voice, which just doubled the melodic line. I did the timbral changes completely by hand.[31]

One of Spiegel's early microcomputer works was *A Harmonic Algorithm* (1980), composed with an Apple II computer. This piece is comprised of a program that "goes on composing music as long as the program is allowed to run,"[32] making it the ultimate self-fulfilling prophecy of process composition.

The Sheer Frost Orchestra (1999) by Marina Rosenfeld is a performance work combining elements of process (time and structure controls) with improvisation. The work calls for seventeen women to play electric guitars or computers. The guitars are placed on the floor in front of each performer. Rosenfeld teaches the players six techniques for playing the guitar with a nail polish bottle (hence the "Sheer Frost" brand name of the title). The score specifies various combinations of players using these techniques over the course of 110 thirty-second segments played without pause for the duration of the fifty-five-minute work. A large digital clock is mounted in the space so that the performers can keep time. Rosenfeld also combines elements of process control and improvisation in her solo work for turntable, *theforestthegardenthesea* (1999), part of a larger work called *Fragment Opera*. The sound material for this work consists of sounds composed and recorded by Rosenfeld onto acetate discs. A live performance involves playing and processing a sequence of the disc sounds, all of which is modified in real time using turntable techniques and audio processors. She explains her approach:

> These are compositions that are superimposable, or modular. With each suite of records I am assuming that the beginning of the performance will somehow start with an unmanipulated superimposition of the "fragments" and as the performance evolves, transformations start to take place with new juxtapositions and so on. . . . It's improvisation but there is usually a structure that is notated at some point. My scores have to do with a sequence of events, but they are not exact instructions to go from point A to point F with B-C-D-E regimented in between. I don't make scores for myself when I perform solo but as soon as I am in an ensemble situation there is usually some kind of score which might look more like a grid, a sequence of events, or something like that.[33]

An approach to process that is not as frequently used is that of gradually changing dynamics in a sound field, perhaps coupled with a steady increase of a given isolated dynamic, such as volume. Iannis Xenakis's defiant *Bohor* (1962) was a tape piece using the amplified sounds of Asian jewelry and a Laotian mouth organ. This was during a period in which he was exploring the gradual transformation of sounds within a cloud of seemingly unchanging density. "You start with a sound made up of many particles, then see how you can make it change imperceptibly, growing, changing, and developing, until an entirely new sound results." Xenakis said he likened this process to the "onset of madness, when a person suddenly realizes that an environment that had seemed familiar to him has now become altered in a profound, threatening sense."[34] The piece has also been likened to the experience of listening to the clanging of a large bell—from *inside* the bell.[35]

The clangorous tones of *Bohor* begin quietly and then steadily build to an extremely loud conclusion that ends so abruptly that it must have been cut off with a pair of scissors. The twenty-two-minute work is largely about the process of increasing volume, and is so extreme in its execution that even Pierre Schaeffer, to whom it was dedicated, could do little but make fun of it. Referring back to Xenakis's *Concret PH*, the pleasant piece composed of the sounds of burning embers and played in the Philips Pavilion at the 1958 World's Fair along with Varèse's *Poème electronique*, Schaeffer said:

> No longer were we dealing with the crackling of small embers [Concret PH], but with a huge firecracker, an offensive accumulation of whacks of a scalpel in your ears at the highest level on the potentiometer.[36]

The crowd that witnessed a live performance of *Bohor* in Paris in 1968 was strongly divided about the work. According to one observer, "By the end of the piece, some were affected by the high sound level to the point of screaming; others were standing and cheering."[37]

Music of the Environment: Ambience, Meditation, and the Art of Being Where You Are

In April 1971, I attended an open rehearsal and discussion of the Merce Cunningham Dance Company and his musicians, John Cage, David Tudor, and Gordon Mumma. During a question-and-answer session, someone asked Mumma what he was currently working on. He replied saying in part that he was working on "music that sounds like it was recorded at a great distance." I hadn't considered such a thing before. The idea struck me as documentary minimalism—audio verité—a coincidental blend of the natural sounds of nature with music. I tried to imagine what it would sound like. Any kind of music heard from a distance would be quiet, certainly. But it would also be muted by the natural filtering of the environment. Melodies would unspool. Themes would break apart and drift off on the breeze. Accents, rhythms, and patterns would float indiscriminately, disembodied, losing their association with the whole. Yet the idea didn't seem antimusical. It struck me as an acknowledgment that the experience of music occurs on many levels of consciousness. Music could connect you with the environment, fasten you to your surroundings through the sensation of hearing and the consequent thoughts conjured up by your mind. It wasn't until recently that I actually heard the specific piece of music that Mumma was referring to. It was the extraordinarily quiet second part of his piece *Retrospect* and was called *Phenomenon Unarticulated* (1972). I later learned that Mumma had used a similar "distant" sound-composition technique in the music for Merce Cunningham's choreography *Signals* (1960).[38]

What Mumma had planted in my mind was the concept of *ambient* music, several years before there was any music described as such. This was my first recognition of an idea that had been lurking about in new music for many years and which has since evolved into a multifaceted idiom of its own.

Ambient and environmental music had roots in the '50s and '60s, particularly in the work of Cage and Tudor, who drew attention to ambient sounds through the inclusion of silent patches in their works, *4'33"* (1951) for a pianist—Cage's so-called silent sonata—being the earliest unequivocal plea to embrace ambient sound as part of music. Cage had an affinity for ambient sounds that he voiced throughout his career. In a piece written in 1950, he spoke about the experiential context within which his plundering of silence would take place:

> This psychological turning leads to the world of nature, where, gradually
> or suddenly, one sees that humanity and nature, not separate, are in this
> world together; that nothing was lost when everything was given away. In
> fact, everything is gained. In musical terms, any sounds may occur in any
> combination and in any continuity.[39]

So strongly did he feel about his innate appreciation of the sounds of the world around us that he could jokingly wonder out loud about the value of writing music at all.

In practice, the '60s were a showcase for experimental music that made use of ambient sounds. Cage and Tudor amplified remote sounds from rooms and piped them into an auditorium (*Variations IV,* 1964). Alvin Lucier has an extensive body of work exploring the natural acoustics of a given performing space. Max Neuhaus, widely credited with inventing the sound "installation," provided continuously playing music within the context of public spaces. David Behrman composed what could be called the first musical composition of electronic sounds with environmental sounds in 1968 for the Robert Watts (1923–1988) film *Cascade*. It was a tape work consisting of highly audible environmental sounds with electronics murmuring underneath and has much of the atmosphere and flavor associated with later experimental ambient works. He called it a collage piece at the time. He remembered that its composition was done independently of the motion picture: "I had seen the film before making the music, but didn't coordinate any of the sounds with any specific action in the film."[41] The film made the rounds of art house theaters at the time but was not highly visible and therefore does not seem to qualify as a major influence on other composers. Thankfully, the music is now available on CD in the form of a piece called *Sounds for a Film by Robert Watts* (Italy, Alga Marghen, Plana B 5NmN.020, 1998). With the exception of a little Cage and Lucier, much of this kind of music was not recorded or released on record and so became the stuff of live performance legend.

Three artists released recordings during the '70s that defined and anticipated a growing interest in music that combined elements of the acoustic environment with musical ideas. Considered individually, one might not normally draw comparisons between the work of Wendy Carlos, Annea Lockwood (b. 1939), and Brian Eno. Each was responsible, however, for experimenting in ambient sound composition in ways that would be much imitated in the future.

Wendy Carlos composed the remarkable *Sonic Seasonings* in 1972, combining synthesized sounds with environmental sounds. Nobody knew quite what to make of it at the time, since it fit none of the convenient names being given to record bins in the store. It consisted of two LPs' worth of quiet, subtle sounds, carefully composed to gently bob the imagination. They were mood pieces, intended to invoke the essence of the four seasons. Carlos's own words explain the concept best:

> *Sonic Seasonings* has the form of a musical suite, made of four contrasting movements. Each is loosely based on images of the four basic seasons on our planet: Spring, Summer, Fall, and Winter. . . .
>
> There is no real plot in any of the movements. Instead they suggest a cyclic point of view that moves onto a few other musical locations, and eventually returns to a similar setting to whence it began.[42]

Carlos wrote musical parts, ever so minimal at times, to accompany recorded sounds of nature. For "Spring," a theme was written to blend with birdsong. For "Summer," an "impressionistic throb and 'klangfarbenmelodie' of timbre" is joined by a slowly arpeggiating melody. "Fall" faces off with the ocean with "majestic" and "folky" musical themes. "Winter" begins sparsely, builds with a drone and is eventually lifted mysteriously by a processed human vocalization by Rachel Elkind responding to a chorus of howling wolves.

By the early '70s, composer Annea Lockwood had created a niche for herself in new music as the lady who burned and drowned pianos and made electroacoustic music with shards of glass. She had worked widely with choreographers and visual artists and was very much in tune with the environmental aspects of the performance space. It was about this time that she turned her attention to the creation of pieces and installations using recorded sounds from the natural world. She had been making remote recordings of natural phenomena such as river sounds since the late '60s, and many of these elements figured prominently in her remarkable *World Rhythms* (1975). *World Rhythms* was a musical travelogue of nature sounds that was pieced together as carefully as a dovetail joint to mesh the rhythms of one segment with those of the next. It was all about the natural world of rhythms in which we exist, making that connection between the listener and the environment that is at the heart of ambient/environmental music.

Lockwood's approach to using taped sounds differed significantly from musique concrète. Like Steve Reich, she was interested in using sounds as themselves so that their intrinsic qualities could be heard. She did not want to mask them with excessive electronic manipulation or even the kind of loop editing that Reich used to transform natural sounds into complex rhythms. She let sounds unfold on their own. Her process has been that of selecting and carefully organizing natural sounds. She explains:

> I've never done much manipulation of the sound sources I'm working with. What I *have* been doing all of this time is selecting what I want to record very carefully, listening to it very closely, and figuring out angles, situations, and times of day in which to record to get maximum presence. I'm really interested in acoustic commonalities amongst various disparate sounds and tracing them. That's been one of my focal points for my electroacoustic works rather than treating these sounds sources as intrinsically raw material and then working them over and transforming them. I regard them all as self-sufficient, certainly as intricately complex and complete audio phenomena in and of themselves. I'm looking at the relationships amongst them.
>
> In terms of assembling the sound materials for a piece . . . very often what will lead me to select sound X to follow what I am currently doing rather than sound Y is something very specific in their respective rhythms or something to do with the frequency band. *Similarity* which can show that I can make a transition, a smooth sort of interface transition between the two sounds. I'm interested in making those sorts of transitions where you really don't realized that you've slipped over into another sound until a second or so.[43]

World Rhythms wasn't only conceived as a recorded work, however, and had an important beginning as a live performance piece:

> *World Rhythms* was composed in 1974–75 and was a ten-channel live improvised mix, together with a performer on a very large tam-tam. The ten speakers formed a circle around the audience, placed at various heights (the speakers!). The gong player and person mixing both sat in the center. The gong part is designed to create an actual biorhythm, not an analog for the heartbeat or anything like that. The player strikes the gong then turns inward, tracking her/his body's responses to that action (not to the mix or even to the sound of the gong per se). When all responses seem to have ebbed away, sh/e sounds the gong again. So it is a rhythm of action and response which is being added to the general mix, but which is created independently of the mix.[44]

Following *World Rhythms*, Lockwood's fascination with river sounds led to the creation of *The River Archive*—a library of natural river sounds that continues to grow to this day. "I've not counted how many rivers the Archive now has, contributed by friends and acquaintances, as well as my own collecting."[45] The idea was triggered by a passage she once read in a book about a Peruvian culture that believed that the sound of a river had healing powers. They were taking people who were off-balance in various ways, out of balance, to rivers for entire days at a time because they felt that that environment rebalanced mental processes. That really stuck in my head. I was living near London and not long after that living in Manhattan and was drawn to river sounds in any case from childhood memories but also because of their textural complexity. They are really complicated masses of interlocking rhythms. That interested me greatly. I came up with the idea of collecting river recordings and making installations from them for city people who were deprived of rivers.[46]

The archive includes the watery pinnacle of her installation work, *A Sound Map of the Hudson River* (1980), a two-hour continuously playing/looping tape comprised of sounds recorded at twenty-six sites, from the source to the mouth of the Hudson River.

These works by Carlos and Lockwood laid the foundation for environmental and ambient music by deftly blending electronics and the recorded manipulation of natural sounds. The next step—a decidedly musical one—was taken by Brian Eno with the release of *Music for Airports* in 1978. His was not music *from* the environment but music *for* the environment, much like Mumma's earlier experiment with *Phenomenon Unarticulated*. It consisted of short pieces of electronic background music, splashes of sound for the blank audio canvas of imaginary airports. Eno used the term "ambient" in describing the work:

An ambience is defined as an atmosphere or a surrounding influence: a tint. My intention is to produce original pieces ostensibly (but not exclusively) for particular times and situations with a view to building up a small but versatile catalogue of environmental music suited to a wide variety of moods and atmospheres . . . Ambient Music must be able to accommodate many levels of listening attention without enforcing one in particular: it must be as ignorable as it is interesting.[47]

This was a new way of listening as much as it was a new way of composing with sound. It assumed that there was a quieter side of the human psyche to which music could appeal. The ambient work of Eno and Harold Budd, his first collaborator in this style, invoked a resilient strength that many found soothing. Some called it *meditative* music, and this led to the idea of *healing* music and the phenomenon of *new age* music. Although ambient is widely accepted today as an alternative style of music, pioneers such as Eno did not find record companies to be too receptive to the idea back in the '70s:

Ambient music was a completely obscure and oblique idea. I remember taking that into record companies, and them saying, "Nobody wants to listen to music that doesn't have a beat, doesn't have a melody, doesn't have a singer, doesn't have words." All they could see were all the things it didn't have. Well, it turns out they were wrong: people's tastes have very much drifted in that direction, and people are very able to handle long pieces of music with or without structures and key chord changes.[48]

Harold Budd is a pioneer of ambient music by virtue of his association with Eno. However, "ambient" is not a term he ever uses to describe the work, and he strongly disagrees with people who find something "meditative" or "healing" about this music. He remarked that the trouble with most "new age" and "meditative music" was that "it had absolutely no evil in it."[49] His music comes from a darker corner of the human psyche: "I find that it comes from a rather *unpeaceful* sort of place. I think an element of danger and a kind of unsettled quality. Unresolved issues. I don't find it meditative at all, just the opposite. If that were meditation, I for one would give it up immediately."[50]

About the time that Eno composed *Music for Airports*, he heard a cassette of a work by Budd that had been performed at Wesleyan University. *Madrigals of the Rose Angel* (1972) was written for female chorus, harp, percussion, and keyboard. Budd had conceived of a piano part that was so radically quiet that he couldn't get anyone to play it adequately. "There didn't seem to be any way to notate it," he explains:

> I could say, "play softly," or "play at the very edge like you're just about to ruin the whole piece." So I decided that in my role as composer I really had to switch over to be the performer as well because I was the only one that really understood what should be done. By default, I became a keyboard player not out of any great desire to express myself but out of the desire to protect my idea.[51]

The piece was performed in the mid-'70s at Wesleyan and, unbeknownst to Budd, a cassette began circulating around the music world. Gavin Bryars and Michael Nyman had a copy of the tape and gave it to Brian Eno. Eno was soon on the phone to Budd asking him if he wanted to turn the work into a commercial recording project.

The *Madrigals* became part of a collection of pieces that were called the *The Pavilion of Dreams* (1978), consisting of four chamber works composed between 1972 and 1975. Following that, Brian recruited Budd to collaborate with him on "something that no one had ever done before."[52] This became the *Ambient 2: The Plateaux of Mirror* (1980), a seminal work of musically inclined ambient music. It was followed by a second piano-based collaboration between the two called *The Pearl* (1984). These two studio works established a quiet, moody style of music of translucent beauty. Budd's elemental musical themes were the ideal foil for Eno's whispery electronic treatments.

It surprised me to learn that the haunting afterimages of sound and beautifully engineered works that comprise *The Plateaux of Mirror* and *The Pearl* were all improvised. Budd would work things out on the keyboard and Eno added his treatments, delays, and mutational processes to the music in real time:

> As you can tell, I am not a professional piano player. My fingerings are all incorrect. I have no athletic skill at the keyboard. I have no formal training at the keyboard. It's all very much what I can come up with at the point of actually doing it. The music is improvised, by and large, or at least extemporaneous. Which is different from something that you can do with a large ensemble of pieces. Neither one of us knew how it was going to turn out. So, we just started. You have to start somewhere so we started inside the studio, inside a pop music studio, with all the Lexicons and the electronic loops and all that stuff that is taken for granted. We didn't know. We didn't have a clue. The quality of the sound is very much due to Brian's skill, period. It wasn't added afterward. It was real time.[53]

Like that bootleg tape of the *Madrigals of the Rose Angel* that compelled Eno to bring Budd into the studio, anyone who heard the recordings of *The Pavilion of Dreams* or *The Plateaux of Mirror* were instantly drawn to them. Budd and Eno seemed to have discovered a rarity in new music these days: a blank canvas. They invented a new palette of sounds and directed the softest of electronic brush strokes to create a dazzling body of highly evocative sound paintings.

The more "musically composed" work of Carlos, Eno, Budd, Jon Hassell, Jon Gibson, and Michael Snow led directly to what is called ambient music today: subtle rhythms and electronic drones. Tetsu Inoue, one of the '90s generation of electronic composers, made his mark with a hybrid form of ambient music that deftly blended world rhythms, documentary sounds, and twittering electronics into a less edgy form of house music. There is also a persistent strand of quieter, harmonious ambient music that is placed under the heading of "new age" music.

It is difficult to draw a line showing where ambient music ends and "other" music begins. One might say that the feature that distinguishes ambient music is nothing more than its voltage or energy level. If recorded music is a high-definition medium—a *hot* medium—as McLuhan suggests, then ambient music must surely be at the low-definition end of the scale.[54] It provides much less structure and content, opening a gap that must be completed or filled by the listener. Perhaps this is why some people think that environmental or ambient music is something *less* than other music. It serves a different purpose. It leads us into an attachment with the space in which we are. Ambient music draws you out to connect with your surroundings; other music gushes out and drenches you with its inescapable rhythm and structure.

Turntablism

Twentieth-century culture has had a love affair with the record player. The turntable has always been a technology of mass consumption. Those of us who were raised prior to the coming of the audio CD—I guess that means every human being on earth who is older than twenty—has childhood memories accompanied by the remembered sounds of scratchy, skipping, vinyl records. For us, the sound of a record being played is charged with such memories. This artifact of "contemporary household culture," as Thurston Moore calls it, has had a long history in the performance of music as well.[55]

In 1936, Varèse had experimented with turntables that could play in reverse and had variably adjustable speeds.[56] In Cage's apocryphal credo on experimental music written in 1937, he mentioned turntables as one of several electrical instruments that would help usher in a new era in the history of music.[57] Recordings of music on 78 rpm discs were widely available at the time and provided the only practical means for making sound recordings until the availability of the tape recorder by about 1950. Cage composed a piece for prerecorded discs called *Imaginary Landscape No. 1* in 1939, for which test records were played simultaneously and their speeds variably adjusted according to Cage's instructions. In 1948, Pierre Schaeffer completed his first work of musique concrète—the *Etudes de bruits*—using turntable technology to collect, play back, and record the final version of the piece.

Turntablism is the use of the turntable as a musical instrument. A vital and broadening DJ performance culture has emerged during the past thirty years. Since about 1977, when Grand Wizard Theodore invented the "scratch" technique, turntablism has been at the center of several musical idioms, most notably hip hop, techno, electronica, and other kinds of house or dance music. Each style has its own use of the turntable. What they have in common is an affinity for active sound mixing as a performance element and the application of electronic effects and synthesizer modules to broaden the sound spectrum of the turntable.

A repertoire of DJ skills has evolved. *Scratching* is the manual reversal of the spin of a record to run the needle backwards over the sound in a quick, rhythmic swipe. The manipulation of beats is another intrinsic characteristic of turntablism. A spinning record is itself a loop, especially when the needle is made to hug a groove rather than move ahead with the natural spiral of the track. *Beat juggling* uses either two identical turntable recordings or one disc and a digital sampler to repeat the same sounds as a "breakbeat." Digital looping and delay are also common to beat manipulation. These techniques are for the turntablist what finger exercises are for the piano player.

Like any performance medium, turntablism has its radicals, its experimentalists, who push the form in unexpected directions. The omnipresence of turntable music in today's culture has been likened to an earlier generation that grew up emulating rock-and-roll artists. "The electric guitar is an instrument that's fifty years old," remarked turntablist Christian Marclay (b. 1955). "It's already become a nostalgic instrument for baby boomers. Today's new guitar is the turntable."[58] These experimental artists use the same equipment as their more popular DJ counterparts, but with a different musical object in mind. They are no different than composers who write experimental works for other instruments and remain vastly outnumbered by those who write conventionally for the widest commercial appeal. They view their instrument as a resource for new musical possibilities.

Marclay is a key figure in the revival of experimental turntablism. He began in 1979 when hip-hop turntablism was emerging. Nicolas Collins calls him the "in-between man" in the development of this style. Marclay approached the music from the perspective of an art school student. He sometimes shared the stage with hip-hop artists, but also organized installations and events that were more common to the gallery scene. After ten years or so devoted to turntable music, he returned to art again. Now he is back and in great demand as a music improviser. Collins thinks that maybe "he's been forgotten by a generation. A lot of DJs came up and started doing the same stuff. He came back in and people noticed him."[59]

Marclay's approach to his instrument is much like Cage's towards the piano. He does not use the trendiest turntable technology, preferring to lug around industrial-strength record players that look like they came from a garage sale at an elementary school. Some of these are not always in the best of working order. He has also repurposed the content of the music on old recordings through his real-time editing of old sounds into new forms, the ultimate recontextualization of reality in music. His palette is rich and he is as likely to break a record as preserve it for future use. He is *not* a collector of records: he is a living channel through which the recorded history of our culture is collected and expressed, a human audio filter.

Marclay also brought black boxes to turntablism. He would be

Christian Marclay in performance. In preparation, he lays his vinyl discs out on any convenient surface, in this case the top of a grand piano. Photo by Thom Holmes (2001).

equally at home setting up shop for a Merce Cunningham performance as for a club date in the East Village. He stacks his records, unsheathed, so that they *will* be scratched and damaged, adding to the noise elements that become an intriguing subtheme of turntable music. Watching him perform is not unlike watching any other highly focused musician. He is intent on the next moment, anticipating changes, listening to haphazard collisions of sound that sometime coalesce, all under his watchful eye. He works with four to eight turntables, digital delay, distortion boxes, and other gizmos thrown together to produce a live mix. His recordings are often prepared using "abusive manipulation": rubbing two records together, cracking them, breaking them apart and gluing them back together, and allowing them to get extremely dirty.[60]

In a recent compilation of his early work, he explained his approach to performance this way:

> I worked on these pieces until I found the right combination of records, then integrated them into my set. Usually lasting between 20 and 30 minutes, the set was an uninterrupted flow of records mixed on multiple turntables—four, six, or sometimes up to eight turntables. It evolved continuously, as records got damaged beyond use and new ones were found. The records were annotated, numbered and stacked in original piles. These stacks of prepared records were my score. Later I preferred improvising with just a few markings on the records, which were ordered only by sound types. I do not remember specifically which records were used on most of these mixes; to my ears they were only sounds, very abstract and detached from their original sources. They lost their identity and became fragments to be mixed—a loop, a texture, a transition, a beat, an intro, a word.[61]

Marclay's most provocative avant-garde statement may have been his 1989 installation piece called *Footsteps*. For this work, he first pressed 3,500 copies of a vinyl disc featuring the sound of recorded footsteps. For six weeks during the summer of 1989, these discs were laid out on the floor of one of the Shedhalle Galleries in Zurich. Visitors to the gallery had to walk on top of the loosely piled recordings, marking the discs with scratches, cracks, dirt, and other physical elements of wear and tear. Each record suffered its own unique form of damage, producing the kind of "abusive manipulation" en masse that Marclay applied individually to his performance discs. After six weeks, 1,100 of the records were packaged and sold (one hundred as a signed edition). The recordings were art objects with an aura of impermanence. Marclay had done something like this on a smaller scale in 1985 with his legendary *Record without a Cover*. Thurston Moore notes, "Christian encouraged the owner to progressively *destroy* the edition. This destruction enabled the listener to create a personal stamp and therefore eradicate any question of value to the object."[62]

A turntablist who has been influenced by Marclay is DJ Olive, the Audio Janitor (Gregor Asch). Like Marclay, he has an art background and became involved in turntablism when he had to provide music for installations. He uses the standard-issue equipment for most DJs, two or three Technics SL-1200 turntables. Rather than working with recordings of recognizable or popular music, his tendency is to shape abstract sounds, electronic or electroacoustic in origin. Using digital delay and sampling, he jockeys sound fragments back and forth, progressively mutating them in conceptual ways that are close to the roots of tape composition. His work sometimes emulates Stockhausen's work with the Springer machine, suspending sounds in time, eradicating all tempo, and then gradually transforming them into something else. His use of recording techniques in real time adds a dimension of complexity to turntablism that is critical to the overall effect of his work. His turntable sources share the audio space with ghosts of themselves that persist sometimes long after the records have been switched.

While Marclay's "score" consists of a stack of records, DJ Olive has devised what he calls the "vinyl score," as a way to extend his work to other turntablists. A vinyl score is a collection of sounds that DJ Olive has created and committed to disc so that other DJs can use them. Each disc includes about fifty tracks. His instructions are simple. "The rules are that you have three turntables. You mix between ten and twenty minutes. Record it and send it to me."[396] This approach brings out the improvisatory nature of turntablism, which is purposefully encouraged by DJ Olive's less-than-rigorous rules of engagement:

What you would paint and what I would paint with a disc would have to
be completely different. What you would pull out of it and what I might
pull out of it would be totally different. And you can't play the whole
thing because you can only play for ten or twenty minutes. So you can
just kind of find some stuff you like and make your interpretation this
time like working just this one band. This is open-ended composition. It
can never be played the same way twice and there is no correct way to
play it. It kind of shows you what the DJ does and what the instrument is.
I've done shows with five different DJs and you see one after the next play
it and it sounds so radically different. You sense, OK, it's the DJ that's
making a difference.[64]

A recording featuring largely improvised experimental electronic
music by DJ Olive, Ikue Mori, and Kim Gordon was released by Sonic
Youth Records (SYR). In performance, this trio complements each other
in a manner that you might expect from a traditional rock guitar-bass-
drum trio, only they do so with the often unpredictable nuance of electronic music. "My part is pretty open," explains electronic musician
Ikue Mori, who plays improvised sounds on her PowerBook. "Olive has
this beat. Kim's singing is kind of fixed. She has songs and lyrics to sing.
When she sings, we imagine all kinds of sounds."[65] Gordon steps up
front, guitar slung over her shoulder, and becomes the visual focus of the
performance as a hail of often calamitous sounds emanates into the
space. It is the perfect demonstration that the turntable and PowerBook
have arrived as the garage-band instruments of the new century.

Another artist riding the experimental edge of turntablism is DJ
Spooky, That Subliminal Kid (Paul D. Miller, b. 1970). He is the most
widely known of the abstract turntable artists. Also based in New York,
he was one of the early performers on the protoplasmic "illbient" scene
in the East Village in the '90s. This was a music without dance rhythms,
yet it was neither trance nor ambient in conception. It was too harsh,
too urban for that. Illbient artists use the noise and energy of the city to
weave their soundscapes. DJ Spooky's gigs are part performance and
part installation, sometimes piping in room noise from other locations,
an environment reminiscent of Cage and Tudor's work in 1964 on
Variations IV. He mixes audio verité to form a kind of real-time
musique concrète, weaving electronic tones into the mix, sampling,
dubbing, and rearranging chunks of sound like pieces of time. It is a
heavy brew of noise, voice, electronic distortion, sampling, and an occa-
sional musical or rap riff.

DJ Spooky is also a prolific writer and immersed in questions of
ontology and the semiotics of popular media and urban culture. His
artistic references span the gamut of the avant-garde. He makes his

sources known in the detailed notes that accompany each of his commercially available recordings, dropping the names of Cage, Stockhausen, Olly Wilson, Gertrude Stein, Pauline Oliveros, Iannis Xenakis, Philip Glass, Ben Neill, Vernon Reid, Bill Laswell, and a host of others. His language is imbued with the vocabulary of a graduate student in philosophy. He takes a classroom discussion of the social significance of music culture to his audience through his liner notes: "Translating the untranslatable in a prismatic fashion through the union of form and content, the DJ refracts meaning from the dense locale of culture and places the rays of meaning, in a rhizomatic fashion, back in their original locale in the human mind."[66]

Despite this academically tuned prose, DJ Spooky has not lost touch with the social significance of the DJ culture and club scene. His thoughts on the place of electronic music in our culture are some of the clearest ever expressed:

> Electronic music is, in a way, the folk music of the 21st century. Instead of, say, the '20s, where you had everyone who knew a blues riff playing a guitar, you now have everyone who knows certain beats and things like that putting them together and then circulating them—this scene is about mixing and mix tapes. Technology is making the creative process democratic.[67]

Marina Rosenfeld represents yet another discipline in turntable performance. Rosenfeld is a schooled composer, having studied composition at Cal Arts with Mel Powell. She acknowledges that Morton Feldman is one of her most beloved influences. She has worked with turntable composition and performance as one of several outlets for her work.

Rosenfeld's *Fragment Opera*, mentioned earlier in the discussion of process music, utilizes a set of acetate discs that she created herself. These form the sound palette for a live performance of the work that follows a structural sequence suggested by her instructions for the performer. Like Marclay, Rosenfeld diddles with the physical material of her recorded discs to create manipulative patterns and noises. She is attracted to the physicality of turntable performance and often prepares her discs by gluing nails to them:

> I like the fact that the turntable *is* mechanical. It's mechanical like the way a piano is mechanical. I was a pianist first, and still feel like my hands have to make the music on some level. My hands are where all the ideas are hiding, plus, from the point of view of a performance, where the idea is to expose the music and not conceal it, or conceal your means of production. It's a plus that you *and* the audience can see the whole thing in

front of you and go anywhere without rewinding something or fast-for-warding something or pressing a button. It's a visual medium and visually exposed.

In my first pieces with turntables, all of my records had nails or pins inserted in them. Like everyone else who ever got into this technique, I was into loops that you could *see*. I was making these pieces where the arm of the record player was going in and then it hit a nail and started to make a bouncing noise. So, you could see it's a loop—and hear the possibly obnoxious bumping noise it made each time the loop repeated. The benefit was that there was something so concrete about it. Not even descriptive. It was a loop. You could *see* it. You could hear it. I like to look at the instrument that way. I think eventually I'm going to get tired of the precomposition that goes into making the LPs first and spinning them later, and will do it from scratch on the spot.[68]

Another Marclay-inspired turntablist with a twist is Philip Jeck from England. He first saw Marclay perform while visiting the United States on a work assignment. It was about the same time that he was beginning to explore turntablism. The experience liberated his thinking about what he could do as a composer using previously recorded works. Jeck has been more interested in composing a wall of vinyl sounds, often repeating loops in long sequences. He places stickers on his records to keep the tone arm stuck in a given groove. His works are long and extended excursions that owe as much to the continuously droning energy of La Monte Young and Terry Riley as to Marclay. He builds layers and loops of interweaving sounds and repeating patterns that change gradually over time. His *Vinyl Requiem* (1993) was the most ambitious piece of turntable industrialism yet conceived. It consisted of a performance for 180 Dansette record players and a visual show provided by twelve slide projectors and two movie projectors.

Following the examples of these composers, and many others who are working in this field, a new generation of turntablists has clearly reclaimed the record player as an instrument of the avant-garde.

Chapter 12

ELECTRONIC MUSIC IN THE MAINSTREAM: A LOSS OF HISTORY

There has been a quiet transition taking place in the world of electronic music. After several decades of rapid technological evolution—from vacuum tubes to transistors to integrated circuits to microprocessors to software—we seem to have landed on the hospitable terrain of a digital world. The technological obstacles that once limited composers—processing speed, computer memory, and permanent electronic storage—have been overcome. For the most part, memory is cheap, processing power is fast enough, and digital storage (CDs, minidiscs, DVDs) is adequate to allow composers and musicians the flexibility they need to create music. What does this do to the music? What does this do to the listener?

The digital transition has transformed the field of popular music. Techniques that were once considered radical and experimental are now a part of the common sound kit of the digital composer. With this transition comes a loss of history. It is a time of opening new doors on the future of music and closing a few doors on the past. Thurston Moore, of the band Sonic Youth, explains: "Musicians working records, turntables, mixers, and various effects do not employ anything desirably 'nostalgic' to their art. In fact, they see and hear what they do as a sort of future-music."[1]

I wrote this book largely to document the history of ideas and techniques that made so much of today's music possible. Until recently, one could trace the influences of new composers back to the lines of experimentation begun by Cage, Stockhausen, Oliveros, Ashley, and others. Nicolas Collins, one of the direct descendants of the post-Cagian school, senses that we are experiencing an "endgame of postmodernism," the close of an era:

It is at an end with us. The emerging musics in Europe and America at the moment are not a continuation of that tradition. They're coming out of pop. They are obviously embracing the same technology that we are using. And the same sound palette and a lot of the same ideas. Ambient music and electronica owe a lot to everything from early La Monte Young and Steve Reich and James Tenney [b. 1934] and Behrman and Niblock [b. 1933] as it does to turning on a circuit and just letting it run. DJ technology goes back to musique concrète and tape manipulation and Cage pieces and the weird early sampling work that was happening in the late '70s and early '80s. There is a lot of common ground there. The rate of change at which the pop world is moving at the moment is kind of fast. The DJs are making those connections much faster. That is what the majority of younger people are listening to. That is what they are going to be building their music on.[2]

Collins recently took a teaching post at the School of the Art Institute of Chicago, his first in twenty years. He immediately noticed that many of his students were not interested in the history behind the music. His fellow instructor John Corbitt made the observation that in the past, if one were to hear an interesting recording of music by Xenakis, one might go find another record and go find out more about Xenakis the man, what made him tick, and how he composed: "Now, if they find the Xenakis record interesting they say, 'Great!' And they might use the Xenakis record in a mix. They might sample it or they might just say, 'that was a nice experience.' But there is no drive to pursue the context of it. It's like a color swatch."[3] This suggests that some new composers listen to sound with an unprecedented freshness, with a lack of contextual bias.

Collins continues:

I think that the reality of the DJ is that a record is a record. A CD is a CD. It doesn't have any other information other than audio. The CD of Stockhausen that they cue in and out of the techno track on the beat doesn't come with any more information than the techno track does. It is just audio. It is equal to everything else.[4]

Exciting and highly original electronic music is still being made, and it is more accessible than ever before in its history. Some young composers *will* dismiss the past; isn't that part of the process of experimentation? There will be a proliferation and sameness of common ideas simply because it is easier to do these days: the bins will continue to be filled with countless techno, electronica, ambient, and other CDs that are barely distinguishable from one another in form and substance. Hasn't this always been the case with popular and even classical music?

What is successful will be imitated. But arising from this common mass are the works of a new generation of composers who reject the norm and create highly original works because they understand the intimate relationship between the human spirit and music of the imagination.

In a world where technology now infiltrates every nuance of our existence, one realizes that the arts succeed where computers fail in elevating the human being in us all. It just could be that the current generation of composers has succeeded in doing what past generations could not: absorbing the use of technology as a means for making music rather than battling with it.

Listening to Electronic Music: A Footnote

I remarked in the beginning of this book that electronic music makes new demands on the listener. I often ask composers about this. Here are two of the most lucid responses, the first from Alvin Lucier, whose process music is often a challenge to a new listener:

> There's no central meaning, as you get in Beethoven, for example.
> Beethoven has his story and he tells it to you and you understand it. In
> my work, it's more that the listener is becoming aware of how he is listen-
> ing. When I play something like *I Am Sitting in a Room* and I can see the
> audience, lights bulbs are going on one by one. Oh, *that's* what's happen-
> ing. Self-realization. The listener has to learn that.[5]

Environmental composer Annea Lockwood takes Lucier's idea about self-realization a step further when she describes her hopes for the listener:

> I guess the experience of no distinction between the listener's self and the
> sound. An experience of oneness. I learned a lot of whatever I realized
> about my relationship with the physical world through my ears, through
> listening. It was through listening that I could find myself at one with a
> river. I was living in a part of the country that was permeated with rivers
> and moving water. Of course my work is permeated by rivers and moving
> water. My ears became a channel for identifying with the world as an
> antidote to separation from the physical world.[6]

What remains to be said about listening to electronic music is best reserved for the inner chambers of one's own human experience. Go listen.

> 1951: Music is dead. Long live electronic music.
> 2001: Electronic music is dead. Long live music.

The World's Most Influential Works of Electronic Music

A book about music will hopefully lead to the listening and creation of music. With this in mind, it seems only fitting to recommend some places to start a further exploration of electronic music.

This is mostly a list of older works, many reaching back to the beginning of whatever style of electronic music they spawned. In selecting the works, I was looking for pieces that were well enough known in their day to influence other people working in the field. Many of these works have been mentioned to me repeatedly by composers and musicians. Some are widely known by the public, while others are rarely heard outside of the circle of composers and patrons who make-up the limited audience for avant-garde music, dance, and installations.

The works are organized alphabetically by the last name of the composer.

Automatic Writing (1974–79), by Robert Ashley. Was it ambient music? Was it minimalism? Was it text-sound composition? It was actually an early Ashley opera. Consisting of text in the manner of involuntary speech, it is but one of this composer's continuing string of storytelling pieces for new media. And a somnambulistic entry it is.

Ensembles for Synthesizer (1961–63), by Milton Babbitt. This is perhaps the most exquisite piece ever to come out of the RCA synthesizer at the Columbia-Princeton Electronic Music Center. It is also one of the most appealing works composed using the serial techniques that were prevalent at the time.

Runthrough (1967–68), by David Behrman. Homemade synthesizers and photosensitive mixers put the controls in the hands of musicians and nonmusicians alike. This work was a breakthrough for the soldering composers and improvised electronic music, and was also one of the earliest interactive works, of which Tudor's *Rainforest IV* is the hallmark.

On the Other Ocean and *Figure in a Clearing* (1977), by David Behrman. These are two early works of interactive microcomputer music. For *On the Other Ocean*, a KIM-1 would sense the order and timing of six pitches being played by two performers, causing it to react by sending "harmony-changing messages to two homemade synthesizers." The computer reacted directly to pitches being played by the performers, and the performers, in turn, were "influenced in their improvising" by the computer's responses. *Figure in a Clearing* did much of the same but with a live performer playing cello. The latter was Behrman's first interactive music piece using a microcomputer.

Thelma–Omaggio a Joyce (1958), by **Luciano Berio**. An early tape composition in which the sound of the voice is the only source material. In this case, it is a single fragment of text read in English, French, and Italian by Cathy Berberian, Berio's wife.

Williams Mix (1952), by **John Cage**. Representing the introduction of chance operations in the composition of electronic music, this work was also the antithesis of all other electronic music being done at the time in Germany, France, and at Columbia University. Cage's work established the most experimental branch of avant-garde music, which continues to this day.

Switched-On Bach (1968), by **Wendy Carlos**. This work single-handedly popularized the Moog synthesizer and started a new industry for commercial electronic music instruments. It also proved that electronic music did not have to be dissonant and disagreeable.

Sonic Seasonings (1972), by **Wendy Carlos**. One of the first composed works that could be called ambient music. It combined the sounds of the Moog synthesizer with nature sounds. It is the reason why, even today, Carlo's work is stashed in the new age bin instead of the classical music section of the record store.

Music for Airports (1978), by **Brian Eno**. This was the first ambient album with purely tonal substance, not using nature sounds. Eno coined the term "ambient" by putting it in his liner notes.

Dripsody (1955), by **Hugh Le Caine**. An early tour de force of basic tape composition techniques using the sound of a drop of water falling into a bucket.

World Rhythms (1975), by **Annea Lockwood**. Simply the first great work of environmental music using only natural sounds as sources.

I Am Sitting in a Room (1970), by **Alvin Lucier**. Everyone mentions this piece as an influence, including those who have only heard *of* it. This fundamental process piece employed the acoustic space itself as a filter for the recorded performance. Nicolas Collins alternates between this work and Lucier's *Vespers* (1968) when choosing "the most significant piece of music of the twentieth century."[7]

Record without a Cover (1985), by **Christian Marclay**. He revived the field of experimental turntablism during the early and mid-'80s. This work, the vinyl recording which bears no protective sleeve, is meant to get increasingly scratched and damaged with each successive handling.

Hornpipe (1967), **by Gordon Mumma.** A performance piece for live waldhorn and French horn, with adaptive analog circuits that responded to the horns by making their own sounds. Mumma's work in this area, dating back to the '50s, was the archetype for the real-time electronic processing of sounds during a performance.

I of IV (1966), **by Pauline Oliveros.** An early work in which the use of tape delay became the key structural element of the music. Many composers are rediscovering what Oliveros did in 1966, whether they realize it or not.

Come Out (1966), **by Steve Reich.** The composer's response to musique concrète was to explore the phasing relationships of tape loops. Of his many phase pieces during that period, this seems to be the one that most people remember. It was a minimal approach to tape composition, but not minimal music.

A Rainbow in Curved Air (1969), **by Terry Riley.** This minimalist ode to the electric organ still dazzles. Its long, entangled melodies took the breath out of electronic music.

Symphonie pour un homme seul (**Symphony for a Man Alone,** 1949–50), **by Pierre Schaeffer and Pierre Henry.** This was the piece that started the modern era of electronic music. Many composers were shopping for tape recorders after hearing this seminal work of musique concrète.

The Expanding Universe (1975), **by Laurie Spiegel.** One of the first works composed with a large-scale computer to put the human back in the algorithm.

Gesang der Jünglinge (**Songs of the Youth, 1955–56), by Karlheinz Stockhausen.** This is the work that leveled the wall between musique concrète and elektronische Musik forever. Composers mention this to me as a major influence more than any other single work of electronic music. It was significant for several reasons. Its sound signature was not cold and scientific but organic and alive. It had a unique sound palette, avoiding the often-heard "bippity-bop" clichés of electronic music of the '50s. It introduced the spatial projection of electronic music by surrounding the audience with five loudspeakers. Finally, it was meticulously planned and scored as only Stockhausen could, and stands as a major aesthetic contribution to the art of electronic music thinking and composition.

Hymnen (**Anthems, 1966–67), by Karlheinz Stockhausen.** This is the *Pet Sounds* of electronic music, possibly even more influential than Stockhausen's earlier *Gesang der Jünglinge*. This pensive work represents the pinnacle of classic tape composition technique. At about two hours long, it elevated the stature of electronic music from being that of a quick parlor trick to an experience of operatic proportions. It also influenced a younger generation of German musicians in the early '70s that spawned "space music," popularized by Can, Klaus Schulze, and Tangerine Dream.

Silver Apples of the Moon (1967), by Morton Subotnick. The first electronic composition conceived and recorded specifically for release as a commercial recording. (Stockhausen can claim to have edited the four parts of *Hymnen* the prior year so that they would fit on four sides of two discs, but his work was conceived for live performance.) It uses the Buchla synthesizer and was the first widely recognized work by this important composer of electronic music.

Rainforest IV (1973), by David Tudor. When it comes to interactive, ambient, homebrewed electronic music, *Rainforest IV* (the installation version) is clearly the most often-mentioned work of the twentieth century. It is like an organism that continues to grow and change with each manifestation. Gordon Mumma deserves mention as an important collaborator on this work.

Sonic Contours (1952), by Vladimir Ussachevsky. This piece of tape composition was based solely on recorded piano sounds. It was composed using only tape speed changes, reverberation, and tape editing. It is an early example of tape composition using traditional instruments. It was played at the first recital of electronic music in the United States at the May 9, 1952, Composers Forum in New York City.

Déserts (1954), by Edgard Varèse. The first work to combine a live orchestra and a magnetic tape part in performance.

Poème électronique (1958), by Edgard Varèse. The culmination, if not the end, of musique concrète.

Bohor (1962), by Iannis Xenakis. The influence of this thundering mass of ever-loudening clangings is epochal. It marked the germination of noise and industrial music that flowered in the late '60s and '70s and still blooms periodically.

Orient-Occident (1960), by Iannis Xenakis. One of the loveliest works of classic musique concrète. Were there such a thing as romanticism in electronic music, this piece would represent its defining moment.

APPENDIX

RECOMMENDED RECORDINGS OF ELECTRONIC MUSIC

Describing electronic music in words is no substitute for listening to it. My hope is that you will go from these pages and seek out recordings of the works discussed here.

The organization of the discography is topical and generally follows the order in which these subjects were discussed in the book. When possible, I have represented every example of music found in these pages with a corresponding CD that was available at the time of this writing in the fall of 2001. Over 230 CDs are listed. Within each subject heading, collections of works are listed first, followed by recordings from individual artists listed in alphabetical order by the last name of the artist or composer. Multiple works by a given artist in a given category are listed chronologically by composition, beginning with the earliest works. Note that many of these recordings have been reissued on CD from previously released vinyl versions; the dates of composition are often much earlier than the date of a CD release.

A printed discography can never be up-to-date or comprehensive enough. Hence, this is a list of "recommended" electronic music recordings of important works and does not claim to be a catalog of every work by every artist. With very few exceptions—such as *In C* by Terry Riley—this list only comprises works that exist because of the use of electronics.

What you will find in the CDs listed here are hundreds of works of electronic music covering its long and wonderful history, from the Theremin to the PowerBook.

Musical Precedents to Electronic Music
Erik Satie
The Minimalism of Erik Satie (Hat Hut, hatOLOGY 560, 2001). Includes several interpretations of *Vexations* by Satie, considered by some to be the first purposefully minimal composition.

Parade/Relâche (EMI, CDC 7494712, 1988). Includes Satie's *Parade* (1917), music for the ballet that included noise instruments such as a siren, typewriter, and roulette wheel.

George Antheil
Ballet mécanique (Music Masters Inc., 01612–67094–2, 1992).

Early Electronic Music Performance Instruments

Theremin Music

The Art of the Theremin—Clara Rockmore (Delos, DE 1014, 1987). Performances of classic Theremin works by the late Clara Rockmore. These recordings were made in 1975, and are primarily transcriptions of music originally intended for other instruments.

Dr. Samuel J. Hoffman and the Theremin. A boxed set containing three Hoffman LPs: *Music Out of the Moon* (1947), *Perfume Set to Music* (1948), and *Music for Peace of Mind* (1950). (Basta Audio/Visuals, 9093, 1999).

Fuleihan: Theremin Concerto (Symposium, SYM 1253, 2000). Featuring *Concerto for Theremin* by Anis Fuleihan, featuring Clara Rockmore (Theremin), recorded in 1942.

Lydia Kavina: Music from the Ether (mode records, mode 76). Classic and contemporary works for the Theremin performed by the world's foremost living master of the instrument.

The Day the Earth Stood Still (Arista, 11010, 1993). Original soundtrack recording from the 1951 science-fiction movie featuring the music of Bernard Herrmann and the Theremin playing of Samuel Hoffman.

Ed Wood: The Soundtrack (Hollywood Records, 162002, 1994). A standout album of campy orchestral music composed by Howard Shore for the Tim Burton film, featuring outstanding Theremin solos on the main themes. The Theremin was played by none other than Lydia Kavina.

The Beach Boys

Smiley Smile (Capitol Records, CDP 7 93696 2, 1967/1990). Includes the song *Good Vibrations*, which used the electro-Theremin.

Pet Sounds (Capitol Records, 72435-21241-2-1, 1967/1999). Includes the Beach Boys' first song to be recorded using the electro-Theremin, *I Just Wasn't Made for These Times*.

The Kurstins

Gymnopédie (Rouge Records, 2000). New and interpreted music by Theremin duo Pamelia and Greg Kurstin.

Ondes Martenot Music

Olivier Messiaen: Turangalîla-Symphonie (Deutsche Grammophon, 2GH 431-781, 1992). This is a recording of the most famous classical music work featuring the Ondes Martenot. This recording features Jeanne Loriod, the instrument's most famous virtuoso.

Ondes—Estelle Lemire, Adrienne Park (SNE, 616, 1997). Features classical works, some older, written for the Ondes Martenot and piano, performed by Estelle Lemire (Ondes Martenot) and Adrienne Park (piano).

Les Ondes Musicales—The Age of the Impressionists (SNE, 642, 1999). Collection of older classic impressionist pieces arranged for the Ondes Martenot.

Suspended in Amber—Peebles, Harada, Mizushima (Innova, MN 506, 1996). A recent collection of new works featuring the Ondes Martenot and other electronic instruments.

Honegger: Film Classics (Marco Polo, 8.223466, 1993). Film music by Arthur Honegger featuring two works scored for Ondes Martenot: *Crime et châtiment* and *L'Idée*.

Trautonium and Mixturtrautonium Music

Oskar Sala

Elektronische Impressionen (Erdenklang, 81032, 1998). Includes: *Elektronische Impressionen* (1978) by Oskar Sala; 7 *Triostüke für Trautonien* (1930) and *Konsertstück für Trautonium mit Begleitung des Streichorchesters* (1931) by Paul Hindemith. Music for the Trautonium and Mixturtrautonium.

Subharmonische Mixturen (Erdenklang, 709621, 1997). Includes: *Sechs Capricen für Mixturtrautonium Solo* (1992–95), *Chaconne électronique* (1945), and *Der Würger von Schlob*

Blackmoor (1963) by Oskar Sala; plus the first work composed for the original Trautonium, *Langsames Stück und Rondo für Trautonium* (1930), by Paul Hindemith. All works produced and played by Oskar Sala.

The Birds (Universal motion picture, DVD, 1963/2000). Oskar Sala used the Mixturtrautonium to compose all of the music and bird sound effects for this film by Alfred Hitchcock.

Signal Degeneration, Echo, Feedback, Tape Delay, and Loops

Brian Eno
Discreet Music (EEG, 23, 1975/1990).

Robert Fripp
God Save the Queen/Under Heavy Manner (EEG 9,1981/1990)

Robert Fripp/Brian Eno
The Essential Fripp and Eno (Virgin EG Records, CAROL 1886-2 17243 8 39045251). Eight works of the Fripp-Eno collaborations, spanning the years 1973 to 1994.

Scott Johnson
John Somebody (Nonesuch/Icon, 9 79133-2, 1986). Includes: *John Somebody* (1981–83), *No Memory* (1981–83), music for voice, tape loops, guitar, bass, woodwinds, percussion, and electronics.

David Lee Myers
Ourobouros, Processor Music (Pulsewidth, PW01, 2001), www.pulsewidth.com. Music for electronic feedback.

Alvin Lucier
I Am Sitting in a Room (Lovely Music Ltd., LP/CD 1013, 1981/1990).

Pauline Oliveros
Pauline Oliveros: Electronic Works (Paradigm, PD04, 1997). Includes Oliveros classics *I of IV*, *Big Mother Is Watching You*, and *Bye Bye Butterfly* (1965).

New Music for Electronic and Recorded Media (CD 728 CRI, 1977–97). A compilation of electronic music by women composers.

Pauline Oliveros: Alien Bog and Beautiful Soop (Pogus 1997). Electronic music composed in real time with the Buchla Box at Mills College circa 1966–67.

Steve Reich
Steve Reich: Early Works (Elektra/Nonesuch, 9 79169-2, 1987). Early experiments with tape loops and phasing, including *It's Gonna Rain* (1965), *Come Out* (1966), *Piano Phase* (1967), and also *Clapping Music* (1972).

Terry Riley
Music for the Gift (Organ of Corti, 1, 1998). The first known recordings of early tape delay music using the technique of regeneration pioneered by Riley and also used extensively by Oliveros.

Classic Tape Composition and Musique Concrète

Cologne–WDR: Early Electronic Music (BVHAAST, CD 9016).

Columbia Princeton 1961–1973 (New World Records, CD 80521-2, 1998).

Early Modulations—Vintage Volts (Caipirinha Music, CAI.2027.2, 2000). An excellent compilation of classic electronic music featuring *Imaginary Landscape No. 1* (1939) by John Cage, *Etude aux chemins de fer* (1948) by Pierre Schaeffer, *Piece for Tape Recorder* (1956) by Vladimir Ussachevsky, *Incantation* (1953) by Otto Luening, and other works.

Electro Acoustic Music Classics (Neuma, 450-74, 1993).

Electro Acoustic Music 5 (Neuma, 450-92, 1997).

Electronic Music Pioneers (CRI, CD 611).

Imaginary Landscapes: New Electronic Music (Elektra/Nonesuch, 979235-2, 1989). A collection of electronic works assembled by composer Nicolas Collins.

Inventionen '98: 50 Jahre Musique
Concrète (ed.RZ, 10009/10, 1999).
Newly composed works of musique
concrète.

*OHM: The Early Gurus of Electronic
Music, 1948–1980* (Ellipsis Arts,
CD3670, 2000). Forty-two original
tracks, some excerpted, of classic electronic music that chronicles the studio
age on three compact discs.

Robert Ashley

Automatic Writing (also includes *She Was
a Visitor* and *Purposeful Lady Slow
Afternoon*) (Lovely Music Ltd., CD
1002, 1996).

Louis and Bebe Barron

Forbidden Planet (GNP Crescendo
Records, PR-D-001, 1989). The original motion picture soundtrack for the
1956 MGM film.

Luciano Berio and Bruno Maderna

Berio/Maderna (BVHAAST, CD 9109)
Includes Luciano Berio, *Momenti,
Thema–Omaggio a Joyce, Visage*;
Bruno Maderna, *Le Rire, Invenzione
su una voce* (featuring Cathy
Berberian).

Konrad Boehmer

Konrad Boehmer (BVHAAST, CD 9011).
Incudes *Aspekt* (1966–67), *Cry of This
Earth, Apocalipsis cum Figuris*.

Earle Brown

*The New York School # 2—Wolff,
Brown, Cage, Feldman* (Hat Hut, Hat
Art, CD 6146, 1994). Featuring *Octet
I*, Earle Brown's tape piece composed
in 1953 while he was a part of Cage's
Project of Music for Magnetic Tape.
Also included are nonelectronic works
by Brown, Cage, Feldman, and Wolff.

John Cage

*The 25-Year Retrospective Concert of the
Music of John Cage*, (Wergo, 6247,
December 9, 1994). This three-disc set
was recorded live at a Town Hall concert in New York in 1958. Although

most of the music is not electronic, the
set is historically important and features recordings of *Imaginary
Landscape No. 1* (1939) and the
extraordinary tape piece *Williams Mix*
(1952*)*, complete with audience disap-
proval (and approval).

The City Wears a Slouch Hat—original
radio broadcast of turntable music,
1942 (organ of Corti, 14, 2000).

Philip Corner

Philip Corner: From the Judson Years
(Alga Marghen, plana C 4NMN019).
Tape music from 1962–63 using inexpensive tape recorders and household
objects.

Morton Feldman

Morton Feldman: First Recordings: 1950s
(mode records, mode 66, 1999). The
first available recording of Feldman's
Intersection (1953) for magnetic tape,
a piece he composed as part of Cage's
Project of Music for Magnetic Tape. It
has a likeness to Cage's early tape
music using chance operations. The
CD also includes other works for
acoustic instruments.

Bruce Haack

Electric Lucifer Book 2 (Normal Records,
CD 037, 1979/2000). Includes *The
Electric Lucifer Book 2* for homemade
electronics and synthesizer.

Luc Ferrari

Luc Ferrari (BVHAAST, CD 9009)
Includes *Petite Symphony intuitive
pour un paysage de printemps,
Strathoven, Presque rien avec filles,
Héterozygote* (1963–64).

Interrupteur/Tautologos 3 (Blue
Chopsticks, BC1). Recordings originally made in 1970 of *Interrupteur*
(1967) for ten instruments, and
Tautologos 3 (1970) for eleven instrumentalists and magnetic tape.

Pierre Henry

Variations pour une porte et un soupir—
ballet version (Mantra, 093-662036-

ARC 332). This shorter version of the original concert work (1963) was created for a ballet by Maurice Béjart in 1965.

Le Voyage/Messe pour le temps présent (French Philips Classics, PHI 412 706-2). Includes *Le Voyage* and *Messe pour le temps présent* (1967).

Messe de Liverpool/Fantaisie messe pour le temps présent (French Philips Classics, PHI 464-402-2, 2000). Includes *Messe de Liverpool* (1967) and a remixed version of *Fantaisie messe pour le temps présent* (1967).

L'Homme à la caméra (Mantra, 092/WMD 332-642350). Includes *L'Homme à la caméra* (1993).

Intérieur/Extérieur (French Philips Classics, PHI 46213-2, 2000). Includes *Intérieur/Extérieur* (1996), short musique concrète pieces.

Une Tour de Babel/Tokyo 2002 (French Philips Classics, PHI 464 400-2, 2000). Includes: *Une Tour de Babel* (1999), a fifty-seven-minute-long work, and the short *Tokyo 2002* (1998).

Hugh Le Caine

Compositions, Demonstrations, 1946–1974 (JWD Music, JWD 03, 1999). A collection of experimental tape compositions and demonstrations by synthesizer pioneer Le Caine. Includes two versions of *Dripsody* and many other short compositions and "humorous" sketches.

Bruno Maderna

Bruno Maderna: Electronic Music (Stradivarius, STR 33349). Includes *Notturno* (1956), *Syntaxis* (1957), *Continuo* (1958), *Musica su due dimensioni* (1958 version), *Dimensioni II—Invenzione su una voce* (1960, with Cathy Berberian, voice), *Serenata III* (1961), *Le Rire* (1962). Works composed in the Studio di Fonologia in Milan.

Gordon Mumma

Studio Retrospect (Lovely Music Ltd., LCD 1093, 2000). Featuring

Retrospect (1959–82), *Music from the Venezia Space Theater* (1964), *The Dresden Interleaf 13 February 1945* (1965), *Echo-D* (1978), *Pontpoint* (1966–80), and *Epifont* (1984).

Live Electronic Music (Tzadik, 7074, 2001).

Arne Nordheim

Arne Nordheim: Electric (Rune Grammofon, RCD 2002, 1998). Includes *Solitaire* (1968), *Pace* (1970), *Warsaw* (1970), *Colorazione* (1968), *PolyPoly* (1970). Realized in Warsaw by the influential Norwegian composer.

Henri Pousseur

Henri Pousseur (BVHaast, 9010). Includes *Scambi* (1957), *Troi Visages de Liège* (1961), and *Paraboles-Mix* (1972).

Dick Raaijmakers (aka Kid Baltan)

Dick Raaijmakers: Complete Tape Music (Donemus, CV NEAR 09–11, 1998).

Pierre Schaeffer

Pierre Schaeffer: L'Oeuvre Musicale (EMF Media, CD 010). The collected works of Pierre Schaeffer, beginning with his earliest musique concrète.

Solfège de l'objet sonore (INA-GRM, INA-C 2010/12, 1998). Schaeffer's spoken discourse with audio demonstrations for his "Treatise on Musical Objects," the building block of musique concrète theory.

Raymond Scott

Manhattan Research Inc. (BASTA Audio/Visuals, 90782, 2000). A retrospective of Raymond Scott's work.

Soothing Sounds for Baby, Volumes I, II, III (BASTA Audio/Visuals, 90642, 90653, 90662). Reissues of Scott's "ambient" music for babies, originally released in 1963.

Karlheinz Stockhausen

Karlheinz Stockhausen retains the rights to his recorded electronic music and has been painstakingly remastering it and rereleasing it on privately issued compact discs with extensive liner notes that are often the size of small books. (Go to www.stockhausen.org.) The following are selected recordings of his electronic music.

Etude (1952); Studie I; Studie II (1953–54); Gesang der Jünglinge (1955–56); Kontakte (1959–60) (Stockhausen 3).

Mixtur (1963–67) for orchestra, sine wave generators, and ring modulators (two versions) (Stockhausen 8).

Mikrophonie I (1964) for tam-tam, two microphones, two filters with potentiometers (six players); Mikrophonie II (1965) for choir, Hammond organ, four ring modulators; Telemusik (1966) (Stockhausen 9).

Hymnen (1966); Hymnen (1966–67) with soloists (Stockhausen 10).

Prozession (1967) for tam-tam, Electrochord, Electronium, piano, filters, potentiometers; Ceylon for Electronium, camel bells with triangles and synthesizer, modulated piano, tam-tam, Kandy drum (Stockhausen 11).

Kurzwellen (1968), six players and short-waves (Stockhausen 13).

Electronic Music with Sound Scenes of Friday (1990–91), from Light (Stockhausen 49).

Also by Stockhausen:

Kontakte (Wergo, WER 6009-2 286009-2, 1964/1992). Realization by David Tudor (piano and percussion) and Christoph Caskel (percussion). This version of Kontakte (1959–60) was first performed by Tudor and Caskel in 1960. This recording dates from 1964.

Edgard Varèse

Varèse: The Complete Works (PolyGram Records, 460208, 1998). Includes Déserts (1954) and Poéme électronique (1958).

Iannis Xenakis

Xenakis: Electronic Music (EMF Media, CD003, 1997). Includes Diamorphoses (1957), Concret PH (1958), Orient-Occident (1960), Bohor (1962), Hibiki-Hana-Ma (1970), S.709 (1992).

Synthesizer Music
Gavin Bryars

BIPED (GB Records, BCGBCD02, 2001). Includes BIPED (1999) for electric keyboard, double bass, electric guitar, cello, violin, and handheld percussion, was commissioned by the Merce Cunningham Dance Company and used for a dance piece of the same name.

Wendy Carlos

Wendy Carlos retains the rights to her recorded music and has been digitally remastering it for release on compact disc. The CDs are accompanied by extensive notes and often feature bonus tracks. (Go to www.wendycarlos.com.)

Switched-On Boxed Set (East Side Digital, ESD 81422, 1999). A collection of all of her albums featuring interpretations of Bach on the Moog synthesizer.

Clockwork Orange—Complete Original Score (East Side Digital, ESD 81362, 1998). The entire score produced by Carlos for the 1972 Stanley Kubrick film, featuring some of her first original electronic compositions using the Moog.

Digital Moonscapes (East Side Digital, ESD 81542, 2000). Original electronic compositions from 1984 using alternative tunings and digital orchestrations.

Beauty in the Beast (East Side Digital, ESD 81552, 1986). Original electronic music compositions using alternative tunings, microtonality, and digital orchestrations. From the standpoint of composition, it is one of her most important albums.

Tales of Heaven and Hell (East Side Digital, ESD 81352, 1998). Original electronic music compositions using alternative tunings and digital orchestrations.

Tom Hamilton

Sebastian's Shadow (Monroe Street Music, msm 60103, 1997). Includes electronic variations on a short Bach fugue. Hamilton is a longtime collaborator of Robert Ashley.

Mother Mallard's Portable Masterpiece Co.

Like a Duck to Water (CUNEIFORM RUNE, 147, 1976/2001). Perhaps the first all-synthesizer ensemble, used Moogs in the late '60s and '70s. Players included David Borden, Linda Fisher, Judy Borsher, and Steve Drews. This was the group's second and final release.

William Orbit

Pieces in a Modern Style (Maverick, 9 47596–2, 2000). Interpretations of works by Samuel Barber, John Cage, Erik Satie, and others.

Terry Riley

Shri Camel (CBS Records, MK 35164, 1980). Music for a Yamaha YC-45–D electronic organ tuned in just intonation and modified using digital delay.

Morton Subotnick

Subotnick: Silver Apples of the Moon, The Wild Bull (Wergo, 2035, 1994). Two early Buchla works from the late '60s. Includes *Silver Apples of the Moon* (1967) and *The Wild Bull* (1968), the first two commercial recordings of voltage-controlled synthesizer music.

And the Butterflies Began to Sing (New World Records, 80514–2, 1997).

Morton Subotnick Volume 1: Electronic Works (mode records, mode 97, 2001). Includes the works *Touch* (1969) for four-channel tape, *A Sky of Cloudless Sulfur* (1978) for eight-channel tape, and *Gestures* (1999–2001) for 5.1 surround sound with Joan LaBarbara, voice.

The Key to Songs, Return by Morton Subotnick with the California EAR Unit (New Albion, 1996).

Computer Music

Computer Music Currents 13 (Wergo, WERGO CD 2033–2, 1995). A historical retrospective of early computer music.

Consortium to Distribute Computer Music (CDCM) Series

The extensive Consortium to Distribute Computer Music (CDCM) computer music series from Centaur Records consists of thirty-two CDs of computer music spanning the period 1988 to 1999.

IRCAM

IRCAM: The 1990s (IRCAM Recordings). A historical retrospective of computer music composed at IRCAM, the landmark center for music technology development in Paris. Some narration.

New Computer Music (Wergo, CD 2010–50). Includes Michel Waisvisz, *The Hands* (excerpts), for gestural performance device; Clarence Barlow, *Relationships for Melody Instruments*; James Dashow, *Sequence Symbols*; Stephen Kaske, *Transition Nr. 2*; Paul Lansky, *Idle Chatter*; Curtis Roads, *nscor*.

Jon Appleton

Contes de la mémoireempreintes DIGITALes (IMED, 9635,1996). Retrospective of Appleton's electroacoustic music. Ten works, including *Georganna's Fancy* (1966), *Chef d'œuvre* (1967), *Newark Airport Rock* (1969), *Dima Dobralsa Domoy* (1993).

Martin Bartlett

Martin Bartlett: Burning Water (Periplum, P 0020). Interactive computer-aided improvisations by Bartlett, a student of David Tudor at Mills College in 1968. The works date from 1979 to 1988 and evoke much of the black-box virtues of Tudor and Behrman's work.

John Bischoff

The Glass Hand (Artifact Recordings, ART 1014, 1996). Includes music created using software tools of Bischoff's design that could randomly search for sounds on a MIDI synthesizer, saving and recalling them, transforming them, and interacting with a performer using a MIDI keyboard.

Joel Chadabe

CDCM Computer Music Vol. 7 (Centaur, 2047, 1996). Includes *Modalities for*

Interactive Computer System (1989) by Chadabe, and works by Neil Burton Rolnick, Pauline Oliveros, Julie Kabat, and Barton McLean. Originally released in 1990.

Works by Chadabe/Eastham/Walker/ Willey (Centaur, 2071, 1996). Includes *Rhythms VI* by Chadabe, and works by George Walker, Clark Eastham, and James Willey.

The Composer in the Computer Age VII (Centaur, 2310, 1997). Includes Chadabe's *Follow Me Softly* (1984), composed using the very first Synclavier digital synthesizer. Other works by Cort Lippe, Larry Austin, James Dashow, and Rodney Waschka.

Larry Fast

Computer Experiments, Volume 1 (Passport Records, SYNCD 94, 1980). Includes executions by a self-composing microcomputer system. Sounds were executed using a Sequential Circuits Prophet 5 synthesizer controlled by a Paia 8700 6503-based microcomputer using a specially designed interface made by the composer.

Paul DeMarinis

Music as a Second Language (Lovely Music Ltd., CD 3011, 1991). Explores speech melodies extracted from sources such as language instruction recordings, hypnotists, and television evangelists and modified using digital music instruments.

The Hub

Wreckin' Ball: The Hub (Artifact Recordings, ART 1008, 1994). A networked computer ensemble including John Bischoff, Tim Perkis, Chris Brown, Scot Gresham-Lancaster, Mark Trayle, and Phil Stone, who performed using interconnected microcomputers.

Jim Horton

Simulated Winds and Cries (Artifact Recordings, ART 1013, 1996). Computer-controlled and synthesized ambient works adjusted in real time by the composer.

Tetsu Inoue

Psycho-Acoustic (Tzadik, TZ 7213, 1998). Works for computer.

Fragment Dot (Tzadik, TZ 7229, 2000). Works for computer.

Waterloo Terminal (Caipirinha Music, cai2015, 1998). In which the composer used software to transform graphical scans of the architectural plan for a British Channel Tunnel railway terminal into electronic music.

Object and Organic Code (IEA, 2, 2001). Digitial sound processing and composition with source recordings by Inoue and Andrew Deitsch.

pict.soul (Cycling 74, c74–005, 2001). Digital composition, with Carl Stone.

Field Tracker (Anomalous Records, Nom 9, 2001). Digital sound processing and composition, with Anfrew Deutsch.

Ikue Mori

Hex Kitchen (Tzadik, TZ 7201, 1995).

Garden (Tzadik, TZ 7020, 1996).

Painted Desert (Avant Records, 30, 1997).

B-Side (Tzadik, TZ 7508, 1998).

One Hundred Aspects of the Moon (Tzadik, TZ 7055, 2000) Music for instruments and computer featuring John Zorn, Anthony Coleman, Eyvind Kang, and others.

Jean-Claude Risset

Jean-Claude Risset (Wergo, 2013–50). Compositions by computer music pioneer Risset. Includes *Songes*; *Passages* for flute and tape; *Computer Suite* from *Little Boy*; *Sud*.

Matt Rogalsky

Resonate (mrogalsky.web.wesleyan.edu, 1997/2000). Matt worked with Alvin Lucier and David Tudor. Includes two minimalist computer works for synthesized strings and dense, clustered sounds: *Tones* (1997), *Noise/Tones* (2000).

Kaija Saariaho

Private Gardens (Ondine, ODE 906–2). Saariaho has worked at IRCAM. Her works use electronics to transform instrumental and vocal sounds, forming an electronic ambient soundscape for her music. Includes: *Lonh*, for soprano and electronics; *Pres*, for cello and electronics; *Noanoa*, for flute and electronics; *Six Japanese Gardens*, for percussion and electronics.

Laurie Spiegel
New Music for Electronic and Recorded Media (CRI, CD 728, 1977–97). A compilation of electronic music by women composers. Includes *Appalachian Grove* (1974) by Laurie Spiegel, composed using GROOVE , a musical programming language that provided computer control for analog synthesis. This was Spiegel's first computer composition and one of the first instances of computer software being used for generating music in real-time under interactive human control.
Unseen Worlds (Aesthetic Engineering, 11001-2, 1994). Computer-generated music composed primarily using Music Mouse, Spiegel's software program for the Macintosh and other computers.
Obsolete Systems (EMF Media, EMF CD 019, 2001). Pioneering analog electronic music works from the 1970s and 1980s created wtih the aid of a variety of synthesizers, computer systms, and experimental instruments.

James Tenney
Tenney: Selected Works 1961–1969 (Artifact Recordings, CD 1007, 1993). Early works for large-scale computers from Bell Labs. Includes *Collage #1* ("Blue Suede," 1961), *Analog #1: Noise Study* (1961), *Dialogue* (1963), *Phases (For Edgard Varèse)* (1963), *Music for Player Piano* (1964), *Ergodos II (For John Cage)* (1964), *Fabric for Che* (1967), *For Ann (Rising)* (1969).

Mark Trayle
Etudes and Bagatelles (Artifact Recordings, ART 1010, 1994). Computer works written in the C pro-

gramming language between 1988 and 1992, running on an Amiga computer using low-fidelity digital sampling.

Trevor Wishart
Red Bird/Anticredos (EMF Media, CD 022). Computer music works by Trevor Wishart in which acoustical sources, such as voices, are radically transformed. Includes *Red Bird* (1980), *Anticredos* (1980).

Live Electronic Music Performance and Improvisation
Flav-O-Pac: Memograph, Vol. 1 (Home Entertainment, 9002, 1999). A varied collection of electronic improvisers and composers ranging from illbient to abstract turntablists.

AMM
AMMusic 1966 (ReRecords, ReR AMMCD). Performances of the British electronic improvisational group AMM, recorded in a studio in 1966. The CD includes five pieces and a track of silence (for programming "wherever you wish").
Laminal (Matchless Recordings, MRCD31). Three recordings of live AMM concert performances on threee CDs: Aarhus, Denmark, 1969; London, 1982; New York, 1994. Various members featured.

Robert Ashley
Superior Seven and *Tract* (New World Records, 80649-2, 1996).

David Behrman
David Behrman, Wave Train—Music from 1959 to 1968. Featuring performances by David Tudor, Christoph Caskel, Gordon Mumma, Robert Ashley, and Alvin Lucier (Alga Marghen plana B 5NMN.020, 1998).
Leapday Night (Lovely Music Ltd., LCD 1042, 1991). With Ben Neill (mutantrumpet), Takehisa Kosugi (violin), and others. This is interactive music for homemade computers and performers and includes *Leapday*

Night, A Traveler's Dream Journal, and *Interspecies Smalltalk.*

Unforeseen Events (Experimental Intermedia Foundation, XI 105, 1991). With Ben Neill (mutantrumpet). Pieces for interactive performance with computer.

John Cage

Indeterminacy (Smithsonian/Folkways, CD SF 40804/5, 1959/1992). This recording, originally released by Folkways in 1959, captures on disc a collaborative piece that Cage and Tudor took on the road for many years. It features Cage reading short anecdotes while Tudor provides electronic music accompaniment. The electronics were created using an assemblage of homemade circuits and amplified small sounds. The reading and the electronics are only related in that they take place at the same time. This startling and often funny piece turned many new composers in the direction of Cage.

Music for Merce Cunningham (mode records, mode 24, 1991). Performed by Takehisa Kosugi, Michael Pugliese, and David Tudor.

Rainforest II & Mureau (New World NW 80540, 2000). Includes the only available recording of *Rainforest II* (1972) by Tudor.

Bird Cage (EMF, CD 013, 2000). A marvelous record of a Cage installation work, which was usually performed "continuously through eight loudspeakers during the course of an entire evening." This performance consists of a studio version by William Blakeney in 1998, but the disc also includes conversations with Cage and Joel Chadabe, David Tudor, and several students preceding the first performance of *Bird Cage* (1973) at the State University of New York in Albany in 1973.

Nicolas Collins

100 of the World's Most Beautiful Melodies (Trace Elements Records, CD 1018, 1988). Features 42 short improvised duos with fifteen musicians.

It Was a Dark and Stormy Night (Trace Elements Records, TE-1019CD, 1992), With David Moss, Ben Neill, Robert Poss and others. Features Collins's trombone-propelled electronics on *Tobabo Fonio* as well as his "backwards electric guitar" and modified CD-player electronics.

Sound without Picture (Periplum, P 0060, 1999) With Ben Neill and the Kammerensemble Neue Musik Berlin, featuring compositions spanning from 1992 to 1998.

A Host, of Golden Daffodils (Plate Lunch, PL07, 1999). By Peter Cusack and Nicolas Collins.

Kim Gordon, Ikue Mori, and DJ Olive

Kim Gordon, Ikue Mori, DJ Olive (SYR 5, 2000). Featuring improvisation-based works for voice and guitar (Gordon), turntable (DJ Olive), and PowerBook (Mori).

Tom Hamilton

Slybersonic Tromosome (Penumbra Music, CD007, 2000). Real-time works for synthesizer, electronics, trombone, valve trombone, irrigation hose, didgeridoo, "beat thing, mouthpiece extender, and superfunnel," performed by Tom Hamilton and Peter Zummo.

Toshii Ichiyanagi

Cosmos of Toshi Ichiyanagi III—1960s & 1990s (Camerata Records, 25CM 552/3, 1999). Includes the tape composition *Parallel Music* (1962).

Diane Labrosse, Ikue Mori, Martin Tétrealult

Île bizarre (Ambiances Magnétiques Etcetera, AM 055, 1998).

Daniel Lentz

Missa Umbrarum (New Albion Records, NA 006CD, 1991). Includes: *O-Ke-Wa* (1974) for twelve voices with bells,

rasps, and drums; *Missa Umbrarum*
(1973) for 8 voices with wineglasses
and 118 "sonic shadows" produced
using a 30-second tape delay technique;
Postludium for full chorus and rubbed
glasses; *Lascaux* for wineglasses.

MEV (Musica Elettronica Viva)
MEV (IRML, 02). A previously unre-
leased MEV improvisational performance recorded in London in 1968.
Performers include Alan Bryant (early
synthesizer), Alvin Curran (trumpet,
percussion), Jon Phetteplace (amplified
cello), and Frederic Rzewski (amplified
percussion, singing).
Rome Cansrt (IRML, 04). Original MEV
members recorded in a live concert in
Rome in 1968.

Pauline Oliveros
Deep Listening (New Albion, NA022,
1989).
Crone Music (Lovely Music Ltd., CD
1903, 1990).
The Ready Made Boomerang (New
Albion, NA 044, 1991).
Sanctuary: Deep Listening Band (mode
records, mode 46, 1995). With Tom
Buckner, Julie Lyon Balliet, Joe
McPhee, Margarit Shenker, Nego
Gato, Carlo Chappell, Jason
Finkelman, and Women Who Drum.
Carrier (Deep Listening, DL-8–1998).
With Andrew Deutsch and Peer Bode.
Non Stop Flight (Music & Arts, CD1030,
1998). The Deep Listening Band
recorded live at Mills College, 1996.
Ghostdance (Deep Listening, DL7 1998).
With Pauline Oliveros (accordion),
Julie Lyon Rose (voice), David Gamper
(djembe/Expanded Instrument System).
Pauline Oliveros in the Arms of Reynols
(White Tapes, whi21.CD, 1999). A
remix of live concerts of Oliveros and
the Deep Listening Band with Reynols.
Limited, numbered, and spray-painted
edition of 100.

Zeena Parkins
Nightmare Alley (Tote, 1, 1992).
No Way Back (Atavistic, ALP64CD, 1998)

Pan-Acousticon (Tzadik, TZ 7049, 1999).
Zeena Parkins with the Gangster Band.

Marina Rosenfeld
*the sheer frost orchestra-drop, hop,
drone, scratch, slide & a for anything*
(Charhizma, 018 2001).

Sonic Youth
Anagrama (SYR, 1, 1997).
Slaapkamers Met Slagroom (SYR, 2, 1997)
Sonic Youth & Jim O'Rourke (SYR, 3,
1998)
Goodbye 20th Century (SYR, 4, 1999).
Sonic Youth with guests.

David Tudor
Rainforest (mode records, mode 64).
Includes the original dance version as
well as the legendary *Rainforest IV*
installation version.
Three Works for Live Electronics (Lovely
Music Ltd., LCD 1601, 1996).
Includes *Untitled* (1972), *Pulsers*
(1976), and *Phonemes* (1981).
Dialects (excerpt). On *Imaginary
Landscapes* (Elektra/Nonesuch,
79235-2, 1989).
Neural Synthesis No. 2 (Ear-Rational,
ECD 1039, 1993).
Neural Synthesis Nos. 6–9 (Lovely Music
Ltd., LCD 1602, 1995).

Mixed Media/Opera
Robert Ashley
in memoriam . . . KIT CARSON (opera,
excerpt). On *Ten Years of Essential
Music* (Monroe Street, MSM 60101,
1964/1997).
*In Sara, Mencken, Christ and Beethoven
There Were Men and Women* (Cramps,
CRSCD 103, 1974/1991).
Private Parts (The Record) (Lovely Music,
Ltd., LP 1001; CD 1001, 1978/90).
Perfect Lives, (Lovely Music Ltd., CD
4917 (3 CDs), 1983/1991). An opera
for television (1983).
Atalanta (Acts of God) (Lovely Music
Ltd., CD 3301, 1985/1997).
Your Money My Life Goodbye (Lovely
Music Ltd., CD 1005, 1999).
Dust (Lovely Music Ltd., CD 1006, 2000).

John Cage

Variations IV (Legacy International, Legacy 439, 1965/1997). Assisted by David Tudor. This is a reissue of a two-record set originally released by Everest Records in 1966. It provides documentary evidence of the live performances given by Cage and Tudor with their table of black boxes. This one took place at the Feigen/Palmer Galleries in Los Angeles in August 1965.

Roaratorio (Wergo, 6303, 1994). Includes *Roaratorio* (1979), during which Cage reads his text from *Writing for the Second Time through Finnegan's Wake* (1978). Irish musicians play and sing, and sounds mentioned by Joyce in *Finnegan's Wake* are played as assembled by Cage on a 62–track tape collage.

Electronic Drones and Minimalism

Philip Glass

Philip Glass (Elektra/Nonesuch, 9 79326–2, 1973/1994). Includes *Two Pages* (1968) for electric organ and piano; *Music in Fifths* (1969) for electric organ, soprano saxophones, and electronics; *Music in Similar Motion* (1969) for electric organs, soprano saxophones, flute, and electronics; *Contrary Motion* (1974) for electric organ.

Toshimaru Nakamura/Sachiko M

Do (Erstwhile Records, 013, 2001). Works of extremely minimal change for electronics using Nakamura's "no-input mixing desk," a mixing board with its output connected to its input to create an internal electronic loop. The results in this case are long, slowly changing sounds and drones.

Phil Niblock

Music by Phil Niblock (Experimental Intermedia, XI 111, 1993). Includes *Five More String Quartets* (1991) for string quartet, and *Early Winter* (1991) for flute, string quartet, 38 computer controlled-sampled and synthesized voices, and an eight-channel recording of bass flute. These works feature dense, loud, perpetually shifting note clusters

and "unplayed pitches" resulting from the combination of played pitches.

Steve Reich

Different Trains/Electric Counterpoint (Elektra/Nonesuch, 9 79176–2, 1989).

Terry Riley

In C (Sony, 7178, 1968/1990). *In C* (1965) is the highly influential work of repeating phrases that defined much of what came to be called minimalism as a genre of pulses and slowly developing melodic changes.

A Rainbow in Curved Air (CBS Masterworks, MK 07315, 1969). Includes *A Rainbow in Curved Air* (1969), *Poppy Nogood and the Phantom Band* (1969).

La Monte Young

Inside the Dream Syndicate Volume I: Day of Niagara (1965) (Table of the Elements, TOE-CD-74, 2000). Includes previously unavailable recordings of Young's Dream House music from the early '60s in New York. Performers include John Cale (viola), Tony Conrad (violin), Angus MacLise (percussion), La Monte Young, and Marian Zazeela (vocals, amplification, sine waves). This is a rare recording of the drone music created by this ensemble.

Process Music

Toshii Ichiyanagi

Cosmos of Toshi Ichiyanagi III—1960s & 1990s (Camerata Records, 25CM 552/3, 1999). Includes *Music for Electric Metronomes*.

Alvin Lucier

Music on a Long Thin Wire (Lovely Music Ltd., LP/CD 1011, 1980/1992).

Crossings (Lovely Music Ltd., CD 1018, 1990).

Clocker (Lovely Music Ltd., CD 1019, 1994). For amplified clock, performer with galvanic skin response sensor, and digital delay system.

Panorama (Lovely Music Ltd., CD 1012, 1997). Includes *Music for Piano with*

Amplified Sonorous Vessels and other works.

Theme (Lovely Music Ltd., LCD 5011, 1999). Includes *Music for Piano with Magnetic Strings* and other works.

Still Lives (Lovely Music Ltd., CD 5012, 2001).

Gen Ken Montgomery

Psychogeographical Dip (GD Stereo, GD 013, 1997). With *Washing the Hare*.

DRONSKIPCLICKLOOP (generator-soundart.org, 1998). A portable sound installation. A set of four three-inch CD-Rs.

The Sound of Lamination (Firework Edition Records, FER1016 1999). <http://user.tninet.se/~ore291s/fer_lamination.html.>

Steve Reich

Reich: Phase Patterns, Pendulum Music (Wergo, WER 6630, 1999). Includes the seldom-performed *Pendulum Music, Piano Phase, Four Organs*, and *Phase Patterns*.

Environmental and Ambient Music

The Dreams of Gaia (EarthEar Records, 1999). A compilation of soundscapes and environmental music.

David Behrman

David Behrman, Wave Train—Music from 1959 to 1968.

Gavin Bryars

The Sinking of the Titanic (Point Music, 446–061–2, 1994). Includes the definitive recording of Bryar's *The Sinking of the Titanic* (1969–72), which has become what might be called the first ambient symphony.

Harold Budd

The Pavilion of Dreams (Editions EG, EEGCD 30, 1978).

Ambient #2: The Plateaux of Mirror (Editions EG, EEGCD 18, 1980). Harold Budd and Brian Eno.

The Pearl (Editions EG, EEGCD 37, 1984). Harold Budd and Brian Eno with Daniel Lanois.

The Room (Atlantic Records, 2A-83382, 2000).

Wendy Carlos

Sonic Seasonings (East Side Digital, ESD 81372, 1998). Early ambient music from 1972 using nature sounds and the Moog.

Yves Daoust

Bruits (Empreintes Digitales, IMED 0156, 2001). Includes electroacoustic and environmental works by Daoust from 1997 to 2001: *La Gamme* (1981, rev. 2000); *Ouverture* (1989); *Impromptu* (1995); *Children's Corner* (1997); *Nuit* (1998); *Fête* (2001).

Brian Eno

Ambient 1: Music for Airports (Editions EG EEG 17, 1979/1990).

Apollo: Atmospheres & Soundtracks (E. G. Records 53, 1983/1990).

Roger Eno

Voices (Editions EG, EEGCD 42, 1985). Haunting melodic music for instruments and electronic ambience, somewhat in the reductionist style of Harold Budd.

Thomas Gerwin

Wattenmeer-Suite (IAP 011, 1996). Environmental sound composition commissioned by the German National Nature Park Waddensee.

Tetsu Inoue

World Receiver (Instinct Ambient, amb6002–2, 1996).

Mark Isham

Vapor Drawings (Windham Hill Records, WD-1027, 1983).

Annea Lockwood

A Sound Map of the Hudson River (Lovely Music Ltd., CD 2081, 1989).

SINOPAH (Experimental Intermedia Foundation, XI 118, 1998). Featuring

World Rhythms by Annea Lockwood and *I Come Out of Your Sleep* by Ruth Anderson.
Breaking the Surface (Lovely Music Ltd., LCD 2082, 1999). Included *Delta Run.*

Gen Ken Montgomery
Icebreaker (Staalplaat, STmCD 020, 2000). A composition for octophonic presentation in the total darkness of an installation space, all of the sounds were originated using a kitchen ice breaking machine.

Pete Namlook
From Within I (Minus Inc., FW 1/4, 1994). Pete Namlook and Richie Hawtin.
Psychonavigation (Subharmonic, SD 7005-2, 1994). Pete Namlook and Bill Laswell.
The Dark Side of the Moog (FAX+49–69/450464, PK 08/143, 1998). Pete Namlook with Klaus Schulze and Bill Laswell.
The Fires of Ork, Vol. 2 (FAX 44, 2001).

Bruce Odland and Sam Auinger
O+A Resonance (O + A, 002, 1997). Ambient works exploring the natural resonance of objects such as tubes, water harps, wind, and other sources, composed using digital filtering.

Hildegard Westerkamp
Transformations (Empreintes Digitales, IMED 9631,1996). A compilation of soundscape composer Westerkamp. Includes *A Walk through the City* (1981); *Fantasy for Horns II* (1979), using sounds of horns such as trains, boats, and foghorns; *Kits Beach Soundwalk* (1989); *Cricket Voice* (1987), based on the sounds of a cricket in a Mexican desert; *Beneath the Forest Floor* (1992).

Darrin Verhagen
Soft Ash (Dorobo, DOR LTD5). A soundscape based on environmental sounds recorded in Australia, India, Belgium, England, and Russia, with voices.

Turntablism
DJ Olive, the Audio Janitor
Kim Gordon, Ikue Mori, DJ Olive (SYR, 5, 2000). Featuring improvisation-based works for voice and guitar (Gordon), turntable (DJ Olive), and PowerBook (Mori).

Philip Jeck
Loopholes (Touch Records, 26, 1995).
Surf (Touch Records, 36, 1999).
Vinyl Coda I–III (2 CDs) (Intermedium, rec. 002, 2000).
Vinyl Coda IV (Intermedium, rec. 008, 2001).

Christian Marclay
Records 1981–1989 (Atavistic Records, 62, 1997).
Moving Parts (Asphodel Records, 2001, 2000).
Fuck Shit Up (Victo, 71, 2000).

Raz Mesinai
The Unspeakable (BSI Records, BSI 016-2, 2000).

Marina Rosenfeld
theforestthegardenthesea, Music from Fragment Opera (Charhizma, 003, 1999). For turntable.
Bitstreams: Sound works from the exhibition at the Whitney Museum of American Art, (JdK 06, Amsterdam, 2001).
Vinyl discs:
the heavens(fragment), 1999, 7" (Yerba Buena Center for the Arts).
theforestthegarden, 1998, 7" (self-released).

DJ Spooky, That Subliminal Kid
Songs of a Dead Dreamer (Asphodel Records, 961, 1996).
Necropolis: The Dialogic Project (Knitting Factory, 185, 1996).
Viral Sonata (Asphodel Records, 976, 1997).
RIOOIM WARFARE (Outpost Recordings, OPRD-30031, 1998).
File under Futurism (Caipirinha Music, 2025, 1999).

ELECTRONIC MUSIC RESOURCES

Publications and Information

Calendar for New Music
http://www.soundart.org/
"New York City's source for information on concerts of contemporary music in all its forms: Avant Garde, Classical, Electronic, Computer, Experimental Jazz and ???" This calendar is published monthly but also posted to its website. It is produced by the SoundArt Foundation, Inc.

Electronic Musician Magazine
http://industryclick.com/magazine.asp?magazineid=33&SiteID=15

The Hyperreal Music Archive
http://music.hyperreal.org/
Fan sites, recordings, sources, ambient, techno, world electronic music scene. Produced by Hyperreal since 1992, this site is a many-faceted resource for those in search of products, music, news, calendars, and message boards about electronic music.

Leonardo: Journal of the International Society for the Arts, Sciences and Technology
http://mitpress.mit.edu/e-journals/Leonardo/index.html
"Founded in 1967, Leonardo provides an international channel of communication between artists and others who use science and technologies in their creations. The journal covers media, music, kinetic art, performance art, language, environmental and conceptual art, computers and artificial intelligence, and legal, economics, and political aspects of art as these areas relate to the arts, tools and ideas of contemporary science and technology."

Moogarchives.com
http://www.moogarchives.com
"A personal collection of rare documents, photographs, and memorabilia from the Moog companies; designers and manufacturers of electronic music instruments."

Motion
http://motion.state51.co.uk/
Calling itself a "focal point for new music," Motion is a London-based website featuring interviews and reviews of new music. It covers a wide variety of artists and idioms, from African to electronic improvisation, always with a slant toward the unusual in contemporary sounds.

Raymond Scott
http://RaymondScott.com/
A website "created, owned and operated by Jeff Winner." This is the authoritative source for information about electronic music pioneer Raymond Scott.

The Recorded Music of John Cage
http://www.newalbion.com/artists/cagej/discog/
An online discography of Cage's work originated by Thom Holmes.

Signal to Noise
http://www.signaltonoisemagazine.org/
"Signal to Noise: the journal of improvised and experimental music is a quarterly publication dedicated to documenting and supporting great progressive jazz, with a special emphasis on grassroots production and promotion."

The Sound Projector
http://www.supergraphics.demon.co.uk/soundprojector/excerpts.html
"The Sound Projector is a magazine written and drawn by British Underground Cartoonists who like music. Steer clear if all you want is obsessive trainspotter information, or 100% authentic facts."

Companies and Organizations

Audities Foundation
http://www.audities.org/
David Kean, President and Founder.
"The Audities Foundation['s] mission is the preservation of electronic musical instruments and the documentation associated with them for use in museums, recording studios, modern instrument research and new music works. The instrument collection comprises over 150 instruments and spans the last 70 years of instrument development."

Big Briar Inc.
http://bigbriar.com/
Big Briar is the home of synthesizer inventor Robert Moog where he continues to design and manufacture Theremins, synthesizers, and synthesizer modules.

Buchla and Associates
http://www.buchla.com/index.html
Learn about Don Buchla's inventions and currently available products from one of the legends in electronic music instrumentation.

Electronic Music Foundation
http://www.emf.org/
Joel Chadabe, President.
"Founded in September 1994, the Electronic Music Foundation (EMF) is a not-for-profit organization dedicated to increasing public understanding of the role that electronic music, in its myriad forms and technologies, plays in our world."

Groupe de Recherches Musicales de l'Institut National de l'Audiovisuel (GRM/INA)
http://www.ina.fr/GRM/
French institute for research in music and audiovisual arts. The original home of musique concrète and Pierre Schaeffer.

Harvestworks Digital Media Arts Center
www.harvestworks.org
"Harvestworks Digital Media Arts Center is a non-profit organization founded in 1977 to cultivate artistic talent using electronic technologies. Harvestworks' programs provide the artist with production studios, grant opportunities, education, communal lab practice and distribution."

Institut de Recherche et Coordination Acoustique/Musique (IRCAM)
http://www.ircam.fr/
IRCAM is the French research institute dedicated to the development of new media and arts, including electronic and computer music.

Experimental Musical Instruments
http://www.windworld.com/
"Experimental Musical Instruments is an organization devoted to unusual musical sound sources. For many years our leading activity was the production of a quarterly journal devoted to the subject. . . . Over the years we became increasingly involved in producing other sorts of materials relating to musical instruments, including books, CDs, cassettes and so forth."

steim
www.steim.nl/
STEIM (the Studio for Electro-Instrumental Music) is the only independent live electronic music centre in the world that is exclusively dedicated to the performing arts. The foundation's artistic and technical departments support an international community of performers and musicians, and a growing group of visual artists, to develop unique instruments for their work."

Michel Waisvisz
http://www.xs4all.nl/~mwais/
"Michel Waisvisz is known for his highly physical, sensitive and ecstatic electronic music shows using The Hands (a gestural sensor instrument) he developed at the STEIM foundation in Amsterdam. Waisvisz has since the late sixties developed whole new ways to achieve a physical touch with electronic music instruments; sometimes literally touching the electricity inside the instruments and thereby becoming a thinking component of the machine. He was one of the first to use synthesizers on stage and the first to develop and perform with what is now called gestural MIDI controllers. He also is the inventor of the CrackleBox and The Web."

Mills College Center for Contemporary Music
http://www.mill.edu/LIFE/CCM/CCM.homepage.html

Wild Sanctuary
http://www.wildsanctuary.com/frameset.html

"Wild Sanctuary is an internationally renowned resource for natural sound and media design. Based on one of the largest and most comprehensive wildlife sound libraries in private hands, our collection includes 3,000 hours of material representing nearly 15,000 species. Most of these holdings are stereo digital recordings."

Radio Programs
Echoes
http://www.echoes.org/
New Sounds with John Schaefer
http://www.wnyc.org/new/music/new-sounds/playlists/index.html

Hearts of Space
http://www.hos.com/

Star's End
http://www.starsend.org/bkgrnd.html

Record Companies and Sources
Artifact Recordings
http://63.198.107.167/artifact/

CDeMUSIC
http://www.cdemusic.org/

Centaur Records
http://www.centaurrecords.com/

Composers Recordings Inc. (CRI)
http://www.composersrecordings.com/index.html

Experimental Intermedia
http://XIrecords.org/

FAX+49-69/450464
http://music.hyperreal.org/labels/fax/index.html

Hat Hut Records
http://www.hathut.com/

Lovely Music Ltd.
http://www.lovely.com/

mode records
http://www.mode.com/main.html

New Albion Records
http://www.newalbion.com/

New World Records
http://www.newworldrecords.org/

Organ of Corti
http://www.cortical.org/index.shtml

TELLUS Media
www.harvestworks.org/tellus/

Tzadik
http://www.tzadik.com/

Selected Artist Sites
Wendy Carlos
http://www.wendycarlos.com/

Merce Cunningham Dance Company
http://www.merce.org/

Gordon Mumma
http://brainwashed.com/mumma/

The Pauline Oliveros Foundation
http://www.pofinc.org/

Karlheinz Stockhausen
http://www.stockhausen.org/
Fax: 02268-1813

David Tudor
http://www.emf.org/tudor/

All Things Theremin
Big Briar Inc.
http://bigbriar.com/

PAiA
http://www.paia.com/

Theremin Enthusiasts Club International
http://www.he.net/~enternet/teci/teci.html

Wavefront Technologies
http://home.earthlink.net/~wavefront/

NOTES

Chapter 1

1. Aaron Copland, *Copeland on Music* (New York: Norton, 1963), 27.
2. Charles Ives, *Essays before a Sonata: The Majority and Other Writings* (New York: Norton, 1962), 4.
3. Karl. H. Wörner, *Stockhausen: Life and Work* (Berkeley, University of California Press, 1976), 123.
4. Wendy Carlos, interview with Thom Holmes, August 8, 2001.
5. John Cage, *Silence* (Middletown, CT: Wesleyan University Press, 1961), 68–69.
6. Igor Stravinsky, *Poetics of Music in the Form of Six Lessons* (New York: Vintage, 1947), 125.
7. Ibid., 29.
8. Robert Ashley, interview with Thom Holmes, September 8, 1982.
9. Richard L. Gregory, "Perceptions of Knowledge," *Nature*, 410 (March 1, 2001), p. 21.
10. Pierre Henry, quoted in Peter Shapiro, ed., *Modulations* (New York: Caipirinha, 2000), 22.

Chapter 2

1. Quoted from Busoni's "Sketch of a New Aesthetic of Music" in Herbert Russcol, *The Liberation of Sound: An Introduction to Electronic Music* (Englewood Cliffs, NJ: Prentice-Hall, 1972), 33.
2. John Cage, *Silence*, 4.
3. Ibid., 9.
4. Allen Strange, *Electronic Music: Systems, Techniques, and Controls* (New York: Wm. C. Brown, 1972), 7.
5. Joel Chadabe, *Electric Sound: The Past and Promise of Electronic Music* (Upper Saddle River, NJ: Prentice-Hall, 1997), 196.
6. Michel Waisvisz, "A Short Biography," at the STEIM website, www.steim.nl/.
7. Joel Chadabe, *Electric Sound,* 228.
8. Robert Ashley, liner notes, *Superior Seven* (New York, New World Records, 80460–2, 1995).
9. Robert Ashley, liner notes, *Superior Seven* (New York, New World Records, 80460–2, 1995).
10. Robert Ashley, interview with Thom Holmes, September 8, 1982.
11. Ibid.
12. Steve Reich, interview with Jason Gross, "OHM: The Early Gurus of Electronic Music," http://www.furious.com/perfect/ohm/reich.html.

13. David Lee Myers, personal communication with Thom Holmes, April 4, 2001.

Chapter 3
1. John Cage, Roger Shattuck, and Alan Gillmor, "Erik Satie: A Conversation." *Contact: A Journal of Contemporary Music* 25 (Autumn 1982), 24.
2. David Ewen, *The Complete Book of 20th Century Music* (Englewood Cliffs, NJ: Prentice-Hall, 1959), 348.
3. Joseph Machlis, *Introduction to Contemporary Music* (New York: Norton, 1961), 388.
4. Luigi Russolo, *The Art of Noise*, trans. Barclay Brown (Stuyvesant, NY: Pendragon, 1986).
5. One of the factors leading to the disturbance was the fact that Marinetti and Russolo had a habit of overbooking their venues. Alessandro Rizzo, "Zang Tumb Tumb; Las Musica Futurista, Futurism," http://www.futurism.fsnet.co.uk.
6. Futurist, *120 Years of Electronic Music (update v3.0)*, http://obsolete.com/120_years/machines/futurist/index.html.
7. Philippe Blanchard, "Plea for a Republication of the Book of G. Franco Maffina," *Publication Electronique*, revue 2 (November 1995), http://homestudio.thing.net/revue/content/asr2p70.html.

Chapter 4
1. Reynold Weidenaar, *Magic Music from the Telharmonium* (Metuchen, NJ: Scarecrow Press, 1995), 182.
2. Ibid., 213.
3. Ibid.
4. Ibid., 253.
5. Ibid.
6. RCA Theremin Service Notes, collection of the author (New York, Radio-Victor Corporation of America, 1929), 5.
7. John Cage, *Silence,* 4.
8. Caramoor.com, "A Garden of Great Music" http://www.caramoor.com/about/index.html.
9. Olivia Mattis, *Lincoln Center Festival 2000 program notes* (New York: Lincoln Center, July 19, 2000), 20B.
10. Lucie Bigelow Rosen, from the *Caramoor Estate Archives* (transcribed by John Snyder, as reproduced on the pages of the Lucie Bigelow Rosen website, http://www.korrnet.org/pipermail/levnet/1997–October/001218.html.
11. David Miller, personal communication with Thom Holmes, May 9, 2001.
12. Albert Glinsky, *Theremin: Ether Music and Espionage* (Urbana: University of Illinois Press, 2000), 158.
13. William W. Austin, *Music in the 20th Century* (New York: W. W. Norton, 1966), 374.
14. Albert Glinsky, *Theremin,*
15. Albert Glinsky, *Theremin,* 190.
16. Charlie Lester, personal recollection communicated to Thom Holmes, April 20, 2001.
17. Charlie Lester, Samuel J. Hoffman webpage, *Ethéreal Esotérica* 137 (2000), http://137.com/me/.
18. As noted in Samuel Hoffman's personal scrapbook and transcribed by Charlie Lester. Charlie Lester, Samuel J. Hoffman webpage, *Ethéreal Esotérica* 137 (2000), http://137.com/me/. Verification of titles, alternative titles, and dates contributed by Saul Fisher.
19. Robert Moog, interview with Thom Holmes, March 4, 2001.
20. David Miller, personal communication with Thom Holmes, April 23, 2001. Miller is a personal acquaintance of both Paul Tanner and Robert Whitsell and has a website dedicated to Theremins: http://www.geocities.com/Vienna/4611/.
21. David Miller, personal communication with Thom Holmes, May 5, 2001.

22. Ibid.
23. Cy Schneider, liner notes, *Music for Heavenly Bodies* (Omega, OSL-4, 1958).
24. David Miller, personal communication with Thom Holmes, May 5, 2001.
25. Ibid.
26. Robert Moog, personal communication with Thom Holmes, April 23, 2001.
27. Claude-Samuel Levine, "Historique de la facture des ondes," http://www.chez.com/ciom/Historique.html.
28. David Kean, president and founder, Audities Foundation, personal communication with Thom Holmes, May 5, 2001.
29. Ibid.
30. Ibid.
31. Jeanne Loriod, liner notes, *Music for Ondes Martenot* (Musical Heritage Society, MHS 821, circa 1970).
32. Oskar Sala, liner notes, *Subharmonische Mixturen* (Germany, Erdenklang 70963), 27–28.
33. Doepfer Musikelektronik, "The Trautonium Project," http://www.doepfer.de/traut/traut_e.htm.
34. Greg Armbruster, ed., *The Art of Electronic Music* (New York: Quill, 1984), 40.
35. Oskar Sala, liner notes, *Subharmonische Mixturen* (Germany: Erdenklang 70963), 28.
36. Oskar Sala, as related to Georg Misch, "The Difference Engine," *The Wire*, 43.
37. Oskar Sala, *Elektronische Impressionen* (Germany, Erdenklang 81032), 7.
38. Oskar Sala, as related to Georg Misch, "The Difference Engine," *The Wire*, 45.
39. Ibid.
40. William W. Austin, *Music in the 20th Century*, 379.
41. Doepfer Musikelektronik, "The Trautonium Project."
42. Greg Armbruster, ed., *The Art of Electronic Music*, 41.
43. Remi Gassman, liner notes, *Electronics* (Westminster Recording, XWN-18962, 1961).
44. Pete Namlook, personal communication with Thom Holmes, March 2, 2001.
45. Greg Armbruster, ed., *The Art of Electronic Music*.
46. Ibid.
47. Alan Douglas, *The Electronic Musical Instrument Manual* (Blue Ridge Summit, PA: TAB Books, 1976), 109.

Chapter 5

1. John Cage, interview with Thom Holmes, April 1981.
2. David Paul, "Karlheinz Stockhausen," interview, *Seconds Magazine* 44 (1997). Accessed on the Stockhausen.org website.
3. Karlheinz Stockhausen, *On Music* (London: Marion Boyars, 1989), 95. From his 1971 lecture "Four Criteria of Electronic Music."
4. Alvin Lucier, interview with Thom Holmes, February 24, 2001.
5. Pauline Oliveros, *Software for People: Collected Writings 1963–80* (Baltimore: Smith Publications, 1984), 43.
6. Pauline Oliveros, personal communication with Thom Holmes, April 14, 2001.
7. Terry Riley, liner notes, *Music for the Gift* (Organ of Corti, 1, 1998).
8. Pauline Oliveros, liner notes, *Electronic Works* (Paradigm Discs, 4, 1997).
9. Hugh Davies, *Répertoire international des musicques électroacoustiques* (International Electronic Music Catalog), (Cambridge, MIT Press, 1967), a joint publication of Le Groupe de Recherches Musicales de l'ORTF (Paris) and the Independent Electronic Music Center Inc. (Trumansburg, NY). My figures are based on an analysis of the studio listings in this historic book.
10. The work was broadcast over French radio in eight one-hour segments.

Carlos Palombini, "Musique Concrète Revisited," *Electronic Musicological Review* 4 (June 1999), palombini.htm#SCHAEFFER,%20Pierre.%201950.

11. John Dack, "Pierre Schaeffer and the Significance of Radiophonic Art," in *Contemporary Music Review* (Harwood Academic Publishers, 1994), http://world.altavista.com/urltrurl?lp=fr_en&url=http%3A%2F%2Fwww.mdx.ac.uk%2Fwww%2Fsonic%2Fdackpierre.html.

12. Pierre Schaeffer, *Machines à communiquer* (Paris: Editions du Seuil, 1970), 108–9.

13. Carlos Palombini, "Musique Concrète Revisited."

14. Ibid.

15. Ibid.

16. Pierre Henry, interview with Ios Smolders, ESTWeb, 1995, http://taz3.hyperreal.org/intersection/zines/est/intervs/collins.html.

17. Maurice Béjart, liner notes, *Variations for a Door and a Sigh* (Limelight, LS 86059, 1966).

18. Ibid.

19. Pierre Henry, interview with Ios Smolders, ESTWeb, 1995.

20. Pierre Schaeffer, "The Musical Object," *The Musical Review*, 212 (1952), 142–156.

21. Pierre Schaeffer interview with Tim Hodgkinson, *Recommended Records Quarterly*, 2(1) (1987).

22. Tetsu Inoue, interview with Thom Holmes, January 15, 2001.

23. Ibid.

24. Konrad Boehmer, interview with Jason Gross, *OHM: The Early Gurus of Electronic Music*, Ellipsis Arts, 1999, http://www.furious.com/perfect/ohm/eimert.html.

25. Pierre Schaeffer, interview with Tim Hodgkinson, *Recommended Records Quarterly*.

26. Christopher K. Koenigsberg, "Karlheinz Stockhausen's New Morphology of Music Time" (unpublished paper), Mills College,

December 1991, http://www.music.princeton.edu/~ckk/smmt/serialism.3.html.

27. H. H. Stuckenschmidt, *Twentieth-Century Music* (New York, McGraw-Hill, 1970), 214.

28. Tom Rhea, "Beginning of the Modern Age," from Alan Douglas, ed., *The Electronic Musical Instrument Manual* (Blue Ridge Summit, PA: TAB Books, 1976), 61.

29. Robert Beyer, 1954, "First Experiments," WDR website by Marietta Morawska Buengeler, http://www.musikwiss.uni-halle.de/musicweb/elemusik/technik.htm.

30. Karl. H. Wörner, *Stockhausen: Life and Work*, 122.

31. Konrad Boehmer, interview with Jason Gross.

32. Konrad Boehmer, liner notes, *Cologne—WDR, Early Electronic Music*, (Acousmatrix, 6 CD 9106, 1999).

33. Karlheinz Stockhausen, personal communication with Thom Holmes, April 10, 2000.

34. Otto Luening, *The Odyssey of an American Composer: The Autobiography of Otto Luening* (New York, Charles Scribner's Sons, 1980), 512.

35. Ibid., 512–16.

36. Ibid., 513.

37. Ibid., 528.

38. Ibid., 533.

39. Harry F. Olson, *Music, Physics, and Engineering* (New York: Dover, 1967), 424. This is a reissue of Olsen's important 1952 work *Musical Engineering*, originally published by McGraw-Hill.

40. Ibid., 448.

41. Ibid., 434.

42. Otto Luening, *The Odyssey of an American Composer*, 554.

43. Wendy Carlos, interview with Thom Holmes, June 6, 2001.

44. Wendy Carlos, liner notes, *Electronic Music* (Turnabout, TV24004S, 1965).

45. Charles Wuorinen, liner notes, *Time's Encomium* (Nonesuch Records, H-71225, 1970).

Chapter 6

1. John Cage, interview with Thom Holmes, April 1981.
2. David Tudor, interview with Teddy Hultberg, Dusseldorf, May 17–18, 1988.
3. David Revill, *The Roaring Silence: John Cage: A Life* (New York, Arcade, 1992), 143.
4. Bebe Barron, interview with Thom Holmes, April 9, 2001.
5. Ibid.
6. David Revill, *The Roaring Silence*, 146
7. Richard Kostelanetz, *John Cage: An Anthology* (New York, Da Capo, 1991), 130.
8. The Wolff piece was identified by Matt Rogalsky in a personal communication with Thom Holmes, August 24, 2001.
9. Bebe Barron, interview with Thom Holmes, April 9, 2001.
10. Ibid.
11. Ibid.
12. Ibid.
13. Frederick S. Clarke and Steve Rubin, "Making Forbidden Planet," *Cinefantastique* 8(2–3) (1979), 42.
14. Bebe Barron, interview with Thom Holmes, April 9, 2001.
15. Ibid.
16. Ibid.
17. Frederick S. Clarke and Rubin, "Making Forbidden Planet," 42.
18. John Cage, interview with Thom Holmes, April 1981.
19. John Cage, interview with Thom Holmes, April 1981. Having been the official keeper of Cage's discography, I can attest to the fact that he did not even own a record player.
20. John Cage, interview with Thom Holmes, April 1981.
21. Matt Rogalsky, *Live Electronic Music Practice and Musicians of the Merce Cunningham Dance Company*, master's thesis, Wesleyan University, May 15, 1995 (revised November 1996), 2.
22. John Cage, interview with Thom Holmes, April 1981.
23. Ibid.
24. Merce Cunningham, *Changes: Notes On Choreography* (New York: Something Else Press, 1969), 28.
25. Matt Rogalsky, *Live Electronic Music Practice*, 2–3.
26. John Cage, in *Conversing with Cage*, ed. Richard Kostelanetz (New York: Limelight, 1988), 191.
27. Gordon Mumma, personal communication with Thom Holmes, March 17, 2001.
28. William Duckworth, *Talking Music* (New York, Da Capo, 1999), 196–97.
29. Richard Kostelanetz, *John Cage: An Anthology*, 21.
30. Joel Chadabe, *Electric Sound: The Past and Promise of Electronic Music*, 82.
31. Robert Moog, interview with Thom Holmes, March 4, 2001.
32. Ronald J. Kuivila, personal communication with Thom Holmes, March 12, 2001.
33. Gordon Mumma, personal communication with Thom Holmes, January 17, 2002.
34. Richard Kostelanetz, *John Cage, An Anthology*, 54.
35. John Cage, *Silence*, 18.
36. John Cage, interview with Thom Holmes, April, 1981.
37. William W. Austin, *Music in the 20th Century*, 377.
38. Herbert Russcol, *The Liberation of Sound: An Introduction to Electronic Music* (Englewood Cliffs, NJ: Prentice-Hall, Inc., 1972), 62.
39. S. A., review of a concert of contemporary music at the Village Gate Café in New York City on November 9, 1958, *Musical America*, December 1, 1958, 29.
40. Karlheinz Stockhausen, "From Tape Loops to MIDI: Karlheinz Stockhausen's Forty Years of Electronic Music," an interview by Michael Manion, Stockhausen.org

LIVERPOOL JOHN MOORES UNIVERSITY
LEARNING & INFORMATION SERVICES

website, http://www.stockhausen.
org/tape_loops.html.
41. Ibid.
42. Ibid.
43. Ibid.
44. Karlheinz Stockhausen, " . . . how
time passes . . . ," (1959), *Die Reihe*,
No. 3, trans. Cornelius Cardew, 10.
45. Robin Maconie, ed., *Stockhausen on
Music: Lectures and Interviews*
(London: Marion Boyars, 2000),
95–111.
46. Karl. H. Wörner, *Stockhausen: Life
and Work*, 41.
47. Ibid.
48. Karlheinz Stockhausen, Facsimile
Edition of *Gesang der Jünglinge*
(score; gesang-der-junglinge.pdf),
Stockhausen Verlag, 2001, p. 2.
49. Karl. H. Wörner, *Stockhausen: Life
and Work*, 41.
50. Jon H. Appleton and Ronald C. Perera,
ed. *The Development and Practice of
Electronic Music* (Englewood Cliffs,
Prentice-Hall, 1975), 109.
51. Karlheinz Stockhausen, liner notes,
Telemusik, Mixtur (Deutsche
Grammophon, 137 012, 1967).
52. Karlheinz Stockhausen, liner notes,
Es und Aufwärts (Deutsche
Grammophon, 2530 255, 1971).
53. Ibid.
54. John Cage, personal correspondence
with Thom Holmes, January 15, 1973.
55. Karl. H. Wörner, *Stockhausen: Life
and Work,* 61.
56. Karlheinz Stockhausen, liner notes,
Hymnen (Stockhausen, 10 A-D,
1959), 130–131.
57. Karl. H. Wörner, *Stockhausen: Life
and Work*, 68.
58. Robin Maconie, ed., *Stockhausen on
Music: Lectures and Interviews*, 103–4.
59. Karlheinz Stockhausen, notes for
Stockhausen Edition No. 26, Sirius,
Stockhausen website,
http://home.swipnet.se/sonoloco7/sto
ckhausen/26.html.

Chapter 7

1. There were a few exceptions.
Between 1975 and 1981, electronic

music historian Tom Rhea (and former Moog employee) authored articles for *Keyboard magazine* about
many hits and misses in the development of electronic musical instruments; ten paragraphs devoted to
Scott appeared in reprint form in the
book *The Art of Electronic Music*
(1984), edited by Greg Armbruster.
But it is only recently that Scott's
work has been rediscovered in grand
fashion by the reissuing of several
recordings of his music and the hand-
some CD/book combination
Manhattan Research Inc. (2000).
2. Gert-Jan Blom and Jeff Winner, from
an article written by Joseph Kaselow,
July 19, 1960, for the *New York
Herald Tribune. Manhattan Research
Inc.* (Holland, Basta 90782, 2000), 9,
46.
3. Ibid., 40–45.
4. Ibid., 31.
5. Robert Moog, interview with Thom
Holmes, March 4, 2001.
6. Raymond Scott advertisement, circa
1957, courtesy the Raymond Scott
Archives, *Manhattan Research Inc.*,
49.
7. Gert-Jan Blom and Jeff Winner,
Manhatten Research Inc. 85.
8. George Martin, ed., *Making Music*
(New York: Quill, 1983), 229.
9. Greg Armbruster, ed., *The Art of
Electronic Music*, 55.
10. Ibid.
11. Joel Chadabe, *Raymond Scott,
Inventor and Composer* (1999), from
Gert-Jan Blom and Jeff Winner,
Manhattan Research Inc., 20.
12. Gert-Jan Blom and Jeff Winner,
Manhattan Research Inc., 54–55.
13. Gert-Jan Blom and Jeff Winner,
Manhattan Research Inc., 51.
14. Robert Moog, interview with Thom
Holmes, March 4, 2001.
15. Liner notes, *Song of the Second
Moon*, (Limelight, LS 86050, circa
1967).
16. Jean-Jacques Perrey, interview with
Dana Countryman, *Cool and Strange
Music!* magazine, 10 (1998),

http://members.aol.com/coolstrge/per-
rey.html.

17. Jean-Jacques Perrey, interview with
Arnaud Boivin, http://www.fly.co.
uk/jjp.html.

18. Dick Hyman, personal communication with Thom Holmes, August 7,
2001.

19. Harry Spiridakis, personal communication with Thom Holmes, July 25,
2000.

20. Gayle Young, "Hugh Le Caine
Biography," *Hugh Le Caine—An
Inventor's Notebook*, 1999,
http://www.hughlecaine.com/en/.

21. Gert-Jan Blom and Jeff Winner,
Manhatten Research Inc., 35.

22. Gayle Young, liner notes, *Hugh Le
Caine: Compositions,
Demonstrations 1946–1974* (JWD
Music, JWD 03, 1999), 1.

23. Pauline Oliveros, personal communication with Thom Holmes, May 4,
2001.

24. Heidi Von Gunden, *The Music of
Pauline Oliveros* (Metuchen, NJ:
Scarecrow Press, 1983), 57.

25. Pauline Oliveros, personal communication with Thom Holmes, May 4,
2001.

26. Elliot Schwartz, *Electronic Music: A
Listener's Guide* (New York: Praeger,
1975), 131.

27. Hugh Le Caine, quoted in Greg
Armbruster, ed., *The Art of
Electronic Music,* 54.

28. Canada Science and Technology
Museum, "Early Synthesizers,
Keyboard and Performance
Instruments," http://www.science-
tech.nmstc.ca/english/collection/music
8.cfm.

29. Gayle Young, "Hugh Le Caine
Instruments," *Hugh Le Caine—An
Inventor's Notebook*, 1999,
http://www.hughlecaine.com/en/.

30. Hugh Le Caine, his narrated intro-
duction to a demonstration recording
of the Sackbut Synthesizer, *Hugh Le
Caine: Compositions,
Demonstrations 1946–1974* (JWD
Music, JWD 03, 1999).

Chapter 8

1. Robert Moog, interview with Thom
Holmes, March 4, 2001.
2. Ibid.
3. Ibid.
4. Ibid.
5. Wendy Carlos, interview with Carol
Wright, *New Age Voice*, November
1999. Quoted from a transcription at
Synthmuseum.com, http://www.syn-
thmuseum.com/magazine/0102cw.ht
ml.
6. Wendy Carlos, interview with Thom
Holmes, August 8, 2001.
7. Robert Moog, interview with Thom
Holmes, March 4, 2001.
8. Ibid.
9. Wendy Carlos, interview with Thom
Holmes, August 8, 2001.
10. Some of her photographs of solar
eclipses are so exquisite that they
have graced the cover and pages of
Sky and Telescope magazine.
11. Wendy Carlos, interview with Thom
Holmes, June 6, 2001.
12. Wendy Carlos, interview with Thom
Holmes, August 8, 2001.
13. Wendy Carlos, interview with Carol
Wright, *New Age Voice*, November
1999. from a transcription at
Synthmuseum.com.
14. Ibid.
15. Wendy Carlos, interview with Thom
Holmes, August 8, 2001. The homemade eight-track tape machine was
created by cannibalizing off-the-shelf
equipment. It was made from Ampex
model 300 and 351 tape recorder
parts, EMI tape heads, and a custom
control panel for "Sel-Synching"—
synchronizing—the tracks. Sel-
Synching was an Ampex
trademarked technique of routing the
record head into the playback pre-
amps so that you could monitor the
same spot on the tape where you
were recording instead of from the
playback head itself, which was an
inch or two to the right and was
slightly delayed from the moment of
recording. It was a critical feature for
a multitrack tape machine, on which

one could build a piece of music one track at a time. Sel-Synching enabled one to synchronize new tracks with previously recorded tracks.

16. Wendy Carlos, interview with Thom Holmes, August 8, 2001.
17. Wendy Carlos, interview with Thom Holmes, June 6, 2001.
18. Wendy Carlos, interview with Thom Holmes, August 8, 2001.
19. Mark Vail, *Vintage Synthesizers* (San Fransisco, Miller Freeman, 2000), 41. Reprint of an interview with Bob Moog by Connor Freff Cochran called "The Rise and Fall of Moog Music," which originally appeared in *Keyboard* magazine. Moog was correct about the relative success of the three records, but was fooled by the so-called bowl of reefers. David Behrman, who was also in attendance at the press party, knew the secret behind the bowl of joints. "My boss, John McClure, who was the head of Columbia Masterworks, made these fake marijuana cigarettes that had tobacco in them and put them in a big bowl. John McClure was being on the safe side."
20. Wendy Carlos, interview with Thom Holmes, August 8, 2001.
21. Ibid.
22. Wendy Carlos, interview with Carol Wright, *New Age Voice*, November 1999, www.newagevoice.com, copyright 1999 by Carol Wright.
23. Ibid.
24. Wendy Carlos, interview with Thom Holmes, June 6, 2001.
25. Wendy Carlos, liner notes, *Digital Moonscapes* (East Side Digital, ESD 81542, 2000), 2–3.
26. Wendy Carlos, interview with Thom Holmes, June 6, 2001.
27. Ibid.
28. Larry Fast, interview with Paul Clark, April 1997, electronicmusic.com/features/interview/larryfast.html.
29. Wendy Carlos, interview with Thom Holmes, June 6, 2001.
30. Wendy Carlos, interview with Thom Holmes, August 8, 2001.
31. Glenn Gould, liner notes to *Switched-On Boxed Set* (East Side Digital, ESD 81422, 1999).
32. Wendy Carlos, interview with Thom Holmes, August 8, 2001.
33. Joel Chadabe, remarks during "Electronic Music Pioneers @ Hofstra," a seminar sponsored by the Hofstra University Department of Music, March 16, 2001, transcribed by Thom Holmes.
34. Ibid.
35. Robert Moog, remarks during "Electronic Music Pioneers @ Hofstra."
36. Gordon Mumma, foreword to Allen Strange, *Electronic Music: Systems, Techniques, and Controls,* Second Edition (Dubuque, IA: W.C. Brown, 1983).
37. Robert Moog, remarks during "Electronic Music Pioneers @ Hofstra."
38. Ibid.
39. Pauline Oliveros, interview with Christoph Cox, The *Wire* 209 (July 2001), 35.
40. Morton Subotnick, quoted at the CDeMusic website (Electronic Music Foundation, Ltd.), http://www.cdemusic.org/artists/subotnick.html.
41. William Maginnis, personal communication with Thom Holmes, 1984.
42. Morton Subotnick, as quoted by Mark Vail, *Vintage Synthesizers,* 106–7. Reprint of the article "Buchla's First Modular System," which originally appeared in *Keyboard* magazine.
43. Charles Cohen, personal communication with Thom Holmes, May 3, 2001.

Chapter 9

1. Les Paul was among the first to use multiple tracking to build several guitar and vocal parts using just himself and his wife, Mary Ford (b. 1928).
2. Gordon Mumma, personal communication with Thom Holmes, March 17, 2001.

3. Robert Ashley, interview with Thom Holmes, March 22, 2001.
4. Ibid.
5. Robert Ashley, "Autobiographie," *MusikTexte*, MT88, February 2001, English version provided by Ashley to Thom Holmes.
6. Ibid.
7. Gordon Mumma, "The ONCE Festival and How It Happened," *Arts in Society* (Madison, WI) 4(2) (1967) (Minor revisions, August 1970).
8. Ibid.
9. Ibid.
10. Robert Ashley, "Autobiographie," *MusikTexte*.
11. Gordon Mumma, "The ONCE Festival and How It Happened," *Arts in Society*.
12. Ibid.
13. This performance in 1968 was not one of the official ONCE festivals, but one of the follow-up concerts involving the ONCE group of performers.
14. Alvin Lucier, interview with Thom Holmes, February 24, 2001.
15. Gordon Mumma, personal communication with Thom Holmes, August 6, 2001.
16. Gordon Mumma, personal communication with Thom Holmes, March 15, 2001.
17. Alvin Lucier, interview with Thom Holmes, February 24, 2001.
18. David Behrman, liner notes, *Wave Train—Music from 1959 to 1968* (Italy, Alga Marghen, Plana B 5NmN.020, 1998), 10.
19. Robert Ashley, interview with Thom Holmes, March 22, 2001.
20. Matt Rogalsky, *Live Electronic Music Practice and Musicians of the Merce Cunningham Dance Company*, master's thesis, Wesleyan University, May 15, 1995 (revised November 1996), 148.
21. Robert Ashley, "Autobiographie," *MusikTexte*.
22. Ibid.
23. Gordon Mumma, personal communication with Thom Holmes, March 17, 2001.
24. Robert Ashley, interview with Thom Holmes, March 22, 2001.
25. Alvin Lucier, interview with Thom Holmes, Feb. 24, 2001.
26. David Behrman, interview with Thom Holmes, March 13, 2001.
27. Gordon Mumma, liner notes, *The Sonic Arts Union* (Mainstream, MS/5010, 1971).
28. Robert Ashley, interview with Thom Holmes, March 22, 2001.
29. David Behrman, liner notes, *Wave Train—Music from 1959 to 1968*, 10.
30. David Behrman, interview with Thom Holmes, March 13, 2001.
31. Robert Ashley, interview with Thom Holmes, September 8, 1982.
32. Ibid.
33. Ibid.
34. Ibid.
35. Alvin Lucier, interview with Thom Holmes, February 24, 2001.
36. Ibid.
37. Ibid.
38. David Tudor, interview with Larry Austin, April 3, 1989 (included in the narrative material for the Larry Austin composition *Transmission Two: The Great Excursion*, 1990).
39. Heidi Von Gunden, *The Music of Pauline Oliveros* (Metuchen, NJ, Scarecrow Press, 1983), 52.
40. Pauline Oliveros, *Software for People*, 195.
41. Ibid., 196–97.
42. William Maginnis, personal communication with Thom Holmes, 1984.
43. Pauline Oliveros, *Software for People*, 197.
44. Maggi Payne, personal communication with Thom Holmes, May 18, 2001.
45. Pauline Oliveros, *Software for People*, 197. John Bischoff and Maggi Payne, personal communication with Thom Holmes, May 18, 2001.
46. Robert Ashley, interview with Thom Holmes, March 22, 2001.
47. Ibid.
48. Maggi Payne, personal communica-

tion with Thom Holmes, August 21, 2001.

49. John Bischoff and Maggi Payne, personal communication with Thom Holmes, May 18, 2001.

50. Robert Ashley, interview with Thom Holmes, March 22, 2001.

51. Maggi Payne, personal communication with Thom Holmes, May 18, 2001.

52. Robert Ashley, interview with Thom Holmes, March 22, 2001.

53. Maggi Payne, personal communication with Thom Holmes, August 22, 2001.

Chapter 10

1. Joel Chadabe, *Electric Sound,* 208–9.

2. Joel Chadabe, remarks during "Electronic Music Pioneers @ Hofstra," a seminar sponsored by the Hofstra University Department of Music, March 16, 2001, transcribed by Thom Holmes.

3. E. E. David Jr., "Digital Simulation in Perceptual Research," *Bell Telephone System Monograph No. 3405–1,* 1958.

4. A press release from Bell Labs in November 1965 proclaimed the results of a listening test, "In listening to the computer-generated tones, 20 persons, several of whom were professional musicians, were unable to tell the difference between the computer trumpet sound and the real one."

5. Joel Chadabe, remarks during "Electronic Music Pioneers @ Hofstra."

6. Laurie Spiegel, personal communication with Thom Holmes, December 19, 2001.

7. Nicolas Collins, interview with Thom Holmes, April 2, 2001.

8. I must give Nicolas Collins credit for this nickname, much as I would like to take credit for it myself.

9. Nicolas Collins, interview with Thom Holmes, April 2, 2001.

10. David Behrman, interview with Thom Holmes, March 13, 2001.

11. David Tudor, interview with Teddy Hultberg, Dusseldorf, May 17–18, 1988.

12. David Behrman, interview with Thom Holmes, March 13, 2001.

13. Gordon Mumma, personal communication with Thom Holmes, August 6, 2001.

14. Ibid.

15. David Behrman, interview with Thom Holmes, March 13, 2001.

16. Hubert Howe, remarks during "Electronic Music Pioneers @ Hofstra."

17. Nicolas Collins, interview with Thom Holmes, April 2, 2001.

18. David Behrman, liner notes, *Wave Train—Music from 1959 to 1968* (Italy, Alga Marghen, Plana B 5NmN.020, 1998), 10.

19. David Tudor, interview with Teddy Hultberg, Dusseldorf, May 17–18, 1988.

20. Gordon Mumma, personal communication with Thom Holmes, June 27, 2001.

21. David Behrman, interview with Thom Holmes, March 13, 2001.

22. Nicolas Collins, interview with Thom Holmes, April 2, 2001.

23. Time Perkis, liner notes, *Wreckin' Ball: The Hub* (Artifact Recordings, ART 1008, 1994), 1.

24. Nicolas Collins, interview with Thom Holmes, April 2, 2001.

25. Laurie Spiegel, from the ReadMe file for Music Mouse.

26. Laurie Spiegel, personal communication with Thom Holmes, June 27, 2001.

27. Nicolas Collins, interview with Thom Holmes, April 2, 2001.

28. Gordon Mumma, personal communication with Thom Holmes, June 27, 2001.

Chapter 11

1. John Cage, interview with Thom Holmes, April 1981.

2. William Duckworth, *Talking Music* (New York, Da Capo, 1999), 197.

3. John Cage, personal communication with Thom Holmes, December 29, 1985. Reproduced with permission of the John Cage Trust.

4. Pauline Oliveros, "The Roots of the Moment: Interactive Music," *NewMus MusNet* 1 (April 1995).
5. Zeena Parkins, interview with Thom Holmes, March 15, 2001.
6. Thurston Moore, interview with Thom Holmes, January 23, 2001.
7. Pauline Oliveros, "The Roots of the Moment: Interactive Music."
8. Ibid.
9. Cornelius Cardew, liner notes, *Live Electronic Music Improvised* (Mainstream, MS-5002, 1968).
10. Marina Rosenfeld, interview with Thom Holmes, February 2, 2001.
11. Alvin Lucier, interview with Thom Holmes, February 24, 2001.
12. William Duckworth, *Talking Music*, 274.
13. Terry Riley, liner notes, *Music for the Gift* (Organ of Corti, 1, 1998).
14. William Duckworth, *Talking Music*, 210.
15. Ibid., 233.
16. Michael Nyman, *Experimental Music: Cage and Beyond* (New York, Schirmer, 1974), 69.
17. Laura Kuhn, executive director of the John Cage Trust, quoted in *The Scotsman*, August 24, 2001, http://www.festival.scotsman.com.
18. As reproduced in Michael Nyman, *Experimental Music: Cage and Beyond*, 70.
19. William Duckworth, *Talking Music*, 253.
20. Ibid., 277.
21. Ibid., 282.
22. Harold Budd, interview with Thom Holmes, February 19, 2001.
23. Hugh Davies, *Répertoire international des musiques électroacoustiques* (International Electronic Music Catalog), (Cambridge, MIT Press, 1967), a joint publication of Le Groupe de Recherches Musicales de l'ORTF (Paris) and the Independent Electronic Music Center Inc. (Trumansburg, NY), vii.
24. Brian Eno, liner notes, *Discreet Music* (Editions EG, EGS 303, 1975).
25. William Duckworth, *Talking Music*, 296.
26. Steve Reich, liner notes, *Three Dances & Four Organs* (Angel Records, S-36059, 1973).
27. Alvin Lucier, liner notes, *Clocker* (Lovely Music Ltd., 1994), 1.
28. Alvin Lucier, liner notes, *Panorama* (Lovely Music Ltd. 1997), 1.
29. Laurie Spiegel, liner notes, *The Expanding Universe* (Philo Records, Inc., 9003, 1980.)
30. Ibid.
31. Ibid.
32. Ibid.
33. Marina Rosenfeld, interview with Thom Holmes, February 2, 2001.
34. Iannis Xenakis, liner notes, *Electro-Acoustic Music* (Nonesuch Records, H-71246, 1969).
35. Makis Solomis, liner notes, *Xenakis: Electronic Music* (EMF Media, EMF CD003, 1997).
36. Pierre Schaeffer, *Regards sur Iannis Xenakis* (Paris: Stock, 1981), 85.
37. James Mansback Brody, liner notes, *Electro-Acoustic Music* (Nonesuch Records, H-71246, 1969).
38. Gordon Mumma, personal communication with Thom Holmes, August 6, 2001.
39. John Cage, *Silence*, 8.
40. Deleted.
41. David Behrman, personal communication with Thom Holmes, August 19, 2001.
42. Wendy Carlos, liner notes, *Sonic Seasonings* (East Side Digital, ESD 81372, 1972/1998).
43. Annea Lockwood, interview by Thom Holmes, February 19, 2001.
44. Annea Lockwood, personal communication with Thom Holmes, July 25, 2001.
45. Annea Lockwood, *The River Archive*, http://www.halcyon.com/robinja/mythos/AnneaLockwood.html.
46. Annea Lockwood, interview with Thom Holmes, February 19, 2001.
47. Brian Eno, liner notes to the vinyl release of *Music for Airports* (Editions EG, EGS 303, 1978).
48. Brian Eno, "Strategies for making

sense," an interview with Paul Schütze, *The Wire* 139 (September 1995).

49. Harold Budd, interview with Thom Holmes, February 19, 2001.
50. Ibid.
51. Ibid.
52. Ibid.
53. Ibid.
54. Marshall McLuhan, *Understanding Media: The Extensions of Man* (New York: McGraw-Hill, 1965), 22–23.
55. Thurston Moore, liner notes, *Records, 1981–1989* (alp62cd, 1997), 4.
56. Herbert Russcol, *The Liberation of Sound* (Englewood Cliffs, New Jersey, Prentice-Hall, Inc., 1972), 71.
57. John Cage, *Silence*, 6.
58. Christian Marclay, interview with Mike Doherty, *Eye*, November 30, 2000, http://www.eye.net/eye/issue/issue_11.30.00/music/marclay.html.
59. Nicolas Collins, interview with Thom Holmes, April 2, 2001.
60. Christian Marclay, liner notes, *Records, 1981–1989* (alp62cd, 1997).
61. Ibid.
62. Thurston Moore, liner notes, *Records, 1981–1989* (alp62cd, 1997), 4.
63. DJ Olive interview with Thom Holmes, January 30, 2001.
64. Ibid.
65. Ikue Mori, interview with Thom Holmes, January 23, 2001.
66. DJ Spooky, liner notes, *Necropolis: The Dialogic Project* (Knitting Factory Works, KFW 185), 1.
67. DJ Spooky, interview with Jon Garelick, *Boston Phoenix*, November 28 - December 5, 1996, http://www.bostonphoenix.com/alt1/archive/music/reviews/11–28–96/DJ_SPOOKY.html.
68. Marina Rosenfeld, interview with Thom Holmes, February 2, 2001.

Chapter 12

1. Thurston Moore, liner notes, *Records, 1981–1989* (alp62cd, 1997), 4.
2. Nicolas Collins, interview with Thom Holmes, April 2, 2001.
3. Ibid.
4. Ibid.
5. Alvin Lucier, interview with Thom Holmes, February 24, 2001.
6. Annea Lockwood, interview with Thom Holmes, February 19, 2001.
7. Nicolas Collins, interview with Thom Holmes, April 2, 2001.

SELECT BIBLIOGRAPHY

Appleton, Jon H., and Perera, Ronald C., eds. *The Development and Practice of Electronic Music*. Englewood Cliffs, NJ: Prentice-Hall, 1975.

Armbruster, Greg, ed. *The Art of Electronic Music*. New York: Quill, 1984.

Barr, Tim. *Techno: The Rough Guide*. London: Rough Guides Ltd., 2000.

Cage, John. *Silence*. Middletown, CT: Wesleyan University Press, 1961.

———. *A Year from Monday: New Lectures and Writings by John Cage*. Middletown, CT: Wesleyan University Press, 1967.

Chadabe, Joel. *Electric Sound: The Past and Promise of Electronic Music*. Upper Saddle River, NJ: Prentice-Hall, 1997.

Copland, Aaron. *Copland on Music*. New York: Norton, 1963.

Cott, Jonathan. *Stockhausen: Conversations with the Composer*. New York: Simon and Schuster, 1973.

Cowell, Henry. *New Musical Resources*. New York: Something Else Press, Inc., 1969. Originally published in 1930 by Alfred Knopf.

Curtis, David. *Experimental Cinema: A Fifty-Year Evolution*. New York: Delta, 1971.

Davies, Hugh. *Répertoire international des musiques électroacoustiques* (International Electronic Music Catalog). Cambridge: MIT Press, 1967. A joint publication of Le Groupe de Recherches Musicales de l'ORTF (Paris) and the Independent Electronic Music Center Inc. (Trumansburg, NY).

Deutsch, Herbert A. *Synthesis: An Introduction to the History, Theory, and Practice of Electronic Music*. New York: Alfred, 1976.

Farnsworth, Paul R. *The Social Psychology of Music*. Ames, IA: Iowa State University Press, 1969.

Glinsky, Albert. *Theremin: Ether Music and Espionage*. Urbana: University of Illinois Press, 2000.

Kostelanetz, Richard, ed. *John Cage: An Anthology*. New York: Da Capo, 1991.

Luening, Otto. *The Odyssey of an American Composer: The Autobiography of Otto Luening*. New York: Charles Scribner's Sons, 1980.

Maconie, Robin, ed. *Stockhausen on Music: Lectures and Interviews*. London: Marion Boyars, 1989.

Nyman, Michael. *Experimental Music: Cage and Beyond*. New York: Schirmer. 1974.

Oliveros, Pauline. *Software for People: Collected Writings 1963–80.* Baltimore: Smith Publications, 1984.

Olson, Harry F. *Music, Physics and Engineering.* 2nd ed. New York: Dover, 1967.

Revill, David. *The Roaring Silence: John Cage: A Life.* New York: Arcade, 1992.

Russcol, Herbert. *The Liberation of Sound: An Introduction to Electronic Music.* Englewood Cliffs, NJ: Prentice-Hall, 1972.

Schaefer, John. *New Sounds: A Listener's Guide to New Music.* New York: Harper & Row, 1987.

Shapiro, Peter, ed. *Modulations—A History of Electronic Music: Throbbing Words on Sound.* New York: Caipirinha, 2000.

Strange, Allen. *Electronic Music: Systems, Techniques, and Controls.* New York: Wm. C. Brown, 1972.

Stravinsky, Igor. *Poetics of Music in the Form of Six Lessons.* New York: Vintage, 1947.

Toop, David. *Ocean of Sound: Aether Talk, Ambient Sound and Imaginary Worlds.* London: Serpent's Tail, 1995.

Treib, Marc. *Space Calculated in Seconds* (Princeton, NJ: Princeton University Press, 1996).

Trythall, Gilbert. *Principles and Practice of Electronic Music.* New York: Grosset & Dunlap, 1973.

Vail, Mark. *Vintage Synthesizers.* San Francisco: Miller Freeman, 2000.

Von Foerster, Heinz, and Beauchamp, James W., ed. *Music by Computers.* New York: John Wiley and Sons, 1969.

Von Gunden, Heidi. *The Music of Pauline Oliveros.* Metuchen, NJ: Scarecrow Press, 1983.

Weidenaar, Reynold. *Magic Music from the Telharmonium.* Metuchen, NJ: Scarecrow Press, 1995.

Whitney, John. *Digital Harmony: On the Complementarity of Music and Visual Art.* Peterborough, NH: Byte Books, 1980.

Wörner, Karl H. *Stockhausen: Life and Work.* Berkeley, CA: University of California Press, 1976.

INDEX

The following index includes the names of inventors, composers, instruments, and principles associated with electronic music. Musical compositions are listed under the names of individual artists. Page references in italics denote a photograph or illustration of a subject. Specific recordings listed in the discography beginning on page 281 *are not* listed individually in the index.